Central Bank Reserves and Sovereign Wealth Management

Also by Arjan B. Berkelaar, Joachim Coche and Ken Nyholm

INTEREST RATE MODELS, ASSET ALLOCATION AND QUANTITATIVE TECHNIQUES FOR CENTRAL BANKS AND SOVEREIGN WEALTH FUNDS (edited)

Central Bank Reserves and Sovereign Wealth Management

Edited by

Arjan B. Berkelaar

Joachim Coche

and

Ken Nyholm

palgrave
macmillan

First published 2010 by
PALGRAVE MACMILLAN

Palgrave Macmillan in the UK is an imprint of Macmillan Publishers Limited, registered in England, company number 785998, of Houndmills, Basingstoke, Hampshire RG21 6XS.

Palgrave Macmillan in the US is a division of St Martin's Press LLC, 175 Fifth Avenue, New York, NY 10010.

Palgrave Macmillan is the global academic imprint of the above companies and has companies and representatives throughout the world.

Palgrave® and Macmillan® are registered trademarks in the United States, the United Kingdom, Europe and other countries.

ISBN: 978–0–230–58089–3

This book is printed on paper suitable for recycling and made from fully managed and sustained forest sources. Logging, pulping and manufacturing processes are expected to conform to the environmental regulations of the country of origin.

A catalogue record for this book is available from the British Library.

A catalog record for this book is available from the Library of Congress.

10 9 8 7 6 5 4 3 2 1
19 18 17 16 15 14 13 12 11 10

Printed and bound in Great Britain by
CPI Antony Rowe, Chippenham and Eastbourne

Contents

Illustrations

Tables

Figures

Box

Preface

On 24–25 November 2008 a conference on Strategic Asset Allocation for Central Banks and Sovereign Wealth Funds was held, jointly organised by the Bank for International Settlements, the European Central Bank and the World Bank Treasury. A total of 35 speakers presented their perspectives on asset allocation, quantitative investment strategies and risk management.

The proceedings of that conference are published in two books. This book contains papers on the themes of Reserves Management and Sovereign Wealth Fund Management.

Papers on the themes of Interest Rate Modelling and Forecasting, Portfolio Optimization Techniques and Asset Class Modelling and Quantitative Techniques are collected in the book *Interest Rate Models, Asset Allocation and Quantitative Techniques for Central Banks and Sovereign Wealth Funds*, edited by Arjan B. Berkelaar, Joachim Coche and Ken Nyholm and published by Palgrave Macmillan in 2009 (ISBN 978-0-230-24012-4).

Notes on Contributors

Arjan B. Berkelaar is Head of Risk Management at Kaust Investment Management Company and was Principal Investment Officer at the World Bank. He is responsible for developing investment strategies and advising the various internal and external clients of the World Bank Treasury on asset allocation and related policy matters. Arjan advises central banks on reserves management issues and Sovereign Wealth Funds, including oil funds and national pension reserve funds on asset allocation and investment strategies. He joined the World Bank in July 2000. Before joining the World Bank, he worked at Ortec Consultants, a pension consultancy firm in the Netherlands. Arjan has published several papers in international journals and is a regular speaker at international conferences. He holds a Ph.D. degree in Finance from the Erasmus University Rotterdam; M.Sc. in Mathematics (summa cum laude) from the Delft University of Technology and is a CFA charter holder.

Joachim Coche works as Senior Asset Management Specialist at the Bank for International Settlements (BIS) in Basle where he advises central bank clients on the management of foreign exchange reserves. Prior to joining the BIS, he worked at the World Bank Treasury where he focused on the development of asset allocation strategies for the Bank's fixed income portfolios. Before joining the World Bank, he was a Senior Economist at the European Central Bank. His main interests include strategic asset allocation, asset and liability modelling and central bank reserves management. Joachim holds an M.Sc. and a Ph.D. in Economics from the University of Osnabrück.

Ken Nyholm works in the Risk Management Division of the European Central Bank, focusing on the practical implementation of financial and quantitative techniques in the area of fixed-income strategic asset allocation for the bank's domestic and foreign currency portfolios, as well as asset and liability management for pensions. Ken holds a Ph.D. in finance and has published numerous articles on yield curve modelling and financial market microstructure. He has extensive teaching experience and communication experience obtained from university courses at the master's level, as well as conference speaking engagements, and central banking seminars.

Dr. Roland Beck is Principal Economist at the European Central Bank where he is in charge of monitoring and forecasting macroeconomic and financial developments in oil-exporting countries, in particular Russia, and also follows developments in the international use of the euro. In this capacity, he has published research articles on Sovereign Wealth Funds and optimal reserve composition in Emerging Markets, among others. Prior to his current affiliation, Roland has been a senior economist at Deutsche Bank Research. He completed his graduate studies in Economics at the University of Maryland (USA) and Bonn University and holds a Ph.D. in Economics from the Goethe University in Frankfurt.

Javier Bonza is currently Head of Financial Research at Fondo Latinoamericano de Reservas (FLAR). He joined FLAR in 2002, as a risk and research analyst. He was responsible for the development and implementation of market and credit risk models as well as of the US economic research monitoring. In 2005, he was promoted to Quantitative Research Manager (QRM). Before joining FLAR, Javier served as Macroeconomic Policy Advisor at the Colombian Ministry of Finance from 1999 to 2001. He was responsible for assisting the vice minister with economic growth projections and providing economic outlook for multilateral institutions. Javier started his career as risk analyst at Sudameris Bank in 1996. In 2002, Javier obtained a M.Sc. in Quantitative Finance from Cass Business School, City of London, through academic scholarship granted by the Colombian foundation Colfuturo. Currently he is a Level II CFA Candidate. Javier also holds an M.A. in Economics (1998) and a B.S. in Economics (1997), both from Universidad de los Andes in Bogotá, Colombia, where he collaborates on specialized finance courses at the Andes University Business School.

Stephen John Fisher, managing director, is a client portfolio manager in the International Fixed Income Group based in Singapore. Initially an employee since 1992, Stephen rejoined in September 2000, after a period working with Merrill Lynch Investment Managers. Prior to this, Stephen was Regional Head of Capital Markets Research for Asia-Pacific from 1996 to 1998. Before this, Stephen worked in the Capital Markets Research group in New York. Stephen's expertise is in fixed income, equities, asset allocation and derivatives. He obtained an M.S. in finance from the University of Rochester and a B.Ec. from the University of Sydney, Australia. Stephen also earned a Ph.D. in finance from the W.E. Simon Graduate School of Business Administration, University of Rochester.

Alex Joia joined the BIS in August 2000 and moved to the BIS Representative Office for Asia and the Pacific in Hong Kong in May 2008. Prior to joining the BIS, he worked at Dresdner Kleinwort Benson in London. Alex has a doctorate from the department of applied mathematics and theoretical physics at Cambridge University and spent four years conducting post-doctoral research at the Ecole Centrale de Lyon. At the BIS Alex has conducted analysis on the Bank's strategic asset allocation and has been involved in the development of systems to support the BIS banking operations. In his current role he is responsible for the management of the Asian Bond Fund I, for servicing and providing technical assistance to BIS Asset Management clients in the region and for providing quantitative support to the business.

Urmila Kisoen is risk manager at the Financial Markets Division of the Dutch Central Bank (De Nederlandsche Bank), and is currently working on developing an ALM model for the balance sheet of the Dutch Central Bank. In her role as risk manager, Urmila Kisoen is involved in strategic asset allocation and reserve management. The main focus of her attention is on market risk and credit risk. Prior to joining De Nederlandsche Bank, Urmila Kisoen worked as a consulting actuary involved in many assignments and projects related to ALM for pension funds and insurance companies.

Jerome Kreuser is the Executive Director and Founder of The RisKontrol Group GmbH in Bern, Switzerland. He holds a Ph.D. in Mathematical Programming/Numerical Analysis and a Master's and B.A. with Honors in Mathematics from the University of Wisconsin. He specializes in strategic asset, liability and risk management for sovereigns, (re)insurance, pension funds, hedge funds, etc. He develops and consults on state-of-the-art systems applying dynamic stochastic optimization models integrated with stochastic processes for risk management that have their origins in a research project that he undertook at the World Bank. Mr. Kreuser worked for 24 years at the World Bank in various positions (1974–1998). He has headed projects, developed and implemented portfolio models, cash flow models, industrial planning models, health sector models, economic models and other project sector models. He undertook the model development for three World Development Reports. He has advised the Finance Complex on modelling applications on derivatives and the World Bank pension fund. He implemented one of the first commercial dynamic asset and liability optimization models under uncertainty that was applied in the World Bank's Treasurer's Department in the seventies. He has taught workshops on modelling applications in economics and finance and on asset and liability management, and international workshops on risk management for central banks and ministries of finance. He is an adjunct Full Professor of Operations Research at George Washington University where he has regularly taught graduate courses on the Applications of Linear and Nonlinear Optimization to Economics and Finance since 1982. He has served as an International Reserves Management advisor for the International Monetary Fund. He has published several papers on theory and applications in his areas of interest.

Eduard Ponds (1958) is Professor in Economics of Collective Pension Plans at Tilburg University. He has been employed at APG since 1995, subsequently as actuary and senior researcher in investments. He is currently the head of research economics of collective pensions. He graduated in Economics. In 1995 he obtained his Ph.D.; his thesis was entitled: *Supplementary pensions, intergenerational risk sharing, and welfare*. He is also an affiliated researcher at Netspar. Eduard Ponds has expertise in the economics of pensions and collective pension plans, in particular in the fields of pension funds, pension plan (re)design, risk management, actuarial aspects, intergenerational risk sharing and classic and value-based ALM. His publications are mainly on collective pensions, in particular related to the pension fund sector in the Netherlands and elsewhere (http://www.tilburguniversity.nl/webwijs/show/?uid=e.h.m.ponds).

David Rogal is an analyst in BlackRock's Multi-Asset Portfolio Strategies (MAPS) group, which is responsible for developing, assembling and managing investment solutions involving multiple strategies and asset classes. Within MAPS, he is part of the Strategic Advice team where he focuses on various research and analytical projects, and is responsible for asset allocation analysis and liability-based portfolio structuring for taxable clients and prospects, as well as maintaining relationships with several of the firm's hedging clients. Mr. Rogal began his career at BlackRock in 2006 as an analyst in the Financial Institutions Group. He earned a B.A. degree in economics and genetics from Cornell University in 2006, and is a member of Phi Beta Kappa.

Krzysztof Rybinski was born on 1 March 1967 in Warsaw. He holds master's degrees in mathematics and computer sciences, and master's and doctorate degrees in economics, all from the University of Warsaw. In his very busy professional carrier he worked as a software engineer in Tokyo, as a World Bank consultant (labor market issues), a Central European University research fellow (privatization in CEE) and a Warsaw University assistant professor (teaching math, econometrics and economics). He organized and served as a director of the economics program financed by the largest US foundations, which offered economics training to some 700 faculty members from 20 post-communist countries. Dr Rybinski has worked as chief economist in three commercial banks in Poland. He was rated several times among the top five financial markets economists covering Central and Easter Europe by international financial magazines. He was also selected the best financial markets' economist in 2000 in Rzeczpospolita ranking. In March 2004 Dr. Rybinski was appointed to the National Bank of Poland deputy governor position where he served until February 2008. He managed eight different departments, including research, reserves management, financial risk, payments systems, cash and international affairs. He represented Poland as the NBP delegate at the Economic and Financial Committee of the European Union and served as the World Bank alternate governor for Poland. He was also a member of the Polish Financial Services Authority and Government Economic Committee. In April 2008 Dr. Rybinski joined Ernst & Young as Partner. He serves as a supervisory board member of several financial sector companies (bank, VC/PE and alternative investments). Dr. Rybinski is the author of more than 50 scientific articles on various topics in economics and finance. He has published several hundred articles in Polish press and is often featured in electronic media. In 2007 he published the book *Three*

Faces of Globalization – Offshoring, Global Imbalances – Monetary Policy (in Polish). In May 2008 he published the book *Gordian Knots of the 21st Century* (in English), which predicts the end of Pax Americana and beginning of the new world order, where Asia will play an important, if not dominant, role.

Vahe Sahakyan is an Asset Management Specialist at the Bank for International Settlements and is a Ph.D. candidate in Quantitative Finance at the Swiss Finance Institute, Zurich. He also holds a Candidate of Science (equivalent to Ph.D.) in Mathematical Methods in Economics from the Yerevan State University, Master of Arts in Economics from the Central European University, Budapest, and Master of Science in Finance from the Universitat Pompeu Fabra, Barcelona. Vahe Sahakyan's experience includes work at the World Bank as a consultant for private sector development and competition policy, work at Central Bank of the Republic of Armenia (RA) and work at the Ministry of Economy of RA. Vahe Sahakyan also has extensive teaching experience in econometrics, corporate finance and game theory. He has published about ten articles and his research interests are in microeconomics of banking and financial markets, corporate finance, regulation economics, and asset management and mathematical finance.

Bernd Scherer is global head of Quantitative GTAA. He joined Morgan Stanley in 2007 and has 14 years of investment experience. Prior to joining the firm, Bernd worked at Deutsche Bank Asset Management as head of the Quantitative Strategies Group's Research Center as well as head of Portfolio Engineering in New York. Before this he headed the Investment Solutions and Overlay Management Group in Frankfurt. Bernd has also held various positions at Morgan Stanley, Oppenheim Investment Management, Schroders and JPMorgan Investment Management. He has authored and edited six books on quantitative asset management and more than 40 articles in refereed journals. Bernd received Master's degrees in economics from the University of Augsburg and the University of London and a Ph.D. from the University of Giessen. He is visiting professor at Birkbeck College (London) as well as WHU (Koblenz), Board member of the London Quant Group and external adviser to the Swiss Finance Institute.

Fred Weinberger is a managing director and asset-liability specialist in BlackRock's Multi-Asset Portfolio Strategies Group. Before joining BlackRock in 1999, Mr. Weinberger was a managing director in Investment Policy & Strategy at Trust Company of the West from 1995. In this role, he was responsible for both the Investment Policy & Strategy and Quantitative Analysis & Development Groups. Previously, he was a director in the Bond Portfolio Analysis Group of Salomon Brothers, where his responsibilities included the development of quantitative approaches and tools for asset allocation and asset-liability management decisions. Mr. Weinberger holds an M.B.A. from McGill University.

Introduction

Reserves and Asset Accumulation

Over the past decade public entities, i.e., governments, central banks and other public intuitions have accumulated significant investable assets, especially in the areas of central bank foreign exchange reserves, commodity savings funds, and pension reserve and social security funds.

Foreign exchange reserves (excluding gold) have grown to about USD 7 trillion by the end of 2008. While a discussion about reserves adequacy in the context of recent market events is ongoing, there continues to be a view that reserves in many countries are in excess of what is deemed adequate to protect against exogenous shocks or adverse external financing conditions. Consequently, some countries have therefore officially established reserves investment corporations out of excess central bank reserves to seek higher returns. In other countries central banks have notionally split the reserves portfolio into separate tranches, including an investment tranche that might be invested in a broader set of asset classes that goes beyond the traditional investment universe of central bank reserves managers, covering just government instruments, agencies and instruments issued by supranational institutions. An enhanced investment universe allows for additional exposures to credit risk obtained, for example, via asset classes such as agency bonds and mortgage backed securities (MBS), and in some cases the enhancement even includes idiosyncratic risk, in the form of corporate bonds and equities. While risk aversion globally (including that of central banks) has increased as a result of the recent global financial crisis, the long-term trend of reserves diversification will likely continue.

With rising commodity prices in the past couple of years, several commodity exporting countries have accumulated large amounts of foreign currency assets. Many countries have established commodity funds to form a buffer against volatile commodity prices and manage their newfound riches more efficiently. By some estimates commodity funds have accumulated about USD 2 trillion. These funds serve different purposes including stabilization of fiscal revenues and intergenerational saving. Stabilization funds typically invest in high-grade fixed income instruments, while savings funds seek to invest in investment-grade fixed income, public and private equity and hedge funds.

Finally, as a result of aging populations and demographic shifts, many countries have established pension reserve funds and social security funds to support pay-as-you-go pension systems. Pension reserve funds are established and funded by the government through direct fiscal transfers. Social security funds are part of the overall social security system. Inflows are mainly surpluses of employee and/or employer contributions over current payouts, as well as top-up contributions from the government through fiscal transfers. According to estimates by the OECD (International Monetary Fund), pension reserve and social security funds total around USD 2 trillion (excluding the US social security trust fund which does not have investable assets).

Many of the funds identified above have been classified as 'sovereign wealth funds' (SWFs) by the financial press. There is no single, universally accepted definition of a SWF but one simple working definition is an investment fund controlled by a sovereign and invested (at least partially) in foreign assets. Table I.1 shows a list of various large public investment funds across the world, including central banks, sovereign wealth funds as well as pension reserve funds. Estimated assets under management by the largest 50 funds total over USD 11 trillion. A total of 44 funds are in emerging or developing countries managing over USD 3 trillion.

Out of the 50 largest funds listed in Table 1, 23 are institutions other than central banks. Many of these sovereign wealth funds were established in the last 10 years[1]. These new public funds' investment strategies are likely to follow the lead of established funds, and other institutional investors, moving from fixed income investments into equities, and even hedge funds, private equity and other alternative investments.

Table I.1 The 50 largest public investment funds

Country	Name of the fund	Estimated AUM (in USD bn)*
China	Central Bank Reserves	1530
Japan	National Reserve Funds	1218
Japan	Central Bank Reserves	974
UAE	Abu Dhabi Investment Authority (ADIA)	875
Russia	Central Bank Reserves	542
Saudi Arabia	Various Funds	433
Norway	The Government Pension Fund	401
Singapore	GIC	330
China	SAFE Investment Company	312
India	Central Bank Reserves	303
Kuwait	Kuwait Fund for Future Generations	264
Korea	Central Bank Reserves	258
Korea	National Pension Service	229
Euro area	Central Bank Reserves	222
Brazil	Central Bank Reserves	206

Continued

Table I.1 Continued

Country	Name of the fund	Estimated AUM (in USD bn)*
China	China Investment Corporation	200
Singapore	Central Bank Reserves	177
China-HK	Hong Kong Monetary Authority	173
Hong Kong SAR	Central Bank Reserves	158
Russia	Reserve Fund	141
Algeria	Central Bank Reserves	141
Singapore	Temasek	134
Sweden	National Pension Funds (AP1-AP4 and AP-6)	133
Canada	Canadian Pension Plan	111
Malaysia	Central Bank Reserves	109
Thailand	Central Bank Reserves	100
Libya	Libya Investment Authority (includes LAFICO)	100
Mexico	Central Bank Reserves	99
Libya	Central Bank Reserves	87
Dubai	Dubai Investment Corporation	82
Turkey	Central Bank Reserves	77
China	National Social Security Fund	74
Poland	Central Bank Reserves	71
Nigeria	Central Bank Reserves	62
United States	Central Bank Reserves	61
United Arab Emirates	Central Bank Reserves	61
Qatar	Qatar Investment Authority	60
Indonesia	Central Bank Reserves	57
Norway	Central Bank Reserves	50
Algeria	Fonds de Régulation des Recettes de l'Algérie	47
Argentina	Central Bank Reserves	46
Switzerland	Central Bank Reserves	45
Spain	Fondo de Reserva de la Seguridad Social	45
Australia	Future Fund	44
Canada	Central Bank Reserves	43
United Kingdom	Central Bank Reserves	42
France	Fonds de Reserve pour les Retraites	42
Romania	Central Bank Reserves	39
Kazakhstan	National Fund	38
Ukraine	Central Bank Reserves	37

Note: *Data reflect latest available figures as reported by individual entities or authoritative sources. Various reporting dates between 2004 and 2008.

Public Investment Funds: Objectives and Liabilities

We cannot paint all public investment funds with the same broad brush. To better understand investment objectives, governance arrangements and investment behaviour, it is helpful to classify the funds according to their policy objectives and liability structure. Similar to Rozanov (2007)[2] we distinguish between five types of public investment funds:

- stabilization and buffer funds and central bank FX reserves,
- reserves investment corporations,
- savings and heritage funds,
- pension reserve and social security funds, and
- government holding management companies.

Stabilization and buffer funds as well as central bank reserves are typically invested with a focus on safety and liquidity. These funds face a contingent liability that is subject to volatile prices such as exchange rates and/or commodity prices. Stabilization funds may need to transfer significant money to the government budget when commodity prices drop precipitously. Central banks may need to intervene in the foreign exchange markets when the domestic currency comes under pressure. Capital preservation, either in nominal or in real terms, is therefore of paramount importance. The investment horizon in most instance ranges from 1 to 3 years and managing credit and liquidity risk are critical. We include traditional central bank reserves in the first category, while so-called excess reserves[3] are included under the category of reserves investment corporations – whether a country has actually established such an organization or not – as the asset allocation problem for both is the same.

It should be noted that the discipline of central bank reserves management is evolving dramatically with the tremendous growth of central bank reserves, stronger balance of payments positions and global capital flows. As emerging market reserves have increased – both in outright terms and beyond that needed for external financial stability – the investment return and negative carry[4] associated with holding reserves has become more of an issue. Central banks have pursued mainly two strategies to address this problem. Some countries have engaged in asset/liability management at the national level and used 'excess' reserves to pay down foreign denominated debt, thus reducing the cost of carry on the national balance sheet. Beyond debt repayment, central banks have also sought to increase long-term returns through more efficient or aggressive investment strategies to reduce the negative carry. This has been done in various ways:

1. shifting excess reserves into a sovereign wealth fund (e.g. China Investment Corporation) in a swap arrangement with the Ministry of Finance;

2. setting up a separate investment agency to manage the long-term investment tranche of the foreign currency reserves (e.g. Korea Investment Corporation); or
3. managing the investment tranche within the central bank (e.g. the Swiss National Bank, the Central Bank of Botswana).

The investment tranche is typically invested in broader investment instruments and over a longer investment horizon with less need for immediate liquidity. The implicit liability of Central Bank reserves is typically characterized by domestic short- to medium-term debt that has been issued for sterilization purposes.

Savings and heritage funds are typically established out of commodity revenues and represent net wealth for a country – unlike central bank reserves which are borrowed. The objective of these funds is to sustain government spending after commodity resources have been depleted. Decision makers are faced with two trade-offs that will, together, determine the ultimate size and life of the fund: current versus future level of spending and the investment strategy for the fund's assets. Transfers to and from the fund are typically determined by a savings or spending rule.

Broadly, there are two types of savings and spending rules. The first is based only on fiscal considerations and any saving is a residual. In this case commodity revenues typically flow into the budget first and a portion is transferred to the fund. Transfer rules include balanced budget requirements whereby allocations to the fund are made only after balancing the budget and there is no cap on the amount of deficit financing available from commodity extraction and sales. Also included in this category are those rules that rely on an administrative oil price to divide oil revenues between the budget and savings. While these rules may stabilize the volatility of government revenues, they do not ensure any capital accumulation to support future spending needs. The second type puts an explicit cap on the spending of oil revenues ensuring some level of capital accumulation over time. In this case commodity revenues typically flow into the fund first and a portion is transferred to the budget. Various ad-hoc spending rules have been devised, but a general principle is that if the fund is to have a permanent nature, the average real spending rate over time should not exceed the expected real return on the portfolio.

Savings and heritage funds tend to have a perpetual investment horizon: they are expected to provide for current and future generations for perpetuity. The asset allocation problem of savings and heritage funds is comparable to that of endowments and foundations, but there are important differences as well. Many savings and heritage funds are in emerging market countries. Typically commodity exporting countries receive commodity revenues in US dollars. When commodities represent a large portion of a country's economic base, commodity price volatility can easily be transmitted to economic volatility leading to the so-called Dutch disease[5]. One of the purposes of the commodity savings fund is to accumulate wealth in US dollars and only transfer a portion of the fund to the government budget that then will be converted into the domestic currency. The bulk of the assets of the fund will therefore be kept in foreign currency. Consequently, most – if not all – of the assets will be in foreign investments. Managing exchange rate risk therefore becomes important – particularly if the domestic currency appreciates against e.g. the US dollar. Savings fund are restricted, however, in their ability to hedge foreign currency risk exposure relative to the domestic currency[6].

Our fourth category is pension reserve and social security funds. Unlike savings funds and foreign reserves, these funds have explicit and clearly defined liabilities. Also these funds typically have a significant allocation to domestic assets. Some observers refer to such funds as sovereign pension funds and define them a separate group of sovereign wealth funds. This group is not well-defined, however. Pension reserve funds are funded by the government from general tax revenues and have been set up to partially or fully pre-finance future pension liabilities of the government, particularly in the light of an aging population. The purpose is to smooth the expected rising fiscal burden on the public pay-as-you-go system. The assets of these funds are owned by the government and fully at their disposal. These funds are rightfully labelled sovereign wealth funds and are typically found in OECD countries where populations are aging rapidly.

Pension reserve funds are usually established with a finite horizon of about 40 to 50 years. The objective of these funds is to set aside and invest a significant portion of financial resources over the next 20 to 25 years during a so-called accumulation phase, making the accumulated assets gradually available thereafter during a so-called withdrawal phase that also lasts about 20 to 25 years at the discretion of the government or as mandated in applicable pension reserve laws. During the accumulation phase withdrawals from the fund are not allowed (typically by law). Consequently, pension reserve funds can allocate a significant portion of their assets to illiquid and risky investments. During the withdrawal phase managing liquidity becomes more important and the allocation should gradually be rebalanced to fixed income assets. Pension reserve funds have only been established in the last 10 years and so all of these funds are currently in the accumulation phase.

Social security funds, on the other hand, are part of the overall social security system. These funds invest contributions from employers and/or employees and are not typically funded by government revenues[7]. In other words, the money does not belong to the government. The government or a separate arms-length agency is acting as fiduciary. These funds should therefore not be classified as sovereign wealth funds. A third group that is sometimes (mistakenly) included under the label sovereign pension funds are pension plans that cover government workers. Unlike pension reserve funds, many social security funds do not have an explicit end-date and are currently paying out social security benefits to the eligible citizens.

The fifth category is government holding companies. Government holding companies are typically funded by privatization proceedings from former national companies. Investments are mostly direct equity stakes in various domestic companies on behalf of the government. Some government holding companies have also bought direct stakes in foreign companies. These types of investments have received a lot of attention in the press and are the subject of debate and concern in the developed world. Government holding companies tend to behave more like private equity funds and less like institutional investors. They do not have any identifiable liability.

It could be argued that there is a sixth category: development funds. These funds are set up with the specific goal of developing the domestic economy by taking large stakes in critical infrastructure projects. It should be noted that this objective could also be achieved through the spending policy of savings and heritage funds or even through domestic investments by savings and heritage funds. Domestic investments require care, however, to avoid contracting a bad case of Dutch disease and politicization (or even corruption) of investment decisions.

Table I.2 presents a summary and overview of the five types of public investment funds that we discussed above, including traditional central bank reserves and social security funds. The table highlights the distinct objectives of each type of fund, their typical liability structure and risk appetite as well as the types of asset classes that these funds might invest in. Many of the recently established funds are still far from the ideal asset allocation. The process of moving from the current asset allocation towards a more appropriate portfolio will likely be gradual. At first, funds will probably be managed conservatively, in ways not dramatically different from how official reserves are managed.

Strategic asset allocation

The strategic asset allocation decision for any investor sets out the optimal long-term portfolio, i.e. the portfolio with the highest expect total return given overall objectives, investment horizon and risk tolerance. It is generally accepted, among practitioners and academics, that the strategic asset allocation (SAA) is the main driver of the risk and return profile of any investment portfolio. The investment policy is typically determined through portfolio optimization. The asset allocation should have a long-term focus but be reviewed periodically – e.g. every one to three years.

Table I.2 Types of public investment funds

Type of fund	Objective	Source of funds	Type of liability	Risk appetite	Types of asset classes
Stabilization funds and central bank adequate reserves	Stability, liquidity and return	Commodity revenues, FX reserves	Contingent liability (depends on unpredictable and volatile variables such as commodity prices and exchange rates)	Low	High-grade fixed income
Reserves investment corporations and central bank excess reserves	Minimize opportunity cost of holding excess reserves	FX excess reserves	Domestic short- to medium-term debt – issued for sterilization purposes	Medium	Investment-grade fixed income and public equities
Savings and heritage funds	Share wealth across generations by converting nonrenewable assets in financial assets	Commodity revenues, fiscal revenues	Contractually defined interim payouts (typically governed by a spending rule) with perpetual investment horizon	Medium to high	Equities and alternative investments
Social security funds	Fund social security benefits	Contributions by participants (employees and employers)	Fixed liabilities in domestic currency that are contractually defined	Medium to high	Investment-grade fixed income, public equities, and some alternatives
Pension reserves funds	Pre-finance all or a portion of future public pension liabilities and act as a fiscal smoothing mechanism	Fiscal revenues	Contractually defined obligations in domestic currency. Typically drawdowns are prohibited for the first 15 to 20 years.	High – particularly during the accumulation stage. Risk appetite will decrease during payout stage.	Equities and illiquid alternative investments
Government holding management companies	Maximize investment return subject to acceptable level of risk	Fiscal revenues, privatization	No identifiable liability	Very high	Equities and illiquid alternative investments

A typical decision framework for setting the strategic asset allocation is:

1. articulate the objectives for overall investment management and the eligible investment universe;
2. specify the risk measures used to define the Board's tolerance for investment risk (e.g. the probability of adverse outcomes, value-at-risk and expected shortfalls), and set out what are unacceptable outcomes;
3. define the investment horizon over which the risk profile and success of the strategic asset allocation in meeting the objectives should be assessed;
4. formalize the methodology for developing the strategic asset allocation proposal – including the determination of capital market assumptions for each of the eligible asset classes and the techniques for deriving optimal risk-efficient portfolios;
5. operationalize the strategic asset allocation by setting out portfolio weights to each of the eligible asset classes, appropriate benchmarks, the rebalancing strategy, and an overall budget for active risk.

Academic research has, historically, focused on portfolio choice for individuals and defined benefit pension funds. Asset allocation for public institutions, on the other hand, appears to be somewhat neglected. While many of the techniques developed in the academic and practitioner literature can be applied to public investors, the unique circumstances and the investment universe of public investment funds require additional attention.

Some examples include:

- Public investment funds face policy objectives tied to their liabilities that may differ from those of other institutional investors. These may include, for example, reducing the cost of sterilization for central banks and reserves investment corporations, stabilization of government revenues due volatile exchange rates and oil prices and domestic (infrastructure) investments to support and grow the domestic economy.
- Balance sheet considerations at the national level are important and governments want to avoid what is called 'mental accounting' in the discipline of behavioral finance, which can loosely be defined as: 'the left hand doesn't know what the right hand is doing'. The simplest example is one where a country has sizeable foreign debts and, at the same time, holds significant foreign currency reserves. Financially, this country would be better off by repaying its debts before it accumulates foreign assets. Coordinated financial management at the national level is particularly important for a country that has significant excess reserves, an oil savings fund and/or a national pension reserve fund.

- Broader macroeconomic implications should be considered when designing investment policies and saving (funding) and spending (withdrawal) rules. Many sovereign wealth funds, for example, are forced to invest abroad (as the source of their revenues is in foreign currency and the country wants to avoid contracting Dutch disease) – unlike other institutional investors that typically have a large allocation to their domestic market. The fund(s) need to be integrated into the government budget.
- Another reason that public investment funds might need to invest a significant portion of their assets abroad is the size of their domestic markets. Many public investment funds are in developing or emerging market countries where domestic markets are not (yet) liquid and deep enough. If the fund is large in relation to domestic financial markets the actions of the public investment fund might move the markets, forcing them to go overseas with their investments. While investors in developed countries typically hedge a significant amount of their foreign investments back into the domestic currency this is not available to sovereign wealth funds in emerging markets due to the absence of depth and liquidity in forward currency markets.
- The investment universe for some public investors might be somewhat different from that of individual investors and defined benefit pension funds. Central banks invest mostly in fixed income securities. Modelling yield curve dynamics over time is therefore important in constructing the appropriate asset allocation. Pension reserve and social security funds typically invest a (large) portion of their assets in domestic markets. Modelling the returns on domestic assets can be challenging due to lack of data availability.
- Finally, investments by public funds are exposed to the public spotlight and reputational considerations play a more important role than for other institutional investors. This has implications for how best to design governance arrangements to ensure that assets are managed as efficiently as possible.

As can be surmised from the examples above, the asset allocation problem for public investment funds requires additional attention and analysis. While research interest in central bank reserves management and sovereign wealth funds has increased in recent years (see Figure I.1), these topics still appear to be an under-researched field in economics and finance (see Figure I.2).

Against this background, the Bank for International Settlements, the European Central Bank and the World Bank Treasury organized a conference on Strategic Asset Allocation for Central Banks and Sovereign Wealth Funds on 24–25 November 2008. A total of 35 speakers presented their perspectives on asset allocation, quantitative investment strategies, and risk management. Many of the speakers were representatives from public investment funds.

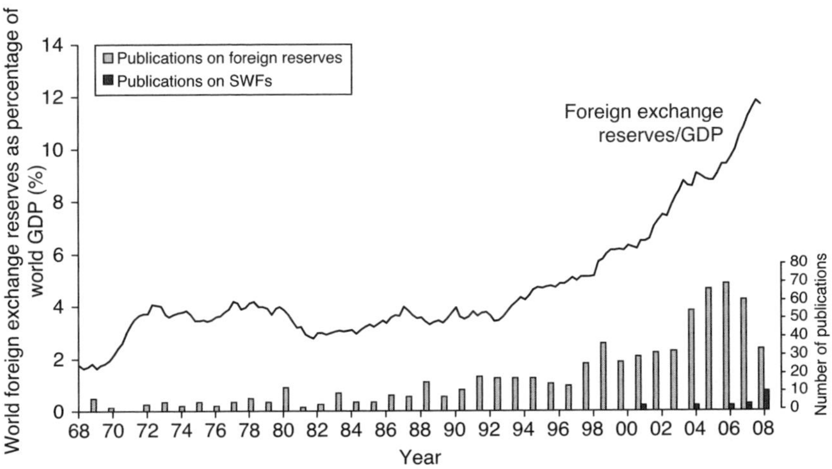

Figure I.1 Reserves growth and the number of academic publications on reserves and sovereign wealth management

Note: The ratio of global foreign exchanges reserves as a percentage of World GDP. Number of publications in the fields of foreign reserves and sovereign wealth funds as identifiable on basis of title, keywords and abstracts in the EconLit database maintained by the American Economic Association.

Source: IMF, *Econlit*

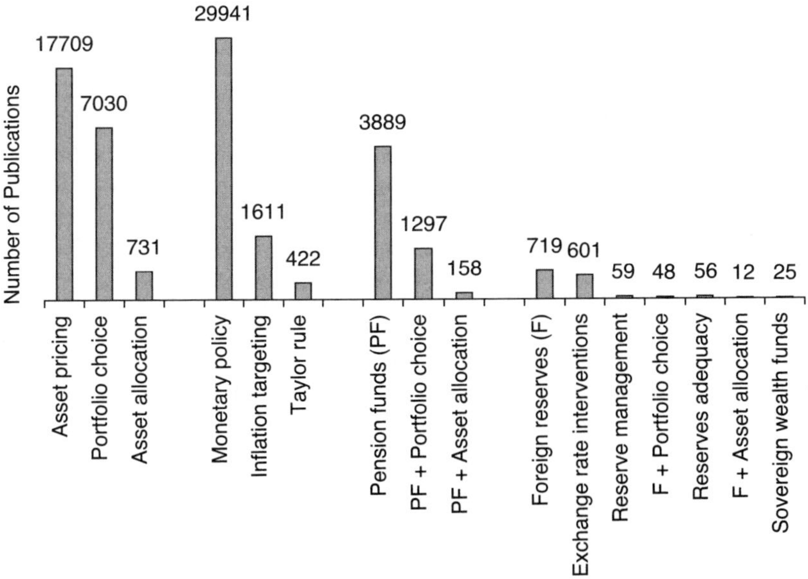

Figure I.2 Research fields in economics and finance: number of publications

Note: Number of matches in keywords, titles and abstracts of publications in EconLit database maintained by the American Economic Association. Numbers are based on contributions published between 1968 to 2008.

Source: *Econlit*

The presentations of that conference can be broadly grouped into five different themes:

1. reserves management,
2. sovereign wealth fund management,
3. interest rate modelling and forecasting,
4. portfolio optimization techniques, and
5. asset class modelling and quantitative techniques.

This book is a collection of papers that were presented which cover themes 1 and 2 (themes 3, 4 and 5 are collected in a second book Interest Rate Models, Asset Allocation and Quantitative Techniques for Central Banks and Sovereign Wealth Funds).

The next section provides a brief summary of each of the papers in this book.

Overview of the book

Theme 1: Reserves management

Central bank reserves have grown considerably in the past 10 years from less than USD 1.5 trillion to over USD 7 trillion. Central banks typically invest their foreign exchange reserves conservatively, guided by principles of liquidity and safety, and are concerned with market losses over the accounting cycle. The investment universe for central bank reserves largely consists of short- to medium-term government bonds issued by the United States and governments in the Eurozone. In many cases, the growth of reserves has been accompanied by sterilization costs where domestic interest rates exceed the rate of return on the foreign assets in which the reserves are invested. More importantly, many central banks have experienced significant foreign exchange losses as a result of the appreciation of their domestic currencies relative to reserve currencies.

With the rapid increase in foreign reserves in many emerging market countries, these costs have become too big to ignore and in several cases even result in a deterioration of central bank capital. Krzysztof Rybinski and Urszula Sowa propose the concept of OCHAR – Opportunity Cost of Holding Ample Reserves – which is defined as forgone GDP growth resulting from overly conservative reserves management by central banks. They estimate OCHAR for a sample of 33 countries which accounted for 80% of total central bank reserves in 2007. In their view, central banks – collectively – have embarked and will continue to embark on a reserves diversification journey. They put forward several hypotheses of the possible consequences of this diversification journey. They believe that relative prices of various assets will find new steady states, which may have little in common with relative valuations seen in the twentieth century. They also expect that slowly, over time, the so-called 'exorbitant privilege' of the United States will be eliminated. Finally they consider global stability risks in the context of the new reserves management style adopted by central banks.

Joachim Coche and Alex Joia identify and discuss the major choices faced by central banks in setting their strategic asset allocation. The strategic asset allocation (SAA) for investors is one of the most important factors affecting the risk and return characteristics of their overall portfolio. Identifying the appropriate SAA for a central bank is a complex process that seeks to ensure that reserves are invested in a manner consistent with the purpose for holding reserves and more specifically that policy constraints, as well as forward-looking risk and return expectations, are embedded in the portfolio. At many stages those responsible for SAA are faced with complex conceptual choices that have a profound impact on the resulting allocation. An example of an SAA process is provided that illustrates a possible and practical solution that balances quantitative and qualitative inputs.

Javier Bonza, Norma Gómez and Reinaldo Pabón propose a new approach to strategic asset allocation for central banks that balances short-term liquidity needs and real capital preservation. They estimate liquidity needs using a put option valuation approach. Monitoring the 'distance to a liquidity crisis' can be useful as an early warning signal of potential liquidity events. Bonza et al. also estimate the maximum financial needs for a central bank as a percentage of real GDP. Robust statistical methods and Monte Carlo simulation of real asset returns are used to establish a set of strategic asset allocation for the excess liquidity tranche of a central bank. The objective of the strategic asset allocation is to preserve the inflation-adjusted value of foreign reserves. Optimization results indicate that the suggested strategic asset allocation outperforms the typical asset allocations of central banks, in terms of real capital preservation risk and expected real return, without sacrificing the typical central bank risk tolerance. Finally, the role of Sovereign and Pooling Reserve Funds in attaining long-term capital preservation is considered. A contingent claim methodology is used to estimate potential loan demands of member countries to a Pooling Reserve Fund.

Urmila Kisoen presents an asset liability model applied to a central bank's balance sheet which incorporates various investment constraints. Economic variables are used as input into the balance sheet and simulated to produce future balance sheets for several years. The objective of these simulations is to gain insight into the development of the capital and reserves and the profit and loss account when investment policies, accounting rules and policy rules are separately or simultaneously implemented. Kisoen presents and discusses the outcomes of several simulations based on different sets of investment, accounting and policy rules. They show that ALM techniques can add substantial value in influencing the decision-making process and the design of policies for a central bank.

Central banks hold foreign reserves to intervene in the currency market. The trigger for currency intervention depends on many factors that cannot be predicted – trade flows, domestic shocks, foreign shocks, speculative attacks and financial crises, as well as the monetary and fiscal policies of domestic and foreign governments. 'Intervention risk' – the sudden need to buy or sell foreign exchange to defend the currency – is the major risk facing a central bank's reserve holdings. Stephen Fisher examines intervention risk and the financial tools that can be employed to combat it. Specifically, he focuses on the interaction between intervention risk on the one hand and investment risks contained in a central bank's reserves portfolio. The major finding is that intervention risk can be effectively managed, and even diversified away, by careful asset choice. Intervention is just another asset (or liability) in a central bank's portfolio that has its own return and risk characteristics. Asset allocation and benchmark selection are key to combating intervention risk. In general, the results strongly encourage central banks to adopt more aggressive asset allocations for their reserves. This means that central banks should decrease their allocation to short term bonds and increase their allocations to longer maturity, higher yielding fixed income assets and even equities.

Establishing a reserves management strategy comprises decisions on the level of reserves (reserves adequacy) and the composition of reserves (reserves allocation). Both in the literature and in practice, the reserves management strategy is often the result of a fragmented, hierarchical decision making process. Joachim Coche and Vahe Sahakyan analyze the implications of jointly determining reserves adequacy and composition. They introduce a model to analyze the optimal reserves management strategy for a small country that is subject to external liquidity shocks. Long-term capital investments in this country are funded by short-term borrowing in foreign currency. In this setting the central bank aims at mitigating adjustment costs to the economy implied by the external liquidity shocks by providing foreign currency loans to the private sector. In deciding the reserves management strategy, the central bank balances adjustment costs, costs of funding foreign reserves as well as investment risks and returns. While investment returns and liquidity shocks are exogenous, funding costs are endogenous and a function of the countries vulnerability. Inter alia, Coche and Sahakyan show that both the demand for reserves and the reserves' composition depend on the characteristics of liquidity shocks and adjustment costs as well as on the central bank's risk aversion. Also a highly risk averse central bank will hold reserves and invest part of these reserves in risky assets in the presence of economically meaningful liquidity shocks.

Theme 2: Sovereign wealth fund management

Increasing numbers of nations are facing a new challenge in managing significant accumulations of national wealth. This sovereign wealth has arisen from a number of sources, including revenues from oil and other natural resources, large trade surpluses, and significant foreign investment in rapidly growing economies. There is an increasing consensus that the appropriate investment policy for such assets is one that is less conservative than the traditional strategies for central bank reserves. The first challenge in managing a sovereign wealth fund is to establish the appropriate asset allocation for the fund. This requires an understanding of the purposes of the fund, the nature and timing of future spending, and the risk preferences of its sponsors.

Bernard Lee, David Rogal and Fred Weinberger consider two types of sovereign wealth funds: stabilization funds and savings funds. They discuss the intended purposes of each, and importantly, the key differences in the nature of their future spending. Using Monte Carlo simulation and assumed risk preferences, asset allocation benchmarks for stabilization and savings funds are evaluated. A key differentiator from stabilization funds is that for savings funds, spending is more discretionary. Nonetheless, the spending decision should not be arbitrary, which leads to the notion of a spending rule. The spending rule should be developed in conjunction with an asset allocation policy to meet an objective of 'intergenerational equity' while achieving a high level of real spending.

Bernd Scherer reviews the financial economics of portfolio choice for oil-based sovereign wealth funds. The optimal asset allocation problem is viewed as a decision-making problem with nontradable endowed wealth (i.e. oil reserves). Optimal portfolios combine speculative demand (optimal growth) as well as hedging demand (hedging resource fluctuation risk) and their level of risk taking should depend both on the fraction of financial wealth to resource wealth as well as the oil shock hedging properties of its investments. As a novelty in the theoretical literature Schrerer introduces background risk for a sovereign wealth fund in the form of oil reserve uncertainty. Sovereign wealth funds with large uncertainty about the size of their reserves should invest less aggressively and vice versa. The optimal speed of the extraction policy (oil to equity transformation) is also identified as a driving force for portfolio adjustments across time. A dynamic programming approach is presented to approximate portfolio adjustments. In a second chapter, Schrerer derives closed form solutions for the optimal dynamic asset allocation for a sovereign wealth fund. He derives a three-fund separation result that splits the optimal portfolio for a sovereign wealth fund into speculative demand as well as hedge demand against oil price shocks and shocks to the short term risk-free rate. A small empirical example with equities, bonds and listed real estate is provided to illustrate the framework.

Stijn Claessens and Jerome Kreuser present a generic framework for analyzing the specific strategic investment and risk management issues facing sovereign wealth funds. They allow simultaneously for general objectives, multiple risk constraints, dynamic rebalancing, variations in stochastic processes over time, extreme events, and diverse classes of assets and liabilities to be managed. These features are presented in a dynamic stochastic optimization model that allows for easy adjustments and adaptation to different macroeconomic and microeconomic -based approaches to sovereign wealth management. Scenario generation, model formulation, solution analysis and the estimation of density functions of outcomes are presented in general terms. The framework is then applied to the case of the Government Pension Fund Global (GPFG) of Norway. The asset allocation produced by the model is compared with the current asset allocation of GPFG.

Yueyan Zhang and Xianhua Wei study the optimal size, asset allocation and target return of sovereign wealth funds (SWFs), taking the China Investment Corporation (CIC) as an example. They use Deaton's precautionary savings model[8] to calculate the optimal size of foreign exchange expenditures. Improvements to the model are made by differentiating between risky and non-risky assets in order to determine the optimal asset allocation and investment strategy for sovereign wealth funds. The optimal size and asset allocation of a sovereign wealth fund mainly depend on the expected trend and fluctuations of future foreign exchange earnings and expected investment returns. When foreign exchange earnings show an upward trend, the scale of the sovereign wealth fund should not be expanded even when the expected investment return is high, and the ratio of risky assets should be kept stable and high. When foreign exchange earnings are stabilized and its growth rate slows down, the size of the sovereign wealth fund has a positive correlation with the degree of earnings fluctuation and the expected return on investment. When foreign exchange earnings decrease, the size of the sovereign wealth fund should be expanded even when the expected investment return is low.

Roland Beck and Michael Fidora from the European Central Bank analyze the impact of sovereign wealth funds on global financial markets. They simulate the potential impact of a transfer of traditional foreign exchange reserves to sovereign wealth funds on global capital flows. If sovereign wealth funds would allocate foreign assets according to market capitalization rather than liquidity considerations, the 'bias' towards the major reserve currencies would be reduced. As a result, more capital would flow 'downhill' from developed to developing economies, in line with standard neoclassical predictions. More specifically, the Euro area and the United States could be subject to net capital outflows while Japan and emerging markets would attract net capital inflows. The findings are sensitive to alternative assumptions for the portfolio objectives of SWFs. Finally, Beck and Fidora discuss whether a change in net capital flows triggered by SWFs could have an impact on stock prices and bond yields.

Roderick Molenaar, Roy Hoevenaars, and Eduard Ponds propose the method of so-called value-based generational accounting to evaluate the (re)distributive effects of collective saving plans such as pension funds and oil savings funds for the younger and older generations. The first building block of the proposed method is generational accounting as developed in public finance to investigate intergenerational distributional effects of fiscal policy. This method is used to frame a collective plan in terms of generational accounts. The second building block is the valuation of these generational accounts as embedded options similar to option valuation in the financial markets. The third building block is to employ an asset liability management model – traditionally used by banks, pension funds and insurance companies. The framework provides insights into the redistributive effects of fund redesign.

Asset Allocation in a General Equilibrium Framework

Bob Litterman, Goldman Sachs

Dinner Speech at the Public Investors Conference 2008, Strategic Asset Allocation for Central Banks & Sovereign Wealth Funds, European Central Bank, 24 November 2008.

My topic tonight sounds rather abstract, "What are the implications of a general equilibrium framework for asset allocation policy?" but I hope to convince you of its relevance for official institutions.

How you address this issue should impact important decisions you make in managing your reserves. In particular, even the most basic question, "How much risk should you take?" may change depending on whether you think in terms of partial or general equilibrium. Perhaps more important, how governments in general respond to this issue may also affect the overall stability of financial markets.

I suspect that you, like most investors, have probably not thought about the issue and that by default you are probably taking a partial equilibrium approach. I will argue that, unlike most investors, governments, in particular, should address this issue and should take a general equilibrium approach.

Now, what is the issue, and what is the difference between a partial equilibrium and a general equilibrium approach? If you frame the question, in managing your assets along the following lines, "Given my expectations for how the markets will behave, how can I maximize my return for any given level of risk?" then you are taking a conventional, partial equilibrium, approach. You are asking what is optimal for you; and implicitly you are assuming that your answer does not affect how others will behave.

The word "partial" in this context refers to the assumption that your behaviour is independent of others. In a "general" equilibrium model you and other investors are assumed to take each other's behavior into account in forecasting the behaviour of the market.

It's a question of what comes first: in partial equilibrium, you start with assumptions about the market and you then optimize your own portfolio holding those assumptions unchanged. For most investors that approach makes sense, they are small relative to the total market.

In general equilibrium you and all other investors start by having a concern about how each of you will behave, and you take that into account as you think about the markets. I will argue, and I think it is actually rather obvious, that when governments think about the markets they have to take a general equilibrium approach – in other words, they have to take into account how they and all other governments, as well as private agents will behave. It only makes sense for governments to at least think about the implications of general equilibrium. Collectively, governments are just too big not to do so.

What does this mean in practice for asset allocation policies? How should governments, as opposed to private investors, think about risk, expected return, and liquidity? There is a conventional approach to asset allocation and there are conventional models and ways to think about this topic. But tonight I want to question those conventions: we have to recognize the limitations of our models, particularly in light of the recent instability evident in the financial markets. We also have to recognize that governments are different than private investors and thus the conventional approaches to asset allocation that make sense for individuals probably do not make sense for governments.

Several inadequacies of the standard approaches are highlighted when we ask fundamental questions about government investment policies: why do governments often divide their reserves among multiple institutions, such as central banks and sovereign wealth funds; how do these institutions differ from each other and from other private fund managers; and how should these institutions, acting on behalf of their governments, approach investment decisions and how should they react to recent market developments?

In managing their wealth, governments are concerned with both short-run liquidity, and long-term safety. These two different concerns lead many governments to divide their wealth into separate pools which are managed very differently and with very different investment horizons. But the standard asset allocation framework has only one time interval of unspecified duration. In the conventional approach there are no dynamics and there is no provision for liquidity trade-offs – and yet the need for liquidity and the expected holding period interval are two key dimensions along which central banks and sovereign wealth funds differ with respect to fund management.

Central bank portfolios are generally held in very liquid, relatively low risk portfolios. The portfolio horizon is generally quite short as well, perhaps measured in months. Sovereign wealth funds hold very illiquid portfolios and manage them with very long horizons, perhaps measured in decades. It's very difficult to integrate these approaches. In practice most governments break their total wealth into two or more pools and manage each pool more or less independently.

But my main concern about the standard approach to asset allocation, which leads to my central message tonight, is this: official institutions are unlike other investors in that they are forced to recognize that they operate in the context of a general equilibrium framework. While it may be appropriate for an individual, an endowment, or even a large private pension fund to view the markets as exogenous from a perspective of maximizing their own utility, official institutions have a joint responsibility to consider whether their behavior, if followed broadly, would be consistent with a stable market equilibrium. In practice what this means is that you must each take each other's behavior into account as you formulate your investment policies.

Now let's turn to the question of market stability. There are a number of potential roles that governments may play in a general equilibrium framework. Certainly there are short-term liquidity demands that market economies face, some of which, as we are seeing in the current environment, can grow into systemic banking system solvency issues. Thus, stabilizing the global economy may require significant liquid public reserves. Another potential role of governments is to look out over a very long horizon, saving for future generations. Private individuals certainly save for their future needs, but individuals are likely to have investment horizons and risk preferences that differ systematically from those of governments.

Central banks and sovereign wealth funds have many characteristics in common. They both manage government owned assets, and at least in principle they are participating in a joint optimization on behalf of the government. They also distinguish themselves from most other institutional fund management companies in that they typically do not have explicit liabilities.

But these institutions obviously differ as well. Central banks have many functions in addition to reserve management, but for our purposes the main difference between central banks and sovereign wealth funds in regard to the management of government assets is that they occupy opposite ends of the spectrum in terms of their ability to take risk and their need for liquidity. It's very important to focus on these differences in time horizon and how they affect investment policy.

Having worked on both sides of my firm, Goldman Sachs, I am well aware that we have a similar distinction in risk and liquidity needs between the market making side of our business, the "sell" side, which has a short time horizon, is quite liquid and engages in market making, or "liquidity provision," and our investment side, the "buy" side, which is a liquidity demander and holds positions over long horizons. This distinction between a liquidity demander and liquidity provider is not always so obvious, but as we have seen recently a retreat by liquidity providers can create fragility and volatility in financial markets.

Let's consider this issue through some examples: consider the quant liquidity crunch in August 2007, an recent event that I personally witnessed from a painfully central location as the head of the Quantitative Investment Strategies group in Goldman Sachs Asset Management. Historically there were two types of quantitative algorithms, those that demanded liquidity and those that supplied it.

Quantitative investors like our group used systematic algorithms to take advantage of traditional long-horizon investment themes such as valuation, earnings quality, and momentum. We were liquidity demanders. We built up positions with exposure to factors that predicted returns over periods of months or years.

The success of these strategies, however, over a period of two decades led to an exponential growth in assets in our business, but more generally in assets under management using such quantitative techniques. This growth caused the information in quantitative factors to be incorporated more and more quickly into prices. The decay rate of information began to increase, and as it did, the time horizon of quantitative investors began to shorten.

At the same time this was happening, another style of quantitative management, statistical arbitrage, developed which focused on taking advantage of high frequency patterns in prices. In essence these algorithms were providing liquidity, reacting to the mean reverting price movements created by liquidity demanders. However, with the increased size of the quant space, and their systematic behaviour, liquidity providers began to be able to anticipate the liquidity demands of this group of investors by reacting to the underlying information itself, rather than the price signals, so that the new information, even about long-term factors such as measures of valuation, began to be incorporated almost immediately into prices.

Long-term investment strategies were becoming less effective as more and more capital flowed into both activities in recent years, and in the summer of 2007, driven in part by the growing stresses from the sub-prime mortgage problems, there was a recognition that what had been for decades a successful long-term investment strategy had merged with statistical arbitrage and together they had both become one crowded trade. This realization led to a sudden panic in the first week of August as quant managers tried to unwind their positions, and quant investing imploded. The de-leveraging of the quant space over four days produced negative returns in virtually all quant factors which, when measured in terms of the immediate prior volatility, had a magnitude that was over 30 standard deviations. It felt like an explosion.

It is still amazing to me how this event, which is clearly understood in retrospect, could appear suddenly, seemingly out of nowhere with very few warning signs. It was a phase change in market behavior.

One lesson from this event that applies broadly is that deviations from equilibrium, such as the predictable returns from quantitative factors, are opportunities for investors to create alpha, a very attractive, if illusive, prey. Such opportunities will create market forces, however, which, over time and not necessarily smoothly, will eliminate those deviations. Though perhaps not perfectly efficient, markets are very efficient.

To the extent that inefficiencies in markets do exist, it makes sense for central banks and sovereign funds, like other investors, to try to take advantage of the profit opportunity and in doing so, to push markets toward equilibrium. However, to the extent that such competition between sovereign funds and the private sector could lead to significant liquidity demands emerging suddenly, as it did in the quant space, one can easily imagine how such competition could become destabilizing. Official institutions need to avoid not only creating, on their own, a sudden demand for liquidity, but they have to avoid any sudden response in the private sector due to an anticipation of, or possible reaction to, their actions.

Let me remind you of another example of a market instability arising from investors treating an investment strategy from a partial equilibrium perspective. I'm sure most of you remember a rather simple, and deceptively attractive investment idea developed in the mid-1980s called "portfolio insurance." The idea was that when markets go up investors are wealthier and should be comfortable taking proportionally more risk. And conversely when markets go down investors are poorer and may want to reduce their risk exposure. I don't want to argue that this is rational – although from a behavioral finance perspective we can understand that investors may want to behave this way. It seems to minimize regret.

In any case, this investment strategy can work fine when one investor buys call options to structure such an investment profile in advance. However, as we saw in October 1987, when a large enough fraction of the market tried to create such a profile through synthetic trading of futures, it led to positive reinforcement of market moves, in particular to forced selling, illiquidity, and a market crash. What made sense for one investor was not consistent with a stable market equilibrium.

Now consider a less obvious example of the problem. This example arose in a recent conversation I had with a Chicago economist, John Cochrane. Many institutional investors follow a policy of rebalancing their portfolio back toward a strategic asset allocation benchmark when the relative prices of assets change. In the context of discussing how institutions could react to the recent market declines, I suggested that such rebalancing makes sense. John called me on it, "Not so fast," he said, "rebalancing is not consistent with general equilibrium – not everyone can rebalance at the same time."

I was taken aback. I have advocated rebalancing strategies to institutional investors for many years without ever considering the possible inconsistency between individual rebalancing and general equilibrium.

Let me point out that, unlike portfolio insurance, at least in the short run, rebalancing behaviour on the part of investors would seem to stabilize prices. When a market goes down, rebalancing back to a strategic benchmark calls for purchasing the depreciated assets.

More formally, a risk based argument for rebalancing goes something like this. A strategic benchmark is established based on a long-term risk tolerance and assumptions about the long-term expected return and risk characteristics of risky assets. When the market has gone down, those long-term assumptions haven't changed and a long-horizon fund should buy risky assets in order to return to the benchmark weights. If, in fact, prices have declined to the point that expected returns have temporarily increased a fund might not only want to get back to benchmark weight, but might even want to get tactically overweight relative to its strategic benchmark. But for risk management purposes, per se, you simply want to get back to your strategic benchmark.

Sitting calmly before the fact, the argument for rebalancing seems like a powerful argument: intuitively it seems like buying low and selling high. And historically there is a tendency for short-run price moves to mean revert – for example, the evidence in stocks is very clear that volatility grows over longer intervals at a rate less than the square root of time. But of course it cannot be easy to tell in any particular event that mean reversion will occur – if it were investors would all take advantage of the obvious profit opportunity. In any case, motivated this way the activity is not what I would call risk based rebalancing, but rather it is a simple form of market-timing.

But back to John's point – there is a deeper problem, rebalancing is not a general equilibrium strategy. If the reason equity market prices have declined is because there is new information, then equity prices should be at that lower level and it is not possible for everyone to maintain their previous equity weight, at least not in a stable, rational-expectations equilibrium. Unless we can differentiate investors in terms of information or risk preferences all funds should rationally decide to lower their strategic asset allocations to be comfortable holding the new lower total value of risky assets. Obviously if some funds are rebalancing back up to their unchanged strategic benchmark, then some others must be selling.

Clearly, if all investors have the same risk preferences, then they cannot all rebalance back to a fixed benchmark every time there is news that moves the market. What approach to strategic asset allocation could work in such a world? First, investors must set an equity allocation based on risk preferences at a point in time. Then, as the market moves, the benchmark equity allocation must move up and down over time exactly in step with that of the market valuations.

To put it slightly differently, if a sovereign investor wants to justify a policy of rebalancing back to a strategic benchmark, without explicitly evaluating why prices have changed, then it cannot be a simple risk management argument. Rather, it requires a more subtle argument that differentiates governments from other investors. Perhaps one could argue, for example, that governments should establish contrarian investment, as well as spending policies to offset economic cycles and the over-reactions of private investors.

In fact, William Sharpe made just such an argument in a paper in 1989 called Investor Wealth Measures and Expected Return – except he didn't call his contrarian investors "governments," he called them "long-run" investors.

Sharpe notes that there is ample evidence that most investors become more risk tolerant when their wealth increases. Conversely, when the market goes down substantially most investors become more risk averse and want to sell risky assets. But not all investors can act this way. If some investors are sellers, then other investors must be buyers. If most investors want to sell when the market goes down, then the expected risk premium must go up in order to equilibrate the market. This increased premium will cause some investors, whose risk preferences are less sensitive to wealth than the average investor, to buy equities when the market is down. Sharpe uses the real cumulative market returns relative to trend to measure this wealth effect, and he evaluates what he calls a contrarian tactical asset allocation strategy based on selling equities when the market is above trend and buying equities when it is below trend.

Sharpe advocates such a contrarian strategy for "those who (personally or organizationally) can take a truly long-run view." He continues, "It appears to be a desirable strategy for those long-run investors who can 'take the heat' when it is most uncomfortable to do so. Although the added returns may be modest, in the long run their cumulative effect may be substantial."

Although Sharpe did not advocate this contrarian tactical asset allocation approach specifically for governments, I would think that governments' risk appetites would be less sensitive to market levels than that of private investors, and therefore I would think such a market stabilizing investment strategy might make sense for governments.

Note, however, that this contrarian investment policy does not require rebalancing all the way back to a fixed weight benchmark; it simply means buying equities when the market is below a long-run trend, creating an above market weight, and selling to a position below market weight when the market is above trend.

Let us turn now to the topic that has probably been dominating most of our attention for the past several months, "What is going on in the financial markets and what does it mean for long-term investors?" What we have been watching is both a financial meltdown and a significant weakening of the real economy; and it is certainly too early to reach definitive conclusions about the implications of the crisis for investment policy.

Nonetheless, there are some lessons that already seem clear. We know where this crisis started – in loose credit conditions and in particular in the expansion of credit to unqualified individuals purchasing homes through the development of the sub-prime mortgage market. It is also clear, in retrospect, that a combination of errors including government policies that tried to encourage home ownership, allowed misaligned incentives in credit ratings agencies, and capital markets that distributed and hid credit risks while eliminating accountability in mortgage origination, all contributed to the explosive growth in the sub-prime mortgage market. These policies, in turn, created positive feedbacks that fed a bubble in housing prices.

The positive feedback of housing price increases, further credit extension, speculative purchases and consumption financed against home equity all allowed for a long period of seemingly stable growth which, like the technology bubble before it, was in reality unsustainable. The economy was not following a stable equilibrium path.

I'm not suggesting that the imbalances were obvious, in fact quite the contrary. But I would note that some observers were quite prescient, for example Mohamed El-Erian in his excellent book, *When Markets Collide, Investment Strategies for the Age of Global Economic Change*. While El-Erian was not focused on the sub-prime mortgage problems, he was writing about the unsustainable borrowing and consumption of the US by households based in large part on lending from China and many other developing countries.

The rest of the story is well known, the inevitable end to the growth in housing prices led to insolvencies in overextended borrowers, increased foreclosures, negative feedback on housing prices, spillover into the credit markets, the money markets, the collapse of financial institutions, spillover into global equity markets, increasing insolvencies and unemployment, and the global economic disaster that we currently face.

The incredible magnitude of the global destruction in value was not clear ahead of time, but the existence of a housing price bubble, just like the existence of the technology bubble before it, was widely recognized. The risk such bubbles pose to the economy as a whole, particularly given the other imbalances, was not appreciated by most observers, and to me this is the main lesson that we should learn.

Inexorable growth of a process that is not sustainable is a dangerous situation. Although it is hard to predict when or how such a process will end, governments recognizing such a situation should avoid any implicit or explicit assumption that there will be a smooth transition to a stable equilibrium. Regulators should not depend on the market to self-correct.

Exponential growth is, on some time scale, an explosive process. As we have recently seen, the global economy can stay on an unsustainable path for a long period of time without showing obvious signs of instability or danger. Nonetheless, the nature of growth, in asset prices, in a sector of the economy, or of the economy itself, is that new barriers are regularly encountered and crossed, new territory is constantly covered, and one should expect the unexpected. Although it may be difficult to forecast when, exponential growth cannot go on forever, eventually a tipping point will be reached, equilibrating mechanisms that have historically supported stable growth may be overwhelmed by negative feedback mechanisms and a crash is a likely outcome.

That is what happened to the quant space, and that seems to have been what has happened recently to the economy.

Let us now turn to the topic of asset allocation.

What does the recent event imply about the premiums that are paid to risky assets? Finance theory suggests that assets should generate a risk premium proportional to the covariance of their returns with marginal utility across states of nature, which we often proxy for by measuring the covariance with a global market portfolio. One of the puzzles of finance has been the magnitude of the equity risk premium. Another puzzle has been the high premiums to what some of us call "exotic betas," risks such as those in value and momentum investing, commodities, real estate, emerging markets, and insurance, which have had low historical correlations to the market portfolio.

While we haven't yet seen the full economic consequences of this event, two points concerning risk premiums are suggested. First, conditioned on this event, the equity risk premium puzzle was not as much a puzzle as some thought. The equity premium during good times is as large as it is in order to induce investors to take the risk of loss during bad times. The puzzle was that the average returns to equities were as large as they were given that bad times weren't so bad. This seemed especially true given the so-called "great moderation," the low volatility of output and inflation since the mid-1980s which some thought was a permanent result of structural changes in the economy or improved macroeconomic policies. It appears, in retrospect, that this moderation in economic volatility was temporary in nature.

In the future we will likely look back at current events as having confirmed that very bad economic outcomes are possible, and thus that the variance of marginal utility across states of nature is larger than some economists had thought. The average returns to the market from whatever date you start at are much lower today than they were a year ago. Thus, as a result of the magnitude of this market decline and the associated economic hardship the equity premium in the future will not be as much a puzzle as it seemed. Moreover, the future recognition of this risk, as a result of this event, should help preserve high equity risk premiums at least for a long time forward. Thus, if your risk aversion has not increased, then you should be not only rebalancing back to a fixed benchmark, but actually increasing your equity allocation.

The second point is that the returns of most of the diversifying assets were not as uncorrelated during this event as the return covariances during good times might have suggested. Apparently those exotic betas weren't as exotic as they appeared. Of course many studies had suggested a tighter coupling of global markets in recent years and the high correlations during a period of significant global equity market decline should not have been a surprise. Nonetheless, the existence of hard data documenting the widening of spreads; the collapse of housing, equity, and even commodity prices; the performance of hedge fund indexes, and negative returns in virtually all risky assets other than government bonds during this event will be helpful as we develop asset allocation correlation assumptions going forward.

Finally, let's review the unique features of sovereign wealth and central bank funds relative to other institutional investors and the implications of these unique features: first, and most obviously, many of these funds are quite large, and the total value of assets managed by this group of institutions in aggregate today is large and it is growing rapidly. Second, these institutions typically do not have specific liabilities and rather have as an objective to grow wealth over a very long horizon. Third, they are government entities.

This special situation leads to a unique set of challenges and suggests to me that we need to think carefully about how these characteristics should differentiate sovereigns' approach to asset allocation. We've already discussed the potential for a tactical asset allocation approach based on contrarian rebalancing toward a fixed benchmark. There are many other issues to address, but in order to simplify the discussion, let me have you try to imagine one dimension which puts a passive market portfolio allocation on one end and what I will call the endowment model on the other.

I suspect you are all familiar with what I have in mind for the endowment model, but if not, I would recommend the excellent text, *Pioneering Portfolio Management: An Unconventional Approach to Institutional Investment* by David Swensen, the CIO of the Yale endowment. Relative to the market portfolio, the endowment model relies quite heavily on finding sources of alpha and relies relatively less on exposure to equities. The endowment model tries to diversify across many asset classes with low correlations, using exotic betas, commodities, and so forth, in order to generate returns and includes relatively high exposure to hedge funds, private equity, real estate, infrastructure, and other illiquid asset classes.

Many examples of endowment asset allocations can be easily found by looking at the web sites for the endowments of the leading educational institutions. One of the common characteristics of the implementations of the endowment model is that the asset allocations tend to be reasonably active, shifting from one set of assets to others as expected returns are seen to vary over time. One might characterize this behaviour as representing an attempt to stay ahead of the curve, moving into undiscovered or out-of-favor assets before they become popular, and then moving out when other investors start moving in. Some endowments have used significant leverage and many have used derivatives extensively to refine risk exposures and reduce transactions costs. Although endowments have been hurt along with other investors in this market crisis, as is well known, this model has worked spectacularly successfully over many years for many endowments.

As an aside, I note that interestingly, when writing for a general audience in his book *Unconventional Success: A Fundamental Approach to Personal Investment*, Professor Swenson does not recommend the endowment model. Recognizing the difficulty most personal investors would have gaining access to managers who can consistently produce alpha, who can stay ahead of the curve, or employ the other components of the endowment model, he recommends that individual investors use index funds to create passive portfolios.

For completely different reasons, I suggest that the largest sovereign funds will also find it very difficult to implement the endowment model. Although size provides some advantages in terms of access to information, first calls on attractive investment opportunities, the ability to recruit and develop skilled staff, and economies of scale in terms of operational costs, there is a significant disadvantage of size. The transactions costs associated with moving significant assets quickly make it very difficult to execute many of the components of the endowment model. Large sovereign funds will have significant market impact when changing their asset allocation as quickly as smaller funds. It will thus be especially difficult for them to stay ahead of the curve. And although they may be able to find talented active managers, the capacity of such managers is limited, and the basis point contribution to the overall fund, if positive net of fees, is likely to be small. When searching for alpha it is critical to think in terms of dollars of alpha and scalability of strategies rather than just Sharpe ratios and historical percentage returns.

Exotic betas do have more capacity to absorb funds than active managers, but as we have seen, for example, with commodities in recent years, the process of large investors attempting to create significant allocations pushes prices up to the point where the attraction, expected returns above a long-run equilibrium level, are no longer likely to be available. Timing these betas may be a strategy for endowments, but it may lead to instability and once again size is a significant disadvantage.

But in my mind it is not just the biggest funds that need to be concerned. I think there is a more general principle. At the end of the day, the total return available to all investors is the return of the market portfolio, broadly defined. There is no way all investors can outperform the market. Given different information, different skills, or just the luck of the draw, some investors can outperform others. But not all can be successful, and in fact, in the presence of transactions costs they cannot even on average be successful. Thus, trying to outperforming the market portfolio is a negative sum game.

The more general question is to what degree should sovereign funds be playing this game at all?

Active management is a strategic game, and as we saw in the quant space, it can be a potentially destabilizing game. Moreover, recent market experience suggests that the stability of the economy per se, is more fragile than we thought.

While I don't have a model I can point to, I can easily imagine that if a relatively homogeneous group of large investors engages in a strategic game of trying to outperform each other, there could be similar situations that lead to instabilities in asset prices. Moreover, if there is such a risk, then it is a risk for which there is no aggregate compensation.

Perhaps there is a more complicated game, one in which sovereigns all invest according to active rules which are nonetheless designed to stabilize markets whose dynamics are driven by the actions of private investors, I have in mind the idea of automated rebalancing back toward benchmark. However, I suspect any active rules known to be followed by sovereigns, even though designed to create stability, might eventually lead to destabilizing strategies on the part of private investors.

Certainly in their management of macroeconomic policies central banks have recognized a joint responsibility. I think sovereigns in their wealth management role should think about a similar joint responsibility, rather than to assume that unfettered competition will lead to an optimal outcome. And it seems clear to me that if you imagine such cooperative solution, it would either be passive or somehow designed to stabilize markets. For example, I certainly can't imagine how it could possibly make sense for sovereign funds to cooperate in a way so as to compete more effectively against private investors for a larger share of the global return pie.

Of course, at this point this is only a conjecture about a game that is not well defined, but my conjecture is that, again referring to a dimension with a passive portfolio on one end and an endowment model on the other, with all sovereign funds committed to staying close to the passive end, potentially with a policy of rebalancing toward a constant equity allocation, we will have a more stable and possibly larger global economy than otherwise.

Having just made what I suspect may be a somewhat controversial suggestion; I am now going to pre-emptively admit that it is not so obvious to me what "passively holding the market portfolio" means in practice as an investment strategy. To me a passive market portfolio strategy is one that stays reasonably close to a combination of cash and a strategic benchmark which includes market capitalization weights in as broad a set of investable securities representing ownership of the productive capacity of the economy as possible.

Trying to define the market portfolio in detail raises interesting and difficult questions, though. For example, should the market portfolio include bonds? If so, should it include only government bonds or should it include corporate bonds? Should it include private equity? Is it even possible to have a passive exposure to private equity? There are no simple or obvious answers.

Moreover, when we think about the unique long-run horizon of governments it suggests to me that they definitely should take an unconventional look at what constitutes productive assets. There may be some market imperfections that provide opportunities for long-term investors. Take, for example, the earth's natural resources. Scientists are beginning to focus on valuing the ecosystem services that are provided by nature, clean water from undeveloped land, fish from the ocean, carbon sequestration of growing forests, and so on. Historically, though, these services have not been priced. Is there a role for governments, in this context, not only to preserve their domestic nature preserves as part of their national policy, but also to invest globally in nature as part of their savings?

Investment in natural resources is already a common asset class for sovereign wealth funds, but it's not clear what that should include. It usually refers to investments in commodity futures and the equity of commodity producers. What about investing in, for example, nature funds that may provide dividends based on rights to ecosystem services? Such funds are beginning to appear. Most nature funds are funded by NGOs and governments and do not provide returns. But why not create funds that both protect nature and derive dividends from the ecosystem services that these protected areas provide? I would think such a dividend producing nature fund might be a very natural investment for a sovereign investor dedicated to growing wealth for future generations.

I will conclude quickly by reviewing my key points:

As we have seen recently, there is profound instability in markets. Unlike other investors, I think a minimum requirement for official institutions is that they agree to jointly act in a manner that is at a minimum consistent with a stable equilibrium of the global financial system.

These considerations lead me to suggest that a prudent approach for all governments would be to allocate portfolios to a combination of cash and a passive exposure to the market portfolio. There is more work to be done, however, to specify in detail what that market portfolio might look like in practice, and potentially to justify a counter-cyclical portfolio rebalancing strategy.

Notes

1. Eleven out 23 funds held at institutions other than central banks were established over the past ten years.
2. Andrew Rozanov (2007), *Sovereign Wealth Funds: Defining Liabilities*, SSgA.
3. The notion of excess reserves is not well defined. Typically economists use the so-called Greenspan-Guidotti rule that defines excess reserves as reserves in excess of short-term external debt (outstanding external debt with maturity less than one year).
4. The negative carry emanates from the cost of sterilization foreign currency inflows as in most instances domestic interest rates exceed the rate of return on the foreign assets in which the reserves are invested. In addition, many central banks have experienced significant foreign exchange losses as a result of the appreciation of their domestic currencies relative to reserve currencies.

5. Dutch disease is an economic phenomenon describing the relationship between a boom in foreign currency revenues (e.g. from the exploitation of natural resources) and an appreciation of the real exchange rate (with the consequence of making the manufacturing sector less competitive) as these revenues are converted into domestic currency and spent by the government.
6. Hedging foreign currency risk using forwards or swaps is often not possible due to a lack of deep and liquid markets in many emerging market currencies and even undesirable – particularly if the fund is large relative to the domestic economy.
7. In some instances, however, the government provides top-up contributions via fiscal transfers.
8. Angus Deaton (1991) "Saving and liquidity constraints", *Econometrica*, 59, 1221–1248.

Part I

Central Bank Reserves Management

1
Global Reserves Management

Krzysztof Rybinski and Urszula Krynska

1.1 Introduction

Foreign exchange reserves held by central banks rose to 6.4 trillion dollars in 2007 from 1.5 trillion a decade ago and are expected to rise further in the coming years. Sovereign wealth funds (SWF) manage assets in excess of 2.5 trillion dollars, and total reserves managed jointly by central banks and SWFs are forecasted to top 10 trillion dollars very soon. This chapter presents motives behind this reserves growth and proposes a concept of OCHAR – Opportunity Cost of Holding Ample Reserves – which is defined as a forgone GDP growth resulting from too conservative reserve management by central banks. We estimate OCHAR for a sample of 33 countries which accounted for 80% of total central bank reserves in 2007. We also argue, that unlike in the twentieth century, where central banks used to be very secretive institutions, twenty-first century central banking is characterized by widespread knowledge sharing and transparency. Therefore best practices, such as inflation targeting or efficient reserve management, spread out quickly and are adopted by an increasing number of central banks. Thus central banks collectively embarked on a reserves diversification journey, and it appears that we can speak of the global reserves management in the twenty-first century. At the end of the chapter we put forward several hypotheses of what could be the consequences of this diversification journey. It seems that relative prices of various assets will find new steady states, which may have little in common with relative valuations seen in the twentieth century. We also expect that slowly, over time, US "exorbitant privilege" will be eliminated. Finally we consider global stability risks in the context of the new reserves management style adopted by central banks. We postulate that due to the increasingly global nature of shocks, as long as central banks and governments in countries which are stakeholders of global imbalances focus their actions on maintaining global price and financial stability, central banks in smaller emerging markets can afford to improve reserve management without incurring additional stability risk.

1.2 The origins of the sharp rise in foreign exchange reserves

In 2007 foreign exchange reserves held by central banks and sovereign wealth funds likely topped 9 trillion dollars. According to IMF COFER (Currency Composition of Official Foreign Reserves) database central bank reserves stood at 6.4 trillion dollars at the end of 2007 and assets under management by SWFs were estimated at around 2.5–3 trillion dollars.[1] Oil prices will likely continue to rise in the next decade after the present global slowdown is over and China's large trade surplus will take time to reverse amid the Chinese tradition of saving a large part of their income, which suggests that further growth of central bank and sovereign wealth funds assets should be expected in the coming years.

The large and unprecedented rise of foreign exchange reserves led to many attempts to explain the reasons behind this trend. In January 1999 Martin Feldstein, the President of the National Bureau of Economic Research, the famous US think tank, wrote an article in the aftermath of the Asian crisis arguing for the need to keep large foreign exchange reserves that would serve as source of protection, flexibility and trust.[2] In March 1999 Alan Greenspan, Federal Reserve chairman, spoke on this issue during the World Bank conference.[3] In those days economists focused their attention on the need to build large reserves to hedge emerging markets against capital flight and sudden stops. Economists discussed whether rules of thumb such as maintaining a reserves coverage

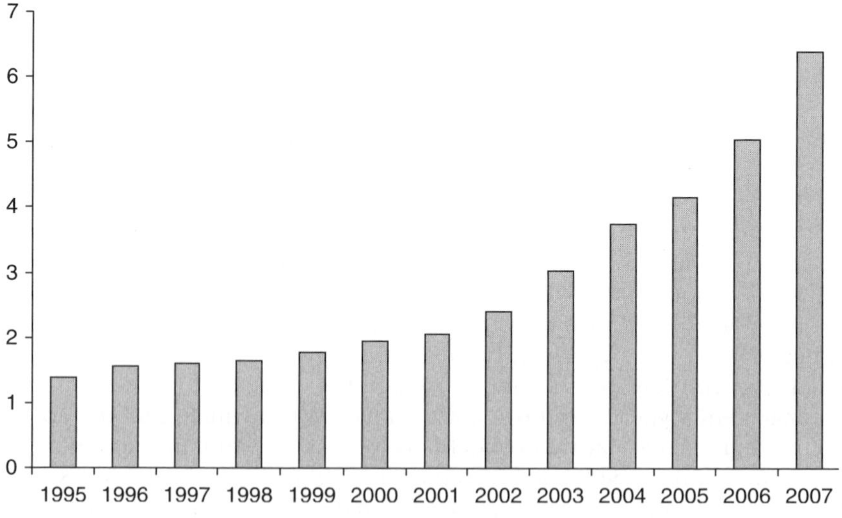

Figure 1.1 The stock of central bank reserves at year end (USD billion)
Source: IMF COFER database, 2007.

ratio of six months of imports is good enough, or whether one should also take into account short-term debt, which shortly after Greenspan's speech was labeled as the Greenspan-Guidotti rule. This rule states that a country should keep its reserves large enough to survive one year without new loans.

From today's perspective it may seem improbable, but it was only eight years ago when economists recommended building up sizeable foreign exchange reserves in emerging markets. Today, as shown in this chapter, many countries amassed reserves well in excess of what can be considered a safe and desirable level. The problem of too few has been replaced in many countries by a problem of too much.

Several papers identified the Asian crisis in 1997 as the time of a series of structural breaks, which explains why in the late 1990s US current account deficit and Asian foreign exchange reserves started to grow simultaneously and which led Dooley et al. (2003, 2004, 2005) to formulate the new Bretton Woods hypothesis.[4] For example, Gruber and Kamin (2005) estimate a model explaining the ratio of current accounts to GDP for a panel of 61 countries during the period of 1982–2003. The standard model, using budget deficit, net international investment position, income per capita, GDP growth, demographic variables, terms-of-trade volatility and openness fails to explain why the US recorded huge current account deficits and why Asian countries posted sizeable current account surpluses accompanied by rapidly rising foreign exchange reserves. However, adding dummies for crisis years in Asia explains the lion's share of current account surpluses in Asian countries. The authors conclude that during the post-crisis period Asian countries adopted macroeconomic policy based on domestic spending restraints, investment spending in particular, and undervalued exchange rates, which required heavy interventions and led to massive reserves accumulation after a few years of such macromanagement. Malecki et al. (2001) use financial markets microstructure analysis to show that it is justified to link the Asian crisis to post-crisis reserves accumulation. They show that the direct cause of speculative attacks on Asian currencies was the low level of foreign exchange reserves on a net basis. The attack on Thai baht took place when markets learned that net foreign reserves in the coffers of the Bank of Thailand were much smaller than those reported in bank assets amid large foreign currency sales in forward transaction conducted by the central bank. In other countries in the region speculative attacks were triggered by market assessments that foreign exchange reserves were too small relative to foreign currency denominated loans taken out at commercial banks. Investors knew that these banks would not be able to renew such loans and that they would have to purchase foreign exchange from the central bank to make payments on existing loans. Anticipation of such massive purchases led to speculation against local Asian currencies.

There is little doubt that the roots of the rapid reserves accumulation lie in the hangover period after the Asian crisis. Much of the literature deals with the explanation of the magnitude of reserve holding increases in the past decade, testing different motives and target size of reserves with mixed success. Examples include Mendoza (2004), Garcia and Soto (2004), Caballero and Panageas (2004a, 2004b), Aizenman and Lee (2005), Gosselin and Parent (2005), ECB (2006), Jeanne and Ranciere (2006), Cifarelli and Paladino (2007) and Green and Torgerson (2007).

There could be many different motives for building a large reserves pool: economics, politics or reputation. Two kinds of economic motives are analyzed in Aizenman and Lee (2005), that is, precautionary motives and mercantilist motives. In the first case, in line with Martin Feldstein's recommendations, reserves are built to hedge the country against sudden stops and against financial markets volatility. In the second case reserve accumulation is a natural consequence of industrial policy based on maintaining an undervalued exchange rate to stimulate exports, which involves central bank interventions to prevent the currency from strengthening. Aizenman and Lee analyze 53 countries in the period 1980–2000. Their results indicate that variables related to trade openness, capital flow openness and financial crises experienced explain the level of foreign exchange reserves quite well, are statistically significant and are economically important. On the contrary, variables related to mercantilist motives such as export growth or exchange rate do not influence reserves accumulation in a sizeable manner, although some are statistically significant.

Gosselin and Patent (2005) analyze the accumulation of foreign exchange reserves in eight Asian countries, and they analyze time series which include the years 2003–2004, when reserves grew rapidly. The authors show that the time series exhibit a structural break in 1997–1998, and that after the Asian crisis demand for foreign exchange reserves at central banks did increase significantly. However, the actual level of reserves observed in 2003–2004 was much higher than the model predicted. This led to the conclusion that if historical relationships between analyzed economic variables[5] still prevail one should expect slower growth of foreign exchange reserves in the years to come, which could create the risk of US dollar depreciation amid the less abundant current account deficit funding available in the future. The frantic pace of reserves growth in 2006 suggests that either relationships between economic variables did change, or there is another factor, missing in the analysis, that has led to acceleration of reserves accumulation.

Jeanne and Ranciere (2006) find that recent accumulation of reserves by Asian central banks cannot be explained by an insurance motive against sudden stops. The authors present a model of the optimal level of foreign exchange reserves and find that the Greenspan-Guidotti rule is a very good approximation of their model results, with an exception – when the short-term debt to GDP ratio is less than 2.5%, then the optimal size of foreign exchange reserves is zero.

The buffer stock model was used by Cifarelli and Paladino (2007) in order to understand the motives of reserves accumulation.[6] The basic model assumes that there are two types of costs related to holding reserves: the opportunity cost of holding reserves and the adjustment cost of reserves restocking, amid the need to generate a balance of payments surplus to build up reserves, which reduces output. As the level of reserves grows the opportunity cost rises and the adjustment cost falls. The authors use cointegration analysis to capture the long term relationships and the error correction method to model the short-term dynamics. Their results suggest that in the long run a precautionary motive is a valid explanation of rapid reserve accumulation in many emerging economies. However, the authors also find that in some countries the short-term dynamics of reserves accumulation does depend on mercantilist motives, as the speed of reserves accumulation increases with appreciation of the real effective exchange rate.

One general conclusion can be formed based on the empirical research to date. It appears that the precautionary motive of reserves accumulation has dominated over other motives in the period following the Asian crisis. Central banks used large foreign reserves as an insurance or hedge against the risk of liquidating long-term investment projects in situations in which the country experiences sudden stop. Existing evidence shows that the cost of such a hedge has been growing over time. Mark-to-market losses on reserves related to local currency appreciation may lead to massive losses in central banks' balance sheets, in extreme cases topping 10% of GDP.[7] Many countries face rising costs from sterilization, which are particularly high in situations where the local interest rates are above the level of interest rates in the US or in the Eurozone.

1.3 Estimates of the costs of excessively prudent reserve management

As discussed above the precautionary motive led to the purchase of a possibly very expensive form of insurance against the risk of sudden stop. However, sterilization costs and local currency appreciation implications may be relatively minor costs in relation to the opportunity cost of holding reserves accumulated over the years. The opportunity cost of holding reserves has been discussed in economic literature since 1960s.[8] There have been many attempts to measure the opportunity cost. For example, Ben-Bassat and Gottlieb (1992) use the difference between return on capital in domestic projects[9] and interest income earned on reserve investment in foreign deposits and fixed income securities. Rodrik (2006) assumes reasonable spreads between the yield on reserve assets and the cost of foreign borrowing, and computes that the income loss to developing countries amounts to close to 1% of GDP. The paper argues that conditional on existing levels of short-term foreign borrowing, this does not seem too steep a price as an insurance premium against financial crises. Paper asks the question why developing countries have not tried harder to reduce short-term foreign liabilities in order to achieve the same level of net liquidity (thereby paying a smaller cost in terms of reserve accumulation) and concludes that it remains an important puzzle.

As shown above there are several definitions of the opportunity cost of holding large reserves, and each of them has shortcomings. Therefore we propose our own concept of the opportunity cost of holding ample reserves. The name implies that the definition applies only to situations in which the level of central bank reserves is beyond what could be considered adequate to fulfill central bank goals related to financial stability and exchange rate policy implementation. We define the opportunity cost of holding ample reserves (OCHAR) as a forgone growth of GDP amid overly conservative central bank reserve management.[10]

The opportunity costs of holding ample reserves (OCHAR) depends on three factors:

1. the size of reserves (the absolute size and the excess over the amount needed to perform central bank stability and exchange rate policy functions);
2. the deviation from the optimal strategy in the long run of the actual investment strategy pursued by a central bank focused entirely on short-term financial and economic stability objectives;
3. the country-specific ability to translate additional income into socially useful projects with a high social rate of return (road, telecom or knowledge infrastructure, education etc.).

Factors (1) and (2) combined correspond to the opportunity cost concept discussed in the economic literature for the past 40 years, but we adopt a more sophisticated measure of forgone profits amid explicit assumptions related to actual and desired asset management styles.

We analyze all three factors below for a selected sample of countries,[11] which accounts for c.a. 80% of global foreign exchange reserves. There are many rules of thumb regarding the proper level of reserves: they should cover above three or above six months of imports of goods and services (depending on the exchange rate regime, the sign and size of trade balance and on the country's rating), they should cover a certain percentage of money in circulation (5–20% depending on currency regime[12]), and they should allow a country to survive without new loans for at least a year. This latest rule is called Greenspan-Guidotti rule and appears to be cited in the

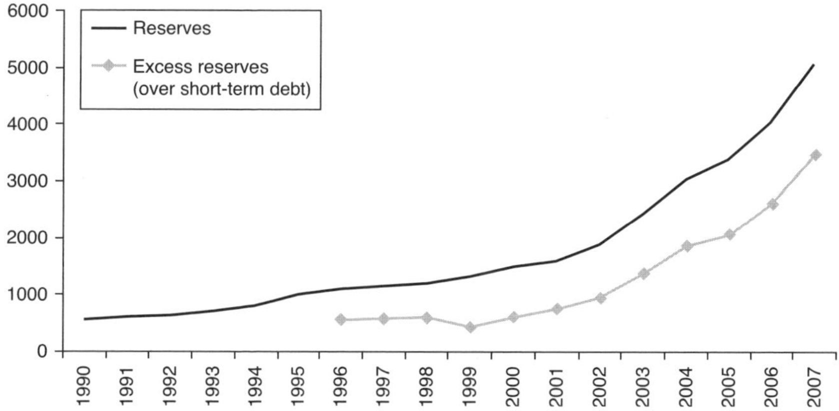

Figure 1.2 Total and excess reserves for the analyzed countries (USD billion)*
Note: *Short-term data for 2007 not available; we used data for 2007 Q2.
Source: IMF, BIS-OECD-IMF-World Bank

literature more often than other rules, so we also take this approach. We adopt the standard definition of the short-term debt and country liabilities payable to non-resident holders within one year, irrespective of the currency in which they are issued.[13]

Figure 1.2 and Table 1.1 below present foreign exchange reserves and outstanding short-term foreign debt for the sample of selected countries. It is evident that reserves are growing fast in every location with exception of developed countries in Western Europe and that reserves above the short-term debt are also rising fast. For the analyzed countries the total excess reserves according to the Greenspan-Guidotti rule likely topped USD 3.5 trillion in 2007 compared with USD 500 billion a decade ago.

Above we calculated the first OCHAR factor, which was the easiest to calculate among the three factors. In order to identify the second OCHAR factor we have to make numerous assumptions. First, data on actual return on foreign reserves is available only for half of the sample of the analyzed countries.[14] So while we calculate the second OCHAR factor for reporting countries, we will also make assumptions regarding what the factor estimate would be if central banks followed certain stylized investment strategy. We will define the typical central bank portfolio as US, Eurozone and UK government bonds with duration 1–3 years. For comparative purposes we will use a long-term focused investment strategy often adopted by pension funds. We will also define a combined strategy which assumes that reserves consistent with Greenspan-Guidotti rule are invested according to the typical central bank style, while reserves above that level are invested according to stylized pension fund investment style.

Table 1.1 Reserves and short-term debt in analyzed countries (USD million)

	2005	2006	2007	2005	2006	2007Q2	2005	2006	2007*
	Reserves			Short-term debt			Reserves exceeding short-term debt		
Germany	101675.9	111637.0	136234.4	988470.0	1091577.0	1344252.0	0.0	0.0	0.0
France	74360.0	98239.1	115717.2	748095.0	1038080.0	1249240.0	0.0	0.0	0.0
Switzerland	57639.6	64497.5	75372.1	411942.0	419299.0	550819.0	0.0	0.0	0.0
Sweden	24890.1	28022.8	31037.4	156919.0	179865.0	202853.0	0.0	0.0	0.0
Poland	42560.9	48474.2	65734.2	16564.0	17130.0	23339.0	25996.9	31344.2	42395.2
Hungary	18603.1	21590.0	24051.8	15899.0	18215.0	22928.0	2704.1	3375.0	1123.8
Czech Republic	29363.8	31220.8	34594.3	11975.0	13005.0	13422.0	17388.8	18215.8	21172.3
Slovakia	15479.6	13364.0	18976.1	5929.0	6725.0	7462.0	9550.6	6639.0	11514.1
Japan	835505.7	880977.4	954144.7	426468.0	383513.0	380547.0	409037.7	497464.4	573597.7
China	825588.0	1072564.0	1534354.0	63106.0	79984.0	103817.0	762482.0	992580.0	1430537.0
Korea	210390.6	238956.2	262224.3	62719.0	100055.0	122804.0	147671.6	138901.2	139420.3
Thailand	52064.9	66984.7	87455.2	12774.0	14452.0	10654.0	39290.9	52532.7	76801.2
Taiwan	257952.1	270840.0	275027.0	38091.0	33184.0	50899.0	219861.1	237656.0	224128.0
Singapore	116172.0	136259.0	162957.0	82888.0	102490.0	123764.0	33284.0	33769.0	39193.0
Hong Kong	124278.3	133210.5	152701.9	79279.0	93368.0	97244.0	44999.3	39842.5	55457.9
Russia	182240.0	303732.4	476390.9	48444.0	57528.0	73553.0	133796.0	246204.4	402837.9

Norway	46985.9	56841.6	60839.6	74349.0	138649.0	181426.0	0.0	0.0	0.0
Saudi Arabia	26759.9	27764.9	34014.4	13644.0	11886.0	19418.0	13115.9	15878.9	14596.4
Nigeria	28279.7	42298.8	51334.4	1930.0	4042.0	3802.0	26349.7	38256.8	47532.4
Venezuela	29636.8	36672.3	33477.1	6728.0	4629.0	5746.0	22908.8	32043.3	27731.1
Kuwait	8971.5	12675.8	16776.3	7320.0	8262.0	10770.0	1651.5	4413.8	6006.3
Mexico	74054.1	76270.5	87109.2	29002.0	31189.0	27554.0	45052.1	45081.5	59555.2
Algeria	56582.4	78207.7	110626.8	1076.9	989.0	910.0	55505.5	77218.7	109716.8
United Arab Em.	21010.3	27617.4	n.a	19608.0	27849.0	29728.0	1402.3	0.0	n.a
Brazil	53799.3	85838.9	180333.7	45583.0	45848.0	52370.0	8216.2	39990.9	127963.7
Argentina	28086.7	32026.0	46116.5	13793.9	13296.0	14883.0	14292.8	18730.0	31233.5
Chile	16932.5	19396.3	16842.2	12426.0	14470.0	16144.0	4506.5	4926.3	698.2
Colombia	14954.6	15437.2	20952.1	5733.0	5710.0	10388.0	9221.6	9727.2	10564.1
South Africa	20629.7	25586.9	32942.9	8615.0	15635.0	16480.0	12014.7	9951.9	16462.9
Sudan	1868.6	1659.9	1377.9	1904.5	1959.2	2105.5	0.0	0.0	0.0
Kenya	1799.1	2416.1	3355.2	529.9	625.8	730.2	1269.1	1790.2	2625.1
Botswana	6309.1	7992.4	n.a	50.0	32.0	46.0	6259.1	7960.4	n.a
Ghana	1897.4	2268.1	n.a	839.1	1194.8	742.8	1058.3	1073.4	n.a

Note: *We used short-term debt for 2007 Q2.
Source: IMF, BIS-OECD-IMF-World Bank.

Stylized central bank portfolio return was calculated on the basis of the rate of return for the weighted average of bond indices for the main reserve currencies (US Treasuries 1–3, EMU Government 1–3, UK Governments 1–3). Currency composition of foreign reserves was obtained from the IMF COFER data. For the observations before 1995 currency composition for 1995 was assumed.

Stylized pension portfolio return was calculated on the basis of stylized central bank portfolio rate of return (with 40% weight) and weighted average of stock index returns for the main reserve currencies (DowJones, DAX and FTSE). We assumed that such weighted average of stocks accounted for 60% of the pension portfolio.

Stylized combined portfolio return was calculated after splitting reserves into two parts: a traditional reserves component and sovereign wealth component[15] (excess over short term debt according to the Greenspan-Guidotti rule). We assumed stylized central bank return for the traditional part of reserves and a more aggressive pension strategy for the sovereign wealth part of reserves.

We begin by looking at the actual returns as reported by central banks in their annual reports. In our sample of 33 central banks only 16 report actual returns, and in 4 cases these returns are measured in local currency (Germany, France, Switzerland and Hong Kong), which makes it impossible to compare these returns with those achieved in other countries. Table 1.2 below presents the results.[16]

It is evident that in the era of low global interest rates central banks are not able to generate high rates of return on their reserves amid conservative investment strategies based on high grade fixed income instruments in most liquid markets. Norges Bank and Hong Kong Monetary Authority are notable exceptions, as they reported higher than typical central bank returns with more diversified portfolios and a more aggressive investment style, which includes equities.[17] In the case of Norway the turmoil on the credit markets triggered by the bursting bubble of the US housing market reduced investment results in 2007, especially in the second half of the year, so the rate of return was lower than in the previous years. Table 1.7 in the Appendix presents the opportunity cost (the first and second OCHAR factors put together) for countries that report actual returns on foreign reserves. For example, this cost for CEE countries is estimated to be 1.2–2.3% of GDP in 2006, for commodity exporters at 0.7–2.5% of GDP, measured against the stylized pension portfolio. In other words if central banks in CEE had pursued an investment style typical for pension funds their profits would have been larger by 1.2–2.3% of GDP, which is a very large sum and often covers a large percentage of the budget deficit in these countries.

Because we have very limited data on actual returns in what follows we assume that central banks allocate their reserves according to a central bank stylized portfolio, and we measure the opportunity cost in comparison with stylized pension and combined portfolios. There are always several caveats for such analyses. Firstly, how far back one should go? With massive changes in the global economy and global financial markets – such as Great Moderation to mention one major structural change – we decided to follow Alan Greenspan's advice and use the last 20 years of data that corresponds to the Great Moderation period.[18] Of course there is an immediate question whether our OCHAR calculations would still hold in the long run in the post Great Moderation period, with more volatility in the markets. Our answer is affirmative and we discuss it in the last part of this chapter.

The second caveat is that even in a Great Moderation period returns on various portfolios vary a great deal, so it makes sense to use multiyear averages. We decided to use a five-year average as it often corresponds to a

Table 1.2 Actual rates of return on foreign reserves

		Actual rates of return (in %)			
		2004	**2005**	**2006**	**2007**
Western Europe	Germany*	–	1.4	1.7	1.5
	France*	2.0	3.5	3.8	3.9
	Switzerland*	2.3	10.8	1.9	3.0
	Sweden	–	–	2.0	5.1
CEE	Poland	2.6	2.6	3.2	5.4
	Hungary	–	2.6	3.6	–
	Czech Republic	2.8	2.6	3.0	–
	Slovak Republic	–	2.2	2.4	–
Asia	Hong Kong*	5.7	3.1	9.5	11.8
Oil exporting countries	Russia	–	3.0	3.8	–
	Norway**	7.8	9.1	7.30	3.4
	Mexico	2.0	1.7	4.9	–
	United Arab Emirates	1.3	2.6	2.7	–
Latin America	Argentina***	3.1	3.1	5.7	–
	Chile	1.8	2.9	2.5	–
	Colombia	–	2.7	3.9	–

Notes: *Indicates that returns were reported in local currency.
**Data refers to investment portfolio only.
***Returns in terms of USD.
Source: Central banks' annual reports and authors' calculations.

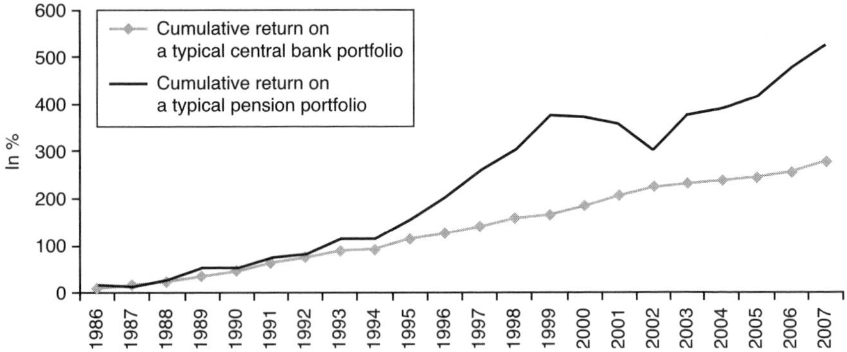

Figure 1.3 Cumulative return, stylized central bank and stylized pension portfolio

Source: Authors' calculations based on Merrill Lynch indices.

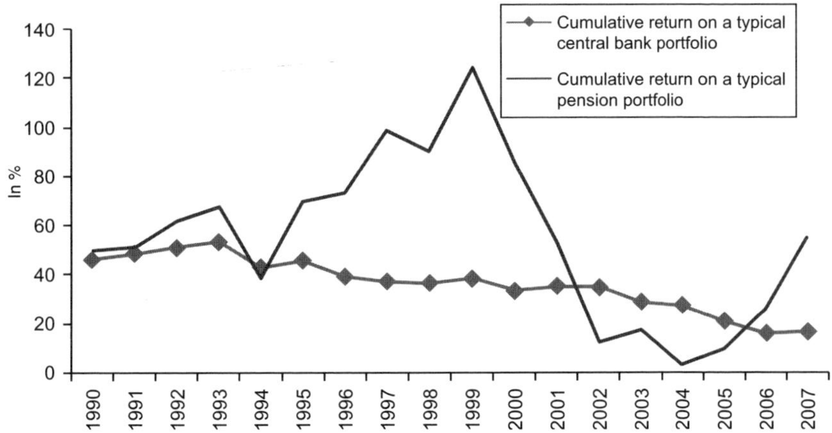

Figure 1.4 Cumulative return over the previous five years

Source: Authors' calculations based on Merrill Lynch indices.

central banker's term in office. In other words when a central banker makes asset diversification decisions she would probably be concerned with how these decisions affect returns on reserve assets during her term, as poor performance may lower chances of reelection.[19]

Figure 1.4 presents rolling cumulative returns for both investment strategies over the period of past five years; the data is plotted for each year between 1990 and 2007. A few observations stand out. First, in a low global interest rate environment stylized central bank portfolio returns exhibit a downward trend. Secondly, in some years stylized pension portfolio returns were two to three times higher than stylized central bank portfolio returns. Finally, in the periods following the burst of the Internet bubble pension portfolios did bring returns below the central bank portfolio, but it has never resulted in a capital loss over the five-year period. So our stylized pension portfolio has yielded a successful capital protection strategy even in the aftermath of the bursting stock market bubble, assuming a five-year verification period. Figure 1.4 shows also that pension portfolio volatility is much higher than central bank portfolio volatility.

In what follows we take the estimated annual differences in returns between central bank portfolios, pension portfolios and combined portfolios, taking into account the size of reserves and measuring the opportunity cost as a percentage of GDP. Figure 1.5 presents these results in the form of a five-year arithmetic average for the whole sample of 33 countries. There are four periods: the low reserves period with low opportunity cost; the pre-internet bubble period, when this cost stands at 0.4–0.9% of GDP; the post-bubble period when opportunity cost turns negative; and the period from 2005 to 2007 when the five-year average opportunity cost turned positive again and reached levels even higher than before the Internet bubble crisis.

The average opportunity cost masks wide differences between groups of countries. As shown in Figure 1.6 in the mid-1990s CEE countries faced the highest opportunity cost of around 1.5% of GDP (measured against pension portfolios), while for remaining groups of countries this cost stood between

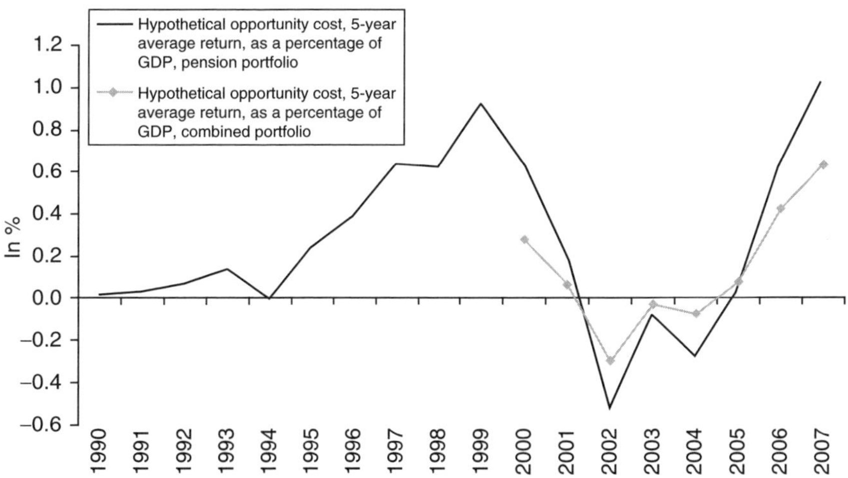

Figure 1.5 Total hypothetical opportunity cost as a percentage of GDP, 5-year average[20]

Source: IMF, BIS-OECD-IMF-World Bank, Merrill Lynch indices and authors' calculations.

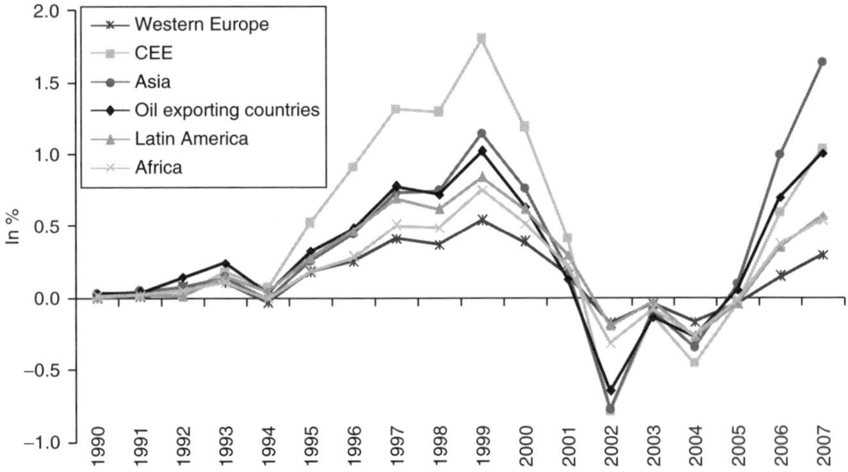

Figure 1.6 Hypothetical opportunity cost as a percentage of GDP, pension portfolio, 5-year average, by groups of countries

Source: IMF, BIS-OECD-IMF-World Bank, Merrill Lynch indices and authors' calculations.

0.5 and 1% of GDP. The reason for that is the high reserves/GDP ratio in CEE countries, which was equal to 18% in 1999. In the same year reserves amounted to 13% of GDP in Asia and not more than 10% in the rest of the analyzed countries. In 2007, however, Asia was the biggest reserve holder with reserves equal to 36% of GDP, while the same ratio for CEE countries amounted to "only" 18 %. In line with the sharp rise of reserves, the highest five-year average opportunity cost was calculated for Asian countries, closely followed by oil exporters and by CEE countries.[21]

Tables 1.3 and 1.4 show opportunity cost estimates for the last four years, in each of these years for both pension and combined portfolios. For 2006 this hypothetical cost for analyzed Asian countries was estimated at 2.7% of GDP or 239 billion dollars. In 2007 the cost decreased to 0.75% of GDP as a result of a significant increase of rate of return on typical central bank portfolios and decrease of return on typical pension portfolios. Opportunity cost estimates for individual countries for the period 2005–2007 are presented in Table 1.8 in the Appendix.

We have estimated two out of three OCHAR factors above. Estimating the third factor is even more difficult, as there are very few studies and very limited data on government ability to generate projects with high social rate of return, and there is hardly any data available to measure what percentage of the "windfall profit" will be spent on such welfare-enhancing projects and what will be spent on current consumption or growth-reducing social handouts, very much in line with windfall proceeds from the first oil shock. Alternatively, governments may decide to

Table 1.3 Total hypothetical opportunity cost for different alternative investment strategies (USD million or % GDP, sample of 33 countries, data for each year)

	2004	2005	2006	2007*
Stylized central bank portfolio return	51 357.3	64 657.4	135 366.5	323 001.2
Stylized pension portfolio return	101 433.5	171 848.7	483 453.5	429 447.8
Stylized combined portfolio return	81 878.2	129 742.7	358 123.5	395 442.8
Hypothetical opportunity cost, pension portfolio	50 076.2	107 191.2	348 087.0	106 446.7
Hypothetical opportunity cost, combined portfolio	30 520.9	65 085.3	222 757.0	72 441.6
Hypothetical opportunity cost as a percentage of GDP, pension portfolio	0.29	0.56	1.69	0.46
Hypothetical opportunity cost as a percentage of GDP, combined portfolio	0.17	0.34	1.08	0.31

Note: *We used short-term debt for 2007 Q2.
Source: Authors' calculations based on IMF, WEO, BIS-OECD-IMF-World Bank data and Merrill Lynch indices.

save part of the proceeds for future generations, as was indeed the case in many commodity exporting countries; Norway, Russia, Venezuela, Trinidad and Tobago, Botswana, Nigeria, Kazakhstan, Korea, Chile and Kuwait have invested part of their foreign exchange reserves through special purpose funds that aim to preserve national wealth.[22] Many oil-exporting countries are investing heavily in improving infrastructure and developing alternative activities, with Dubai Outsource Zone[23] serving as the best example.

In order to estimate OCHAR we will assume that governments invest 100% of extra profits made by central banks in improving the national infrastructure, which is a growth bottleneck in many emerging economies. There are of course other ways of public spending that stimulate long-term growth and potentially have a higher growth multiplier than spending on infrastructure, for instance education or well-targeted research and development. Here, however, we focus on the infrastructure development, but we do acknowledge that the OCHAR estimates based on this spending assumption may be in the lower end of the actual OCHAR, when all desired public investment opportunities are taken into account.[24]

Table 1.4 Hypothetical opportunity cost as a percentage of GDP, by group of countries (USD million)

	2004	2005	2006	2007	2004	2005	2006	2007*
	Hypothetical opportunity cost, pension portfolio				**Hypothetical opportunity cost, combined portfolio**			
Western Europe	4491.7	8134.2	25852.7	7475.2	0.0	0.0	0.0	0.0
CEE	1573.3	3334.9	9801.7	2990.3	957.0	1750.4	5093.1	1589.6
Asia	35836.4	76192.4	239361.8	71523.8	25358.7	52116.0	170365.2	52964.7
Oil exporting countries	6090.4	14928.0	56603.1	18159.5	3736.5	9430.9	39249.5	13933.5
Latin America	1674.6	3579.2	13054.6	5512.0	272.6	1140.0	6273.0	3555.7
Africa	409.8	1022.5	3413.2	785.9	196.1	648.1	1776.2	398.2
	Hypothetical opportunity cost as a percentage of GDP. pension portfolio				**Hypothetical opportunity cost as a percentage of GDP. combined portfolio**			
Western Europe	0.08	0.14	0.43	0.11	0.00	0.00	0.00	0.00
CEE	0.31	0.57	1.50	0.37	0.19	0.30	0.78	0.20
Asia	0.45	0.90	2.72	0.75	0.32	0.62	1.93	0.55
Oil exporting countries	0.27	0.55	1.76	0.48	0.17	0.35	1.22	0.37
Latin America	0.17	0.27	0.83	0.29	0.03	0.09	0.40	0.19
Africa	0.15	0.33	1.00	0.20	0.07	0.21	0.52	0.10

Note: *We used short-term debt for 2007 Q2.
Source: Authors' calculations based on IMF, WEO, BIS-OECD-IMF-World Bank data and Merrill Lynch indices.

An adequate supply of infrastructure services is an essential ingredient for productivity and growth.[25] Aschauer (1989) in his classic study used a Cobb-Douglas production function to analyze 1970s data from the US. He finds that the output elasticity of public investment in core infrastructure was about 0.4. This means that a 1% increase in investment in public infrastructure would lead to a 0.4% increase in the output of the private sector. Wylie (1996) obtains similar results for Canada. He concludes that the investment in infrastructure, especially public one, has significant and positive role to play in national economic growth and productivity.[26] However, elasticities derived from different studies vary significantly. The frame below presents results obtained for the US and Japan. A 1% increase in investment in public infrastructure would lead to a 0.03%–0.39% increase in the output of the private sector. One may expect that output elasticity is higher in developing countries, as road and telecommunication infrastructure are much less developed there. Indeed Calderón and Servén (2003) find that lagging infrastructure accounts for about one-fifth of the GDP growth differential between Latin America and East Asia over the last 20 years – nearly one percentage point per annum. This suggests that the growth payoff from infrastructure catch-up would be quite significant.[27]

Box 1.1 Production Function Estimates of the Output Elasticity of Public Capital by Level of Geographic Aggregation

Author	**Level of Aggregation**	**Specification**	**Output Elasticity of Public Capital**
Aschauer (1989)	National	Cobb-Douglas; Log levels	0.39
Holz-Eakin (1988)	National	Cobb-Douglas; Log levels	0.39
Munnell (1990a)	National	Cobb-Douglas; Log levels	0.34
Costa, Ellson, Martin (1987)	States	Translog; Levels	0.20
Eisner (1991)	States	Cobb-Douglas; Log levels	0.17
Mera(1973)	Japanese regions	Cobb-Douglas; Log levels	0.20
Munnell (1990b)	States	Cobb-Douglas; Log levels	0.15
Duffy-Deno and Eberts (1989)[a]	Metropolitan areas	Log levels	0.08
Eberts (1986, 1990)	Metropolitan areas	Translog; Levels	0.03

Source: Munnell (1992).

In what follows we use the highest estimate presented in Munnell (1992) – see the frame below – to calculate forgone GDP growth. The result is presented in the Table 1.5 below. We calculated average forgone GDP growth for four periods 1990–1995, 1996–1999, 2000–2003 and 2004–2007. In the first, second and fourth periods cost was positive. The third period, which corresponds to the internet bubble burst, was characterized by negative cost. It means that the stylized central bank portfolio was more profitable than the stylized pension portfolio, and as a result central banks transferred more profit to the state budgets than under more diversified investment strategies. It is, however, worth repeating that the cumulative 5-year return was never negative in the analyzed period for any of the analyzed strategies.

As shown in this section OCHAR can be very high. In 2003–2007 hypothetical OCHAR amounted to almost 0.7% of forgone GDP growth for Asian countries, while oil exporters and CEE economies lost almost 0.5% per annum and Latin American countries lost 0.3% of GDP growth in the last three years. Of course in a very bad year, such as the stock exchange crash, the OCHAR can turn negative, as was the case for all countries in the 2000–2002 period. But as shown in Figure 1.3 and Table 1.5 the

Table 1.5 OCHAR estimates 1990–2007*

	1990–1995	1996–1999	2000–2002	2003–2007	1990–2007
		Pension (in %)			
Western Europe	0.01	0.23	–0.27	0.12	0.04
CEE	0.11	0.74	–0.91	0.46	0.18
Asia	0.03	0.50	–0.82	0.66	0.17
Oil exporting countries	0.04	0.42	–0.58	0.42	0.13
Latin America	0.05	0.35	–0.42	0.25	0.10
Africa	0.03	0.32	–0.46	0.23	0.07
		Combined (in %)			
Western Europe	n.a.	0.10	0.00	0.00	0.03
CEE	n.a.	0.42	–0.50	0.26	0.12
Asia	n.a.	0.24	–0.49	0.46	0.15
Oil exporting countries	n.a.	0.14	–0.23	0.25	0.09
Latin America	n.a.	0.04	–0.07	0.08	0.03
Africa	n.a.	0.15	–0.18	0.11	0.05

Note: *Unweighted average, for the elasticity equal to 0.39.
n.a. stands for not available.
Source: Authors' calculations

cumulative return on stylized pension portfolios has been much higher then on stylized central bank portfolios, so the cumulative OCHAR over that last twenty years was positive and high. Average forgone GDP growth for the whole period 1990–2007 was positive, and amounted to 0.18% in CEE, 0.17 % in Asia and 0.13% in oil exporting countries. These estimates are not high, which is mainly the result of negative opportunity cost in the 2000–2002 period. Going forward many countries face very large opportunity costs of holding ample reserves; given forecasts of further reserves growth, forgone GDP growth may top 0.5% per annum in the long run.

These are conservative estimates using infrastructure multipliers; we should assume that if extra central bank profit is invested in R&D or in education, which could have a much higher marginal return in the knowledge economy, then the increase in the potential GDP amid less conservative reserve management could be even larger over the long run.[28]

1.4 Yield enhancement strategy adopted by central banks with ample reserves

OCHAR is a new concept, but is closely related to the opportunity cost idea discussed in the economic literature in the past 40 years. However it was only in the last few years that central banks collectively started to think in these terms when making reserve management decisions. There is overwhelming evidence now that central banks will manage foreign exchange reserves differently in the twenty-first century than they managed in twentieth century. Previously almost 100% weight was given to the following goals: capital preservation, the role of the lender of last resort, intervention needs and preventing financial crises. Nowadays these goals remain very important, but the ample level of reserves has increased the weight attached by central bankers to the return on reserve assets. There are also other factors, nicely put together by Rietveld and Pringle (2007):

> What changed? Countries have become better stewards of their national wealth, with commodity revenues now being channeled into endowment funds for social and economic purposes rather than private bank accounts or politically-inspired investments. The production of manufactured goods has shifted massively to emerging market countries, creating the accumulation of national wealth in the form of foreign currency reserves. Finally, governments have benefited from "windfall" revenues from the privatization of state-owned companies.

There are two different types of strategies being pursued. Some countries (a clear minority, e.g. Mexico, Slovakia and Switzerland) try to estimate what the "optimal" level of reserves is, and achieve this level via various

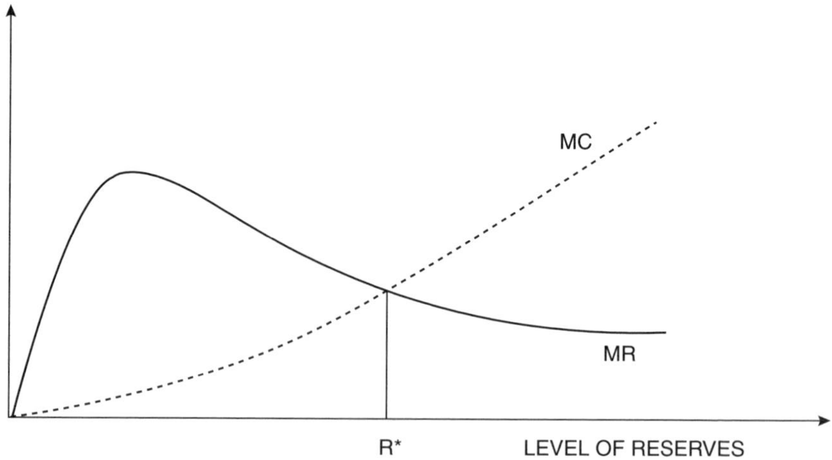

Figure 1.7 Possible reserves marginal revenue and marginal cost, and the equilibrium level of reserves

Source: Green and Torgerson (2007), authors' modifications

transactions on the market or with other local stakeholders. This approach could be modeled using the approach proposed in Green and Torgerson (2007), where the optimal level of reserves R* can be formally determined such that the marginal cost of holding reserves equals marginal revenue.

However the majority of central banks have adopted a different approach. Instead of targeting the optimal level of reserves (which often cannot be precisely determined and changes over time, similar to natural rate and potential output estimates) they choose to increase returns on the existing pool of reserves in order to reduce OCHAR, which can be sizeable as shown in the previous section. This is equivalent to the strategy depicted in Figure 1.8.

A yield enhancement strategy (e.g. by adopting a stylized pension investment style) may lead to higher marginal revenue curve MR' and the higher level of reserves R'>R*, which can also become the optimal level of reserves. For high-rated countries, which face low borrowing costs, this strategy may be very tempting. In the long run the country can borrow at low cost, and due to its high rating will face a slowly upward-sloping marginal cost curve. However a properly diversified investment portfolio with a proper long-term horizon may lead to a high marginal revenue curve, and this would result in a very large equilibrium level of reserve assets. These properties have been used by United States on the macro level, which in the post–Bretton Woods period enjoyed twice as high of a return on its total foreign assets (6.82%) than the cost of its liabilities (3.5%), which was labeled as the "US exorbitant privilege".[29]

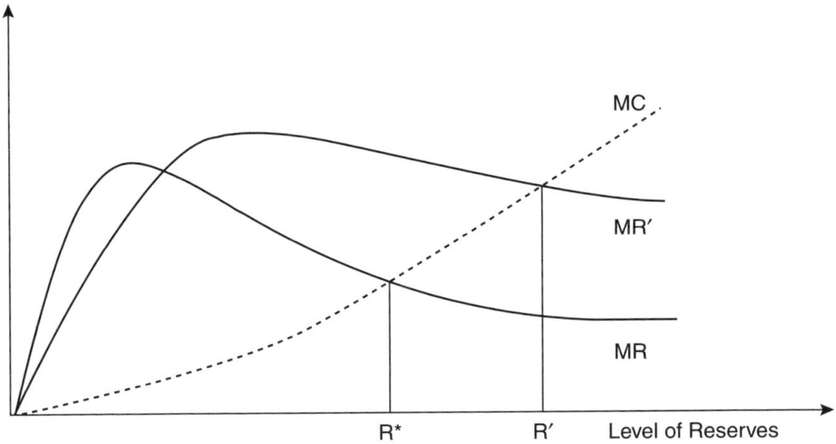

Figure 1.8 Possible reserves marginal revenue and marginal cost under a yield enhancement strategy

Source: Green and Torgerson (2007), with authors' modifications

One can try to formalize the reserves management change process in the following way. A country has a given social preference function related to reserves. We may assume that the central bank utility function is identical to the social preference function. In general terms it can be written as

$$L = f(\overset{(+)}{return}, \overset{(-)}{risk}, \alpha)$$

where first derivatives of utility with respect to return and risk are positive and negative respectively, and α denotes the bank's risk appetite. The central banks face the problem of maximizing such a utility function subject to various constraints, such as the following.

- An appropriate part of the reserves should be invested in liquid markets, which implies that liquidity can be sourced from these markets instantly and the loss of reserves value resulting from such transaction cannot be significant (related to spread, or to the market's ability to absorb sizeable asset sales).
- The currency structure and also general guidelines for the asset structure of reserves should be relatively stable in the short term.
- Changes in central bank investment policy should be market neutral.
- Some countries, depending on the level of reserves, the exchange rate regime or the exports structure may wish to impose other "expert constraints" on the optimization process. For example, a commodity exporter

may wish to reduce exposure to currencies that are positively correlated with commodity prices; some less developed countries may wish to invest in currencies which are used in import invoicing, etc.

To illustrate this problem consider the maximization of a very simple utility function:

$$\max\left(\alpha E(S)-(1-\alpha)Var(S)\right)$$

where S denotes the investment portfolio, and E and Var denote expected return and the variance of returns respectively. In the optimization process the volatility of returns related to exchange rates was higher than the volatility related to interest rate changes by an order of magnitude. Hence it was natural for central banks to determine the optimal currency allocation as a minimum variance portfolio on the efficiency frontier. However, it implied that α was set to zero in the above utility maximization problem. Now it appears that many central banks are gradually raising their risk appetite which corresponds to adopting higher (non-zero) α in the optimization process, and central banks are also moving across different efficiency frontiers, as shown on Figure 1.9.

We are aware that not every central bank used formal optimization techniques in order to optimize currency structure of the reserves portfolio. Often such decisions are taken on the basis of an expert view, are affected by the country's exchange rate regime, its export or import structure, and the need for investment policy changes to be market neutral. However, even in such cases the above modeling framework would apply to the thinking process about reserves management in the twenty-first century.

Central banks are also changing their reserve management strategies by improving risk management, building in house capacity to invest in new asset classes or cooperating with external asset managers. There is a vast literature with examples of such strategies and large investment banks are producing numerous reports on this topic, so it is not necessary to repeat this evidence here. However it is worth looking at the chart below in order to understand the journey the central banks embarked on some time ago.

This stylized journey started some time ago, with central banks pursuing a very conservative capital protection strategy which implied very safe investments, such as deposits with highly rated institutions. This is the lower-left box-mark in Figure 1.9. Then central banks realized that capital protection strategy may be relaxed a bit to allow for a very low likelihood of limited capital loss in the short run. This implied enhancing central bank reserves portfolios by adding treasuries of the largest developed countries, usually US treasuries, German bunds, UK gilts and similar

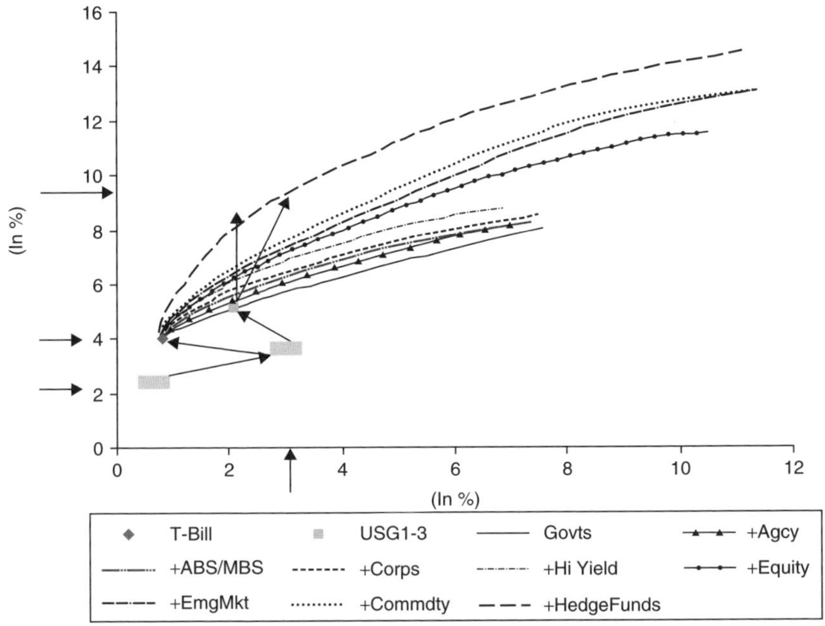

Figure 1.9 The central banks' diversification journey

Source: World Bank Treasury presentation, with authors' modifications; this figure is for illustrative purposes only

instruments denominated in Japanese yen or in Swiss franc, though to a much lesser degree. However the old, very rigid risk limits were still in place, which implied that central banks were not able to achieve risk-return profiles implied by the treasury-efficient frontier. The situation improved with better risk management systems put in place. Then central banks continued their journey, and started diversifying across currencies (in some countries in the eurozone the reverse was observed in order to reduce balance sheet volatility) and adding new instruments. There are some examples of central banks which invest in emerging markets and in hedge funds. On a trip to London one of the authors found that a London-based hedge fund has received a mandate from an Asian central bank to invest in CEE4-currencies. It has been reported, that the Singapore GIC achieved the annual average return of 9.5% in the past 25 years, and the GIC is probably a very good example of a monetary authority that stands on a very high efficiency frontier.

One should also observe that diversification across instruments and currencies makes it possible to move up-left, that is, it is possible to improve returns and reduce volatility of returns at the same time. This is not a free lunch, however; there are other types of risk that do increase, such as liquidity risk, which may become a significant source of capital losses as shown so painfully in the current credit markets turmoil.

1.5 Implications of the global change in reserves management

As documented by actions and by public announcements many central banks have already embarked or are planning to embark on a journey that leads to a more efficient reserves management. Creation of the new investment company in China – China Investment Corporation – new investment funds in Korea and Japan, increasing allocation to equities from 40% to 60% by Norway Pension Fund or more aggressive allocation of Russian oil export proceeds serve as best examples. This will imply slow but sure moves toward more diversified portfolios (across currencies and instruments), while at the same time monetary policy goals and financial stability needs will remain binding constraints.

This trend, which appears to be a commonly shared vision in the vast majority of public sector institutions (central banks and SWFs) jointly managing more than 9 trillion dollars, is likely to result in a shift of relative demand across asset classes. It will likely be associated with further effects, as public institutions actions tend to coordinate with private sector actions around trends.

These trends will probably imply gradual reallocation of reserve assets away from treasury bonds and away from dollar-denominated assets. While many central banks have ruled out net sales of dollars, it is not a universal assumption; for example, the National Bank of Poland was a net seller of dollars and US treasuries in the last two years and the share of US dollars in its portfolio fell from 50% to 40%. So far the IMF COFER data does not indicate that central banks have started to move away from dollars, and public announcements by countries which hold large reserves assets and have currencies pegged to the dollar reaffirm this view.[30]

This long term shift away from dollars and towards riskier assets, *ceteris paribus*, could provide additional safety cushion to emerging markets in the post–Great Moderation period. Global Financial Stability Report published by the IMF in April 2008 argues that there are several risks to the continuation of emerging markets' remarkable stability in the face of the global credit and confidence crisis. Namely, parent banks may pare back funding to their emerging markets subsidiaries, balance sheet contraction may reduce funding and raise funding costs for investments by hedge funds and other institutions investing in emerging markets, emerging markets financial institutions may yet prove vulnerable to financial contagion and a spike in exchange rate volatility could slow or reverse flows into emerging markets fixed income classes. These risks did materialize in 2008, especially in countries with high external imbalances and with large share of short-term financing. Iceland, Hungary, and Ukraine, among others, were forced to accept IMF assistance to avoid bankruptcy. However, at the same time reserves managers may use this opportunity to accelerate asset diversification to benefit from much more attractive stock valuations and much higher credit spreads than in the last few years,[31] thus providing a safety cushion for emerging markets with sound fundamentals. This is also consistent with the weakening of the US dollar[32] and should contribute to reducing the global imbalances problem in the long run.

In the May 2007 version of this chapter we wrote that *ceteris paribus* was not a relevant assumption here. We argued that credit derivatives markets could be a source of large shocks and that the originate-to-distribute business model made it impossible to understand what the risks are and how they are distributed across institutions and across borders. Late 2007 and 2008 did show that this was indeed the case.

The US subprime credit crisis and implosion of the credit derivatives markets indicate that asset valuations in the last few years did not reflect all risks properly and currently markets are in the process of finding a new equilibrium in which liquidity risk will be adequately priced. Similarly the changes in global reserve management imply a continued trend toward a new equilibrium, wherein the relative prices of various asset classes will find their twenty-first century steady state, and some assets prices will likely have very little in common with their historical twentieth-century averages. This trend will probably be interrupted from time to time by bouts of volatility related to sentiment shifts in this or that market (with the subprime crisis as far sigma example of such event). Recent evidence of SWF purchases confirms that such episodes can and will be used by public sector asset managers (including central banks) to accelerate asset diversification.

In the May 2007 version of this chapter we also asked the question what if central banks moved too far with yield enhancement strategy, and they invested in markets that appeared liquid in a world within two-sigma deviations, and a four-sigma global event then hit the markets. Would these markets remain liquid, would central banks be able to take timely actions to preserve liquidity and stability? A few months later such a global shock did happen and we have seen unprecedented action on a global scale. The Bank of England estimated that the total government support for banks and other financial institutions (guarantees, capital injections and purchase of assets) topped 7 trillion dollars.[33] The Federal Reserve and ECB (European Central Bank) flooded the banking sector with an almost unlimited amount of liquidity and organized swap lines with other central banks around the world. So it appears that as long as central banks in charge of global reserve currencies (dollar and euro) can be entrusted with the task of responding to global shocks, central banks in smaller countries can afford to continue their journey to improve returns on their reserves to a certain degree. The list of guardians[34] of global stability will expand in the coming decade, as indicated by the list of countries invited to participate in IMF multilateral consultations[35] on the global imbalances issue.

One more trend, which is slow but deterministic, is the financial deepening in Asia. This is a welcome development, because in the long run the highest returns should be expected in regions with the highest potential growth rates. This is probably Asia in the first 50 years of the twenty-first century, and Africa in the following 50 years. This trend will have a gradual but far-reaching impact on global reserve management. It is likely that in 20–30 years Asian currencies will have a large share in central bank portfolios around the world, and this share could dwarf the dollar and euro if a single Asian currency is created.

Let us restate our main claim in this section. We are in an unprecedented process of finding a new twenty-first century steady state in terms of the relative prices of various asset classes.[36] Actually this equilibrium should have been found already, but the fact that a big chunk of financial intermediation takes place via central banks, who behave in a different manner than private institutions and individuals has delayed the process. But the common, collective mindset to improve reserves management by central banks and sovereign wealth funds will slowly remove this distortion. Let us hope this will be a smooth adjustment.

The global collective move of central banks toward more diversified portfolios will also gradually take away US "exorbitant privilege" by shifting it to reserve-abundant emerging markets. This will not be a zero-sum game, as more diversified and efficient reserve allocation will result in higher global growth, which will be a positive sum outcome, with a higher percentage slice of the bigger pie going to emerging markets.

This section puts forward a number of hypotheses that will be tested in the coming years. Empirical research on the topic of global reserves diversification and its impact on asset prices is still rare,[37] and this issue will certainly attract more attention of researchers in the coming years.

1.6 Conclusions

The foreign exchange reserves held by central banks rose to 6.4 trillion dollars in 2007 from 1.5 trillion a decade ago and are expected to rise further in the coming years. Sovereign wealth funds manage assets in excess of 2.5–3 trillion dollars. This chapter presents the motives behind rapid reserves growth and proposes the concept of OCHAR – Opportunity Cost of Holding Ample Reserves – defined as a forgone GDP growth amid too conservative reserve management by central banks. We estimate OCHAR for a sample of 33 countries which account for 80% of total central bank reserves. We also argue that unlike in the twentieth century, when central banks used to be very secretive institutions, twenty-first century central banking is characterized by widespread knowledge sharing and transparency. Therefore best practices such as inflation targeting or efficient reserve management spread out quickly and are adopted by an increasing number of central banks. Thus central banks have collectively embarked on a reserves diversification journey, which appears to be the central banks' collective mindset, and we can speak of the global reserves management in the twenty-first century. At the end of the chapter we put forward several hypotheses of what the consequences of this diversification journey could be. It seems that relative prices of various assets will find new steady states, which may have little in common with relative valuations seen in the twentieth century. We also expect that slowly, over time, US "exorbitant privilege" will be eliminated. Finally, we consider global stability risks in the context of the new reserves management style adopted by central banks. We postulate that due to the increasingly global nature of shocks, as long as central banks and governments in countries which are stakeholders of global imbalances focus their actions on maintaining global price and financial stability, central banks in smaller emerging markets can afford to improve reserve management without incurring additional stability risk.

In our analysis we encountered significant problems with access to data on central bank reserves, such as investment structure, currency composition and returns achieved in the past. This problem is particularly severe in some Asian countries. We therefore welcome IMF (International Monetary Fund) initiatives such as CPIS (Coordinated Portfolio Investment Survey) and JEDH (Joint External Debt Hub)[38] and we are of the opinion that expanding these initiatives to include an multilaterally agreed format of reporting reserves structure and reserve returns would be a further desirable step in the right direction.

The first version of this chapter was completed in May 2007. Since then the global financial system has experienced a once in a century financial stress. From the crisis perspective many issues presented in this chapter may seem of little relevance. Why worry about forgone GDP growth of 0.2% per year at times when there is a threat of large and prolonged recession in many developed countries, and central banks that did adopt the pension funds' investment style suffered very sharp losses in 2008? We argue that on the contrary, it is a once in a lifetime opportunity for central banks to accelerate their reserves diversification journey and benefit from very low stock valuations and large credit spreads. When the dust of this global financial crisis settles down, investors will notice that the new financial order of the twenty-first century has started to emerge. Central banks and SWFs that keep a large percentage of their assets in US dollars and in government bills and bonds will run significant risk of exposing themselves to large OCHAR.

Appendix

Table 1.6 Actual returns and opportunity cost of reserves compared to combined portfolio (USD million, % GDP)*

		Actual return on reserves			Typical combined return on reserves			Actual opportunity cost			Actual opportunity cost as a percentage of GDP		
		2005	2006	2007	2005	2006	2007	2005	2006	2007	2005	2006	2007
Western Europe	Germany**	1442.6	1948.4	2043.5	1929.4	3711.6	8623.0	486.8	1763.2	6579.5	0.02	0.06	0.20
	France**	2630.9	3733.1	4513.0	1411.1	3266.2	7324.4	−1219.9	−466.9	2811.4	−0.06	−0.02	0.11
	Switzerland**	6225.1	1225.5	2261.2	1093.8	2144.3	4770.7	−5131.3	918.9	2509.5	−1.38	0.24	0.59
	Sweden	–	560.5	1582.9	472.3	931.7	1964.5	–	371.2	381.6	–	0.09	0.08
CEE	Poland	1106.6	1551.2	3549.6	1625.5	4291.3	5045.0	518.9	2740.1	1495.4	0.17	0.80	0.36
	Hungary	483.7	777.2	–	438.1	1006.3	1545.8	−45.6	229.1	–	−0.04	0.20	–
	Czech Republic	775.2	942.9	–	1104.2	2595.3	2631.3	329.0	1652.4	–	0.26	1.16	–
	Slovak Republic	341.7	323.0	–	594.2	1011.9	1441.3	252.5	688.9	–	0.53	1.23	–
Asia	Hong Kong**	3852.6	12655.0	18018.8	3773.9	7835.1	10822.1	−78.7	−4819.9	−7196.7	−0.04	−2.54	−3.48
Oil exporting countries	Russia	5467.2	11541.8	–	7667.3	31146.9	38556.3	2200.1	19605.0	–	0.29	1.98	–
	Norway ***	4266.3	4149.4	2050.3	891.6	1889.8	3850.9	−3374.7	−2259.6	1800.6	−1.12	−0.67	0.46
	Mexico	1226.1	3722.0	–	2822.6	6389.9	6755.9	1596.5	2667.9	–	0.21	0.32	–
	United Arab Emirates	540.8	756.7	–	442.8	918.2	–	−98.0	161.5	–	−0.07	0.10	–
Latin America	Argentina****	873.5	1825.5	–	982.6	2666.1	3570.5	109.1	840.6	–	0.06	0.40	–
	Chile	491.0	475.2	–	463.1	1066.0	1080.6	−28.0	590.8	–	−0.02	0.41	–
	Colombia	410.6	599.9	–	573.9	1344.8	1546.5	163.2	745.0	–	0.13	0.55	–

Notes: *Short-term data for 2007 not available; we used short-term debt for 2007 Q2.
**Actual rate of return were calculated in national currency term, date not comparable with the rest of the countries.
***Data refers to investment portfolio only.
****Return in USD terms.
Source: Authors' calculations based on IMF, WEO, BIS-OECD-IMF-World Bank data, Merrill Lynch indices and central banks' annual reports.

Table 1.7 Actual returns and opportunity cost of reserves compared to pension portfolio (USD million, % GDP)

		Actual return on reserves			Typical pension return on reserves			Actual opportunity cost			Actual opportunity cost as a percentage of GDP (in %)		
		2005	**2006**	**2007**	**2005**	**2006**	**2007**	**2005**	**2006**	**2007**	**2005**	**2006**	**2007**
Western Europe	Germany*	1442.6	1948.4	2043.5	5128.0	13255.7	11464.8	3685.5	11307.4	9421.3	0.13	0.39	0.28
	France*	2630.9	3733.1	4513.0	3750.4	11664.9	9738.2	1119.4	7931.8	5225.2	0.05	0.35	0.20
	Switzerland*	6225.1	1225.5	2261.2	2907.1	7658.4	6342.9	−3318.0	6433.0	4081.8	−0.89	1.66	0.96
	Sweden	–	560.5	1582.9	1255.3	3327.4	2611.9	–	2767.0	1029.0	0.00	0.70	0.23
CEE	Poland	1106.6	1551.2	3549.6	2146.6	5755.8	5531.8	1040.0	4204.6	1982.2	0.34	1.23	0.47
	Hungary	483.7	777.2	–	938.2	2563.6	2024.1	454.6	1786.4	–	0.41	1.58	–
	Czech Republic	775.2	942.9	–	1481.0	3707.1	2911.3	705.8	2764.3	–	0.57	1.93	–
	Slovak Republic	341.7	323.0	–	780.7	1586.8	1596.9	439.0	1263.8	–	0.92	2.26	–
Asia	Hong Kong*	3852.6	12655.0	18018.8	6268.0	15817.4	12850.6	2415.4	3162.4	−5168.2	1.36	1.66	−2.50
Oil exporting countries	Russia	5467.2	11541.8	–	9191.3	36065.1	40090.6	3724.1	24523.3	–	0.49	2.48	–
	Norway **	4266.3	4149.4	2050.3	2369.7	6749.4	5119.9	−1896.6	2599.9	3069.6	−0.63	0.77	0.78
	Mexico	1226.1	3722.0	–	3734.9	9056.3	7330.7	2508.9	5334.3	–	0.33	0.64	–
	United Arab Emirates	540.8	756.7	–	1059.7	3279.3	–	518.9	2522.6	–	0.39	1.54	–
Latin America	Argentina***	873.5	1825.5	–	1416.6	3802.8	3880.9	543.1	1977.3	–	0.30	0.93	–
	Chile	491.0	475.2	–	854.0	2303.1	1417.4	362.9	1827.9	–	0.31	1.25	–
	Colombia	410.6	599.9	–	754.2	1833.0	1763.2	343.6	1233.1	–	0.28	0.91	–

Note: *Actual rate of return were calculated in national currency term. Date not comparable with the rest of the countries.
**Data refers to investment portfolio only.
***Return in USD terms.
Source: Authors' calculations based on IMF, WEO, BIS-OECD-IMF-World Bank data, Merrill Lynch indices and central banks' annual reports.

Table 1.8 Hypothetical opportunity cost (USD million, % GDP)

		Hypothetical opportunity cost			Hypothetical opportunity cost. combined portfolio			Hypothetical opportunity cost as a percentage of GDP			Hypothetical opportunity cost as a percentage of GDP. combined portfolio		
		2005	2006	2007	2005	2006	2007*	2005	2006	2007	2005	2006	2007*
Western Europe	Germany	3198.6	9544.1	2841.8	0.0	0.0	0.0	0.11	0.33	0.09	0.00	0.00	0.00
	France	2339.3	8398.7	2413.8	0.0	0.0	0.0	0.11	0.37	0.09	0.00	0.00	0.00
	Switzerland	1813.3	5514.1	1572.2	0.0	0.0	0.0	0.49	1.42	0.37	0.00	0.00	0.00
	Sweden	783.0	2395.7	647.4	0.0	0.0	0.0	0.21	0.61	0.14	0.00	0.00	0.00
CEE	Poland	1338.9	4144.2	1371.2	817.8	2679.7	884.3	0.44	1.21	0.33	0.27	0.78	0.21
	Hungary	585.2	1845.8	501.7	85.1	288.5	23.4	0.53	1.63	0.36	0.08	0.26	0.02
	Czech Republic	923.8	2669.1	721.6	547.0	1557.3	441.6	0.74	1.87	0.41	0.44	1.09	0.25
	Slovak Republic	487.0	1142.5	395.8	300.5	567.6	240.2	1.02	2.04	0.53	0.63	1.01	0.32
Asia	Japan	26284.2	75317.1	19902.8	12868.0	42529.6	11964.9	0.58	1.72	0.45	0.28	0.97	0.27
	China	25972.2	91696.4	32005.6	23987.0	84858.3	29840.0	1.16	3.47	0.98	1.07	3.21	0.92
	South Korea	6618.7	20429.0	5469.8	4645.6	11875.0	2908.2	0.84	2.30	0.57	0.59	1.34	0.30
	Thailand	1637.9	5726.7	1824.3	1236.1	4491.2	1602.0	0.93	2.77	0.74	0.70	2.17	0.65
	Taiwan	8114.9	23154.8	5736.9	6916.6	20317.9	4675.2	2.28	6.33	1.50	1.94	5.56	1.22
	Singapore	3654.7	11649.1	3399.2	1047.1	2887.0	817.5	3.05	8.53	2.11	0.87	2.11	0.51
	Hong Kong	3909.7	11388.5	3185.3	1415.6	3406.2	1156.8	2.20	5.99	1.54	0.80	1.79	0.56

Oil exporting countries	Russia	5733.1	25966.9	9937.2	4209.1	21048.7	8402.9	0.75	2.63	0.77	0.55	2.13	0.65
	Norway	1478.1	4859.5	1269.1	0.0	0.0	0.0	0.49	1.44	0.32	0.00	0.00	0.00
	Saudi Arabia	841.8	2373.7	709.5	412.6	1357.5	304.5	0.27	0.68	0.19	0.13	0.39	0.08
	Nigeria	889.7	3616.2	1070.8	828.9	3270.7	991.5	0.79	2.46	0.64	0.74	2.23	0.59
	Venezuela	932.3	3135.2	698.3	720.7	2739.5	578.5	0.65	1.70	0.30	0.50	1.49	0.24
	Kuwait	282.2	1083.7	349.9	52.0	377.3	125.3	0.35	1.10	0.31	0.06	0.38	0.11
	Mexico	2329.7	6520.6	1817.0	1417.3	3854.1	1242.3	0.30	0.78	0.20	0.18	0.46	0.14
	Algeria	1780.0	6686.2	2307.6	1746.2	6601.6	2288.6	1.73	5.82	1.75	1.70	5.75	1.74
	United Arab Em.	661.0	2361.1	n.a	44.1	0.0	n.a	0.50	1.45	n.a	0.03	0.00	n.a
Latin America	Brazil	1692.5	7338.6	3761.6	258.5	3418.9	2669.2	0.19	0.68	0.29	0.03	0.32	0.20
	Argentina	883.6	2738.0	962.0	449.6	1601.3	651.5	0.49	1.29	0.37	0.25	0.75	0.25
	Chile	532.7	1658.2	351.3	141.8	421.2	14.6	0.45	1.14	0.21	0.12	0.29	0.01
	Colombia	470.5	1319.8	437.0	290.1	831.6	220.4	0.38	0.97	0.25	0.24	0.61	0.13
Africa	South Africa	649.0	2187.5	687.2	378.0	850.8	343.4	0.27	0.85	0.24	0.16	0.33	0.12
	Sudan	58.8	141.9	28.7	0.0	0.0	0.0	0.21	0.39	0.06	0.00	0.00	0.00
	Kenya	56.6	206.6	70.0	39.9	153.0	54.8	0.30	0.91	0.24	0.21	0.67	0.19
	Botswana	198.5	683.3	n.a	196.9	680.6	n.a	1.87	6.18	n.a	1.86	6.16	n.a
	Ghana	59.7	193.9	n.a	33.3	91.8	n.a	0.56	1.53	n.a	0.31	0.72	n.a

*We used short-term debt for 2007 Q2.

Source: Authors' calculations based on IMF, WEO, BIS-OECD-IMF-World Bank data and Merrill Lynch indices

Notes

Authors are respectively: (1) partner at Ernst & Young, former deputy governor of the National Bank of Poland and former member of the Polish Financial Services Authority; (2) economist at Millennium Bank in Warsaw and former economist at the National Bank of Poland. The views presented in this chapter are those of the authors and do not represent the official position of the institutions that the authors are or were affiliated with. This chapter was inspired by Jennifer Johnson-Calari and Roberts Grava's presentations to the World Bank Treasury, which drew authors' attention to the problem of rising opportunity cost of holding ample reserves. We thank Roberts Grava and Ewa Szafarczyk for helpful comments on the earlier draft; all remaining errors are ours. The first version of this chapter was written in late 2006.

1. MGI (2007) estimates that Sovereign Wealth Funds account for only 60% of petrodollar assets, with the rest managed by wealthy private individuals.
2. Feldstein (1999).
3. Greenspan (1999).
4. Rybinski (2007) discusses all existing theories of global imbalances, showing their strengths and weaknesses (in Polish).
5. The most parsimonious cointegrating relationship contains the following variables: ratio of reserves to nominal GDP, imports to GDP, broad money to GDP, volatility of export revenues and structural changes in coefficients related to imports to GDP and money to GDP after the Asian crisis.
6. Cifarelli and Paladino (2007) discuss previous empirical research utilizing the buffer stock model. In particular they show that two strands of papers emerge. The first one attempts to adopt the buffer stock model to emerging markets characteristics by adding proper institutional variables. The second one focuses on quantitative aspects of the cost-benefit structure, e.g. estimating the relationship between reserves and the probability of costly default. For example Rodrik and Velasco (2000) estimate that the probability of a sudden stop would fall by 10% if a country fulfilled the Greenspan-Guidotti rule.
7. Green and Torgerson (2007).
8. Kenen and Yudin (1965), Courchene and Youssef (1967), Flanders (1971), Frenkel and Jovanovic (1981), Edwards (1985), Landell-Mills (1989) and Ben-Bassat and Gottlieb (1992).
9. They use a maximum of return on business projects and government projects. The latter is approximated by return on investment in infrastructure. The difference between real return on domestic projects and on foreign reserve investments is always positive in the analyzed case of Israel, and remains in the range of 5–15%. This strand of literature uses the opportunity cost of holding reserves to estimate the demand for reserve assets; it does not focus on the forgone potential GDP growth.
10. We limit our analysis to central bank portfolios amid very limited information about asset size and investment styles of many SWFs (truly exceptional in this respect is the Government Pension Fund of Norway which is a very transparent institution).
11. These countries are: Germany, France, Switzerland, Sweden, Poland, Hungary, Czech Republic, Slovakia, Japan, China, Korea, Thailand, Taiwan, Singapore, Hong Kong, Russia, Norway, Saudi Arabia, Nigeria, Venezuela, Kuwait, Mexico, Algeria, United Arab Emirates, Brazil, Argentina, Chile, Colombia, South Africa,

Sudan, Kenya, Botswana and Ghana. We exclude the US from the analysis as we think that it would be odd to add the biggest world debtor into the global assets analysis. The same could apply to Western European countries, as in every case the country's short-term debt vastly exceeds the country's foreign exchange reserves.

12. Wijnholds, Beaufort and Kapteyn (2001).
13. For a recent review of other reserve adequacy rules see Green and Torgerson (2007).
14. See Table 1.6 in the appendix. Only 16 out of analyzed 33 countries reported return on reserves for at least one year in the period 2004–2006. Out of 16 countries, 4 report returns in local currency, which further complicates calculations.
15. Coming from the central banking community we do acknowledge that splitting reserves into "traditional reserves" and a "sovereign wealth component" is controversial. It raises questions regarding whether central banks should act as sovereign wealth managers given the institutional constraints they face (see Bakker and van Herpt (2007)). Hildebrand (2007) asks a question whether it is appropriate at all to treat reserves above any rule the same way we treat assets in sovereign wealth funds. These are important considerations but in-depth discussion of these issues extends beyond the limited scope of this chapter.
16. Actual rates of return were obtained from the central banks' annual reports. They were either reported directly or calculated on the basis of reported interest income on foreign exchange assets.
17. Swiss National Bank also manages a well diversified portfolio which has included equities since 2004; see Hildebrand (2007).
18. In this decision we follow Greenspan (2005) who said: "Over the past two decades, inflation has fallen notably, virtually worldwide, as has economic volatility. Although a complete understanding of the reasons remains elusive, globalization and innovation would appear to be essential elements of any paradigm capable of explaining the events of the past ten years. If this is indeed the case, because the extent of globalization and the speed of innovation are limited, the current apparent rapid pace of structural shift cannot continue indefinitely. While the outlook for the next year or two seems reasonably bright, the outlook for the latter part of this decade remains opaque because it is uncertain whether this transitional paradigm, if that is what it is, is already far advanced and about to slow, or whether it remains in an early, still-vibrant stage of evolution".
19. We assume that central bankers love their jobs and want to be reelected or reappointed.
20. Short-term debt data for 2007 was not available; we used the data for 2007 Q2. For the period 1990–1996 reserves data for some countries (Taiwan, Russia, Czech Republic, Slovak Republic and Hong Kong) are missing; for those years we calculated average opportunity cost excluding countries with missing data.
21. At the National Bank of Poland we conducted the following exercise. We assumed that we were allowed to invest in ten currencies (USD, EUR, GBP, CHF, JPY, DKK, SEK, NOK, AUD and CAD) and that there were no limits on the share of a particular currency. We conducted the optimization procedure, using PLN as the base currency and assumed investments in asset classes that

we actually use (governments and high rated agencies). We then selected the optimal unconstrained portfolio, which had the same volatility as the actual portfolio (the same risk related to volatility of returns). This theoretical portfolio had a return 2.7% higher than the actual one, on average each year, which could have translated into 0.4–0.5% of GDP of additional revenue to the budget each year. The currency structure of the theoretical portfolio would have probably been unacceptable due to the high proportion of shares of CAD and NOK, which are not liquid enough markets given the size of Poland's reserves. But this exercise shows what the magnitude of the opportunity cost is, even before one starts to think about opportunity costs related to diversification across asset classes.

22. Pringle and Carver (2007), Johnson-Calari and Rietveld (2007 presentations at the World Bank Sovereign Investment Partnerships forum, Washington, 16–18 April 2007.
23. www.doz.ae
24. On the other hand, one can assume that going forward a significant percentage of central bank reserves in countries holding ample reserves will be allocated to SWFs (recently in Korea, plans announced in China and Japan). In such an event, if profits of SWFs are retained, our OCHAR estimate may be too high as investments in physical or intellectual assets will not be forgone, but will be shifted to the future. We reiterate that the third OCHAR factor is country-specific as there are "good governments" as well as "bad governments" when it comes to spending extra revenues. Here we assume "average government" for all countries.
25. Calderón and Servén (2004).
26. Wylie (1996).
27. Calderón and Servén (2003).
28. "Government clearly has a role in financing basic research, but government programs to finance commercial R&D have a mixed record. The government often has difficulty in selecting appropriate research projects and in motivating researchers to focus on developing viable projects. Researchers applying for grants have an incentive to present the prospects of success in the best possible light to increase their chances of receiving funding. Research administrators in turn have incentives to tell their superiors that prospects for success are bright in order to increase the budgets of their divisions" (Glennerster and Kremer (2000)). Public R&D spending may thus turn wasteful or unproductive. One can escape from that limitation by using a maximum of return on business projects and government projects (see Ben-Bassat and Gottlieb (1992)) when estimating the opportunity cost. It is equivalent to the assumption that the government either finances R&D by itself, or lowers taxes in order to stimulate private R&D spending.
29. See Gourinchas and Rey (2005).
30. However, one has to acknowledge that the US dollar peg is complicating the macroeconomic situation in some GCC countries. While these countries should be raising rates amid high inflation, the Federal Reserve has been cutting rates to avoid a credit crunch-led recession, which limits the GCC central banks' ability to raise rates.
31. One example of such diversification is a series of investments by emerging markets SWFs in large US, Swiss and British financial institutions in the last few

quarters. There is, however, a debate regarding whether SWFs moved in too quickly and "burnt their fingers" as the mark-to-market valuations a few months after the purchases have shown significant losses. It is, however, worth recalling that SWFs have much longer investment horizons than typical private sector investors and may pay more attention to fundamental valuations that to quarterly mark-to-market outcomes.

32. US dollar perspectives will also depend on the home bias developments in the US. It the last few years US investors have diversified assets internationally and the home bias fell. It remains to be seen whether the weakening of the dollar that took place in 2007 and 2008 will reduce or reverse this process. Rapid dollar appreciation in the second half of 2008 stems from market panic and reflects flight to quality; it should be seen as a short-term phenomenon.
33. See Bank of England (2008).
34. In the late twentieth century the Federal Reserve assumed this responsibility in the face of Russian and LTCM (Long Term Capital Management) crisis. In the twenty-first century it will likely be joined in this role by ECB (European Central Bank) and PBoC (People's Bank of China), with smaller global roles played by BoJ (Bank of Japan) and SAMA (Saudi Arabian Monetary Authority). On the global nature of shocks see for example Ehrmann and Fratzscher (2006).
35. Multilateral consultations coordinated by the IMF with the participation of the US, Eurozone, China, Saudi Arabia and Japan are testing the ability of large stakeholders of global imbalances to deal with this issue. See IMFC statement http://www.imf.org/external/np/sec/pr/2007/pr0772.htm
36. For example B-rated and BB-rated emerging market CDS[Author query: Could you please spell out and give abbreviation on first use] spreads fell below spreads on similarly rated US corporates in 2007; see BIS(2007). Another example is given by PIMCO (2007) research which notes that local and external market debt have been among the most stable asset classes in the episode of market volatility in late February – March 2007. Finally, as documented by J. P. Morgan (2006), the correlation between VXY and EM-VXY, which are volatility indices for G-7 and for emerging markets has gone up significantly in recent two-three years, which reflects the fact that global investors cross asset classes borders much more often than before.
37. A very good survey and some early empirical results are reported in the IMF Global Financial Stability Report (2007).
38. See IMF (2007: 77).

References

Aizenman, J. and Lee, J. (2005) "International Reserves: Precautionary vs. Mercantilist Views, Theory and Evidence", IMF Working Paper WP/05/198, October 2005.

Aschauer, D. (1989) "Is Public Expenditure Productive?" *Journal of Monetary Economics*, Vol. 23, 177–200.

Bakker, A. and van Herpt, I. (2007) "Reserve Management in the Eurosystem: From Liquidity to Return", in Johnson-Calari, J. and Rietveld, M. (eds) *Sovereign Wealth Management*, London: Central Banking Publications, 2007, 273–284.

Bank of England (2008) "Financial Stability Report", No. 24, October 2008.

Ben-Bassat, A. and Gottlieb, D. (1992) "On the Effect of Opportunity Cost on International Reserve Holdings", *The Review of Economics and Statistics*, Vol. 74, No. 2., May 1992, 329–332.

BIS (2007) "BIS Quarterly Review. International Banking and Financial Market Developments", Bank for International Settlements, March 2007.

Caballero, R. and Panageas, S. (2004a) "Contingent Reserves Management: An Applied Framework", unpublished ms., MIT, Department of Economics.

Caballero, R. and Panageas, S. (2004b) "Insurance and Reserves Management in a Model of Sudden Stops", unpublished ms., MIT, Department of Economics.

Calderón, C. and Servén, L. (2003) "Macroeconomic Dimensions of Infrastructure in Latin America", mimeo, The World Bank.

Calderón, C. and Servén, L. (2004) "The Effects of Infrastructure Development on Growth and Income Distribution", World Bank Policy Research Working Paper No. 3400.

Cifarelli, G. and Paladino, G. (2007) "The Buffer Stock Model Redux? An Analysis of the Dynamics of Foreign Reserve Accumulation", Intesa Sanpaolo research paper, February 2007.

Courchene, T. and Youssef, G. (1967) "The Demand for International Reserves", *The Journal of Political Economy*, Vol. 75, No. 4, Part 1., August 1967, 404–413.

Dooley, M., Folkerts-Landau, D. and Garber, P. (2003) "An Essay on the Revived Bretton Woods System", NBER Working Paper 9971, September 2003.

Dooley M., Folkerts-Landau D., Garber P. (2000) "The Revived Bretton Woods System: The Effects of Periphery Intervention and Reserve Management on Interest Rates and Exchange Rates in Center Countries", NBER Working Paper 10332, March 2004.

Dooley, M., Folkerts-Landau, D. and Garber, P. (2005) "Savings Glut and Interest Rates: The Missing Link to Europe", NBER Working Paper 11520, July 2005.

ECB (2006) "The Accumulation of Foreign Reserves", Occasional Paper No. 43, International Relations Committee Task Force, February 2006.

Edwards, S. (1985) "On the Interest-Rate Elasticity of the Demand for International Reserves: Some Evidence from Developing Countries", *Journal of International Money and Finance* Vol. 4, June 1985, 287–295.

Ehrmann, M. and Fratzscher, M. (2006) "Global Financial Transmission of Monetary Policy Shocks", ECB Working Paper No. 616, April 2006.

Feldstein, M. (1999) "Self-Protection for Emerging Market Economies", NBER Working Paper 6907, January 1999.

Flanders M. (1971) "The Demand for International Reserves", *Princeton Studies in International Finance* Vol. 27, 1971.

Frenkel, J. and Jovanovic, B. (1981) "Optimal International Reserves: A Stochastic Framework", *Economic Journal* Vol. 91, June 1981, 507–514.

Garcia, P. and Soto C. (2004) "Large Hoarding of International Reserves: Are They Worth It?", manuscript, Bank of Chile.

Glennerster, R. and Kremer, M. (2000) "A Better Way to Spur Medical Research and Development", *Regulation*, Vol. 23, No. 2, 2000, 34–39.

Gosselin, M. A. and Parent, N. (2005) "An Empirical Analysis of Foreign Exchange Reserves in Emerging Asia", Bank of Canada working paper 2005–38, December 2005.

Gourinchas, P-O. and Rey, H. (2005) "From World Banker to World Venture Capitalist: US External Adjustment and the Exorbitant Privilege", working paper, UC Berkeley, August 2005.

Green, R. and Torgerson, T. (2007) "Are High Foreign Exchange Reserves In Emerging Markets a Blessing or a Burden?", US Department of Treasury Occasional Paper No. 6, March 2007.

Greenspan A. (1999) "Currency Reserves and Debt", Remarks by the Chairman of the Board of Governors of the Federal Reserve System before The World Bank Conference o n Recent Trends in Reserve Management, Washington, D.C., 29 April 1999.

Greenspan, A. (2005) "Globalization", remarks given at the Council of Foreign Relations, New York, 10 March 2005.

Gruber, Joseph W. and Steven B. Kamin. 2005. "Explaining the Global Pattern of Current Account Imbalances". Board of Governors of the Federal Reserve System, International Finance Discussion Papers, no. 846, November.

Hildebrand, P. (2007) "Four Tough Questions in Foreign Reserve Management", in Johnson-Calari J., Rietveld M. (eds) *Sovereign Wealth Management*, London: Central Banking Publications, 2007.

IMF (2007) "Global Financial Stability Report", IMF, April 2007.

IMF (2008a) "Global Financial Stability Report", IMF, April 2008.

IMF (2008b) "COFER database", http://www.imf.org/external/np/sta/cofer/eng/index.htm .

Jeanne, O. and Rancière, R. (2006) "The Optimal Level of International Reserves for Emerging Market Countries: Formulas and Applications", IMF Working Paper 06/229, October 2006.

J. P. Morgan (2006) "Introducing the JPMorgan VXY and EM-VXY", J. P. Morgan Global Currency & Commodity Strategy, 11 December 2006.

Kenen, P. Yudin, E. (1965) "The Demand for International Reserves", *Review* 47, August 1965.

Landell-Mills, J. (1989) "The Demand for International Reserves and Their Opportunity Cost", IMF Staff Papers 36, September 1989.

Malecki, W., Sławiński, A., Piasecki, R. and Żuławska, U. (2001) "Currency crises", *PWN*, Warsaw 2001 (in Polish).

Mendoza, R.(2004) "International Reserve-Holding in the Developing World: Self Insurance in a Crisis-Prone Era?" *Emerging Markets Review* 5(1), 61–82.

MGI (2007) "The New Power Brokers. How Oil, Asia, Hedge Funds and Private Equity Are Shaping Global Capital Markets", McKinsey & Company, October 2007.

Munnell, A. H. (1992) "Policy Watch: Infrastructure Investment and Economic Growth", *The Journal of Economic Perspectives*, Vol. 6, No. 4, 189–198.

PIMCO (2007) "Emerging Markets Watch. Can You (Point Your Fingers and Do the Twist?)", research note by Michael Gomez, PIMCO, April 2007.

Pringle, R. and Carver, N. (eds) (2007) *RBS Reserve Management Trends 2007*, London: RBS and Central Banking Publications.

Rietveld, M. and Pringle, R. (2007) "The Evolution of Sovereign Wealth Management" in Johnson-Calari, J. and Rietveld, M. (eds) *Sovereign Wealth Management*, London: Central Banking Publications, 2007.

Rodrik, D. (2006) "The Social Cost of Foreign Exchange Reserves", *International Economic Journal*, Vol. 20, No. 3, September 2006, 253–266.

Rodrik and Velasco (2000) "Short-Term Capital Flows", in Annual World Bank Conference on Development Economics 1999, April 2000.

Rybinski, K. (2007) "Three aspects of globalization. Offshoring, global imbalances, monetary policy", *Difin*, Warsaw, forthcoming in May 2007 (in Polish). Several topics covered in the book are available in English at www.rybinski.eu

Wijnholds, J., De Beaufort, O. and Kapteyn, A. (2001) "Reserve Adequacy In Emerging Market Economies", IMF Working Paper No. 01/143.

Wylie P.J. (1996), "Infrastructure and Canadian Economic Growth, 1946–1991", *The Canadian Journal of Economics / Revue canadienne d'Economique*, Vol. 29, Special Issue: Part 1., S350–S355.

2
Framework and Process for Strategic Asset Allocation in Central Bank Foreign Exchange Reserves Management

*Alex Joia and Joachim Coche**

2.1 Introduction

Already prior to the international financial crisis, Strategic Asset Allocation (SAA) was a topic of growing interest to central banks. Increasing levels of reserves had shone a spotlight on central banks' reserves management in general and on SAA in particular. The events of the international financial crisis have intensified the interest in SAA as the need for a disciplined approach to reserves management and a careful analysis of investments' risk–return characteristics was highlighted.

The reserves' SAA comprises decisions on allocations to different currencies, asset classes and maturity sectors and is therefore the central determinant of the reserves' risk–return profile. While many central banks have developed robust reserve management frameworks and SAA processes, there are nevertheless lessons to be learnt from the financial crisis. On the one hand, the crisis has highlighted the limitations of some elements of the process such as the modelling and projection of future returns. Consequently assumptions have to be revised and improvements to models made. On the other hand, the crisis has emphasised the importance of other elements of the process such as robustness checks in form of stress testing. Despite such adjustments, the major elements of a robust reserve management framework and SAA process remain the same post-crisis as they were pre-crisis. The purpose of this paper is to present a possible SAA process and describe its integration into the reserves management framework. This process might be used by central banks to gauge to what extent revisions to the institution's risk–return preferences and modelling assumptions affect the reserves' optimal allocation.

* The views expressed in this paper are those of the authors and not necessarily those of the BIS.

While it is obvious that central banks as investors behave differently from private sector institutions, the SAA process presented below also reflects the facts that individual central banks operate under legal frameworks, are given mandates, have opted for governance structures and have accumulated levels of foreign exchange reserves that are markedly different from their peers. Consequently, the purpose for holding foreign exchange reserves and the objectives in managing them differ from one central bank to another. Decision-makers need to reflect the idiosyncratic nature of their institutions when faced with a number of key choices in the design of the SAA process. Choices range from the integration of the SAA into the broader reserves management framework, to decisions on the appropriate unit of account (or numéraire) to be used in asset allocation analysis, and from the tranching of reserves to the specification of risk–return preferences and expectations. These choices dictate the resulting asset allocation and the overall risk–return characteristics of foreign exchange reserves.

The remainder of this paper is organised as follows. Section 2.2 describes the purpose for holding reserves and investment objectives, describes the elements of the reserves management framework, and introduces a common hierarchical approach to asset allocation. Section 2.3 discusses the SAA process and highlights the main choices facing the decision-makers and alternatives as well as pitfalls of each choice. Section 2.4 summarises. Finally, an example of the SAA process illustrating a possible, practical solution that balances quantitative and qualitative inputs is provided as a casestudy in the Annex.

2.2 Reserves management framework

Similar to other institutional investors, central bank reserve managers aim at identifying the asset allocation with risk–return characteristics that are superior to those of all other feasible allocations. However, the definition of superiority and the process by which central banks identify superiority differs significantly from other institutional investors, as the purpose for holding reserves and the institutional decision-making framework is different.

This section addresses the idiosyncratic nature of central banks as investors and how this affects their decision-making with regard to SAA. To this end we first review the purpose of holding reserves and secondly discuss how SAA is integrated into the broader reserves management framework. While Borio, Ebbesen, Galati and Heath (2008) describe some of the high-level elements of foreign exchange reserve management framework, we focus on how the SAA is an integral part of such a framework.

2.2.1 Purpose for holding reserves

The IMF "Guidelines for Foreign Exchange Reserve Management"[1] establish as a primary purpose for holding foreign exchange reserves the support and maintenance of confidence in a country's monetary and exchange rate policy. To this end, foreign exchange reserves are held to build and maintain market confidence so that a country can meet its external obligations and to demonstrate the backing of domestic currency by external assets. Furthermore, reserves allow the government to meet its foreign exchange needs and external debt obligations. Finally, foreign exchange reserves may be held as a reserve for national disasters or other emergencies.[2]

In addition to these traditional purposes, the massive increase in reserves holdings observed over the past years in many countries triggered a discussion on additional purposes for holding reserves. One such purpose is the holding of reserves as a store of national wealth (see, e.g., Genberg et al. 2005). Others (see, e.g., Dooley, Folkerts-Landau and Garber 2003) indicate that these reserves are a by-product of a policy to preserve export competitiveness through intervention in the foreign exchange market.

These general purposes for reserves holdings mean that liquidity, safety and – often to a lesser extent – return are desirable characteristics of the foreign exchange reserves portfolio. These desirable characteristics are reflected in form of investment objectives which we will discuss in detail in Section 2.3. At this point we note that the above outlined purposes generally result in low appetite for market and credit risk as well as specific concern for liquidity and reputational risk. Furthermore, central banks normally have higher accountability and transparency requirements than private sector investors. The fact that central banks are accountable to the government and the general public on investment strategy and performance influences their reserve management decisions. Also, investment constraints are established in order to minimise potential interference of the role that some central banks have in financial stability and supervision with their investment activities. Finally, the central bank balance sheet is part of the consolidated public sector balance sheet. Thus, for example, profit distribution by the central bank to the government may be a consideration in formulating investment objectives.

In summary, the objectives for managing reserves should follow from the ultimate purpose for holding reserves. Since the purpose for holding reserves differs from one central bank to another, so should the objectives and resulting SAA. A good understanding of the purpose for holding reserves is therefore a prerequisite for proper asset allocation decisions.

2.2.2 Governance structure

Central banks do not only differ in investment objectives but also in the way that the SAA process is integrated into the institution's governance structure. As opposed to arrangements often made in the private sector where the top decision-maker fully delegates investment decisions to lower level bodies,[3] the top decision-makers in central banks are typically involved to a substantial degree in the SAA process. At a minimum, senior management imposes constraints and specifies risk–return preferences, allowing a subordinate body to determine the optimal SAA on this basis. In practice the senior decision-makers often prefer to remain more "hand-on" and are, in addition, required to approve the resulting SAA.

Figure 2.1 depicts a possible integration of SAA into the reserves management framework. In this example, management of foreign exchange reserves is implemented in a hierarchical manner with SAA being at the top, followed by Tactical Asset Allocation (TAA) and a portfolio management implementation layer at the bottom.

The inputs into the SAA process are (1) constraints, (2) risk–return preferences and (3) risk–return expectations. Constraints typically take the form of limits on various types of risk (e.g., liquidity risk) and exposures to individual asset classes (e.g. non-government instruments). Risk–return preferences specify the trade-off between financial risk and return and thereby provide a means for comparing the characteristics of different allocations and selecting the one best suited to the institution.[4] Finally, risk–return expectations are required in order to assess the risk and return properties of alternative asset allocations against the specified preferences. In principle, SAA should be reviewed whenever changes in the inputs to the SAA process would lead to a material change in the allocation. The appropriate SAA review frequency therefore depends on the rate of change of these inputs. While constraints and risk–return preferences are expected to remain broadly unchanged over time, risk–return expectations may change frequently over the economic cycle.

The SAA process normally results in a strategic benchmark constructed using a set of indices from one or more external providers or constructed in-house from individual bonds. On the basis of this benchmark portfolio, it is possible to precisely measure the ex-post performance of the SAA decision. Furthermore, the strategic benchmark serves as a reference for active position taking.

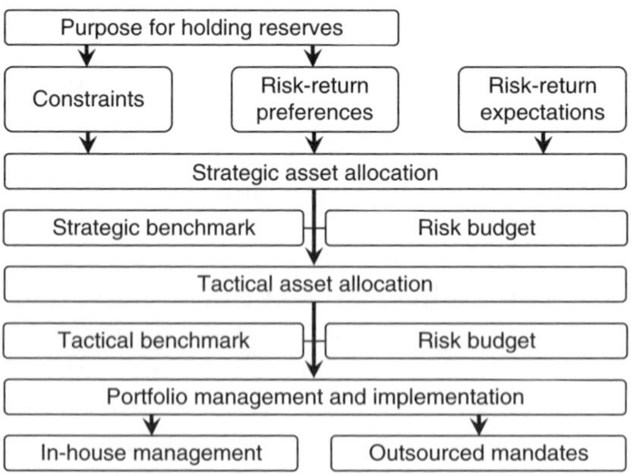

Figure 2.1 Reserves management framework

TAA is based on the assumption that there are market inefficiencies that can be exploited through active position-taking relative to SAA. TAA positions will typically focus more narrowly on enhancing return rather than on the overall risk–return optimality of the resulting allocation.[5] TAA will be able to respond to market developments in a timelier manner than is possible at the SAA level.[6] Furthermore TAA may be used to gain exposure to asset classes and risk factors that are not part of SAA and, in this way, to earn a premium. The size of these active positions is limited by means of a risk budget for active position-taking expressed, for example, in form of a tracking error (or relative Value-at-Risk) limit or a duration deviation band.

The lowest level in the asset allocation hierarchy is the implementation level, which consists of the actual investment of the reserves in financial instruments. This implementation can be performed in-house or through outsourcing to external fund managers. Similar to TAA, position-taking at the implementation level is restricted by a risk-budget.[7] The scope for position-taking at the TAA and implementation levels will depend on the perceived added-value from active position-taking. If there is little or no perceived added-value from active position-taking, the TAA level may be absent altogether and the leeway for position-taking at the implementation level may be small.

Measurement and attribution of performance and risk should be performed at each level of the asset allocation process. Controls need to be in place to ensure that constraints are adhered to and timely reports are available to the units in charge of monitoring investment activity, performance, counterparty and market risk exposures and compliance with investment guidelines. A unit with the capacity for risk–return analysis – such as the risk unit or the middle office – supports the SAA process by periodically reviewing the SAA's risk–return properties and if necessary proposes changes. Furthermore, the ability to appropriately respond to rapidly changing market conditions during periods of stress is desirable.

The hierarchical approach to asset allocation depicted in Figure 2.1 provides a framework for a robust governance structure required to support a broad range of asset classes, facilitates a clear segregation of responsibility and contributes to enhanced transparency and accountability. The entire framework should be documented, with roles and responsibilities clearly defined and accepted by all parties involved.

2.3 The SAA process

In our discussion of the reserve management framework, it became apparent that central banks are individually unique investors, with reserves held for different purposes and with different reserve management objectives that feed through into their asset allocation decisions. This section introduces a SAA process comprising the steps *tranching, definition of investment universe, choice of numéraire and currency composition, risk–return preferences, constraints, risk–return expectations, selection of the SAA* and *implementation.* Various conceptual considerations that central banks face in the specification of these process steps are addressed. Generally our goal in this section is less to make clear recommendations, in the sense of being prescriptive, but rather to identify the main considerations central banks face.

2.3.1 Tranching

The multiple purposes for holding reserves, as outlined in Section 2.2, translate into different objectives in their management. To facilitate implementation, central banks often split their reserves into different *tranches* (or slices), with each tranche designed to meet a narrower purpose.

A common structure is to earmark a working capital, a liquidity and an investment tranche. The currency composition, asset allocation, duration and constraints of each tranche are set separately based on the objectives of the tranche. When multiple tranches exist an important element of SAA is the determination of the appropriate relative size of each tranche.

The working-capital tranche serves to meet the normal day-to-day demand for foreign exchange. The near-term inflows and outflows from this tranche can normally be accurately anticipated and the currency composition and maturity profile of the working-capital tranche is chosen to closely match the anticipated net demand for foreign currency. This tranche is normally held on deposit at commercial banks or international organisations such as the Bank for International Settlements and/or in Treasury bills.

The liquidity tranche serves as a buffer to meet unanticipated and possibly large demands for foreign exchange. As a result this tranche needs to be invested in highly liquid instruments that can be sold in quantity without major impact on market prices. In addition to deposits and Treasury bills, this tranche may be invested in longer-maturity government bonds[8] and in high-grade spread products such as agency bonds or bonds issued by supranational institutions. Historical analysis or stress tests may be used to determine an appropriate size for the liquidity tranche. Alternatively, traditional measures of reserve adequacy such as import coverage ratio, short-term debt coverage ratio or a broad money coverage ratio may be used to estimate the appropriate size of this tranche.

The investment tranche can be regarded as the tranche for surplus reserves, that is reserves that are in excess of what is believed to be required as working-capital and for liquidity purposes. Typically, the investment tranche is invested with a larger focus on generating returns over the long run. Despite this distinction, safety and liquidity continue to be of major concern in the management of the liquidity tranche and return maximisation is constrained by a cautious definition of risk appetite.[9]

The tranching of reserves may introduce inefficiencies as it foregoes the possibility of optimising the reserve allocation "as a whole". Some central banks therefore choose not to tranche their reserves, and instead express liquidity requirements in the form of constraints on the portfolio optimisation exercise. Others central banks limit the number of tranches to two whereby each tranche serves to meet multiple purposes.

2.3.2 Investment universe

Traditionally, central banks have limited their investments to a universe comprising of highly liquid, highly credit-worthy instruments, such as money market instruments, government bonds and bonds issued by high credit-worthy borrowers such as government sponsored agencies, supranational and international institutions. There has recently been a marked trend for central banks to introduce high-grade fixed income instruments such as mortgage-backed securities (MBS), asset-backed securities and corporate bonds into their reserve portfolios and for some to venture into non-fixed income asset classes. The introduction of these asset classes is motivated by the yield pick-up and diversification benefit they offer. The ongoing financial crisis has however made central banks reassess the benefits of diversifying into new asset classes and has vividly demonstrated the multifaceted nature of risks inherent in investing in non-traditional asset classes including liquidity, reputation and legal risk. The financial crisis has furthermore highlighted the need for central banks to adopt a definition of investment universe that can be maintained under severely stressed market conditions.

Generally, central banks determine the investment universe for their foreign exchange reserves on the basis of quantitative as well as qualitative criteria. Quantitative analysis may be used to assess potential diversification benefits from adding an asset class based on the trade-off between expected return and market and credit risk (on the level of individual instruments, asset classes or in a portfolio context). Qualitative considerations may be used to determine the appropriateness of non-government asset classes by an assessment of their liquidity, reputation and credit risk characteristics that are hard to formally quantify. Qualitative considerations may also be used to assess asset class properties during periods of financial stress, the limitation of in-house capabilities, as well as the reputational risk of investing in an asset class in which it is perceived that the bank may benefiting from non-public information in its investment decisions. Furthermore, the perception of losses in individual names or asset classes may differ significantly from portfolio losses and therefore could have an impact on the specification of the investment universe.[10]

2.3.3 Numéraire and currency composition

A unit of account – also known as the numéraire – is required in which the value of reserves is measured and in which performance is reported. The analysis performed in the SAA process also requires a numéraire in which risk–return preference and expectations are expressed.

Typically central banks measure the value of reserves, as well as the associated risk–return profile, either in the domestic currency, a major reserve currency such as the USD or EUR, or a basket of reserve currencies. According to McCauley (2008) the choice of the numéraire is closely related to the purpose of holding reserves. If reserves serve as a store of domestic value, it may be appropriate to use the domestic currency. If reserves are held as a store of international value, a currency basket with import weights may be more appropriate. On the other hand, if reserves are held as a medium of exchange then a major world currency such as the USD or EUR may be appropriate. In practice the choice of numéraire is complicated by the fact that reserves are normally held for multiple purposes.

Similar to the choice of the numéraire, central banks should base their currency allocation decisions first and foremost on considerations related to the purpose for holding reserves. Such considerations may be based on the composition of external debt and trade flows (e.g. Eichengreen and Mathieson (2000) and Dooley, Folkerts-Landau and Garber (2003)). While the numéraire is expected to remain unchanged over time, the currency composition is an allocation to individual currencies that might be reviewed and adjusted on a regular basis. In some cases, the reserves' currency composition corresponds to the numéraire. In other cases the currency composition is necessarily different from the numéraire (as will be the case for central banks that choose the domestic currency as numéraire).

In addition to basing currency allocation decisions solely on fundamental considerations such as external debt and trade flows, the currency allocation decision may also take into account risk–return considerations as measured in the chosen numéraire. For example if return volatility is of major concern, currencies with stable exchange rates against the numéraire may be favoured.

Once the appropriate currency composition of reserves has been determined, there may be limited or no scope for deviations in the actual investment of reserves. Exposures to markets that differ from the corresponding currency weights may nevertheless be permitted on a currency-hedged basis.

2.3.4 Risk–return preferences

The institution's risk–return preferences are one of the primary inputs to the SAA process. Although preferences are conceptually difficult to articulate and quantify, they nevertheless have a profound effect on the SAA and an inappropriate specification may invalidate the entire process. Careful consideration is therefore needed in specifying how the institution should trade-off risks and returns implied by different asset allocations.

A formal specification of the institution's risk–return preferences requires the definition of two elements. This is firstly a definition of what returns represent and how they are measured and secondly rules on how risks and returns are traded-off.

In addition to the choice of the numéraire (as discussed above), the first element also comprises the definition of the investment horizon, a decision on whether returns are measured on a stand-alone basis or in relation to a reference (such as associated liabilities or a risk-free rate) and a choice on whether returns are measured in nominal or real (inflation-adjusted) terms. With a clear definition of what returns represent, the properties of individual asset classes or allocations are characterised by the return distribution. As it is, however, difficult to compare different allocations on the basis of the entire distribution, risk–return preferences are specified in terms of the distribution's mean (expected return) and a suitable risk measure (such as return volatility or a tail-risk measure). Depending on the purpose for holding reserves different representations of return may be appropriate. Furthermore, the appropriate representation may differ between tranches. For example, the investment horizon is expected to be longer for the investment tranche than for the working capital or the liquidity tranches. In addition, if the purpose of the investment tranche is to safeguard and enhance the purchasing power of reserves it may be appropriate to consider real returns rather than nominal returns for this tranche.

With regard to the second element (risk–return trade-off), finance literature prescribes using the concept of utility functions. Alternative forms of utility functions have been discussed in the literature. A standard example is quadratic utility, which implies a linear trade-off between expected returns and squared volatility that is governed by the risk aversion parameter λ, which has to be specified by the decision-makers (a high λ implies a high level of risk aversion). Financial literature gives some indications for the λ of the average investor; it is, however, not obvious what the parameter should be for a more risk-averse central bank.[11]

As an alternative to standard utility functions, Cardon and Coche (2004) suggest that central banks express risk–return preferences in the form of simple rules such as maximising the reserves' expected return subject to a maximum risk tolerance. More precisely the institutional risk–return preferences are specified in terms of a trade-off between expected return and a tail risk measure such as the probability of earning a negative return, Return-at-Risk (RaR) or conditional Return-at-Risk (cRaR).[12] For example, one such rule requires the maximisation of expected returns subject to the condition that there are no losses on an annual basis at a suitably high confidence level. A confidence level of 95% should be used if negative returns are only tolerated in one out of every 20 years and 99% for a possible loss event in one out of 100 years. In practice a broad range of alternative specifications of risk–return preferences can be used.

The financial crisis has made some central banks question the manner in which they specify their risk–return preferences. In particular, the financial crisis has demonstrated that it is not only the frequency of adverse outcomes that counts but also their severity. A risk–return preference that simply limits the probability of a negative return may therefore be inadequate, and may need to be augmented with additional constraints regarding acceptable tail risk such as limiting the cRaR or by specifying the minimum acceptable return under stress test scenarios.

Depending on the purpose for holding reserves one representation of risk–return preferences may be more appropriate than another. In particular, the appropriate representation is likely to differ between tranches. For example, the investment horizon is expected to be longer for the investment tranche than for the working capital or the liquidity tranches.[13] Furthermore if the purpose of the investment tranche is to safeguard and enhance the purchasing power of reserves it may be appropriate to consider a preference definition on the basis of real returns rather than nominal returns for this tranche.

In the quantification of an institution's risk–return preferences, it is important to distinguish between the ability and the willingness of decision-makers to bear financial risks. While potentially central banks have a high ability to bear financial risks due to the special nature of their balance sheets, it can be argued that the willingness to bear risks is rather low due to the dominance of policy consideration and reputational concerns. Consequently, central banks will typically choose an appropriately high confidence level for avoiding losses.

While generally risk return preferences should be specified on the basis of economic considerations, they might not be entirely independent from reporting and accounting considerations. For example, as investment results are typically reported on an annual basis there might be special interest in managing the reserves return distribution over an annual horizon. Therefore, special care is needed to ensure that the investment horizon used in SAA analysis is primarily a function of the true economic horizon that follows from the purpose for holding reserves rather than allowing this horizon to be overly influenced by the reporting frequency. Imposing a strict limit on the probability of suffering a loss over an annual (reporting) horizon may be overly conservative if this specification is solely the result of the reporting frequency. Furthermore, investment returns are typically reported in local currency and on a nominal rather than on a real (inflation-adjusted) basis. This practice may lead to central banks not placing sufficient importance on the effect inflation has on real investment performance and in choosing an allocation to currencies that are relatively stable with respect to the domestic currency. The effect of inflation is of particular relevance when reserves are considered a long-term store of national wealth.

While it is neither possible nor necessarily desirable to fully ignore reporting and accounting considerations in setting the SAA, it is important to ensure that these considerations do not dominate the SAA process. The risk of undue dominance of accounting considerations can be mitigated through clear communication to all stakeholders, including the general public, to ensure that they understand the purpose for holding reserves, the reserve management objectives that follow therefrom and the processes and motivations used in setting the SAA. If this is properly undertaken the public will understand the reason behind any future negative return.

In order to meet long-term objectives, as is typically the case in the context of the investment tranche, it may be practical to use a multi-period approach with risk–return preferences defined over a shorter (one year) horizon. In such a case the preferences need not necessarily be binding on a year-by-year basis, but instead the preferences are intended to apply on an average through-the-cycle basis. Such a through-the-cycle specification of risk–return preferences would result in the central bank accepting temporary (cyclical) fluctuations in the short-term risk–return profile of their reserves.

2.3.5 Constraints

In a broad sense, asset allocation decisions need to consider all elements of risk and the policy objectives in managing reserves. While risk–return preferences are defined over measurable components of market, credit and liquidity risks, investment constraints are aimed at factoring-in policy considerations and limiting a wide range of non-financial risk-exposure including reputation and legal risks as well as the non-quantifiable elements of liquidity, credit and market risks. To this end, constraints may impose limits on the exposure to individual securities, issuers, sectors, asset classes, risk factors, currencies and countries. Furthermore, constraints may involve an upper or lower exposure limit. For example, overall portfolio risk may be constrained by an upper limit on exposure to risky asset classes and minimum liquidity is ensured by imposing a lower limit on exposure to asset classes judged to be sufficiently liquid. In addition, constraints can be expressed as absolute dollar amounts or percentages of the portfolio.

Each constraint may introduce a cost in terms of a reduction in the possible return for a given level of risk. It is therefore advisable to periodically assess these costs to determine whether all constraints remain appropriate.

2.3.6 Risk–return expectations

In order to derive the asset allocation that best corresponds to the institution's risk–return preferences, it is necessary to estimate risk–return characteristics of the different feasible allocations.

To assess the properties of different asset allocations, estimates of the risk–return properties at the individual asset class level (including return correlations) are required. Depending on the chosen numéraire, the investment universe and the scope of the SAA exercise (review of local market exposure versus a comprehensive review of currency as well as asset allocation), risk–return expectations for exposures to currencies and all permitted asset classes are required. Prior to a discussion of alternative approaches to the quantification of risk return-expectations, we review a couple of general requirements.

SAA-selection is the interplay between risk–return expectations and preferences. Therefore, the horizon over which expectations are estimated needs to correspond to that over which preferences are expressed. As discussed above, preferences can be applied strictly on a period-by-period basis or alternatively they can be applied on average over multiple periods. Thus, risk–return expectations should be consistent with the manner in which preferences are expressed. This means that if preferences are applied strictly on a period-by-period basis then risk–return expectations should give precise estimates of the risk-return properties over the forthcoming periods. On the other hand, if preferences need only apply on average, through-the-cycle, then risk–return expectations should be averaged long-term estimates. The averaging approach leads to more stable asset allocations as longer-term expectations change relatively slowly and, in the limit of increasing the period over which expectations are averaged, expectations only respond to structural changes in the market. This stability may, in itself, be viewed as a desirable SAA characteristic.[14]

Furthermore, expectations should strive to be neutral (non-subjective) in the sense that they are based on publicly available information and are obtained using a generally accepted methodology. Thus, the SAA does not aim to include subjective views in order to produce an allocation with superior risk–return expectations to those of other market participants with comparable preferences.

While it is tempting to use historical returns as a proxy for future returns, only under limited circumstances is this approach appropriate. In many instances it is easy to demonstrate that historical returns are biased estimates. For example, data on a number of asset classes such as agency bonds are only available from the early 1980's onward. Over that period, historical returns comprise, in addition to a high coupon income, substantial price appreciation as a results of the secular decline in interest rates. Projecting these returns into the future would necessitate yields falling below their theoretical floor of zero. To overcome this problem, return expectations for fixed income instruments may be based on various assumptions regarding the term structure of yields and spreads which, in turn, translate into expected returns. Specifying expectations on the level of yields and spreads also facilitates plausibility and robustness checks. For example, yields and spreads can be decomposed into individual components and linked to macro-economic considerations.

As an alternative to historic returns, there are various term structure-based approaches that may be used in determining return expectations:

Current term structure: Assuming that term structures remain unchanged on average allows return expectations to be proxied by current yields and spreads. Despite the simplicity of this approach, a drawback is that the derived expectations do not incorporate information on future changes in the term structure that are embedded in the current shape of the yield curve. For example: a steep upward-sloping yield curve may reflect expectations of increases in yield and not necessarily higher expected return for investing in longer maturity bonds.

Average historical term structure: The historical average yield pick-up obtained from duration extension and from investing in spread products offers an estimate of the average premium that investors demanded for assuming duration and credit–liquidity risk. If there is no structural change in the markets, these may offer adequate estimates of future excess returns. A drawback of this approach is that – whilst it may offer a good estimate of average risk premiums – the premiums may be time-varying and their average may be a poor expectation over short investment horizons.

Projecting the term structure: Expected returns can be obtained by estimating the term structure at the end of the investment horizon by making assumptions on how yields and spreads evolve. One possibility is to assume that yields and spreads converge to equilibrium levels at estimated convergence speeds. Incorporating stochastic error terms as well as uncertainty about the equilibrium levels and convergence speeds, returns on fixed income instruments can be determined under different simulated realisations of the term structure. This provides return distributions from which expected returns, volatilities and correlation can be determined. This approach is described in more detail below.

Approaches involving an explicit modelling of the term structure of interest rates potentially allow a more precise estimation of risks and returns. A number of central banks apply a methodology suggested by Diebold and Li (2006) which is based on a combination of a vector autoregressive model and the Nelson-Siegel yield curve model. In a first step projections for the government yield curve are made which, in a second step, are translated into return distributions for instruments of various maturities.[15] If calibrated on historic data, a vector autoregressive model will have yields that converge over time to their historical mean. The model specifies the speed of mean reversion, that is, the equilibrium path, and the stochastic deviations from this path. Instead of convergence to historic averages, the model parameters can be calibrated such that yields converge to levels implied by the forward curve (possibly adjusted for risk premiums), survey expectations or alternative curve scenarios. This approach can be extended to handle exposure to spread products and currencies by adding factors such as spreads and exchange rates to the model. In this way, additional return components can be modelled in a consistent manner.[16]

While the above approaches appear to quantify the risk–return characteristics of alternate asset allocations well during normal market periods, the financial crisis has highlighted that they are not suitable to accurately quantify risk under stressed market conditions. Over the past months yield curve realisations outside of the probability distributions derived on the basis of the Diebold and Li methodology have been observed. In particular, non-normally distributed and serially correlated error terms have been observed. Consequently a debate on the properties of these models during periods of market stress has started. While the outcome of this debate is uncertain, a reversion to a purely judgemental decision-making process is not likely. Instead the discussion might focus on necessary improvements in models and improvements in the way these models are used in the asset allocation process. In particular model limitations should be understood and model results should be carefully reviewed.

With regards to model improvements, alternatives to the normal distribution, the incorporation of regime shifts (shifts in the equilibrium levels of yields, spreads, volatilities and correlations), incorporation of parameter uncertainty and an assessment of the benefit of combining alternative return projection approaches (portfolios of models) is desirable.

With regards to how these models are applied, an assessment of the benefit of combining quantitative and qualitative elements in the projection of asset returns, and the way in which return distributions are translated into asset allocations is necessary. In the meantime, while continuing using model-based risk–return expectations, decision-makers need to be aware of its potential limitations.

2.3.7 Selection of the SAA

SAA selection is an exercise of selecting amongst the allocations that satisfy all constraints the one with the best risk–return characteristics given the institution's risk–return preferences. A typical starting point for this exercise is modern portfolio theory. In a first step mean–variance optimisation is used to determine the efficient frontier which is defined as the set of (constrained) portfolios that maximise expected return at any given level of return volatility.

In a second step, the institution's risk–return preferences are used to select the optimal allocation from the efficient frontier. This can be done using standard utility functions or simple rules such as maximising the reserves' expected return subject to a maximum risk budget.[17] Both approaches have specific limitations. As discussed above, standard utility functions are hard to calibrate while the maximisation of expected return subject to a risk budget disregards incremental risks.[18] To overcome these problems some central banks apply a combination of utility functions and a risk budget approach. For example, the objective can be to choose from the efficient frontier the portfolio with the highest Sharpe ratio subject to avoiding losses at a given confidence level.

Additionally, the analysis should take into account the known limitations of mean–variance optimisation such as the reliance on the assumption of normally distributed returns, the one-period horizon, the tendency for corner solutions where exposure is concentrated in a small number of assets, and the sensitivity of the solution to the estimated input parameters. The robustness and validity of the optimised allocations may be assessed by variations in assumptions and using alternative optimisation techniques as for example re-sampling or Bayesian approaches. In addition, further quantitative analysis can be performed to verify the properties of the asset allocations independently from the assumptions made for the optimisation exercise. This might include the following:

- Historic properties: The risk–return profile of the portfolio determined on the basis of the forward-looking risk–return expectations can be compared to the historic risk–return profile of the portfolio.
- Stress testing: Historical and hypothetical stress scenarios are applied to the portfolio to quantify the impact of unlikely but possible adverse market movements.
- Risk decomposition: Risk decomposition attributes total portfolio risk to factors such as yield curve (level, slope, curvature), credit spread and exchange rate exposures.
- Impact of portfolio management: Analysis may be used to assess the extent to which active management (or imperfect indexing) may change the risk–return characteristics of the portfolio.

Beyond these specific considerations, the financial crisis has demonstrated the limitations of purely model-based approaches to portfolio selection in general. In particular the practice of exhaustively using available risk budgets might be questionable. Prior to the financial crisis, in many institutions the belief was that efficient management implied exhaustive use of available risk budgets. For example, if risk tolerance is defined as no annual losses at a 95% confidence level but the current allocation implies no losses at a 99% confidence level, then the allocation of reserves was considered to be inefficient. However the financial crisis has emphasised the difficulties of making precise estimates of distributions' tail properties and in particular the tendency for model-based approaches to underestimate tail risk. This implies that an exhaustive use of the risk budget based on model results may represent a breach in the risk budget based on the true asset properties.

The procedure described above results in SAA that is defined by specifying weights to different currencies and asset classes. For central banks that are predominantly invested in government bond markets, the asset allocation decision becomes one of determining the appropriate allocation to different maturity sectors of this market. The high correlation that exists between the returns of different maturity sectors means that there is limited diversification benefit from investing across different sectors, and that the risk–return characteristics of different allocations are to a large extent driven by the modified duration, a measure of the allocation's overall exposure to changes in the level of yields.[19] Many central banks therefore specify their SAA as a duration target (even though duration is not an "allocation" as such). When investing beyond government bonds into high grade fixed income spread products, duration remains the main factor influencing the risk–return characteristics of the asset allocation. It may therefore make sense to focus on the duration decision as a first step and then to assess the risk–return benefits of investing in spread products on a duration neutral basis.

2.3.8 Implementation

SAA results in a weighting of currencies, asset class and sectors that have to be translated into a concrete strategic benchmark which serves various functions throughout the reserves management process, as discussed in Section 2.2 of this chapter. The benchmark may be considered as a notional portfolio whose risk exposures and ex-post performance can be determined.

The components or building blocks used to construct the strategic benchmark can either be individual instruments or publicly available indices.[20] Risk–return characteristics of fixed income instruments change over time as the residual maturity of the instrument decreases. Furthermore, relative performance between the different components of the benchmark will result in changes in their weights within the benchmark. The benchmark therefore needs to be rebalanced in order to maintain the desired risk–return profile. Clear rules specifying the rebalancing frequency and the weight of each component are required. A benchmark could, for example, be constructed through monthly rebalancing in which equal weights are given to the on-the-run two-, five- and ten-year US Treasuries. Alternatively a benchmark could be constructed through monthly rebalancing in which equal weights are given to the indices representing the one- to three-, three- to five-, five- to seven- and seven- to ten-year US government bond sectors.

The SAA review may result in significant changes in response to changing risk–return expectations. On top of this, a wider-reaching asset allocation review may introduce new asset classes, changes in the institution's risk–return preferences or changes in the analysis conducted to optimise the asset allocation. Central banks often prefer to phase-in large changes in SAA. For example, if new asset classes have been introduced, it is common practice to build-up this exposure gradually. This build-up permits central banks to gain experience in the new asset class while exposure is low and mitigates the possibility of large early losses if the timing of the switch proves to be inappropriate.

2.4 Summary

In this paper we stress the importance of SAA in the management of foreign exchange reserves and the idiosyncratic nature of central banks as investors, describe a possible reserves management framework and summarise the main issues central banks face in establishing a SAA process. While the ongoing financial crisis may result in a re-assessment of the risk–return characteristics of various asset classes and may change the institution's tolerance for market, credit, liquidity and reputational risk it should not change the framework and the process for SAA as such.

Central banks have to contend with specific considerations in their investment decisions related to monetary and exchange rate policy as well as financial stability. Reserves are public funds that need to reflect specific objectives and may need to be invested in a transparent manner and with a high degree of accountability. As a result reserves are generally managed in a conservative manner with a strong focus on liquidity and safety.

The purpose for holding reserves and the mandate central banks have in managing these reserves vary substantially between central banks and therefore reserve management practices will differ between central banks. In establishing a reserve management framework and in identifying the appropriate SAA, central banks can benefit from reviewing practices adopted at other central banks; however, a good understanding of the purpose for holding reserves and the mandate the central bank has in managing the reserves are necessary to identify what is appropriate on a case-by-case basis.

This chapter identifies many choices faced by central banks in establishing a reserve management framework and in setting the SAA. While choices will not always be clear-cut, in establishing the SAA central banks should bear in mind the trade-off between optimality and complexity

Annex: Case Study

In this Annex we introduce a hypothetical central bank to illustrate the SAA process put forward for discussion in the body of this paper. In this example the central bank holds foreign reserves to meet the day-to-day demand for foreign exchange and to permit occasional exchange rate intervention in order to support its domestic currency. Furthermore, the central bank holds reserves which it deems to be in excess of the amount required to satisfy these two purposes. These excess reserves are invested with a larger focus on generating an attractive risk–return profile over the long term.

Framework

To facilitate their management, reserves are split into three tranches: a working capital tranche that satisfies the day-to-day demand for foreign exchange, a liquidity tranche and an investment tranche. This case study focuses on the allocation of the liquidity and investment tranches as the composition of the working capital tranche is based on the anticipated near-term net demand for foreign exchange in a relatively straightforward manner.

The liquidity tranche provides ready liquidity for intervention needs and to replenish the working capital tranche when necessary. The liquidity tranche comprises 80% USD and 20% EUR. It is invested in cash, government debt issued in domestic currency and USD-denominated supranational bonds. The 80/20 USD/EUR split follows an analysis of the currency composition of external debt, trade patterns and consideration of potential intervention needs.

The investment tranche comprises USD-denominated government, supranational and corporate debt as well as MBS. Furthermore, to exploit diversification benefits, investments in EUR-, GBP- and JPY-denominated government debt are permitted on a currency-hedged basis. An asset-liability analysis supports having a USD-denominated investment tranche since the bulk of reserves are funded through domestic debt issuance and because the country adopted a managed float regime against the USD, resulting in low volatility between the domestic currency and the USD.

The central bank reviews and possibly makes adjustments to the SAA on an annual basis.

Risk–return preferences

The objective for the management of the liquidity tranche is to maximise, for each currency separately, the expected return subject to strict safety and liquidity constraints. The safety constraint is reflected in the need to avoid annual losses in the respective currency at a 99% confidence level. Losses in the USD or EUR portfolios are tolerated in only one out of 100 years. The liquidity constraint corresponds to a minimum allocation to liquid government debt, and a maximum exposure in the USD portfolio of 30% to supranational debt.

For the investment tranche, risk–return preferences are defined in terms of expected return and loss probability measured in USD. The objective is to maximise the expected return subject to avoiding an annual loss at a 95% confidence level. Furthermore, there are maximum allocations of 10% to MBS and to each non-USD market on a currency-hedged basis and a 20% exposure limit for supranational bonds.

While the loss constraint for the liquidity tranche is expected to strictly hold in each individual year, the specification of the loss constraint for the investment tranche is indicative of the institution's long-term risk aversion and it is accepted that in individual years the probability of earning a negative return can exceed 5% if on average, through the cycle, the portfolio remains compliant with the specified risk constraint.

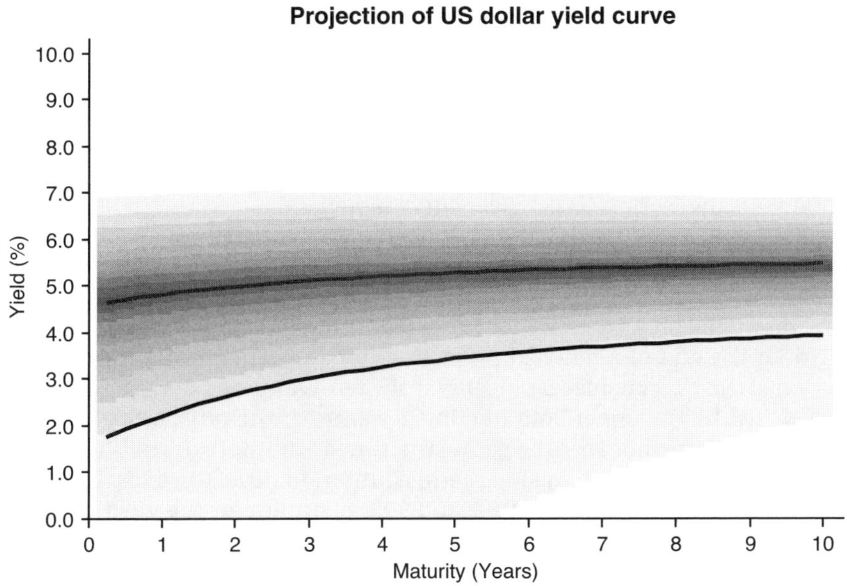

	US Treasuries				Euro-area Government bonds			
Maturity	**3 Months**	**2 Years**	**5 Years**	**10 Years**	**3 Months**	**2 Years**	**5 Years**	**10 Years**
1% Quantile	8.77	9.03	9.32	9.48	9.96	9.57	9.34	9.30
5% Quantile	7.68	7.91	8.11	8.23	8.38	8.19	8.13	8.12
Expected	4.63	4.93	5.25	5.50	4.56	4.65	4.80	4.97
95% Quantile	1.57	1.96	2.40	2.78	0.70	1.08	1.47	1.81
99% Quantile	0.48	0.83	1.19	1.53	0.10	0.12	0.26	0.64

	Japanese Government bonds				UK Government bonds			
Maturity	**3 Months**	**2 Years**	**5 Years**	**10 Years**	**3 Months**	**2 Years**	**5 Years**	**10 Years**
1% Quantile	6.17	6.03	6.08	6.10	12.91	11.99	11.50	11.36
5% Quantile	4.97	4.89	4.92	4.96	11.21	10.58	10.17	10.03
Expected	2.15	2.12	2.19	2.33	7.10	6.98	6.91	6.91
95% Quantile	0.22	0.19	0.18	0.24	2.98	3.37	3.66	3.80
99% Quantile	0.05	0.05	0.02	0.04	1.28	1.96	2.33	2.46

Figure 2.2 Yield Projection

Projections of the term structure of government yields

The evolution of government yields is central to the pricing of the asset classes under consideration. In our example yield curve projections for the government bond markets in the US, euro-area, Japan and United Kingdom are generated based on a methodology suggested by Diebold and Li (2006); these projections are made using a vector autoregressive model in combination with the Nelson-Siegel yield curve model.

The graph in figure 2.2 shows the simulation results for the US dollar curve at the end of the ten-year projection horizon. The lower bold line shows the term structure at the start of the simulation (end-July 2008 in this case). The greyish shaded area represent the probability distribution of yields at the end of a ten-year projection horizon. The mean of this distribution is the expected level of yields at the ten-year projection horizon, and is depicted by the upper bold line in the centre of the probability distribution. In the four markets the term structure at the start of the simulation (end-July 2008) is below the long-term equilibrium level of yields. Expected values as well as the 1%, 5%, 95% and 99% quantiles for the yield distribution at the ten-year horizon are shown in the tables.

Return projections

For each simulation run the return on government bonds is determined by pricing the bonds off the projected yield curve. Returns on USD-denominated spread products (MBS and supranational and corporate bonds) are determined by adding a simulated excess return to the return on maturity-equivalent Treasury bonds. The excess returns are additional factors in the vector autoregressive model and therefore their distribution can be simulated in a manner consistent with historically observed covariances.

The tables in Figure 2.3 show annual return statistics for the various asset classes over the ten-year projection horizon, with each of the ten years in the projection period contributing. Two distinct scenarios are considered. Through-the-cycle return projections are generated by setting the term structure of yields at the beginning of the horizon to their equilibrium values, from which they are projected forward. Returns under the convergence scenario are calculated by setting the term structure of yields at the beginning of the horizon to the actual (current) term structure of yields. As of end-July 2008, government yields in all four markets were below equilibrium levels; yields are expected to rise under the convergence scenario resulting in capital losses and lower mean returns. Consequently, RaR figures and loss probabilities are less favourable under the convergence scenario than they are under the through-the-cycle scenario. Results under the through-the-cycle scenario are relevant in setting the investment tranche while those under the convergence scenario are relevant in setting the liquidity tranche.

The summary statistics shown for the both scenarios represent annualised figurers over the ten-year projection period. While it would have been sufficient to use return projections over a one-year horizon to find an asset allocation that complies with the risk constraint (no losses after one year), a ten-year horizon is used to reduce the frequency and extent of SAA adjustments. It can be argued that return statistics over a projection horizon of only one year would be appropriate since risk–return preferences need to strictly hold on a year-by-year basis. Single-year return projections and correlations are however unstable and may lead to undesirably large changes in asset allocation. The approach adopted here is to use the full ten-year Monte Carlo simulation results to determine the expected return and the correlations between different asset classes. These then form the inputs to a mean–variance optimisation exercise to identify the composition of the efficient portfolios. The full results of the Monte Carlo simulation are then used again to quantify the tail risk of each efficient portfolio.[21]

The above results invariably show lower expected annual returns under the convergence scenario than under the through-the-cycle scenario. This is because the lower starting yield in the convergence scenario results in a lower "running yield" that is further compounded by capital losses as yields revert to equilibrium. Return volatilities are also typically higher in the convergence scenario. The lower expected returns and higher return volatility results in significantly higher tail risk in the convergence scenario.

It is noted that while un-hedged exposure to non-USD-denominated government debt presents significant risk, exposure to these asset classes on a currency-hedged basis entails much reduced risk.

SAA selection for the USD liquidity tranche

Figure 2.4 shows the analysis performed for the selection of the optimal asset allocation for the USD-denominated portion of the liquidity tranche. A similar analysis is performed separately for the EUR-denominated portion of the liquidity tranche.

The top left chart in Figure 2.4 shows the risk–return trade-off for the USD liquidity tranche under the convergence scenario. The efficient frontier is made-up of 11 portfolios and is constrained by a 30% maximum allocation to supranational bonds. The minimum risk portfolio, P1, with an expected return of 3.53% and a volatility of 1.67%, comprises 99% T-bills and 1% T-bonds. The chart also shows for each portfolio on the frontier the implied RaR at a 99% confidence level. For example, the RaR of the minimum risk allocation is 0.23%. Thus in 1 out of 100 years the minimum risk allocation is expected to show a return of less than 0.23%.

From the efficient frontier, three allocations, portfolios P3, P5 and P6, are analysed in greater detail. P3 is selected because the loss probability is close to 1% under the convergence scenario and P5 and P6 are selected because they show loss probabilities close to the assumed constraint of 1%

under the through-the-cycle scenario.[22] P3 has a duration of 1.1 years and an allocation of 10% to supranational bonds, P5 a duration of 1.9 years and a 15% allocation to supranational bonds while P6 with a duration of 2.3 years allocates 20% to supranational bonds.

For these three allocations, the forward-looking risk–return characteristics are shown above. Under the through-the-cycle scenario, P3 has an expected return of 5.10% and a volatility of 1.69%. Moving from P3 to P5 increases the expected return by 37 basis points while the volatility goes up by 46 basis points. Expected return and volatility increase further by 20 and 30 basis points respectively by moving from P5 to P6. While through-the-cycle

Through-the-cycle scenario

	US Treasuries (in %)		US Supras (in %)	US MBS (in %)	US Corporates (in %)	Government bonds (local returns) (in %)		
	Bills	Bonds				Euro-area	Japan	UK
Expected return	4.70	6.47	6.96	7.16	7.56	5.77	3.15	7.18
Volatility	1.54	4.19	4.47	4.48	5.86	3.22	3.54	4.60
RaR return (95%)	2.10	−0.38	−0.31	−0.09	−1.94	0.53	−2.43	−0.19
cRaR return (95%)	1.42	−1.99	−2.08	−1.85	−4.21	−0.79	−3.84	−2.09
RaR return (99%)	0.92	−3.02	−3.27	−3.01	−5.56	−1.53	−4.82	−3.47
cRaR return (99%)	0.50	−4.45	−4.77	−4.45	−7.36	−2.72	−5.84	−4.85
Prob. Neg. returns	0.02	5.80	5.80	5.15	9.57	3.31	17.71	5.43

	Government bonds (USD unhedged returns) (in %)			Government bonds (USD hedged returns) (in %)		
	Euro-area	Japan	UK	Euro-area	Japan	UK
Expected return	5.88	3.19	7.24	5.92	5.78	4.82
Volatility	12.50	12.79	11.99	3.46	3.83	4.63
RaR (95%)	−13.60	−16.62	−11.30	0.35	−0.37	−2.71
cRaR (95%)	−17.59	−20.69	−15.36	−1.08	−2.03	−4.54
RaR (99%)	−20.19	−23.21	−17.58	−2.03	−3.04	−5.68
cRaR (99%)	−22.94	−26.49	−21.02	−3.18	−4.22	−7.19
Prob. Neg. returns	32.60	42.03	28.25	3.98	6.18	14.54

Convergence scenario

	US Treasuries (in %)		US Supras (in %)	US MBS (in %)	US Corporates (in %)	Government bonds (local returns) (in %)		
	Bills	**Bonds**				**Euro-area**	**Japan**	**UK**
Expected return	3.5	4.79	4.86	4.72	3.98	5.05	2.16	5.36
Volatility	1.68	4.28	4.61	4.62	5.92	3.20	3.53	4.62
RaR (95%)	1.08	–2.00	–2.48	–2.62	–5.36	–0.15	–3.25	–1.97
cRaR (95%)	0.56	–3.58	–4.20	–4.36	–7.64	–1.31	–4.62	–3.84
RaR (99%)	0.18	–4.67	–5.36	–5.45	–9.06	–1.99	–5.48	–5.17
cRaR (99%)	0.05	–5.87	–6.74	–6.78	–10.78	–3.04	–6.55	–6.48
Prob. Neg. returns	0.09	12.77	14.50	15.69	25.97	5.57	25.93	11.68

	Government bonds (USD unhedged returns) (in %)			Government bonds (USD hedged returns) (in %)		
	Euro-area	**Japan**	**UK**	**Euro-area**	**Japan**	**UK**
Expected return	5.15	2.22	5.40	4.31	4.03	3.10
Volatility	12.34	12.87	11.56	3.69	3.89	4.69
RaR (95%)	–13.87	–17.63	–12.66	–1.58	–2.15	–4.48
cRaR (95%)	–17.98	–21.76	–16.37	–2.90	–3.67	–6.07
RaR (99%)	–20.53	–24.13	–18.61	–3.85	–4.64	–7.02
cRaR (99%)	–23.38	–27.17	–21.34	–4.80	–5.82	–8.44
Prob. Neg. returns	36.03	45.54	33.68	12.25	14.91	25.74

Figure 2.3 Return projections

P5, with a loss probability of 0.76%, would be compliant with the assumed risk constraint (no losses at a 99% confidence level), P6 shows a loss probability that is slightly higher (1.23%). Therefore, P5 might be considered to be the tranche's "natural allocation", in a sense that through the cycle this allocation appears to be optimal subject to the expressed preferences. However, given the market environment prevailing in July 2008, both P5 and P6 breach the risk constraint with loss probabilities of 3.13% and 4.91% respectively under the convergence scenario. For this scenario, P3 shows a probability of negative returns that is broadly in line with the risk tolerance expressed for the liquidity tranche.

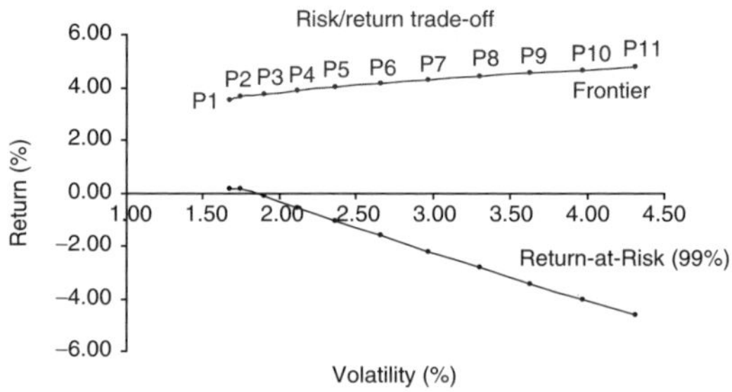

Allocations	P3	P5	P6
USD T-Bills	80%	60%	50%
USD T-Bonds	10%	25%	30%
USD Supras	10%	15%	20%
Duration	1.1	1.9	2.3

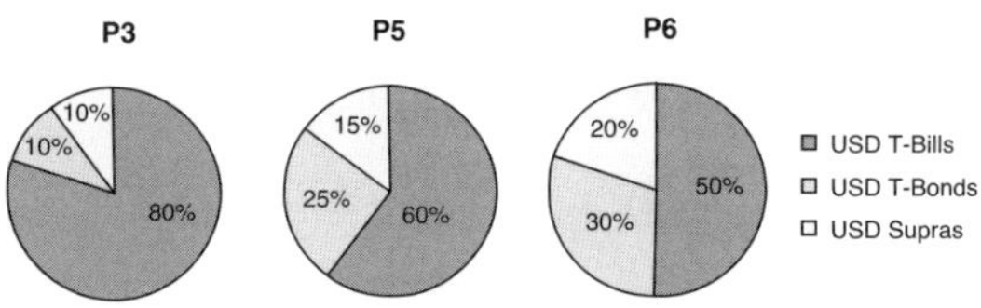

	Portfolio P3		Portfolio P5		Portfolio P6	
	Through-the-cycle	Convergence	Through-the-cycle	Convergence	Through-the-cycle	Convergence
Forward looking risk-return						
Expected return	5.10%	3.77%	5.47%	4.03%	5.67%	4.16%
Volatility	1.69%	1.90%	2.15%	2.36%	2.45%	2.66%
Sharpe ratio	0.22	0.13	0.35	0.22	0.39	0.24
RaR (95%)	2.29%	0.99%	1.92%	0.37%	1.63%	0.03%
cRaR (95%)	1.47%	0.32%	0.91%	−0.45%	0.51%	−0.95%
RaR (99%)	0.89%	−0.13%	0.19%	−1.07%	−0.19%	−1.60%
cRaR (99%)	0.36%	−0.59%	−0.56%	−1.70%	−1.14%	−2.36%
Prob. of neg. returns	0.18%	1.19%	0.76%	3.13%	1.23%	4.91%
Historical risk–return						
Average return	5.67%		6.00%		6.18%	

	Portfolio P3		Portfolio P5		Portfolio P6	
	Through-the-cycle	Convergence	Through-the-cycle	Convergence	Through-the-cycle	Convergence
Volatility	2.20%		2.46%		2.67%	
RaR (95%)	1.72%		1.86%		1.75%	
Stress tests						
Return, Sept 93–Sept 94	2.81%		1.60%		0.95%	
Return, May 03–May 04	0.71%		0.29%		0.06%	
Impact of active management						
Tracking error	0.4%		0.4%		0.4%	
Information ratio	0.5		0.5		0.5	
Expected return	5.30%	3.97%	5.67%	4.23%	5.87%	4.36%
Volatility	1.74%	1.94%	2.19%	2.40%	2.49%	2.69%
RaR (95%)	2.41%	1.12%	2.06%	0.52%	1.78%	0.18%
RaR (99%)	0.98%	–0.03%	0.31%	–0.95%	–0.06%	-1.47%

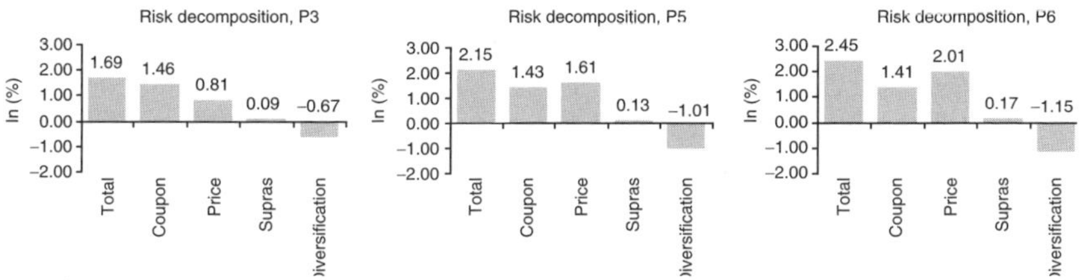

Figure 2.4 USD liquidity tranche

Historically, the portfolios have shown average returns that are somewhat higher than the forward-looking ones computed under the through-the-cycle scenario, which can be attributed to the generally decreasing yields over the period considered for the historical analysis (1986 to 2008). While the historical RaR is lower for P3, the figures for P5 and P6 are comparable to the through-the-cycle scenario. Using the sharp increases in Treasury yields in 1994 and 2004 as stress scenarios, all three allocations would still have realised positive returns over the relevant 12-month period.

The effect of active management on the risk–return characteristics of the portfolio can be determined based on the following assumptions: 1) full utilisation of the available 40 basis points tracking error budget, 2) active returns are uncorrelated with benchmark returns and 3) the skill of the active managers results in an information ratio of 0.5 (net of fees). Active management increases the expected return by the product of the tracking error budget and the information ratio (i.e. 20 basis points). Furthermore, the assumption of uncorrelated active and benchmark returns results in only a marginal increase (about 4 basis points) in return volatility. Under the stated assumptions, active management results in a portfolio with higher expected return and lower tail risk.

Risk decomposition attributes total risk (as measured in terms of volatility of portfolio returns) to fluctuations due to changes in the government yield curve (price risk), coupon reinvestment risk and changes in the spread between government and non-government instruments (risk specific to supranational instruments). As shown in the charts in the lower part of Figure 2.4, this analysis identifies price risk as the most important risk factor for allocations P5 and P6 while reinvestment risk is more important for P3. The higher volatility of allocation P6 compared to P5 can mostly be attributed to the allocation's higher duration. The fact that P6 has a higher allocation to non-government instruments has only a small effect on the overall volatility.

On the basis of the above analysis, management decides to implement P3 as this allocation is deemed to be compliant with the risk constraint under the convergence scenario. The probability of earning a negative return on P3 is actually slightly greater than 1%. It was however deemed to be acceptably close enough to this limit.

Selection for the investment tranche

Figure 2.5 illustrates the selection of the SAA for the USD-denominated investment tranche.

For the investment tranche a universe comprising US government debt, MBS, supranational and corporate bonds as well as currency-hedged investments in government debt denominated in EUR, JPY and GBP is considered. The efficient frontier in the top left of Figure 2.5 is derived for the through-the-cycle scenario constrained by maximum allocations of 10% to MBS and to each non-USD-denominated market and a 20% limit on supranational bonds. The graph shows Returns-at-Risk at both the 99% and 95% confidence levels.

From the efficient frontier, portfolios P8 and P10 are analysed in depth as they show through-the-cycle annual loss probabilities close to the 5% limit. P8 has an expected return of 6.67% and a volatility of 3.81% while the expected return of P10 is higher by 52 basis points and volatility increases by 104 basis points. Both P8 and P10 have relatively low allocations to US

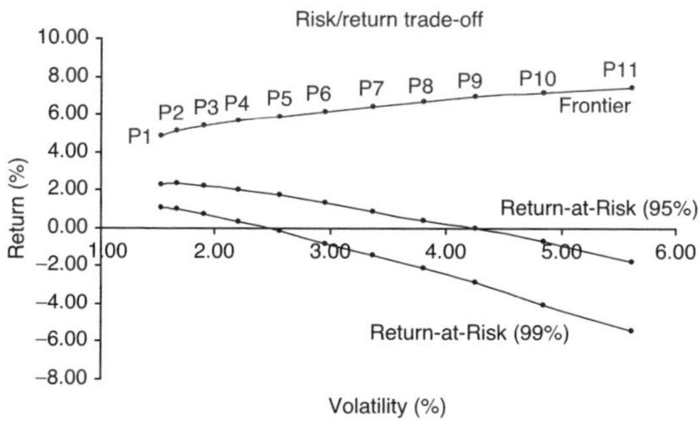

Allocations	P8	P10
USD T-Bills	10%	0%
USD T-Bonds	10%	10%
USD Supranationals	20%	20%
USD MBS	10%	10%
USD Corporates	30%	54%
EUR Government Bonds (hedged)	10%	0%
JPY Government Bonds (hedged)	10%	6%
Duration	5.1	6.5

	Portfolio P8		**Portfolio P10**	
	Through-the-cycle	**Convergence**	**Through-the-cycle**	**Convergence**
Forward looking risk-return				
Expected return	6.67%	4.31%	7.19%	4.32%
Volatility	3.81%	3.99%	4.85%	5.02%
Sharpe ratio	0.47	0.17	0.48	0.14
RaR (95%)	0.42%	–2.05%	–0.72%	–3.66%
C-RaR (95%)	–1.18%	–3.51%	–2.77%	–5.50%
RaR (99%)	–2.14%	–4.38%	–4.05%	–6.66%
C-RaR (99%)	–3.61%	–5.67%	–5.78%	–8.14%
Prob. of neg. returns	3.81%	14.17%	6.84%	20.13%

	Portfolio P8		Portfolio P10	
	Through-the-cycle	Convergence	Through-the-cycle	Convergence
Historical risk–return				
Average return	7.31%		7.71%	
Volatility	3.77%		4.60%	
RaR (95%)	1.14%		0.04%	
Stress tests				
Return, Sept 93–Sept 94	-1.54%		-2.95%	
Return, May 03–May 04	-0.10%		-0.32%	
Impact of active management				
Tracking error	0.75%		0.75%	
Information ratio	0.5		0.5	
Expected return	7.05%	4.68%	7.56%	4.69%
Volatility	3.88%	4.06%	4.91%	5.07%
RaR (95%)	0.68%	-1.79%	-0.44%	-3.37%
RaR (99%)	-3.40%	-5.45%	-5.54%	-7.89%

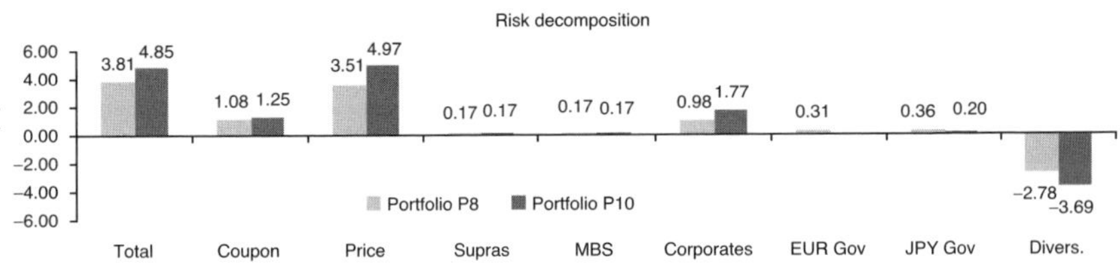

Figure 2.5 Investment tranche

Treasury debt. The optimisation has made full use of the leeway provided for investing in higher-yielding asset classes. The Sharpe ratios of both allocations are broadly similar and the long-run probability of earning negative returns is higher for P10 than for P8.

The above results also show that all tail risk measures are considerably higher under the convergence scenario than they are under the through-the-cycle scenario. Under the convergence scenario P8 has a 14.17% probability of earning a negative return over the forthcoming year. This is a result of the relatively low yield "cushion" under the convergence scenario coupled with capital losses as yields are expected to increase as they revert back to equilibrium.

The forward-looking risk–return profiles under both the through-the-cycle and convergence scenarios are less favourable than the historic returns profile. Historical returns of both allocations have been somewhat higher and volatilities lower than those of the simulated forward-looking return profiles. The combination of higher historic returns and lower historic volatilities naturally results in higher (better) Return-at-Risk figures at the 95% confidence level.

Using the sharp increases in Treasury yields in 1994 and 2004 as stress scenarios, both allocations would have realised negative returns over the respective 12-month periods.

Similarly to the analysis for the liquidity tranche, active management has a positive effect on the risk–return profile of the portfolio. As there is greater scope, that is, a larger number of uncorrelated risk factors that portfolio managers can exploit for active management in the investment tranche than in the liquidity tranche, a larger 75 basis points tracking error budget has been assigned for active position taking. All other assumptions regarding active management are the same in both tranches.

Risk decomposition identifies price risks as the most important source of risk for both allocations. For P10, corporate bond specific risks are the second most important factor, while reinvestment risk ranks third.

Since risk–return preferences for the investment tranche have been expressed on an average, through-the-cycle basis, management selects P8 as this allocation shows the highest expected return while it still satisfies the specified risk constraint of an average loss probability of less than 5%.

Notes

1. http://www.imf.org/external/pubs/ft/ferm/guidelines/2004/081604.pdf.
2. These precautionary motives for holding foreign exchange reserves are mirrored in economic literature. For example Feldstein (1999) discusses reserves holdings to manage risks of currency attacks. Calvo (1998) analyses reserves in the context of sudden stops of capital inflows. The role of foreign reserves in the management of exchange rate volatility is discussed for example by Calvo and Reinhart (2002) and Flood and Marion (2002). Holding reserves for output stabilisation in general is discussed for example by Ben-Bassat and Gottlieb (1992) and Garcia and Soto (2004).
3. For example, in the management of corporate pension plans, executive boards fully delegate investment decisions (including the formulation of risk–return preference and investment constraints) to a Pension Fund Committee.
4. Both constraints and risk–return preferences are tools to manage risk. As such overlap may exist between these two inputs to the asset allocation process. A general distinction we make is that risk–return preferences focus solely on financial (or dollar value) risk and reward whereas constraints will also cover non-financial risk such as liquidity or reputational risk. Furthermore, given the primacy of policy considerations, constraints are often imposed with little regard of for their impact on expected return, whereas risk–return preferences explicitly trade-off the risk of financial loss against the benefit of higher expected return.

5. The institution's risk–return preferences may even not be known at the TAA decision-making level.
6. For example, during the ongoing financial crisis relative value between asset classes may be driven by technical factors (such as the choice of instrument targeted by central banks to implement monetary policy) and may not be fully justified by fundamentals. Relative value trades depend on the ability to take and implement decisions flexibly over short horizons.
7. There may not be a clear distinction between the TAA and the implementation levels. Depending on the institution-specific set-up there is a larger or lesser overlap between TAA and implementation. Furthermore, the absence of the TAA level does not preclude relatively large active positions from being taken at the implementation level. When a distinct TAA level exists it will typically 1) be characterised by a medium-term investment horizon (of between three and 12 months) as opposed to a shorter-term investment horizon (of between one and six months) that is common for position-taking at the implementation level; 2) have leeway for larger position-taking (a larger risk budget) than available at the implementation level; 3) be decided by more senior decision-makers – typically referred to as the Investment Committee – than those responsible for position-taking at the implementation level.
8. The higher market risk inherent in longer-maturity government bonds leads some to question the suitability of these instruments in the liquidity tranche.
9. The financial crisis has shown that rapidly changing fundamentals and sentiment can result in a rapid depletion of reserves. This highlights the need to manage the investment tranche in a conservative manner and with adequate consideration given to safety and liquidity. On the other hand, the ongoing financial crisis has resulted in a large number of foreign exchange swap arrangements between countries and some argue that the liquidity that these provide reduces the amount of liquid reserves central banks need to hold.
10. The notion here is that "A dollar lost to a credit event is worse than a dollar lost to a market move".
11. Given that central banks are often more concerned about tail risk than about return volatility, and given uncertainties about parameter specification, the above approach is seldom used on its own.
12. The RaR is the return which will be achieved at a given confidence level. For example, a RaR of –3% at a confidence level of 99% means that the allocation will return –3% or better with a probability of 99% and less than –3% with a probability of 1%. From this definition we see that RaR is similar to the more commonly used Value-at-Risk, which considers tail risk as a dollar amount rather than a return amount. The cRaR is the expected return conditional on the return being below the RaR. Thus the cRaR is a measure for the expected return in case of adverse market conditions.
13. In order to meet the long-term objectives of the investment tranche it may be practical to use a multi-period approach with risk–return preferences defined over a shorter (one year) horizon. In such cases however the preferences need not be binding on a year-by-year basis but instead apply on average through the cycle. The central bank may therefore be willing to accept temporary (cyclical) fluctuations in the short-term risk–return profile of their reserves.
14. The relative stability of longer-term expectations means that the frequency at which the SAA needs to be reviewed may be reduced and, furthermore, only

relatively small changes in the allocation may be expected. In general, SAA should be reviewed whenever changes to risk–return expectations are large enough to have a meaningful impact on SAA. In particular it is not adequate to have a review period that is longer than that over which risk–return expectations are determined as this would lead to outdated expectation prior to the next review. In practice a large number of central banks choose to review their SAA on an annual basis even if they use a longer period in determining risk–return expectations.

15. In practice, the return distributions are generated by means of Monte Carlo simulation. That is, on the basis of the estimated vector autoregressive model, a large number of possible future outcomes are simulated. For each outcome the shape of the yield curve and consequently asset returns can be determined.
16. While the described approach of explicitly modelling the term structure has the potential to make alternative distributional assumptions, the normal distribution is most commonly used. Therefore, there is a limitation in the accuracy with which the distibutions' tail properties are quantified. This might be a of particular relevance, given the facts that "fat tails" are regularly observed in a number of market segments and, as noted above, the institution's risk–return preferences are often expressed in terms of a tail risk measures.
17. In the case of standard utility functions, risk–return preferences can be represented by the so-called indifference curves. Indifference curves are risk–return combinations that render the same level of utility. Thus risk–return combinations on a given indifference curve are equally preferred by the investor. Being positioned on a higher indifference curve (one with higher expected return for the same amount of risk) is preferable to being positioned on a lower indifference curve. The portfolio that best corresponds to the institution's risk–return preferences is identified by the tangent point of the indifference curve and the efficient frontier.
17. In practice identifying the institution's indifference curves is difficult and, as discussed earlier, the decision-makers will typically be more comfortable in specifying an upper limit to the amount of risk than in expressing their preference in terms of the trade-off between risk and return.
18. That is, higher risks implied by a higher return strategy are ignored as long as the total risks are within the risk budget. Thus under this approach an investor may be willing to accept substantially higher risks even though return expectations are only marginally improved.
19. This means that the risk–return characteristics of a "bullet" allocation (where intermediate maturity sectors have high weights and short and long maturity sectors have low weights) and that of a "barbell" allocation (where intermediate maturity sectors have low weights and short and long maturity sectors have high weights) are similar provided that the overall exposure to market risk–modified duration – is the same for both allocations.
20. Fixed income index providers include: Merrill Lynch; JPMorgan; Barclays Capital; and Citigroup.
21. This approach is justified assuming that the efficient portfolio that minimises return volatility for a given level of expected return is also efficient in that it minimises tail risk.
22. Looking at the risk–return characteristics of P5 and P6 is instructive as it provides an indication of the opportunity cost of specifying our risk–return preference on a year-by-year basis rather than on an average, through-the-cycle basis.

References

Ben-Bassat, Avraham and Daniel Gottlieb (1992) "On the Effect of Opportunity Cost on International Reserve Holdings", Review of Economics and Statistics, Vol. 74, No. 2.

Borio, C., J. Ebbesen, G. Galati, and A. Heath. (2008) "FX Reserve Management: Elements of a Framework", BIS Papers, No. 38, March.

Calvo, Guillermo A. (1998) "Capital Flows and Capital-Market Crises: The Simple Economics of Sudden Stops", Journal of Applied Economics, Vol. 1, No. 1, 35–54.

Calvo, Guillermo A. and Carmen M. Reinhart (2002) "Fear of Floating", The Quarterly Journal of Economics, Vol. 117 No. 2, May, 379–408.

Cardon, Pierre and Joachim Coche (2004) "Strategic Asset Allocation for Foreign Exchange Reserves", In Bernadell, Carlos, Pierre Cardon, Joachim Coche, Francis X. Diebold and Simone Manganelli (Eds) Risk Management for Central Bank Foreign Reserves, European Central Bank.

Diebold, Francis and Canlin Li (2006) "Forecasting the Term Structure of Government Bond Yields", Journal of Econometrics, February, 337–364.

Dooley, Michael P., David Folkerts-Landau and Peter Garber (2003) "An Essay on the Revived Bretton Woods System", NBER Working Paper, No. 9971.

Eichengreen, Barry and Donald J. Mathieson (2000) "The Currency Composition of Foreign Exchange Reserves: Retrospect and Prospect", IMF Working Paper.

Feldstein, Martin (1999) "Self-Protection for Emerging Market Economies", NBER Working Paper, No. 6907.

Flood, Robert and Nancy Marion (2002) "Holding International Reserves in an Era of High Capital Mobility", Brookings Trade Forum, 2001, Brookings Institution, Washington, D.C.

Garcia, Pablo and Claudio Soto (2004) "Large Hoarding of International Reserves: Are They Worth It?", Working Paper, Central Bank of Chile.

Genberg, Hans, Robert N. McCauley, Yung Chul Park and Avinash Persaud (2005) Official Reserves and Currency Management in Asia: Myth, Reality and the Future, Centre For Economic Policy Research.

McCauley, Robert N. (2008). "Choosing the Currency Numéraire in Managing Official Reserves". RBS Reserve Management Trends 2008.

3

Strategic Asset Allocation: Balancing Short-Term Liquidity Needs and Real Capital Preservation for Central Banks

Javier Bonza, Norma Gómez and Reinaldo Pabón

3.1 Introduction

The typical central bank strategic asset allocation is mainly focused on attending short-term liquidity needs, but has secondary consideration for real capital preservation criteria. It is well surveyed that though "conservative and very liquid" allocation of foreign reserves to US short-term treasuries, for instance, provides timely and relatively stable access to funds, it is costly in terms of falling behind the adjusted inflation or GDP growth value of foreign reserves. In fact, the probability of the typical Central Bank portfolio (consisting of US 0–3 year treasuries) of suffering negative real returns in a long-term horizon amply exceeds the chances for a typical pension portfolio allocation (60% stocks/40% fixed income). Summers (2007) finds that for a 10 year holding period the probability of having negative real returns investing in US short-term treasuries is 38%, whereas for the pension portfolio it lowers to 12.5%. Not only the probability but the size of the average loss in real terms increases, from –2.3% to –7.7%.

The unprecedented accumulation of reserves seen in recent years has made less constrained the case for a more return-orientated foreign reserves management (Borio, Galati and Heath 2007). In that sense, the increasing sophistication of central bank reserve management teams and the more notorious visibility of Sovereign and Pooling reserve institutions pave the way for gradually adopting a balanced approach between liquidity and capital preservation.

The purpose of this chapter is to set a Strategic Asset Allocation (SAA) framework that is consistent with the liquidity needs and real capital preservation in the long term for central banks. We propose both a contingent claims approach and a maximum external financial need based approach as a ratio of real GDP, in order to identify the minimal liquidity threshold for foreign reserves. This also allows us to propose an SAA, using robust optimization techniques, for the excess liquidity requirements aligned with real capital preservation goals. The set of SAA proposals is based on target return objectives conditioned on forecasted GDP growth paths.

The proposed SAA framework with real capital preservation is more in the spirit of asset and liabilities management (ALM) rather than only an asset-driven strategy. Although there have been some particular attempts of central banks to broaden the scope for reserve management in an ALM framework, for the bulk of central banks, the reserve management is, in practice, subordinated to monetary and financial stability goals and to some extent investment guidelines reflect the constraints in place. Pooling reserves and sovereign wealth institutions can mitigate these constraints and can be used as a vehicle for accomplishing an ALM framework.

The structure of the chapter is as follows. In the second section, we propose a contingent claim approach in order to estimate liquidity needs for central banks. We also estimate the maximum financing need as a percentage of GDP, using the methodology of Caballero and Panageas (2007). In the third section, we implement robust statistical methods that give less weight to atypical return events (Scherer and Martin 2005) and Monte Carlo Simulations of asset returns. In this sense the results are not biased by abnormal returns and provide more stable and diversified portfolios, increasing Sharpe Ratios with the same level of risk compared to classical optimization techniques. In a second step of the estimation, extreme events are fully considered by ranking SAA (Strategic Asset Allocation) using expected shortfall measures (i.e. CVAR at 95% interval confidence, taking all the information, without adjustments). The fourth part of the study presents empirical results regarding robust optimal portfolios that meet the goal of preserving capital in real terms for Latin American countries. The following section introduces the role that sovereign and pooling reserve institutions have on facilitating central banks to attain real capital preservation objectives. We also propose a Contingent Claim methodology in order to estimate the potential loans demand of countries that belong to a pooling reserve institution. The last section states some conclusions regarding strategic asset allocation linked to balancing short-term liquidity needs and real capital preservation for central banks.

3.2 Methodologies for assessing short-term liquidity needs

3.2.1 Maximum external financing needs

The external financing need is estimated as a percentage of GDP, $\varphi_{(t)}$, using the methodology of Caballero and Panageas (2007). The model is developed in an economy that exhibits current account deficits that are compensated by capital inflows. The risk that the economy faces is related to a potential capital flow reversal (outflow). The external financial need is estimated by dividing the cyclical capital flows by the GDP's long-term trend.

Cyclical financial flows are equal to capital flows valued in USD import prices plus exports valued in import prices, discounting intermediate inputs in the production that is export oriented. The GDP's long-term trend equals the sum of product nontradable goods, Nt and the tradable component of the GDP, which is approximated by the term of trade. The external financing need as a percentage of the GDP, $\varphi_{(t)}$, is:

$$[1]\quad Max\varphi_{(t)} = Max\frac{(\theta_t - 1) * Y}{Y} = Max\frac{\dfrac{E_t * CF_t}{PM_t} + \left[\left(\dfrac{Px_t * X_t}{PM_t} - 0.5 * X_t\right)\right]^{Cyclical}}{[N_t]^{Trend} + \left[\left(\dfrac{Px_t * X_t}{PM_t} - 0.5 * X_t\right)\right]^{Trend}}$$

where: Y corresponds to the GDP; $(\theta - 1)*Y$ corresponds to capital flows; P_x is export price in local currency; X is export volume; PM relates to import price in local currency and N is the GDP's nontradable goods.

3.2.2 Contingent claim approach

Several studies have applied a contingent claim approach in order to estimate a country's sovereign risk such as in the studies of D. Gray, R. Merton and Z. Bodie (2007) and C. Keller, P. Kunzel and M. Souto (2007). These studies quantify the sovereign asset at risk (SAaR).

In addition, D. Gray and S. Malone (2008) introduced the concept of sovereign liquidity at risk (SLaR) and the Contingent Claim framework (modified version of KMV) proposed in this study is based on the SLaR concept in order to estimate the probability and the magnitude of an external liquidity crisis has the following three steps:[1]

1. A country's current international reserve level is compared to a distress barrier of critical liquidity needs in USD, equivalent to 100% of short-term debt,[2] 10% base money[3] plus 20% of imports. This barrier reflects a minimum level of international reserve needed in order to respectively pay the short-term external debt, satisfy a potential speculative attack on the local currency or capital outflows and guarantee at least 20% of imports equivalent to 2.4 months (transactional motives).
2. The probability of an external liquidity crisis event is estimated. It is equivalent to the probability that international reserves are equal or fall below the distress barrier of critical liquidity needs.
3. The magnitude of the liquidity crisis can be estimated by considering an implicit put option in the contingent claim framework.

3.2.2.1 *Liquidity crisis probability*

The external liquidity crisis probability is equivalent to the probability that international reserves are less than or equal to the distress barrier of critical liquidity needs (BCL), in hard currency. Assuming that international reserves follow a lognormal probability distribution with a drift μ_r and a standard deviation σ_r, the liquidity crisis probability is:[4]

$$[2]\ \text{Prob}\left(\text{Reserves}_{(t)} \leq \text{BCL}_{(t)}\right)$$
$$= \text{Prob}\left[\text{Reserves}_{(t-1)} * \exp\left(\left(\mu_r - \frac{\sigma_r^{\ 2}}{2}\right) * t + \sigma_r * \varepsilon * \sqrt{t}\right) \leq \text{BCL}_{(t)}\right]$$

where: ε is a normal random variable with mean zero and unit variance, and t represents the horizon. The distress barrier of critical liquidity needs in USD (or in any other hard currency) corresponds to:

$$[3]\ \text{BCL} = \text{Short-Term External Debt} + 10\%\ \text{Base Money} + 20\%\ \text{Imports}$$

Rearranging equation [2], the liquidity crisis probability referring to the probability that international reserves are less than or equal to the distress barrier of critical liquidity needs, is equivalent to the probability of the normal random variable ε being less than or equal to the distance to liquidity crisis distress ($d2$) in terms of standard deviations:[5]

$$[4]\ \text{Prob}\left(\varepsilon \leq -\frac{\ln\left(\dfrac{\text{Reserves}_{(t-1)}}{\text{BCL}_t}\right) + \left(\mu_r - \dfrac{\sigma_r^{\ 2}}{2}\right) * t}{\sigma_r * \sqrt{t}} = -d2\right)$$

Therefore, the liquidity crisis probability is equal to the standard cumulative normal distribution (ε) minus the distance to liquidity crisis distress ($-d2$). This distance indicates how many standard deviations away international reserves are from a liquidity crisis event. Figure 3.1 shows the liquidity crisis probability taking into account: the international reserves path, the distress barrier of critical liquidity needs of a particular country and the distance to liquidity crisis distress.

In this example, the country is three standard deviations away from a liquidity crisis event, given its current international reserves level and volatility and its distress barrier of critical liquidity needs. The liquidity crisis probability is represented in the area where international reserves are less than or equal to the distress barrier of critical liquidity needs.

3.2.2.2 Magnitude of the liquidity crisis

Following the contingent claim approach, the expected magnitude of the liquidity crisis is estimated through an implied put option, given the present

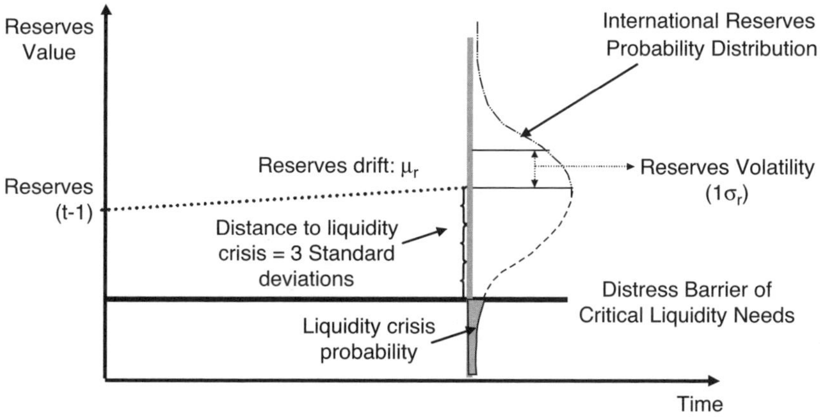

Figure 3.1 Liquidity crisis probability

value of the distress barrier of critical liquidity needs and the level of the country's international reserves:

$$[5]\ \text{Put} = \text{BCL} * e^{-r*T} * N(-d2) - \text{Reserves}_{(t-1)} * N(-d1)$$

where: BCL is the distress barrier of critical liquidity needs, r is the risk free rate; t is the horizon; $N(\,)$ is the standard cumulative normal distribution; $d2$ refers to the distance to liquidity crisis distress and $d1$ is equal to the following equation:

$$[6]\ d1 = d2 + \sigma_r * \sqrt{t}$$

Figure 3.2 shows a GDP weighted average of the distance to liquidity event for several Latin American economies between December 1999 and March 2008.

We estimated that the GDP weighted average of the distance to a liquidity crisis event for several Latin American economies was 1.84 standard deviations away from a liquidity event in October 2008, considering their actual international reserves levels and their distress barriers of critical liquidity needs. The monitoring of the distance to a liquidity crisis can be useful as an early warning signal of potential liquidity events.

The distance of 1.84 standard deviations implies that the probability of a liquidity event is 3%, $N(-1.84)$, which is quite low and indicates that it is the right moment to invest excess liquidity reserves in a SAA that preserves real capital related to real GDP growth.

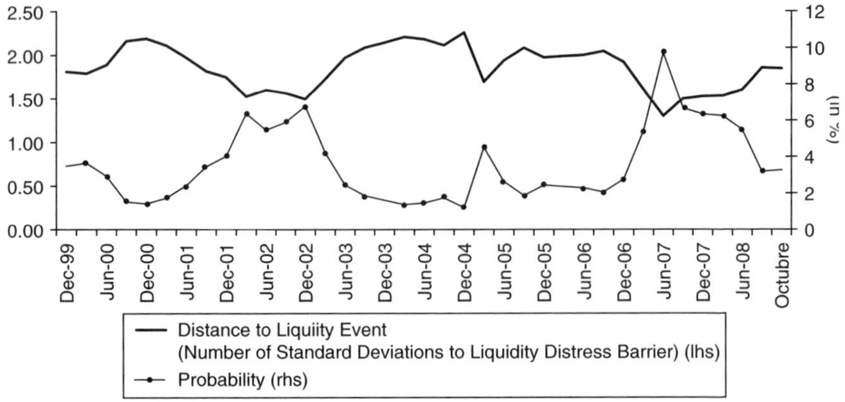

Figure 3.2 Probability and distance to liquidity event for several Latin American countries (December 1999–October 2008)

In addition, it could also be useful to consider a worst case scenario regarding for example the future path of the international reserves level of countries that have access to the pooling reserve mechanisms. In this regard, we apply to the actual level of international reserves as of October 2008 its worst percentage drop registered during the period 1994–2008 with a 99% confidence level. This enables us to estimate the probability of a liquidity event under a specific worst case scenario regarding international reserves. Under this scenario the probability of a liquidity event rises to 18% for Latin American countries.

Other scenarios could also be performed regarding the future paths of the levels of short-term external debt, base money and imports, affecting the distress barrier of critical liquidity needs and therefore the probability of registering a liquidity event.

3.3 Strategic asset allocation for real capital preservation

3.3.1 Robust Methods of Optimization

We used the robust optimization procedure mentioned by B. Scherer and D. Martin (2005). The robust mean of asset $\hat{\mu}$ returns is the solution to the following minimization problem:

$$[7] \min_{\mu} \sum_{t=1}^{n} \rho\left(\frac{r_t - \mu}{s}\right)$$

where: $\hat{s}$ is a scale robust measure of volatility and ρ is a penalty function. It is possible to estimate $\hat{\mu}$ by differencing the objective function [7] with respect to μ. In fact, the equation that estimates the robust mean of returns is given by the following expression:

$$[8] \quad \sum_{i=1}^{n} \psi\left(\frac{r_t - \hat{\mu}}{\hat{s}}\right) = 0$$

where: $\psi = \rho'$. Equation [8] is a similar version of the weighted least square estimator, by fixing:

$$[9] \quad w_t = w\left(\frac{r_t - \hat{\mu}}{\hat{s}}\right)$$

$$[10] \quad w(u) = \left(\frac{\psi(u)}{u}\right)$$

where u is a variable that represents asset return observations.

We can rewrite the estimating equation [8] as a weighted least square equation:

$$[11] \quad \sum_{i=1}^{n} w_t\,(r_t - \mu) = 0$$

When $\rho(t) = t^2$, the ψ function is the identity function of $\psi(t) \equiv t$, and the weights wt are all equal to one. The solution is the least square estimator of μ (i.e. the sample mean). The sample mean is not robust due to the quadratic character of the least square loss function, which causes outliers to have a major effect and is not recommended due to its influence on estimates. By using a ρ that grows more slowly than a quadratic function, we can obtain a robust mean estimate of asset returns. The formula for rho $\rho(t)$ is the following:

$$[12] \quad \rho(u) = \left\{ \begin{array}{ll} 0.5u^2 & |u| \leq 2 \\ c^2 \left\{ \begin{bmatrix} 1.7972 \; 0.972\left(\frac{u}{c}\right)^2 + 0.432\left(\frac{u}{c}\right)^4 \\ 0.052\left(\frac{u}{c}\right)^6 + 0.002\left(\frac{u}{c}\right)^8 \end{bmatrix} \right\}, & 2c \leq |u| \leq 3c \\ 3.25c^2 & |u| \geq 3c \end{array} \right.$$

The purpose of the constant c is to calibrate the efficiency of the estimate to the desired level when the returns are normally distributed. The variance of the least squares estimator divided by the variance of the robust estimator represents the efficiency indicator when the returns are gaussian.

The robust mean estimator is calculated from a function that minimizes the sum of standardized returns adjusted by a penalty parameter, which equals one when the observed return is considered a frequent event and close to zero if it represents an abnormal value. In this form, abnormal and atypical returns are given a lower weight than more frequent and usual returns. A single extreme event can bias the entire mean estimation and generates instability in the mean result.

As an example, Figure 3.3 shows the weights that are given to the Global Emerging Market Bond Index (EMBI Global) returns between 1994 and 2008. Note that the returns observed between 1994–2000 have a lower weight, signaling extreme events with high volatility.[6]

The usual measure of volatility is the standard deviation, which also lacks robustness when considering extreme events. A single extreme event can bias the entire volatility estimation and generates instability in the volatility result.

A robust volatility estimation is obtained by using the mean absolute deviation (MAD) about the median returns, u:

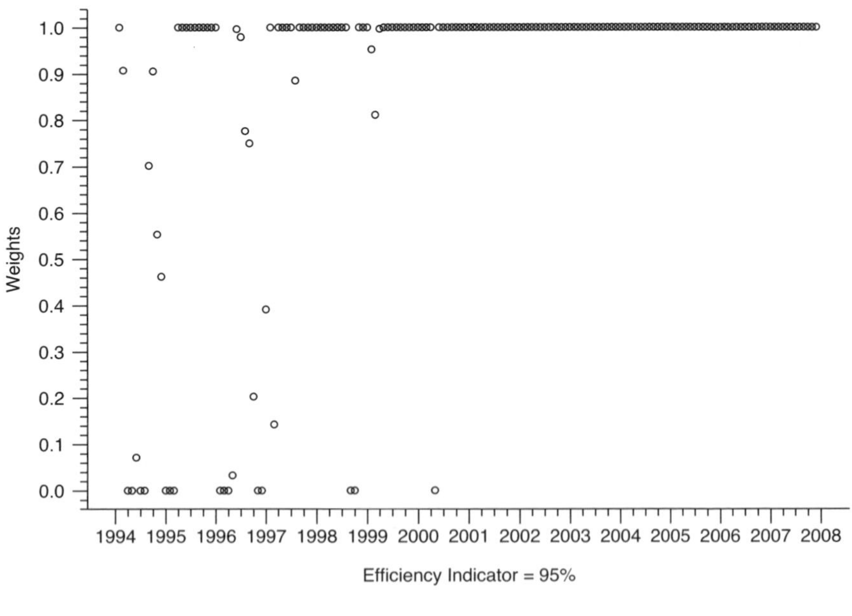

Figure 3.3 Robust weights for the EMBI Global

$$[13]\ \text{MAD} = \text{Median}\left(\mid u_i - \text{Median}(u_i) \mid \right)$$

The standard deviation squares the distances with the mean and therefore high differences have a high impact on the estimator. On the contrary, the magnitude of the distances of a small number of extreme events has a limited impact on the MAD estimator.

The robust correlations between assets classes are estimated taking into account the robust mean and volatility estimates.[7]

3.3.2 Monte Carlo simulation and real capital preservation risk measures

The robust optimization techniques are relevant in a sense that they generate stable optimal portfolios, where extreme and abnormal returns are given a lower importance. Nonetheless, in the risk measures related to these optimal portfolios the extreme events are fully considered by ranking SAA using expected shortfall measures (i.e. CVAR at 95% interval confidence, taking all the information, without adjustments).

For both the robust optimization procedure and risk measures the inputs are 10.000 Monte Carlo simulations based on the historical real assets returns (1997–2008). The advantages of using Monte Carlo simulations methods are the following.

- By increasing the size of the data set, we can have a better knowledge of the returns probability distribution function. Therefore, we can obtain better estimators such as the expected return, volatility and correlation between asset classes. In fact, the Law of Large Numbers states that the expected value of a random sample converges to the expected value of the entire population as the size of data increases.
- Monte Carlo simulation captures nonnormal behavior of asset returns.
- Monte Carlo simulation increases flexibility and precision regarding sensitivity analysis and stress testing.

3.4 Strategic asset location proposals and expected GDP growth paths

3.4.1 Latin America's GDP growth paths

Latin American economies have experienced accelerated growth during the recent years. In particular, the aggregated growth rate of the GDP of the member countries was 6.7% during the period 2003–2007. Long-term growth estimations are subject to uncertainty regarding some aspects such as population growth rate, investment rate, technological progress rate, or multifactor productivity.

However, disregarding the uncertainty and possible margin of error of these types of forecasts, it is useful to establish reference criteria for long-term growth in the economies of Latin American countries. For this purpose, three possible paths were determined in order to achieve GDP growth in terms of US dollars at 2007 prices.

1. Potential GDP growth rate or long-term growth could be found using estimations made in macroeconomic programming documents generated by the Ministries of Finance and central banks, as well as from private analysts.[8]
2. Brazil's expected growth rate, based on estimations made by the investment bank Goldman Sachs[9] for the bigger emerging economies denominated as BRICs (Brazil, Russia, India, China), could be used as the reference criterion. The reason for taking this growth rate as a reference criterion is the fact of considering Brazil as a strong influence and engine of growth for other Latin American countries.[10]
3. The aggregated growth rate of the countries of the region could be formulated under a GDP growth model in terms of employment growth, capital stock, and multifactor productivity.[11]

The real Exchange rate remains constant during the analysis period. Figure 3.4 shows the predicted growth paths during 2008–2050 according to the different methods of estimation.

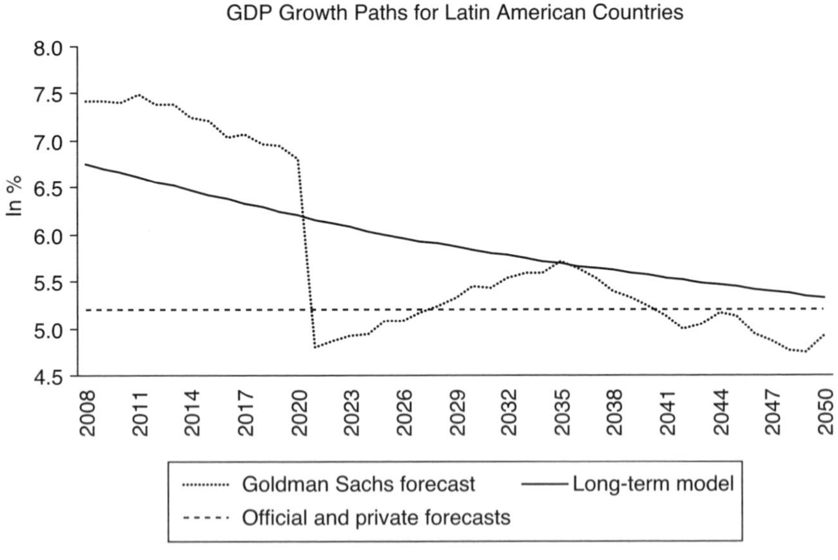

Figure 3.4 Possible economic growth paths (2008–2050)

3.4.2 SAA and real capital preservation for the long term

In the following stage, a simulation is done of the real capital preservation capacity of an investment strategy compared with the real growth of Latin American economies' GDP between 2008 and 2050. A strategic asset allocation that preserves real capital is one that has a similar expected real return compared to the real GDP growth rate. We start to estimate the real capital preservation under a scenario of maintaining a typical central bank strategic asset allocation consisting of US Treasury and Agency Notes of 1–3 years. Table3.1 indicates all the asset classes that are considered in the robust optimization in real terms.

First, an estimation of the growth of Brazil, calculated by Goldman Sachs, is used as an approximation of the real GDP growth of other Latin American countries. The evolution of the maximum credit requirements is determined as a function of the highest historical value of equation (14), as a percentage of the real GDP growth rate.

Table 3.1 Eligible assets classes for the optimization

Assets	Index	Source	Data
Global High Grade FI, Ex USD (USD Unhedged)	Lehman Global Aggregate	Lehman Brothers	Dec 1997–Jun 2008
Emerging Equities (MSCI Emerging Markets)	MXEF	Morgan Stanley	Dec 1997–Jun 2008
Global Equities (G23 Ex USD Hedged to USD)	MXWOU	Morgan Stanley	Dec 1997–Jun 2008
Currency Overlay Strategy (G10)	YAJPFUS8	JP Morgan	Dec 1997–Jun 2008
Commodities (S&P/GSCI)	SPGCCI	Goldman Sachs	Dec 1997–Jun 2008
Global Equities (G23 Ex USD Unhedged)	MVLDWXUS	Morgan Stanley	Dec 1997–Jun 2008
US Equities MidCap (S&P400)	MID	Bloomberg	Dec 1997–Jun 2008
Global Emerging Bonds (EMBI+)	EMBI+	JP Morgan	Dec 1997–Jun 2008
Global High Grade FI, Ex USD (Hedged to USD)	Lehman Global Aggregate	Lehman Brothers	Dec 1997–Jun 2008
High Grade US Fixed Income	US Lehman Aggregate	Lehman Brothers	Dec 1997–Jun 2008
US Equities (S&P500)	SPX	Bloomberg	Dec 1997–Jun 2008
US Equities (S&P600)	SML	Bloomberg	Dec 1997–Jun 2008

$$[14]\ Max\ \varphi_{(t)} = \frac{(\theta_t - 1) * Y}{Y}$$

$$= \frac{\dfrac{E_t * CF_t}{PM_t} + \left[\left(\dfrac{Px_t * X_t}{PM_t} - 0.5 * X_t\right)\right]^{Cyclical}}{[N_t]^{Trend} + \left[\left(\dfrac{Px_t * X_t}{PM_t} - 0.5 * X_t\right)\right]^{Trend}}$$

Consequently, estimations made by macroeconomic programming documents and private analysts are used. Finally, the model of long-term growth is also applied to Latin American countries. In the following simulations of the investment strategies for real capital preservation, we initially suppose that the value of the portfolio is equal to the maximum credit requirements, φ. The real capital preservation is determined by the following equation:

$$[15]\ \text{Real Capital Preservation}_{(t)} = \frac{\text{Portfolio Value}_{(t-1)} * \left(1 + \text{SAA Real Expected Return}_{(t)}\right)}{Max\varphi_{(t-1)} * \left(1 + \text{Real GDP Rate}_{(t)}\right)}$$

In order to preserve real capital, the SAA has to have an expected real return equivalent to the real GDP growth rate:

$$[16]\ \text{SAA Real Expected Return} = \text{Real GDP Growth Rate}$$

3.4.2.1 Current SAA (Treasury and Agency notes, 1–3 years, USA vs. real GDP 5.8%)

Under the scenario of maintaining the current typical central bank asset allocation the real expected return for one year corresponds to 2.31% and therefore, the real capital preservation compared with the real GDP growth will deteriorate significantly, falling from 100% in 2008 to 22% by 2050 as shown in Figure 3.5. The asset return would be much lower than the real GDP growth of Latin American countries, according to estimations of the model of long-term real GDP growth (5.8%).

3.4.2.2 Nominal optimal portfolio strategy: (expected return 3.16% vs. real GDP 5.8%)

At the same time, an important detriment to real capital preservation compared with Latin American countries' real GDP growth rates would be perceived when adopting the optimal portfolio in nominal terms, which has a 3.16% annual expected real return and was established under normal conditions and with no relation with the real GDP growth of Latin American countries (asset structure proposal under nominal capital preservation in an annual horizon). As shown in Figure 3.6, the real capital preservation compared with GDP real growth falls from 100% in 2008 to 30% in 2050.

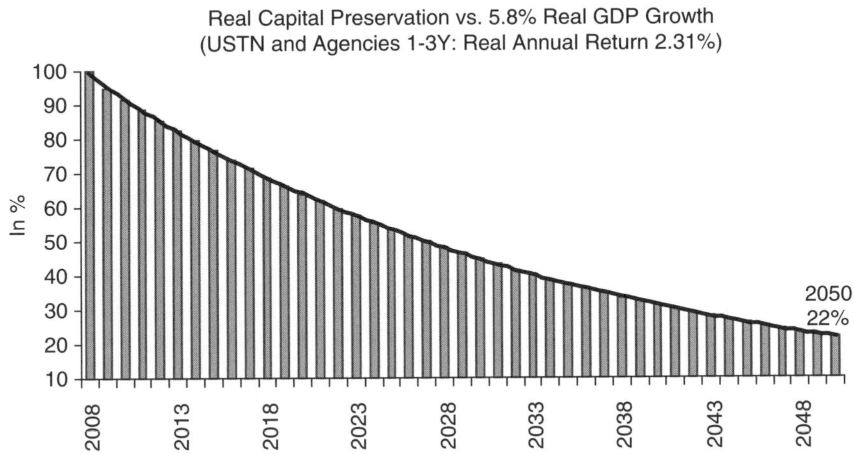

Figure 3.5 Real capital preservation vs. real GDP growth according to the current typical central bank asset allocation

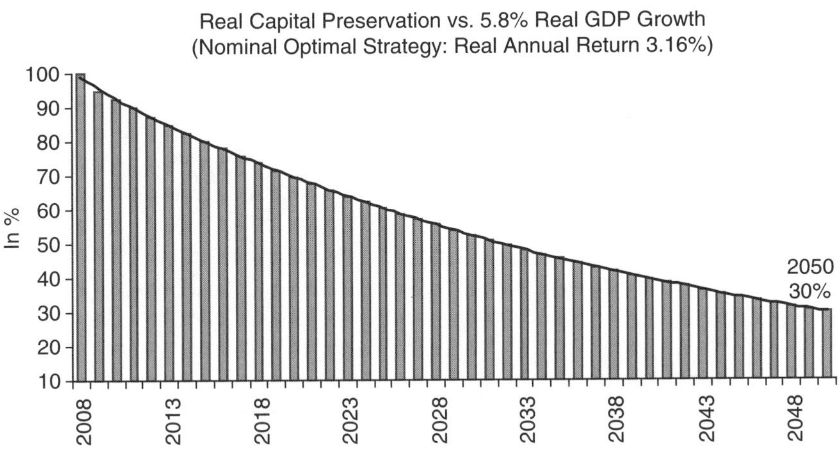

Figure 3.6 Real capital according to the nominal capital preservation structure

3.4.2.3 Strategy of real capital preservation

The Figure 3.7 compares the Robust Efficient Frontier vs. the Classical Efficient Frontier (Markowitz Mean-Variance). The inputs of the optimization procedures are 10.000 Monte Carlo simulations of performed annual moving assets real returns on a monthly basis between 1997–2008.[12]

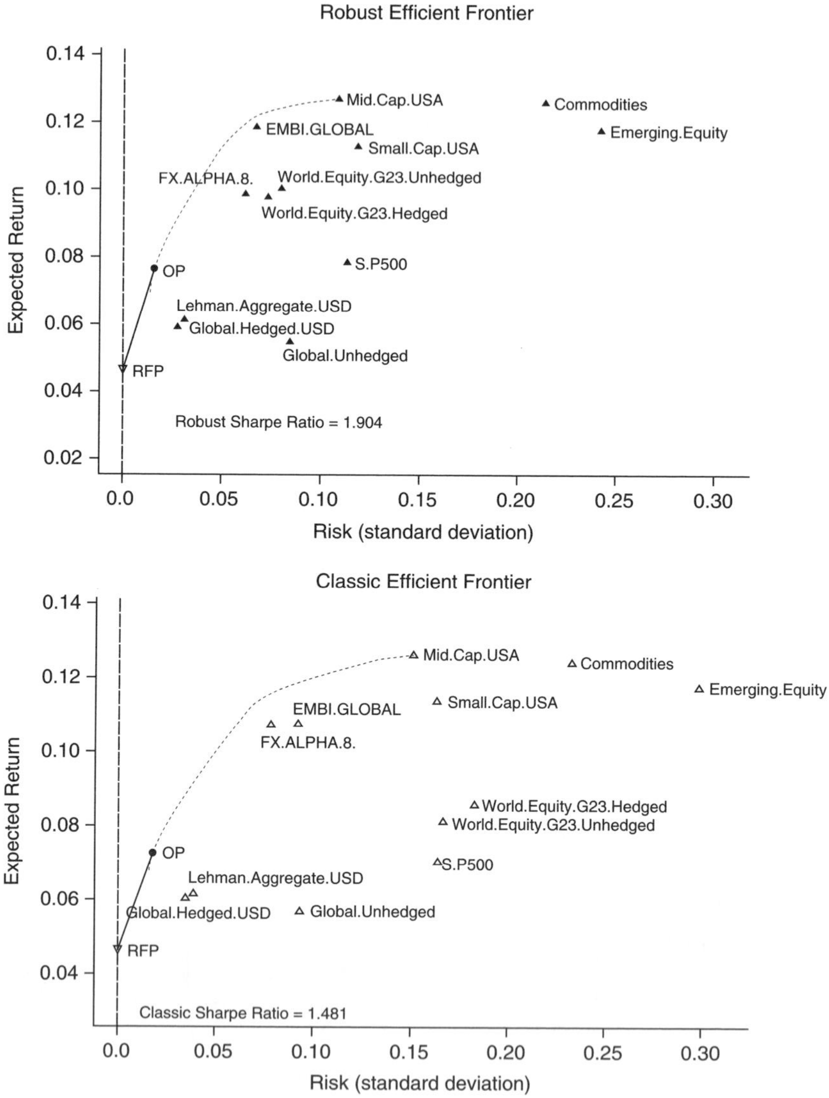

Figure 3.7 Robust efficient frontier vs. classical efficient frontier

The robust optimization technique not only gives more diversified portfolio results but also a higher Sharpe Ratio compared with the classical Mean-Variance analysis (Robust Sharpe Ratio = 1.76 vs. Classical Sharpe Ratio = 1.49). Figure 3.8 describes the robust and classical optimal portfolios' composition in their entire efficient frontiers in real terms.

Figure 3.9 indicates that the optimal robust portfolio in real terms has an expected real return of 6.56%, which is similar to the real GDP growth rate of Latin American economies and therefore preserves real capital.

Table 3.2 shows the capital preservation and the risk in the worst 5% of cases for a range of optimal robust portfolios that have expected real returns between 4.14% and 7.13%, which preserve in the long term the capital preservation vs. real GDP growth rates and compare the results with those obtained for a typical central bank's strategic asset allocation.

These results indicate that a typical central bank's strategic asset allocation (US Treasuries and Agencies of 1–3 years) does not preserve capital in real terms, since the VAR in real terms is –2.40% with a 95% confidence level.

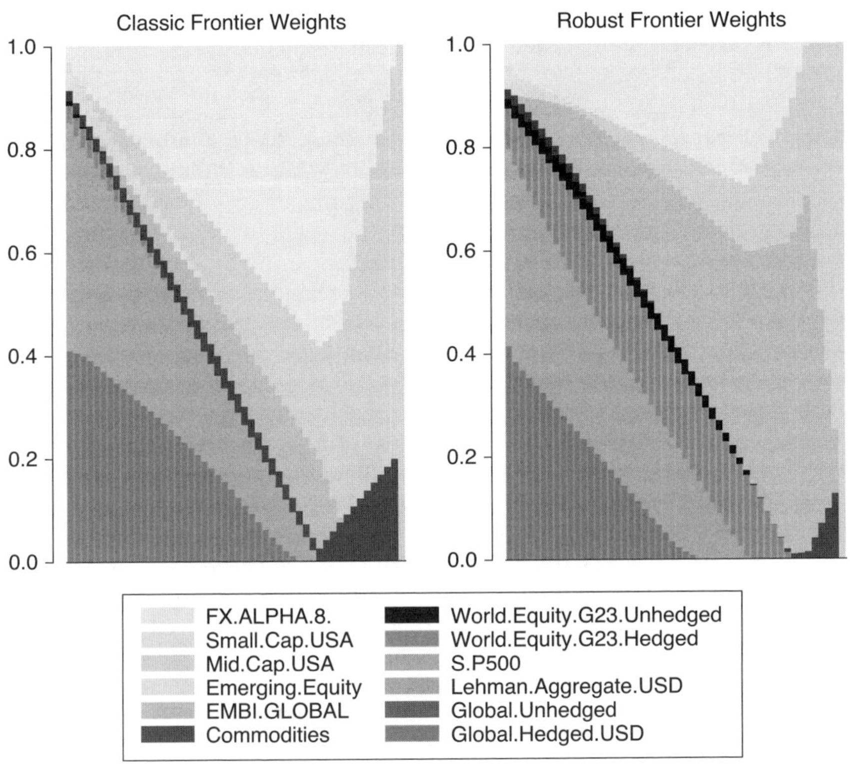

Figure 3.8 Robust and classical optimal portfolios' composition

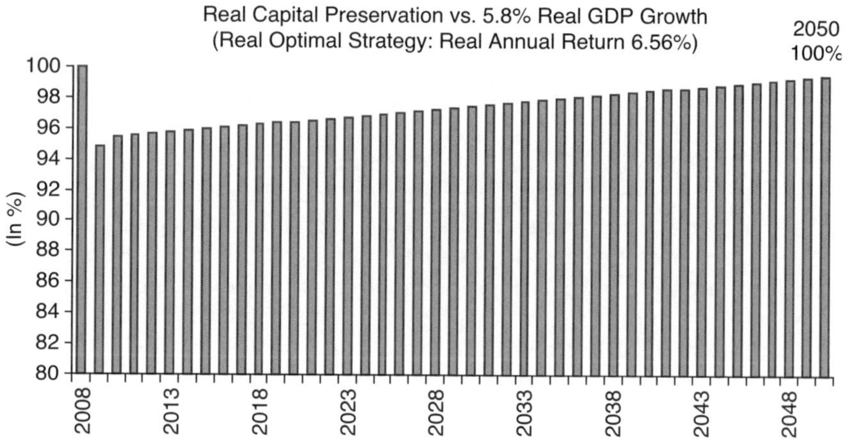

Figure 3.9 Real capital preservation v. real GDP growth

Table 3.2 Expected real return, capital preservation and risk

	Capital preservation		**Risk in 5% worst cases**	
Expected real return annual (in %)	**VAR nominal (95%) (in %)**	**VAR real (95%) (in%)**	**CVAR nominal (in%)**	**CVAR real (in %)**
4,14	3.37	1.06	2.49	0.20
5,09	2.56	0.12	1.66	–1.11
6,03	1.93	–0.82	–0.27	–3.02
7,13	0.64	–2.41	–3.20	–5.83
USTN and Agencies 1–3Y = 2.31	1.02	–2.40	–0.49	–3.11

On the other hand, several real robust optimal portfolios that have expected a real return between 4.14 and 5.09% do preserve capital in real terms and also in nominal terms. Furthermore, the typical central bank´s asset allocation is not efficient since the expected annual real return is less that the one that could be achieve by investing according to an optimal portfolio with the same level of risk measured in VAR or considering the worst 5% of cases (CVAR). Figure 3.10 shows the composition related to these real optimal portfolios, given a specific target return.

Figure 3.11 indicates that the minimum and maximum exposure per asset class are exhibited as shown.

These robust optimization results indicate that strategic asset allocation including emerging market bonds, fixed income global bonds, commodities, equities, active currency strategy and US fixed income aggregate

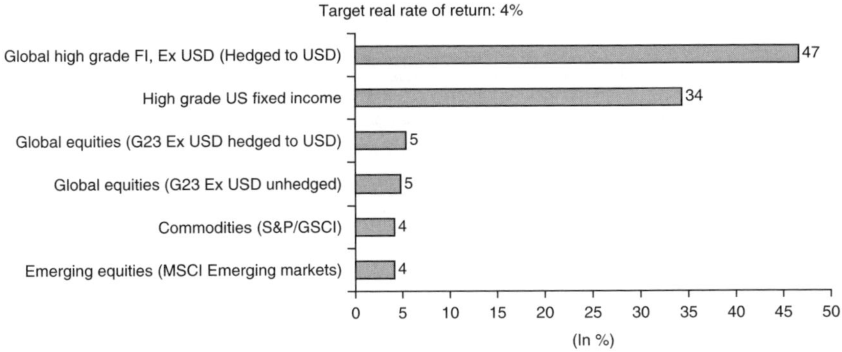

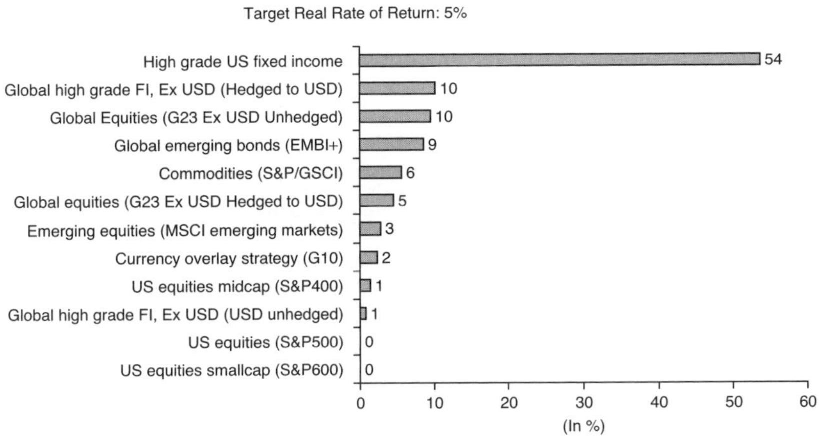

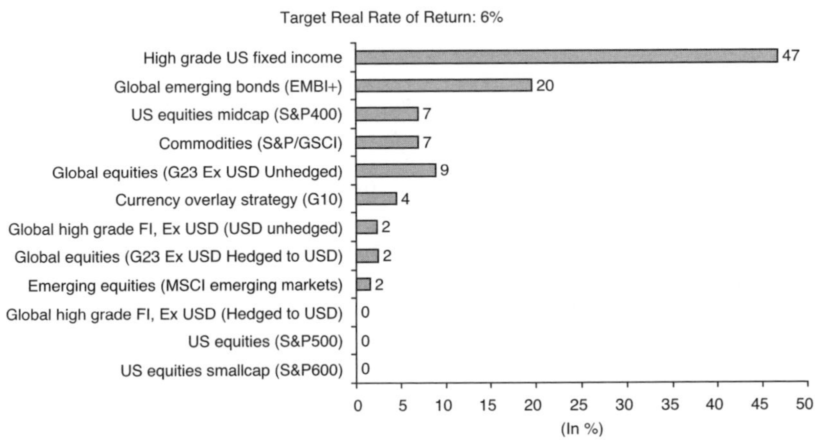

Figure 3.10 Continued

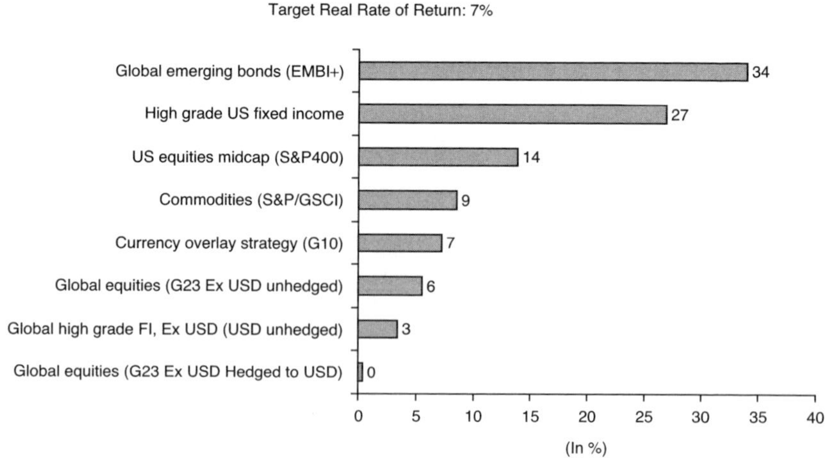

Figure 3.10 Real optimal portfolios composition

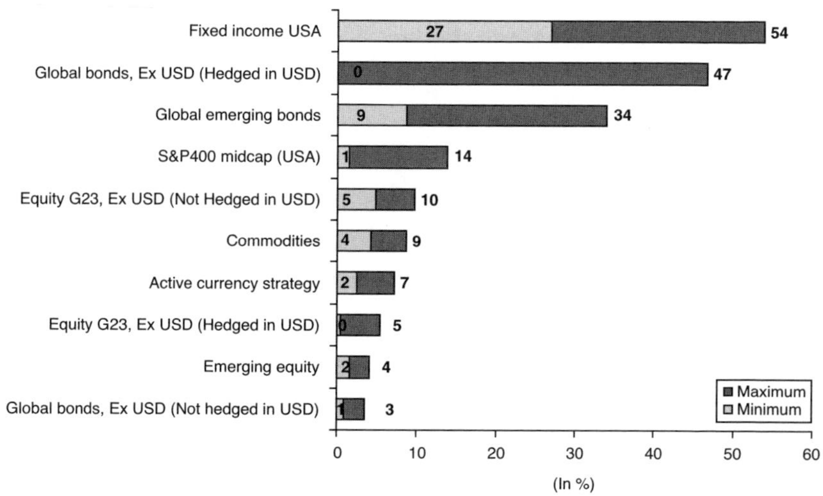

Figure 3.11 Minimum and maximum exposure per asset class

bonds outperformed a typical central bank´s asset allocation related to US Treasuries and Agencies Notes 1–3 years, in terms of real capital preservation (risk) and expected real return.

In Figure 3.12, we compare the cumulative value of these robust optimal portfolios with a typical central bank's asset allocation, in both real and nominal terms. We indicate the final value of each strategy if 100 USD were initially invested in November 1997.

These results indicate that robust optimal portfolios offer cumulative real values that are superior to those obtained by investing in US Treasuries and Agencies of 1–3 years (188 USD vs. 122 USD). The Figure 3.13 shows that this is also the case in nominal terms.

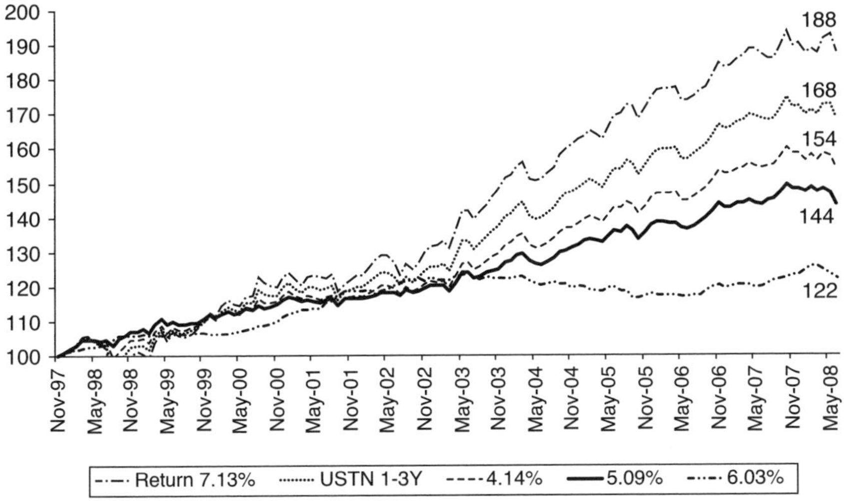

Figure 3.12 Real comparison: optimal portfolios vs. USTN and Agencies 1–3 years

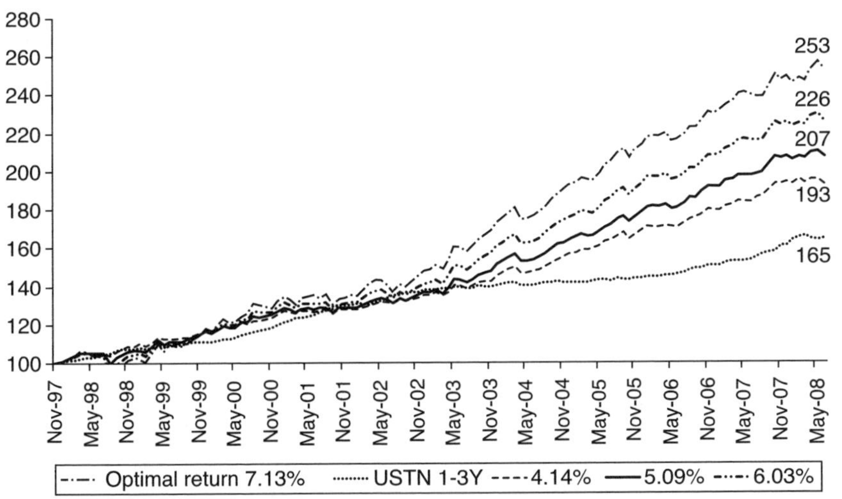

Figure 3.13 Nominal comparison: optimal portfolios vs. USTN and Agencies 1–3 years

These results represent the medium- to long-term optimal portfolios. Nonetheless, it is relevant to consider short-term tactical allocation deviations from the optimal portfolios. In this regard, the F. Black and R. Littermann (1992) model could be used; it combines the CAPM equilibrium theory with the Markowitz Mean–Variance optimization process by incorporating subjective investors' views (Bayesian approach) on future returns in the optimization framework.

In addition, K. Winkelmann and S. Glaubach (2006) show that while markets tend to equilibrium, they are not in equilibrium at any point in time. Furthermore, these authors show that the Black and Litterman model could be used in order to increase the beta of the portfolio by incorporating sources of exotic beta and tilts away from equilibrium market capitalization weights.

3.5 The role of sovereign and pooling reserve institutions and real capital preservation

Although there have been some particular attempts by central banks to broaden the scope for reserve management in an ALM framework, for the bulk of central banks reserve management is, in practice, subordinate to monetary and financial stability goals and to some extent investment guidelines reflect the constraints in place. As Lawrence Summers (2007) has pointed out, the first obstacle to new investment guidelines concerns risk. A more aggressive investment strategy raises the likelihood of preserving real capital over the long term. The second obstacle is related to the agency problem for central bank officials. The main objective of central banks is monetary policy and not reserve-asset management. If they invest in an unusual way and are successful, the reward is practically minimal. If on the contrary they are not successful, they face a high reputation risk.

Pooling reserves and sovereign wealth institutions can mitigate these constraints and can be used as a vehicle for accomplishing an ALM framework. It can also be useful to estimate the credit financial needs that potentially could be addressed to reserve pooling institutions. For example, A. Ghosh, M. Goretti, B. Joshi, A. Thomas, and J. Zalduendo (2008) conclude that the use of IMF resources is likely to decline significantly, from the actual average of 50 billion SDR (special drawing right) in the period 2000–2005 to 8 billion SDR during 2006–2010, using stochastic simulations and alternative scenarios assuming weaker economic conditions.

We next propose a contingent claim framework in order to determine the potential external credit financing needs of countries that have access to pooling reserve mechanisms. For each country of a particular pooling reserve institution (PRI), following a contingent claim analysis we can calculate the expected credit requirement by estimating an implicit put option shown in equation [17]. The total potential credit requirement (TCR) of all countries that have access to pooling reserve mechanisms is equal to the sum of the put options of each country:

$$[17]\ \mathrm{TCR} = \sum_{j=1}^{n} \mathrm{Put}_j$$

where j is a particular country and n is the total number of countries that belong to the pooling reserve institution.

We propose a modified version of the KMV contingent claim approach in order to quantify the expected credit amount required by all the countries that are part of a pooling reserve institution and also its credit assistance capacity. To accomplish this goal we compare the maximum amount the pooling reserve institution can lend to its countries with a total credit requirement barrier, which is equal to the sum of the put options of each country (equation [17]). These put options are financial guarantees that countries have with the pooling reserve institution.

The amount that the pooling reserve institution can lend to the countries represents contingent international reserves that are valued as put options and appear as a contingent asset in a central bank´s balance sheet framework. For the pooling reserve institutions these put options are regarded as a contingent liability in its balance sheet.

In Figure 3.14, we show a simplified version of the interactions between balance sheets between central banks assets and liabilities with the pooling reserve institution in a contingent claim framework. In this example three countries have access to the pooling reserve institution.

Member central banks have the option to receive USD from the pooling reserve institution and therefore have an implicit put option that is regarded as a contingent international reserve in the asset side of its balance sheet. In other words, the pooling reserve institution has "sold" to its countries the right to receive a credit in USD that is valued as a put option and represents a contingent liability to the Institution.

The maximum amount that a pooling reserve institution can lend to its countries is usually a function of the capital paid by the countries. We now propose a method based on a contingent claims approach in order to estimate the institution's credit capacity for assistance to its countries. To accomplish this goal, we compare the maximum amount that the pooling reserve institution can lend with the total credit requirement Barrier by all the countries (Σ put options).

Figure 3.15 describes the methodology used to estimate the probability that the pooling reserve institution cannot satisfy the total credit requirement barrier of the countries that have access to that facility, which is equivalent to the probability that the maximum amount the pooling reserve institution can lend is less than or equal to the total credit

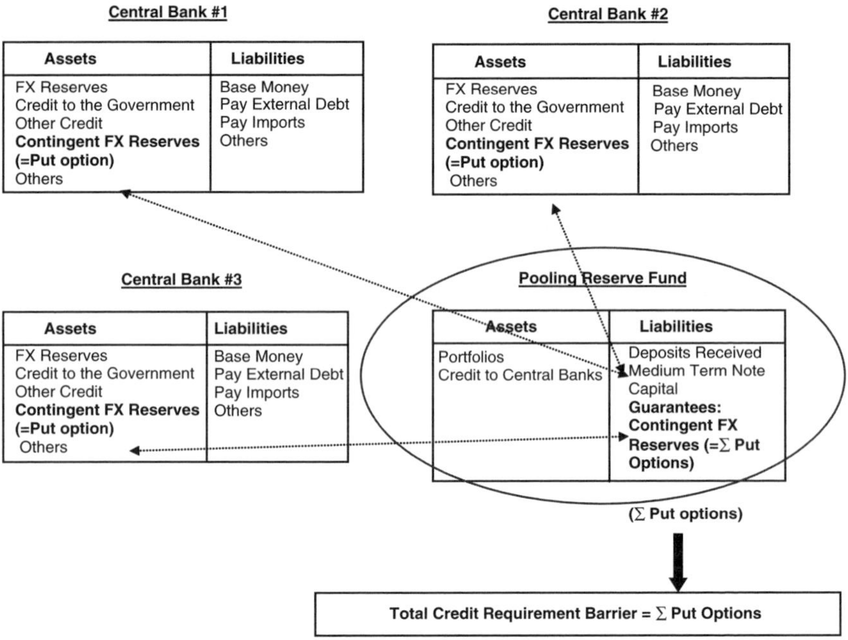

Figure 3.14 Central banks and pooling reserve institution contingent balance sheet

requirement barrier of its countries. Furthermore, as shown in Figure 3.15, we can estimate the distance to not satisfying the countries' credit requirements, in terms of standard deviations. In this example the pooling reserve institution is three standard deviations away from not satisfying the total credit requirement.

Assuming that the maximum amount that the pooling reserve institution can lend to its countries follows a lognormal distribution as in a KMV framework, the probability that the institution cannot satisfy the total credit requirement barrier of its countries (CT) corresponds to the following equation:

$$[18]\ \text{Prob}\left(\text{Max Credit}_{(t)} \leq \text{CT}_{(t)}\right) = \text{Prob}\left[\text{Max Credit}_{(t-1)} * \exp\left(\left(\mu_p - \frac{{\sigma_p}^2}{2}\right) * t + \sigma_p * \varepsilon * \sqrt{t}\right) \leq \text{CT}_{(t)}\right]$$

where: ε is equal to a normal standard random variable with zero mean and unit variance, and *t* is the time horizon. The total credit requirement barrier of the countries that belong to the pooling reserve institution in

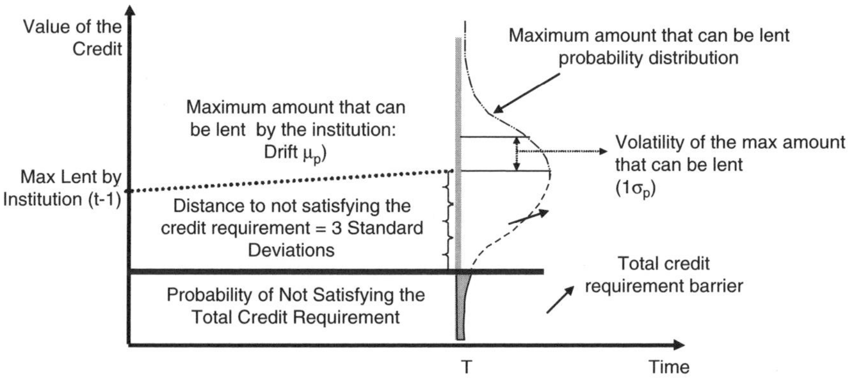

Figure 3.15 Pooling reserve institutions' credit assistance capacity

USD is equal to the sum of the put option of each country as shown in equation [19].

$$[19]\quad CT = \sum_{j=1}^{n} Put_j$$

μ_p, γ, and σ_p are respectively the drift (tendency) and volatility associated with the maximum amount that the institution can lend to its countries. In this regard, the SAA determines both μ_p and σ_p, given an initial paid capital. The SAA's expected return and volatility are equal to the drift and volatility of the maximum amount that the pooling reserve institution can lend to its countries, given an initial paid capital. Therefore, the probability that the maximum amount the Institution can lend is less than or equal to the total credit requirement barrier of the countries that have access to the pooling reserve mechanisms also depends on the expected return and volatility of the strategic asset allocation.

Rearranging equation [18], we find that the probability that the maximum amount the institution can lend is less than or equal to the total credit requirement barrier of its countries is equal to the probability that ε is less than or equal to minus the distance to not satisfying the credit requirement ($-d3$) in terms of standard deviations.

$$[20]\quad \text{Prob}\left(\varepsilon \leq -\frac{\ln\left(\frac{\text{Max Credit}_{(t-1)}}{CT_t}\right) + \left(\mu_p - \frac{\sigma_p^2}{2}\right) * t}{\sigma_p^* \sqrt{t}} = -d3 \right)$$

In this sense, the probability that the credit assistance capacity of the pooling reserve institution is insufficient corresponds to the standard cumulative normal distribution (ε) of minus the distance to not satisfying the credit requirement ($-d3$). This distance indicates how many standard deviations away the maximum amount the Institution can lend is from the total credit needs of the countries that have access to the pooling reserve facility.

Following the KMV approach, it is also possible to determine the expected gap between the credit requirement of countries that belong to the pooling reserve institution and the maximum amount the institution can lend through the valuation of another put option. The following equation indicates the expected amount that the pooling reserve institution cannot satisfy in terms of credit requirement:

$$[21]\quad \text{Put Gap} = \text{CT} * e^{-r*T} * N\left(-d3\right) - \text{Max Credit}_{(t-1)} * N\left(-d4\right)$$

where: CT is the total credit requirement barrier of its countries; r is the risk free rate; t is the horizon; N ( ) is the standard cumulative normal distribution; $d3$ refers to distance to not satisfying the credit requirement and $d4$ is equal to the following equation:

$$[22]\quad d4 = d3\ + \sigma_p * \sqrt{t}$$

3.6 Conclusions

This chapter has established strategic asset allocations by balancing short-term liquidity needs and real capital preservation for central banks, considering robust optimization techniques. A contingent claim analysis was used in order to estimate short-term liquidity needs. A distance to liquidity crisis indicator was estimated for Latin American countries between 1999–2008. The current distance to liquidity distress is equivalent to 1.84 standard deviations and implies that the probability of a liquidity event is 3%, $N(-1.84)$, which is quite low and suggests that it is the right moment to invest excess liquidity reserves in an SAA that preserves real capital related to real GDP growth. An SAA that preserves real capital is one that has a expected real return similar to the real GDP growth rate.

In addition, it could also be useful to consider a worst case scenario regarding for example the future path of international reserves level of countries that have access to the pooling reserve mechanisms. In this instance, we have applied to the actual level of international reserves as of October 2008 its worst percentage drop registered during the period 1994–2008 with a 99% confidence level. This enables us to estimate the probability of a liquidity event under a specific worst case scenario regarding international reserves. Under this scenario the probability of a liquidity event rises to 18% for Latin American countries.

The robust optimization results indicate that SAAs including emerging market bonds, fixed income global bonds, commodities, equities, active currency strategy and US fixed income aggregate bonds outperformed a typical central bank´s asset allocation related to US Treasuries and Agencies Notes 1–3 years, in terms of real capital preservation (risk) and expected real return. Furthermore, these optimal portfolios improve both the risk and return profile compared to typical central bank´s investment strategy and does imply changes in terms of risk tolerance (i.e. they preserve nominal capital at an annual horizon). Sovereign and pooling reserve institutions are suitable vehicle in helping central bank´s meeting real capital preservation in longer terms.

Annex A: Comparison between robust and classical asset allocation parameter estimates

Table 3.3 Comparison between robust and classical mean estimates

	Robust mean (in %)	**Classic mean (in)**	**Difference (in)**
Global High Grade FI, Ex USD (Hedged to USD)	3.2	2.9	0.2
US Equities SmallCap (S&P600)	6.6	6.5	0.2
Global High Grade FI, Ex USD (USD Unhedged)	3.5	3.5	0.1
High Grade US Fixed Income	3.4	3.4	0.0
Treasuires-Agencies, 1–3Y	2.3	2.3	0.0
Liquidity Protfolio	1.8	1.9	0.0
Commodities (S&P/GSCI)	11.8	11.9	0.0
US Equities MidCap (S&P400)	8.2	8.3	−0.1
Emerging Equities (MSCI Emerging Markets)	8.7	8.9	−0.1
US Equities (S&P500)	2.7	3.0	−0.3
Currency Overlay Strategy (G10)	6.1	6.7	−0.6
Global Equities (G23 Ex USD Hedged to USD)	3.9	4.7	−0.8
Global Emerging Bonds	7.4	8.4	−1.9
Global Equities (G23 Ex USD Unhedged)	2.9	4.4	−1.6

Table 3.4 Comparison between robust and classical volatility measures

	Robust volatility (in %)	Classic volatility (in %)	Difference (in %)
Emerging Equities (MSCI Emerging Markets)	30.2	24.5	5.7
US Equities SmallCap (S&P600)	17.1	12.0	5.1
US Equities (S&P500)	17.1	12.1	5.1
Global Emerging Bonds	9.4	4.6	4.8
US Equities MidCap (S&P400)	16.1	11.7	4.4
Currency Overlay Strategy (G 10)	10.8	8.1	2.6
Global Equities (G23 Ex USD Unhedged)	18.2	15.9	2.3
Global High Grade FI, Ex USD (USD Unhedged)	9.6	7.8	1.8
Global Equities (G23 Ex USD Hedged to USD)	19.0	17.8	1.1
Global High Grade FI, Ex USD (Hedged to USD)	3.8	2.8	1.0
Commodities (S&P/GSCI)	24.0	23.3	0.7
High Grade US Fixed Income	4.1	3.9	0.2
Liquidity Portfolio	2.4	2.6	–0.2
Treasuries-Agencies, 1–3Y	3.0	3.3	–0.4

Annex B: Long-term growth model

The model represents a simple GDP (Y) formula in terms of employment (L), capital stock (K), and technological progress or total productivity of the factors (A). We assume that the GDP is approximated by a Cobb-Douglas function:

$$[23] \quad Y = AK^{\alpha}L^{1-\alpha}$$

The capital stock evolves according to the investment rate (I/Y) and assuming a capital depreciation rate of 4% (δ).

$$[24] \quad K_{t+1} = K_t(1-\delta) + \left[\frac{I_t}{Y_t}\right]Y_t$$

The capital share in the income (α) equals one third, according to historical estimations. The series of capital stock were taken from a date generated by the World Bank and the investment rate of 2007 was considered as the base scenario.

Employment is forecasted using expected population growth rates according to data from the Governmental Statistical Agency of Latin American countries. Multifactor productivity was forecasted according to convergent criteria between the economies of the Latin American countries (LC) and the US economy. Seeking to reduce the margin of difference between the income per capita of the economies of the member countries and the income per capita of the US, the technological growth rate captures this convergence according to the following formula:

$$[25] \quad \left[\frac{A_{t+1}}{A_t}\right] = 1.3\% - \beta \ln\left[\frac{\text{Income per capita}_{\text{LC}}}{\text{Income per capita}_{\text{USA.}}}\right]$$

where: 1.3% is the multifactor productivity for the US, and β is the velocity of convergence (1.5%). The income per capita for each of Latin American country, as well as for the US, is adjusted to purchasing power parity according to calculations made by the World Bank.

Using the model of long-term economic growth, the forecast for the GDP in US dollars by 2007 is shown next in Figure 3.16.

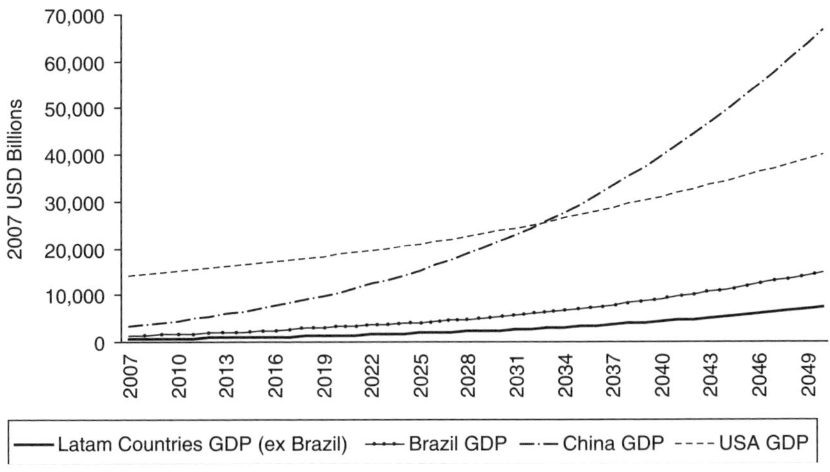

Figure 3.16 GDP growth paths

Table 3.5 GDP long-term growth forecast 2007 USD billions

	Latam countries GDP (ex Brazil)	Brazil GDP	China GDP	USA GDP
2007	623	1325	3252	14074
2008	665	1423	3631	14425
2009	709	1529	4046	14779
2010	756	1642	4495	15126
2011	806	1765	4971	15478
2012	859	1895	5472	15824
2013	915	2036	6000	16167
2014	975	2183	6553	16511
2015	1037	2340	7127	16853
2016	1103	2505	7730	17218
2017	1173	2682	8373	17584
2018	1247	2869	9057	17952
2019	1325	3068	9802	18331
2020	1407	3277	10599	18710
2021	1494	3434	11463	19109
2022	1585	3602	12369	19528
2023	1682	3779	13288	19967
2024	1783	3.965	14268	20423
2025	1890	4167	15312	20904
2026	2003	4378	16412	21432
2027	2122	4605	17589	21990
2028	2247	4.846	18823	22569
2029	2379	5104	20103	23160
2030	2518	5382	21457	23745
2031	2664	5674	22878	24359
2032	2818	5989	24383	25014
2033	2980	6323	25962	25707
2034	3150	6677	27628	26428
2035	3330	7058	29392	27159
2036	3518	7456	31251	27916
2037	3717	7869	33211	28686
2038	3926	8295	35265	29466
2039	4146	8737	37404	30252

Continued

Table 3.5 Continued

	Latam countries GDP (ex Brazil)	Brazil GDP	China GDP	USA GDP
2040	4376	9195	39638	31036
2041	4619	9667	41983	31833
2042	4874	10148	44360	32660
2043	5141	10660	46861	33509
2044	5423	11210	49479	34388
2045	5718	11786	52171	35284
2046	6028	12368	54925	36201
2047	6353	12971	57705	37148
2048	6694	13.588	60599	38111
2049	7052	14232	63579	39092
2050	7428	14933	66645	40081

Notes

We are particular grateful for the useful comments and suggestions of Iker Zubizarreta and Carlos Giraldo. Any errors and omissions are the responsibility of the authors. This study should not be reported as representing the views of Fondo Latinoamericano de Reservas (FLAR). The views expressed in this study are those of the authors and do not necessarily represent those of FLAR.

1. This modified KMV (Kealhofer, Merton, and Vasicek) approach applied to a liquidity crisis event does not require an estimation of the "implicit market value of international reserves" (assets) since reserves are directly market to market. On the other hand, in a traditional KMV approach, the equity value (call option) and its volatility enables an approximation of the asset's market value.
2. The short term external debt was used as a proxy of the short term debt denominated in foreign hard currency, due to a lack of information.
3. It is also possible to include deposits denominated in foreign currency, especially those that are held by non residents, since they could be withdrawn during a speculative event.
4. The traditional KMV framework also assumes that asset's market value follows a Lognormal distribution.
5. It is also possible to estimate an adjusted or risk neutral probability of a liquidity crisis event, by using the risk free rate, r, instead of the international reserves drift, μ_r.
6. However, during the current financial crisis, it could be useful to measure the sensitivity of results by giving a higher weight to extreme negative returns and a much lower weight to "normal" returns. Tail risk event protection could be achieved by for example buying exchange traded out of the money put options. In addition, it is possible to include liquidity risk in the optimization process. This could be done by incorporating liquidity constraints in the optimization framework such as assets and portfolio turnover and bid/ask spreads metrics as indicated

by A. Lo et al. (2003). Efficient Frontiers can de determined by considering these liquidity metrics. In a similar way, credit risk could also be explicitly incorporated in the optimization framework as a constraint (target CreditVAR, probability of default, etc...).

7. The estimates of mean and volatility returns are presented for both classic and robust methodologies in Annex A.
8. According to the consulted numbers, the aggregated potential growth rate for Latin American countries is 5.2%.
9. See J. O'Neill et al.
10. Estimated growth rate of Brazil is 5.8% in average for the period 2008–2050.
11. The forecasted aggregated growth rate for some Latin American countries is 5.9% on average for the period 2008–2050. The methodology in detail is presented in the attached Model of Long Term Growth Forecast.
12. Robust and Classical Optimization were performed using the software Splus 8.0.

References

Black, F. and R. Litterman (September 1992) "Global Portfolio Optimization", Financial Analysts Journal, September, 28–43.

Caballero, R. and S. Panageas (2007). "A Global Equilibrium Model of Sudden Stops and External Liquidity Management" MIT Department of Economics Working Paper No. 08–05.

Galati, G, C. Borio and A. Heath, FX reserve management: trends and challenges, BIS Paper No. 40, May 2008.

Ghosh, A., M. Goretti, B. Joshi, A. Thomas and J. Zalduendo (2008) "Modeling Aggregate Use of IMF Resources – Analytical Approaches and Medium Term Projections", IMF Staff Papers, Vol. 55, No. 1.

Gray D. and S. Malone (2008) "Macrofinancial Risk Analysis", *Wiley Finance*, 59–185.

Gray, D., R. Merton and Z. Bodie (2007) "Contingent Claims Approach to Measuring and Managing Sovereign Credit Risk", IMF, Harvard Business School and Boston University School of Management.

Keller, C., P. Kunzel and M. Souto (2007) "Measuring Sovereign Risk in Turkey: An Application of the Contingent Claims Approach", IMF Working Paper (WP/07/233).

Lo, A., C. Petrov and M. Wierzbicki (2003) "It is 11Hpm – Do You Know where Your Liquidity Is? The Mean–Variance–Liquidity Frontier", *Journal of Investment Management*, Vol. 1, No.1, 55–93.

O'Neill, J., S. Lawson, D. Wilson, Purushothaman and Roopa (2004) "Growth and Development: The Path to 2050", The Goldman Sachs Group Inc., 23–58.

Scherer, B. and D. Martin (2005) "Introduction to Modern Portfolio Optimization with NuOpt, S-Pus, and S+Bayes", Editorial Springer.

Summers, L. (2007) "Sovereign Wealth Management", *Central Banking Publications*, Treasury-World Bank-Blackrock, 25–27.

Winkelmann, K. and S. Glaubach (2006) "Designing Efficient Return-Generating Portfolios: Tilting Away from Equilibrium toward Alpha and Exotic Beta", Goldman Sachs, Strategic Research.

4

Assets and Liabilities Management for Central Banks

*Urmila Kisoen**

4.1 Introduction

For a central bank to fulfill its key role in maintaining price stability and to fulfill its policy functions in the field of financial stability it is paramount to have a good measure of financial independence, giving it credibility as a critical partner in political decision-making. The current financial turmoil shows the importance of a strong central bank being able to take emergency measures when necessary to enhance financial stability and the smooth functioning of money markets. To achieve these public tasks it is desirable to hold a sustainable capital buffer.

The capital buffer is subjected to operating costs and losses related to financial risk, like currency risks, interest rate risks, equity risk and reputation risks. As a provider of payment services, lender of last resort and in the execution of monetary operations, De Nederlandsche Bank (DNB) is also exposed to credit, market and liquidity risks.

Among the techniques employed to calculate the capital buffer are Value-at-Risk (VaR) analysis, stress-testing and scenario analysis. However, there are some disadvantages to these techniques, like the short-term horizon, dependency of the outcomes on both the choice of scenarios and the assumptions made on market values. Moreover, these techniques have an asset-only approach, and accounting rules are excluded. Notably, the risk of decision-making based on these techniques is the significant volatility of the Profit and Loss (P&L) account due to the realizations immediately following on rises or falls in market values.

To provide a more accurate description of the long-run development of capital needed, simulation techniques like an assets and liabilities simulation of the balance sheet may be used. This type of simulation derives

* The author wishes to thank Carsten Folkertsma, Tessa Wouters and Eloy Lindeijer for their useful contributions. Views expressed are those of the author and do not necessarily reflect official positions of the Nederlandsche Bank.

successive balance sheets and P&L accounts for years to come. Compared to the techniques mentioned above, its strength lies in the possibility to simultaneously model the assets, liabilities, policies and economic assumptions, hence increasing the understanding of the complex interactions between monetary operations, financial assets, accounting and profit distribution rules and investment decision making.

We believe that the aim of such a central bank's assets and liabilities model should be to provide insight into the long-term development of its capital buffer and P&L situation. The purpose is to identify and manage various risks given a set of risk tolerances and constraints.

In this chapter we will demonstrate an assets and liabilities model developed in-house, specifically designed to serve a central bank's needs.[1] We will show the transformation of a stylized balance sheet combined with contingencies mentioned before into a decision-making tool. In the first section the assets & liabilities model will be explained. Subsequently, we will present and discuss illustrations of the balance sheet review.

4.2 Methodology and description of the assets and liabilities model

The assets and liabilities management (ALM) model outlined in this chapter is suitable for a central bank's balance sheet and has been applied to a stylized balance sheet. The model incorporates both internal and external restrictions. The economic variables used as input for the balance sheet are simulated, resulting in stochastic simulations of the balance sheet through time with a horizon of 15 years.

To obtain a reliable output from the ALM model, stochastically simulated data of all the economic variables are required to represent real life economics. Furthermore, the correlation between the variables should generate a consistent economic pattern, e.g. diversification effects and long-term effects. Constructing accurate simulations of economic variables is specialized and time-consuming work. In order to focus our attention on central bank ALM issues, we therefore acquired economic scenarios from a professional provider of simulation models.[2]

ALM is traditionally applied to multi-decision problems. We handled the issue of implementing multi-decision problems by dissecting the model into different modules, each module handling a specific task. The ALM model consists of a stochastic economic module, a balance sheet module, an input and an output module.

4.2.1 The stochastic economic module

Because the economic scenarios we use are obtained from a proprietary model, we cannot give the full details of the model here. However, we do give a general description of the model, which works along the lines of the model described in Boender et al. (2007). The fundamental form of the model is a Vector AutoRegressive (VAR) time-series model for which the parameters are calibrated on a combination of historical time-series data, forward-looking information and economic theory.

The economic module generates scenarios of inflation rates, interest rates, exchange rates, equity prices and gold prices based on predefined stochastic processes. These stochastic processes take into account observed volatilities and correlations, as well as long-run relations and economic theories like interest rate parity and mean reversion. The drift, standard deviation and correlations are estimated from historical observations. Each scenario covers 15 years of inflation rates, interest rates, exchange rates, equity prices and gold prices.

The long-term expected inflation rate is set at 2%, in conformity with the ECB (European Central Bank) target rate. The building blocks of the exchange rate are an interest differential (domestic minus foreign short interest rate) and an "excess" exchange rate return based on the covered interest rate parity. The expected return on equity is based on the long-term return on fixed-income (that is, the average long-term nominal interest rate) and the equity risk premium. Gold is a commodity, and the development of the gold price is therefore regarded as an inflation hedge. This implies that since the Eurozone inflation rate target is 2%, the expected gold return is 2%. In the table below, the values of some key parameters are displayed.

The figures below shows stochastic developments of EUR 100 invested in equity (Figure 4.1) and EUR 1000 invested in gold (Figure 4.2) over a period of 15 years. Ultimately 1000 scenarios with a total of 15,000 possible outcomes for both asset classes will be generated and integrated into the balance sheet module.

The interest rate term structures are produced by a scenario generator based on the Nelson and Siegel (1987) model,[3] which uses four parameters (βs and τ) to describe the yield curve. These parameters take into account the jump movement (overall level), the tilt movement (difference

Table 4.1 Key parameters stochastic simulation – mean and volatility

Ecomomic variable	Mean (in %)	Volatility (in %)
Inflation EUR	2.0	1.0
Inflation US	2.3	1.4
Short rate EUR	3.4	1.8
Short rate US	3.3	2.0
Equities	6.9	15.9
Gold	2.0	24.1

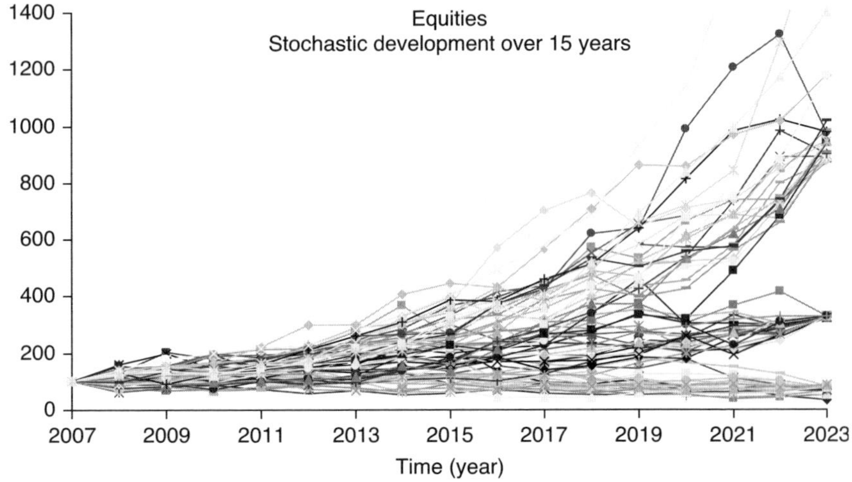

Figure 4.1 Stochastic developments – equity

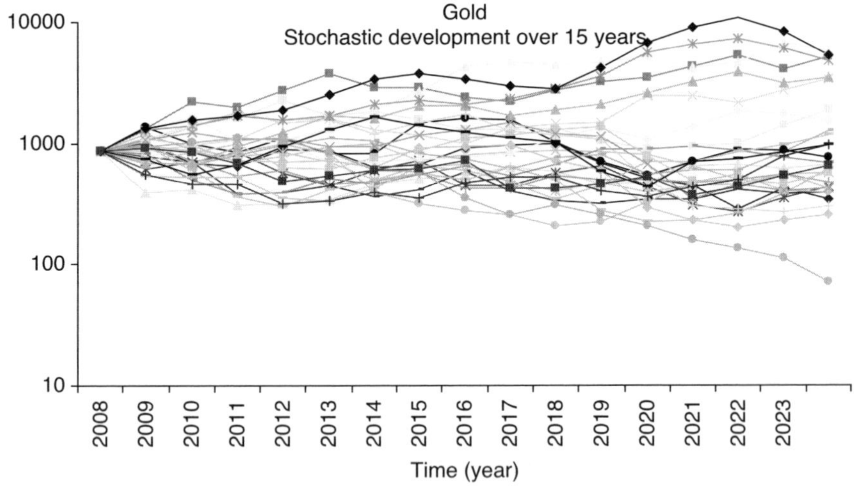

Figure 4.2 Stochastic developments – gold

between long-term and short term interest rate) and the flex movement (the curvature). The fixed-income returns follow from these term structure scenarios, enabling the modelling of different duration strategies.

Figures 4.3 and 4.4 show an example of one stochastic scenario from the thousand scenarios generated from the 15-year development of the interest rate term structures for both the euro region and the US. As one can

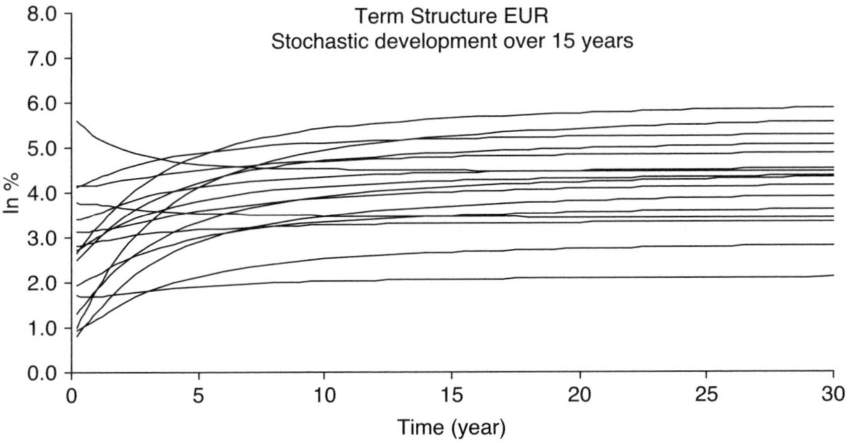

Figure 4.3 Stochastic developments – term structure (EUR area)

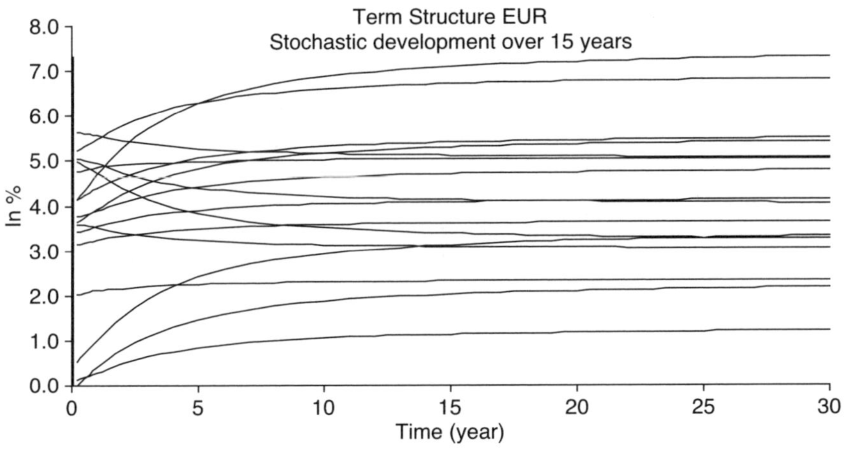

Figure 4.4 Stochastic developments – term structure (USD area)

see, the possibility of inverse term structures also appears in the scenarios. Ultimately 1000 scenarios with a total of 15,000 interest rate term structures will be generated and integrated into the balance sheet module.

The stochastic processes are Monte Carlo simulations.[4] The resulting histogram of the outcomes is effectively a probability distribution, from which we can derive the average as well as other statistics, like the value at risk.

4.2.2 Balance sheet module

A stylized balance sheet of a certain year, as illustrated below (Table 4.2), is the starting point of the ALM analyses. The book entries are gold, a USD

Table 4.2 Stylized balance sheet

Balance Sheet			
Assets		**Liabilities**	
Gold	8.9	Bank notes	21.6
USD fixed-income	5.3	Revaluations accounts	7.4
EUR fixed-income	13.4	Capital & Reserves	4.3
Equities	1.0		
SDR	0.6		
Monetary policy operations (net)	4.1		
	33.3		33.3

fixed-income portfolio, an EUR fixed-income portfolio, equities, an SDR (special drawing right) portfolio and monetary policy operations. The passive side includes the banknotes, the revaluation accounts and the capital and reserves. The balance sheet module incorporates internal as well as external restrictions and policy reactions. An example of external restriction is gold sales. Internal restrictions include targets for currency and equity exposure. A policy reaction could be to increase the duration of fixed-income portfolios after a significant rise in interest rates. In addition, accounting rules are incorporated in this module.

As indicated by the flow chart of the ALM model shown in Figure 4.5, the stochastic economic scenarios generated in the economic module are combined with the balance sheet module. For example, the stochastic scenarios for the euro interest rate term structure will influence the value for the book entry EUR fixed-income in the balance sheet at time *t*. This equally applies for the book entries gold, USD fixed-income, EUR fixed-income, equities, SDR (special drawings right) and monetary policy operations. Through changes in the book entries the P&L account will be affected. Negative changes will only have an immediate effect on the P&L and positive changes if the assets are sold. The latter is dependent on the circulation rate of the portfolios. A circulation rate less then one means intra-year sales and purchases. The circulation rate in the ALM model is assumed to be equal to one. Furthermore dividend depends on the profit distribution mechanism. Ultimately the balance sheet at time (*t*+1) will be constructed from the previous balance sheet on the basis of all investment decisions, policy rules and accounting rules.

The ALM is an annual model. So with 1000 scenarios there will be a total of 15,000 observations of every single economic variable, resulting in 15,000 balance sheets and P&L accounts. In other words: 1000 balance sheets and P&L accounts per year.

However, it would be difficult to interpret 15,000 possible balance sheet paths. Therefore, in the standard setting we decided to display the median,

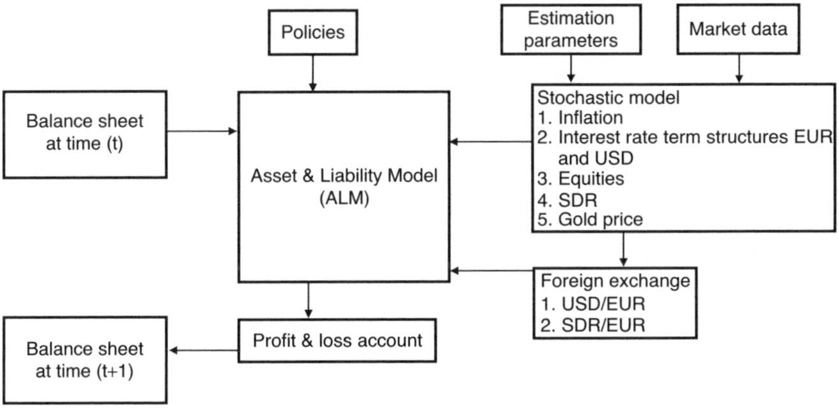

Figure 4.5 Flow chart of the ALM model

the 25 best-case and 25 worst-case scenarios for the capital development and P&L development in the next 15 years.

The portfolios are rebalanced on an annual basis. Rebalancing of the portfolios can be regarded as a system of communicating vessels, all interconnected through the liquidity deficit, i.e. the central vessel. This is necessary to distribute market value changes of the portfolios. These changes are based on the input from the stochastic economic module. Stylized examples are illustrated to explain the dynamics in the balance sheet.

For the EUR fixed-income portfolio the dynamics works as follows. Assume this portfolio is annually set at the market value of EUR 10 billion while the liquidity deficit is set at EUR 8 billion. Assume also that the market value of the EUR portfolio before rebalancing is 10.5 billion. After rebalancing, when the EUR portfolio is set at EUR 10 billion, the surplus of 500 million of the EUR fixed-income portfolio flows into the market shortage, which will increase by 500 million to EUR 8.5 billion.

Conversely, in case of a shortage, assume the market value is EUR 9.5 billion. During rebalancing, 500 million will flow out of the liquidity deficit into the EUR portfolio, resulting in a EUR 10 billion EUR fixed-income portfolio and a EUR 7.5 billion liquidity deficit.

Let us examine a stylized example concerning the USD fixed-income portfolio. Assume this portfolio is set at EUR 4 billion during the annual rebalancing. The flow during rebalancing of the USD fixed-income portfolio runs via the EUR fixed-income into the liquidity deficit. Assume the market value of the USD portfolio is EUR 4.5 billion. Remember the EUR portfolio is EUR 10.5 billion and the liquidity deficit amounts to EUR 8 billion. This gives a surplus of 500 million for the USD fixed-income portfolio, which flows into the EUR fixed-income portfolio, which in turn will increase by EUR 500 million to EUR 11 billion. Simultaneously, rebalancing of the EUR portfolio to EUR 10 billion will cause the 1 billion surplus of the EUR fixed-income portfolio to flow into the liquidity deficit. The liquidity deficit will therefore increase by EUR 1 billion to EUR 9 billion.

Vice versa in case of a shortage; assume the market value of the USD portfolio to be 3.5 billion. When rebalancing, this deficit of 500 million flows into the USD portfolio, causing the EUR portfolio to decrease to EUR 10 billion, while the liquidity deficit remains EUR 8 billion.

Assume the market value of the equity portfolio is 1.3 billion and is set at EUR 1 billion during the annual rebalancing. The EUR portfolio is still EUR 10.5 billion and the liquidity deficit is EUR 8 billion. The flow during rebalancing also runs via the EUR fixed-income into the liquidity deficit. The surplus of 300 million for the equity portfolio flows into the EUR fixed-income portfolio, which will increase by EUR 300 million to EUR 10.8 billion. Simultaneously, the rebalancing of the EUR portfolio to EUR 10 billion will cause to the liquidity deficit to increase, resulting in a market value of EUR 8.8 billion.

Conversely, in case of a shortage, e.g. if the equity market value is EUR 700 million, then EUR 300 million will flow into the equity portfolio and the EUR fixed-income will decrease to 10.2 billion. At the same time, when the EUR portfolio stands at EUR 10 billion after rebalancing, the liquidity deficit will increase to EUR 8.2 billion.

Obviously, the annual rebalancing causes the portfolios to rebalance simultaneously. To illustrate this, assume all portfolios have a surplus. Rebalancing causes the following dynamics. The USD portfolio is set from EUR 4.5 billion to EUR 4 billion . The equity portfolio is set from EUR 1.3 billion to EUR 1 billion. The total surplus of EUR 800 million flows into the EUR portfolio. Simultaneously, the total EUR surplus (EUR 500 million plus EUR 800 million) flows into the liquidity deficit resulting in an increase to EUR 9.3 billion.

Notably, the liquidity deficit has a minimum level. As breaching this minimum will induce other assets to be liquidated, this restricts the maximum outflow to make up for a shortage of the portfolios. The linkage between both sides of the balance sheet is the relationship between the liquidity deficit and the banknotes. Retrieval of bank notes from circulation results in an increased liquidity deficit.

Income from gold sales goes directly into the capital, in conformity with the agreement between DNB and the Ministry of Finance that the profit on gold sales is exempt from dividends. Furthermore, the equity, EUR and USD fixed-income portfolios are each connected with their respective revaluation accounts.

Besides market value changes, effects of accounting rules concerning netting and realizations of P&L are also implemented. Netting is not allowed, i.e. a loss in a portfolio cannot be compensated for by a profit of another portfolio. With respect to P&L, there is an asymmetry in their realization.

Losses go through the profit and loss account, while profit realization depends on the turnover rate of the respective portfolio.

4.3 Evaluating the ALM model

In the previous section we explained the complex interactions of the ALM model. To test the consistency of the model, an expected change is required, which can be calculated theoretically. If the ALM model is economically plausible this calculated change should match the outcome of the model. A convenient way to test this is to compare the effect of impulse responses on the balance sheet with the calculated change of the baseline scenario. The graphs in this section represent capital (graphs on the right) and the P&L distribution (graphs on the left). Capital is defined as the capital without the revaluation accounts.

Changing a single parameter while keeping the other risk factors constant will give relatively straightforward outcomes. At the same time, single parameter changes can be calculated theoretically. For the model to be considered consistent, the effect on capital and on the P&L distribution of these two outcomes should match.

The impulse response strategy is to induce a change in year (t) and reverse the change in year ($t+1$). For example, assume an interest rate of 4%. The impulse strategy will be a change in interest rate from 4% in year 2 ($t-1$) to 14% in year 3 (t) and back to 4% in year 4 ($t+1$).

4.3.1 Baseline

In the baseline scenario, the balance sheet presented in the previous section is used as the starting point. The risk factors are kept constant and no expansion of portfolios is assumed. Risk factors are gold sales and gold price fluctuations, interest rate for both the Eurozone and US region, return on equities and hedging dollar risk. Notably, only the dollar portfolio is hedged against currency risk. Income from gold sales is assumed to flow directly into the capital. Finally, 95% of the profit goes to the stakeholder and losses will be fully compensated over a six year period.

The graphs below show that both the capital development (Figure 4.7) and the profit development (Figure 4.6) are upward-sloping when risk factors are kept constant due to annual interest-related income and return on equities. The graph on the right shows that the annual increase of capital is 5% of the annual profit (shown in Figure 4.6) induced by the profit distribution mechanism.

4.3.2 Gold sales

This impulse response mimics a single 10-ton gold sale in year 2. As mentioned before income from gold sales is assumed to go into capital and reserves. The expected change in capital and reserves of a single 10-ton gold sale is the difference between market value and book value. The market

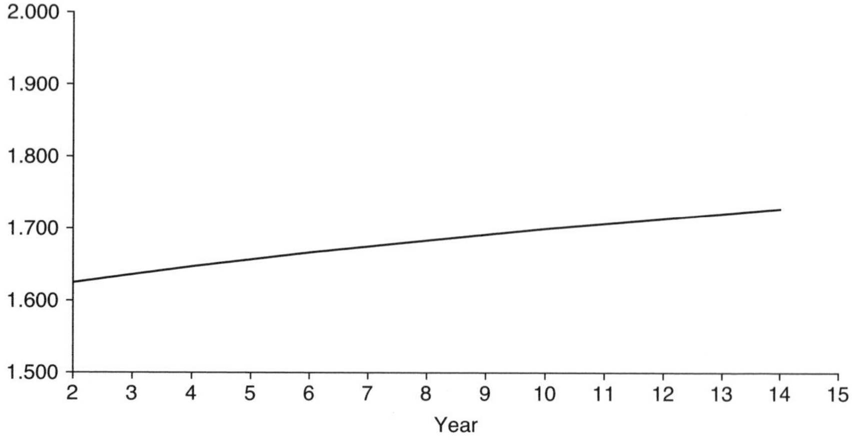

Figure 4.6 Impulse response – P&L (baseline)

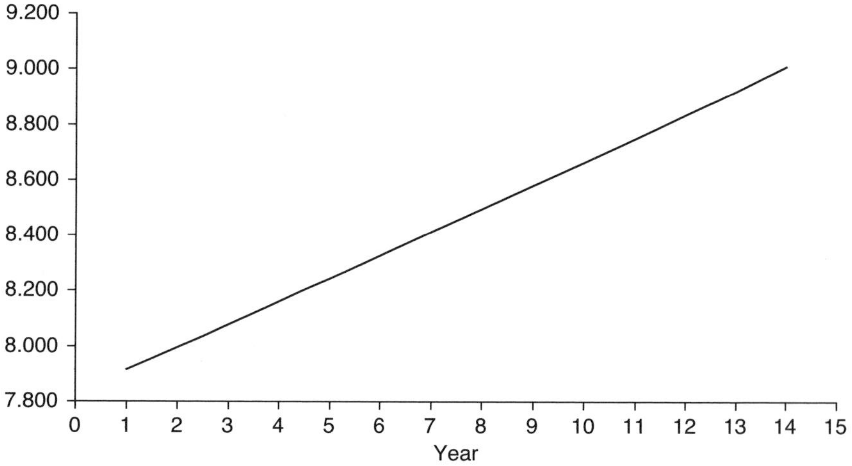

Figure 4.7 Impulse response – capital and reserves (baseline)

value of 10 tons of gold is 192 million and the book value is 18 million. The difference of 175 million will flow into capital. Furthermore, transferring assets from gold into the EUR portfolio has the effect of creating additional interest-related income. The figures below are produced by the model. The additional interest related income is visible in both the capital development (Figure 4.9) and the P&L development (Figure 4.8), and is consistent with the expected effect, i.e. initially a single increase of the capital and reserves

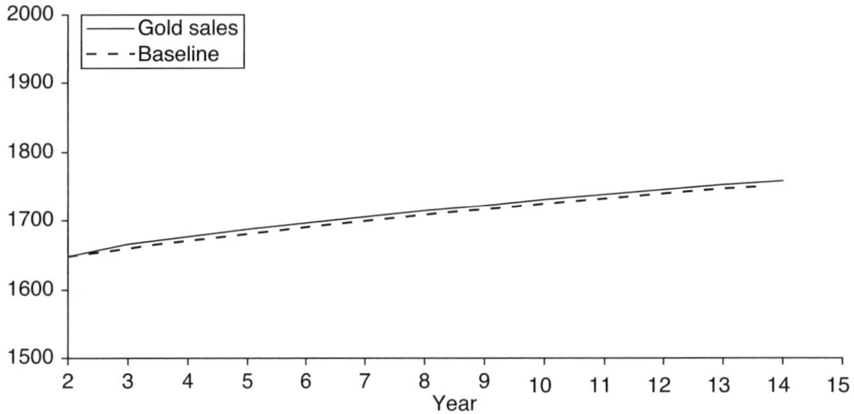

Figure 4.8 Impulse response – P&L (gold sales)

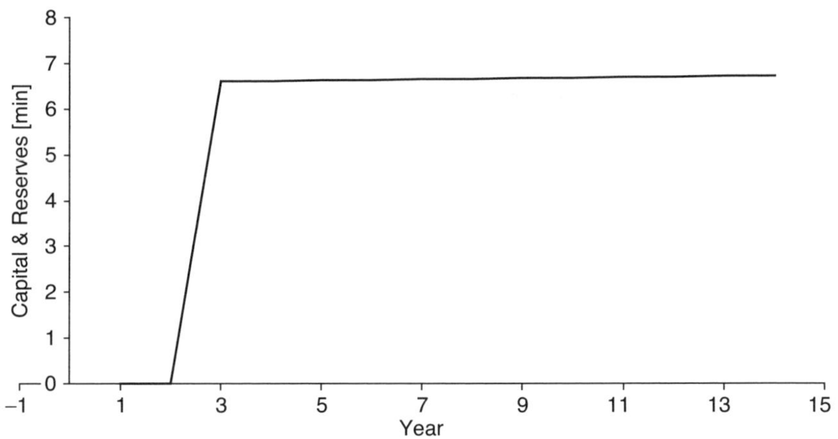

Figure 4.9 Impulse response – capital and reserves (gold sales)

in year 3 followed by a minor additional increase for the remaining years due to the interest-related income.

4.3.3 Fixed-income: EUR and USD portfolios

The impulse strategy here starts with an interest rate of 4.27% for the EUR portfolio (4.58% for the USD portfolio), a 10% increase in interest rate in year 3% to 14.27% for the EUR portfolio (14.58% for the USD portfolio), followed by an equal decrease in year 4 back to 4.27% (4.58% for the USD

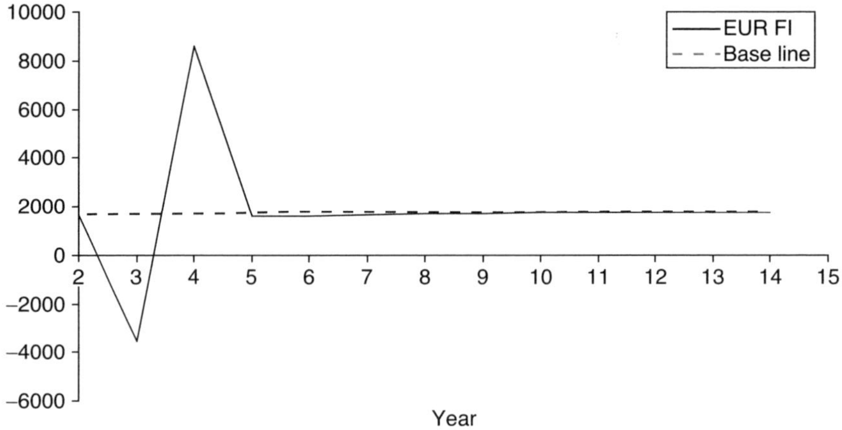

Figure 4.10 Impulse response – P&L (Eurozone interest rate increase)

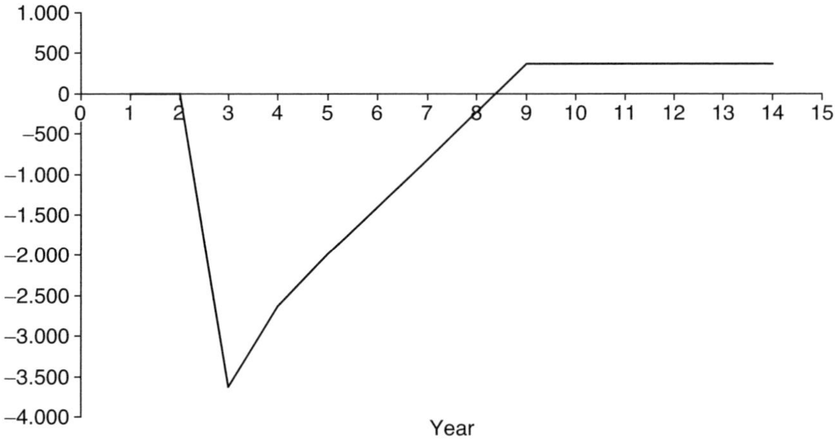

Figure 4.11 Impulse response – capital and reserves (Eurozone interest rate increase)

portfolio). The duration and size are 3.8 and 17 billion for the EUR portfolio and 1.24 and 6.5 billion for the USD portfolio.

Since these portfolios are fixed-income portfolios, an increase in the interest rate has two effects: the market value decreases and interest-related income increases. In year 4 the interest rate returns to its previous level and the market value increases. For the EUR portfolio we expect to endure a bigger loss in market value that can be compensated for by interest related income in year 3. In the figures on the right the P&L for the strategy is compared to the baseline. According to the profit distribution mechanism losses will be fully compensated over a 6-year period.

For the EUR portfolio (Figure 4.10) the P&L becomes negative (a loss). This loss will be fully compensated over a period of six years as a consequence. The surplus after six years can be explained by the difference between 100% loss compensation (income) and 95% dividend payment to the stakeholder (expense). This surplus resembles the 5% of the increase in market value that occurs in year 4 (Figure 4.11). The figures produced by the ALM model consistently describe the expected effects.

The USD portfolio has the same dynamics, but with a less obvious effect. This phenomenon is caused by a shorter duration, the smaller size of the USD portfolio and no need for loss compensation (Figures 4.12 and 4.13).

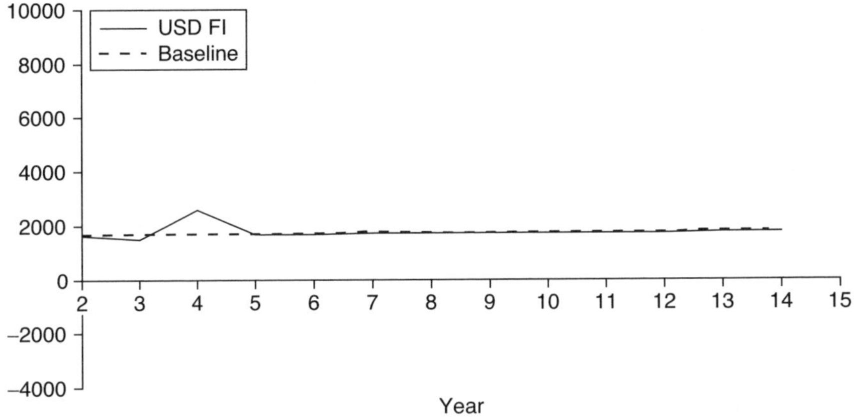

Figure 4.12 Impulse response – P&L (US interest rate increase)

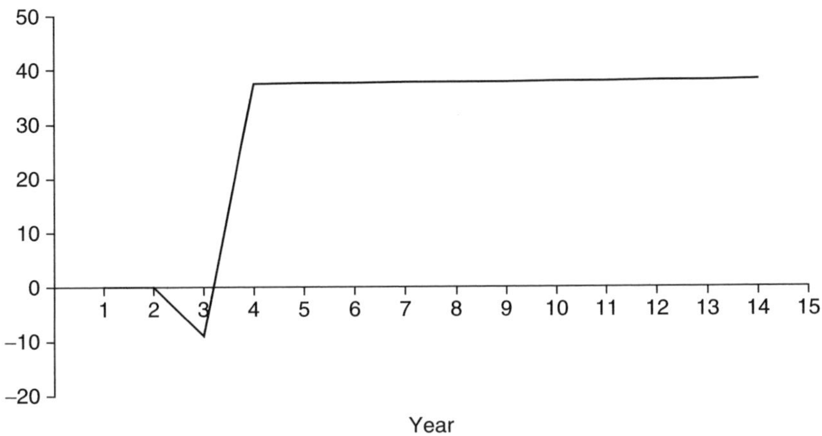

Figure 4.13 Impulse response – capital and reserves (US interest rate increase)

4.3.4 Expansion portfolios of EUR fixed-income and USD fixed-income

The impulse strategy studies the effect of expanding the portfolio by a single fixed amount in year 3. The expansion for the EUR portfolio is EUR 5 billion (a total of EUR 22 billion) and EUR 1 billion (a total of EUR 7.5 billion) for the USD portfolio.

Expanding the portfolios with a fixed amount, while keeping interest rates constant, is expected to result in a proportionally higher interest related income. The expansion of the portfolios is financed by the liquidity deficit. Like the EUR portfolio and the USD portfolio, the liquidity deficit also has an interest related income based on the MRO (main refinancing operations) rate. In this exercise the MRO rate (4%) is lower than the interest rate for both the Eurozone (4.27%) and US region (4.58%). The increase in interest related income will be the difference between the interest rate and the MRO rate for the respective portfolios. When defining the Eurozone (US) term premium as being the difference between the Eurozone (US) interest rate and the MRO, the expected effect is an increase based on this risk premium in the interest related income for both portfolios. Consequently, the profit will increase on the basis of the respective risk premium (Figures 4.14 and 4.15). With the given distribution mechanism and annual rebalancing this results in a linear increase of the capital, which is in fact 5% of the annual profit. The graphs below produced by the model are consistent with this expected effect. For the USD portfolio, matters are complicated by the foreign exchange exposure. Hedging foreign currency risks implies an additional interest rate differential between the Eurozone and US interest rate. Refraining from hedging will save this additional interest rate differential.

In summary, the P&L without hedge will slightly increase due to the minor increase in interest-related income. Including the hedge, the decrease due to the

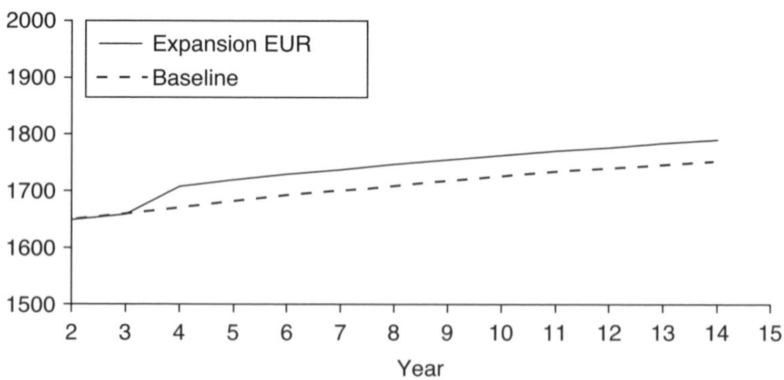

Figure 4.14 Impulse response – P&L (expansion EUR portfolio)

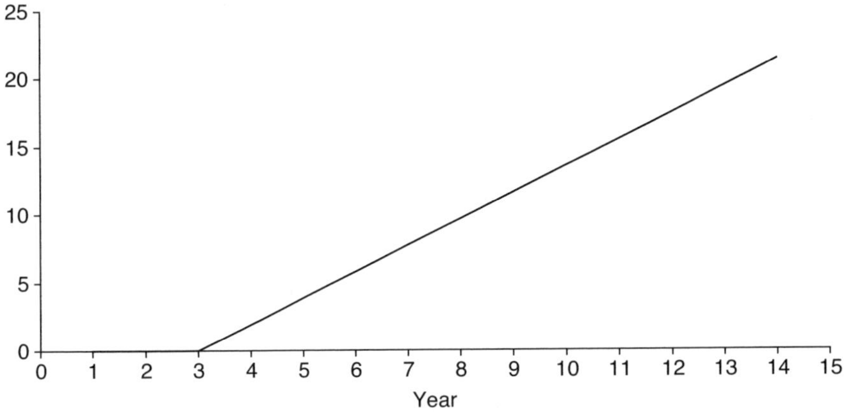

Figure 4.15 Impulse response – capital and reserves (expansion EUR portfolio)

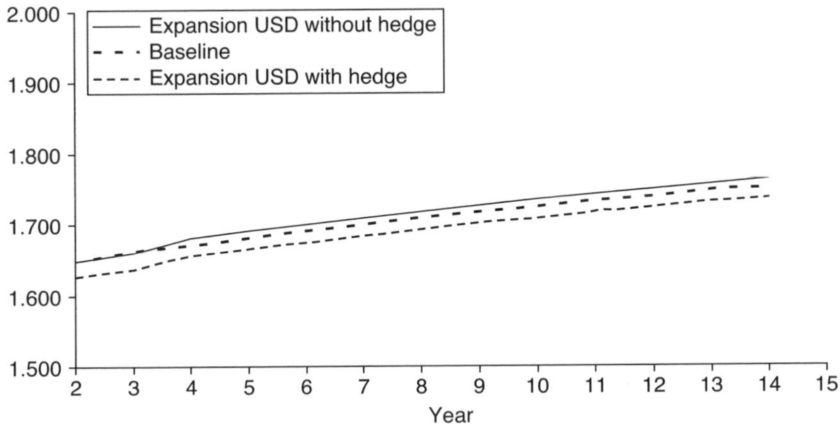

Figure 4.16 Impulse response – P&L (expansion USD portfolio)

interest rate differential will outweigh the increase of interest-related income. The graphs below are in line with the expected outcome (Figure 4.17).

4.3.5 Black Monday

The Black Monday scenario is a stress test, with a one-year 15% decrease of the interest rates and at the same time a 25% reduction in equity market value in year 6. In year 7 the risk factors return to their baseline scenario. Due to interest rate decreases, initially profit rises (Figure 4.18) and, hence, capital rises (Figure 4.19). This profit is due to greater capital gains than the loss in interest related income occurring in year 6. Returning to the baseline scenario in year 7 the profit returns to its original value (Figure 4.19), but

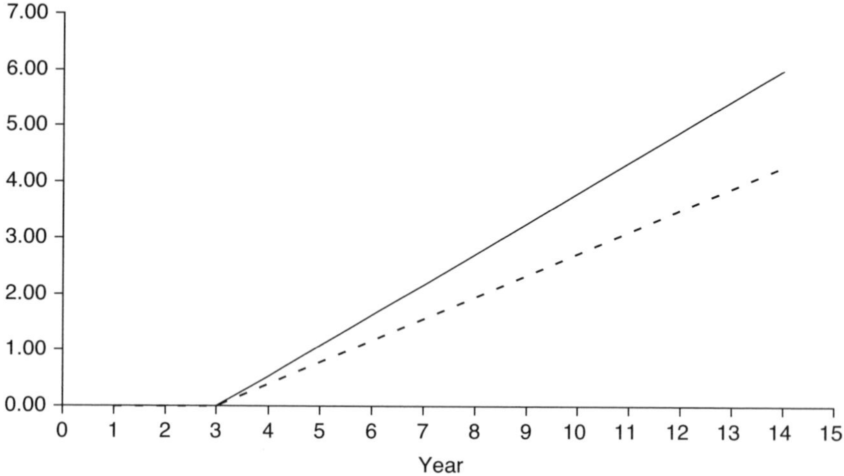

Figure 4.17 Impulse response – capital and reserves (expansion USD portfolio)

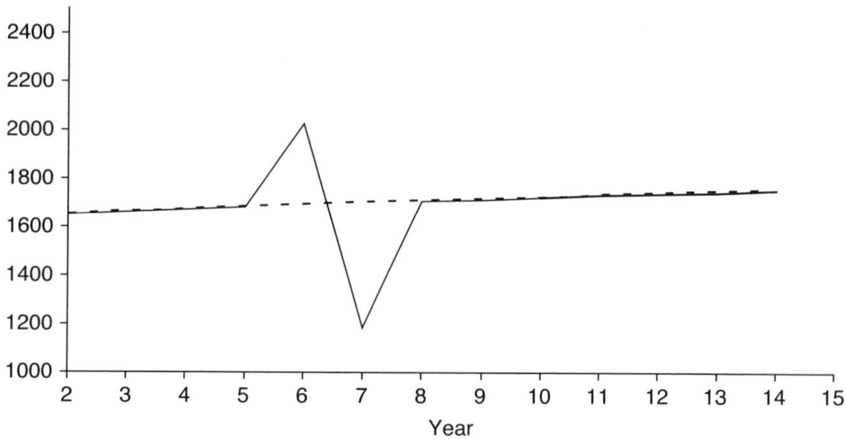

Figure 4.18 Impulse response – P&L (Black Monday)

the capital loss is greater than the increase in interest-related income. Since loss compensation plays no role, this loss in capital will not be compensated and capital will end up at a lower level than the baseline. At the same time, the decrease in equity accelerates the negative effect on capital.

We also tested the ALM model with impulse responses looking at the effect of an increase in rate of return on equities, an equity portfolio expansion, an MRO interest rate rise, and SDR interest rate rise and an increase in the banknotes in circulation. We found all the effects produced by the model consistent with expected outcomes (results not shown).

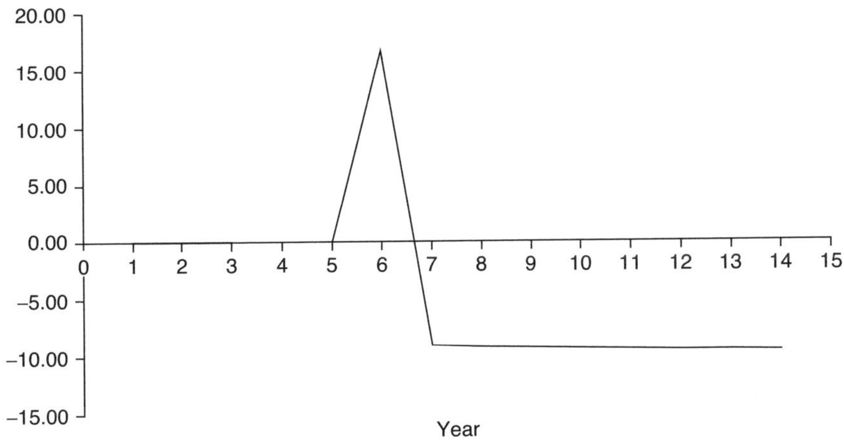

Figure 4.19 Impulse response – capital and reserves (Black Monday)

4.4 Balance sheet review – baseline scenario

In this section we apply the ALM model on the stylized balance sheet shown in the previous section, with starting capital of 4.3 billion. The figure below shows the result of the baseline scenario. In the baseline scenario, banknotes in circulation are assumed constant, no gold is sold and the dollar portfolio, i.e. the exposure to foreign exchange rate risk, is not hedged. Also a profit sharing mechanism and accounting rules are incorporated. The profit sharing and loss compensation mechanism are such that 95% of the profit will go to the stakeholder and losses will not be compensated.

The figure 4.20 shows the capital development over 15 years and represents the baseline scenario, which will serve as the benchmark for the other scenarios. As mentioned before, the median, the 25 best-case and the 25 worst-case scenarios are plotted.

The most striking observation is that the initially upward-sloping median bends downwards after a few years. This implies that in the long-run capital cannot recover from substantial losses due to the high dividend percentage.

The rationale behind this is as follows. High returns are often accompanied with high volatility. High volatility leads to an increase in both gains and losses. Given the current profit distribution mechanism, losses are not compensated. Thus an increase in volatility will result in a decline in capital, i.e. capital erosion, and, consequently, less profit. Therefore, under the given profit distribution mechanism an investment style with low volatility is rewarded, because losses will not be compensated. In other words, a conservative investment style is rewarded.

Furthermore, the 25 worst-case scenarios are not as clustered as the 25 best-case scenarios. The reason for clustering the best-case scenarios is the

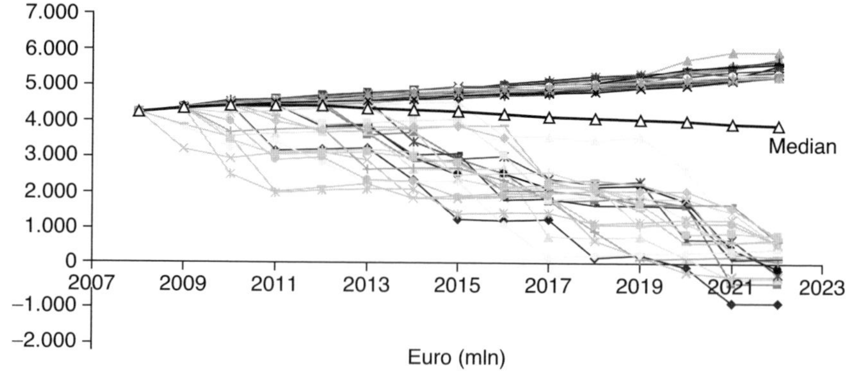

Figure 4.20 Baseline scenario – capital development over 15 years (median, 25 best-case and 25 worst-case scenarios)

Table 4.3 Baseline – useful statistical measures

Statistics	
Measure	**Base line**
Pr{loss}	19.7%
Pr{loss, two years in row}	3.6%
Pr{loss > 1,000}	1.7%
Average growth rate capital	−1.3%
Standard deviation capital	745
Expected profit	691
Standard deviation profit	868

cushioning effect in the case of profit. Only 5% of the profit flows into the capital. For the worst-case scenarios this cushioning effect is absent, i.e. 100% of the loss affects capital. The implemented profit distribution implies that it will be difficult to recover after a loss. In addition, declining capital implies a declining capacity to generate profit, since the size of the total investment portfolio declines. In the long run, capital might even drop below zero. The table above shows some useful statistical measures for interpreting the effect of the ALM study.

The dividend is expected to be approximately EUR 690 million with a volatility of EUR 870 million. Furthermore, the model also provides the VaR and the expected shortfall[5] (ES) of the profit and loss account. Both the VaR and the ES are important parameters to quantify the downside risk and are important input for strategic investment decisions. The value at risk and expected shortfall in this section are given with a confidence interval of

97.5%. The chance of a loss greater than the VaR is 2.5%. In this baseline scenario the VaR is EUR 841 million and the ES is EUR 1.186 billion.

4.5 Balance sheet review – evaluating alternative investment policies

In this section several policy strategies will be analyzed and compared with the baseline scenario. The scenarios we will study are portfolio expansion, hedging foreign exchange exposure, implementing a Hold-to-Maturity portfolio, a longer duration, higher dividend and gold sales.

The capital development over 15 years (median, 25 best-case and 25 worst-case scenarios), and their respective probability distributions are presented. The probability distributions for the different strategies are compared with the probability distribution for the baseline scenarios for both the capital (the graphs on the right) and the P&L account (the graphs on the left). The intuitive outcomes of the different policies will be discussed in light of the probability distributions produced by the ALM model. The probability distributions presented in this section are a representation of all of the 15,000 simulations, a sample of 1000 simulations representing year 2010 and 1000 simulations representing year 2020. The latter two are included to illustrate the dynamics of the distributions throughout the time horizon.

Notably all outcomes are dependent on the balance sheet used as input. This means that different outcomes are possible when another balance sheet is used.

A common feature in all the policy strategies is that the probability distribution for capital tends to be skewed and remains skewed throughout the time horizon. Simultaneously, an increased spread (a volatility measure) is shown by the diverging patterns appearing in the figures for capital development.

4.5.1 Portfolio expansion

In this strategy EUR and USD fixed-income portfolios are simultaneously expanded by a single fixed amount in year 3. The expansion for the EUR portfolio is EUR 2 billion (a total of EUR 15.4 billion) and EUR 1 billion (a total of EUR 6.3 billion) for the USD portfolio.

Expanding portfolios are expected to increase profit due to higher interest-related income (see Section 4.2.2 on expansion portfolios of EUR fixed-income and USD fixed-income). In addition expanding portfolios is also expected to increase the volatility of capital, and hence capital erosion. The latter becomes apparent from the graph given below (Figure 4.21). The median is even more downward-sloping compared to the baseline scenario. Second, the spread increases to EUR 883 million, i.e. the graph is more divergent compared to the baseline. However, the probability of losses and consecutive losses remain almost unchanged (Table 4.4). On the other hand, the probability of losses greater than 1 billion increases.

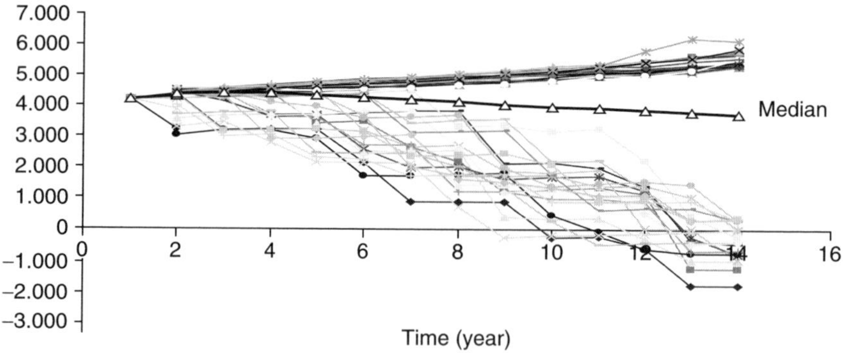

Figure 4.21 Expansion portfolios – capital development (median, 25 best-case and 25 worst-case scenarios)

Table 4.4 Expansion portfolios – useful statistical measures

Statistics		
Measure	**Base Line**	**Expansion**
Pr{loss}	19.7%	19.9%
Pr{loss, two years in row}	3.6%	3.6%
Pr{loss > 1,000}	1.7%	2.7%
Average growth rate capital	–1.3%	–2.0%
Standard deviation capital	745	883
Expected profit	691	773
Standard deviation profit	868	969

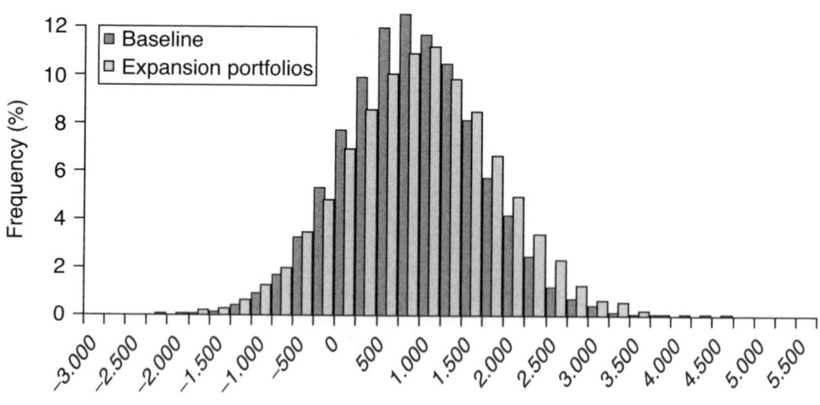

Figure 4.22 Expansion portfolios – P&L probability distribution (representation of all 15,000 simulations) in EUR million

The profit distributions (Figures 4.22 and 4.24) show a shift to the right, mimicking increased profit. Even though the overall profit distribution representing all the 15,000 simulations (Figure 4.22) shows a shift to the right, the profit distribution representing the 1000 simulations for year 2020 shows a significant shift to the left (Figure 4.27). This indicates that, conditionally on the given balance sheet and on the given profit distribution mechanism (losses are not compensated), the long run profit reduces when portfolios are expanded. This may be explained by the increased volatility in the capital distribution (Figures 4.23, 4.25 and 4.27), which leads to capital erosion. The downside risk represented by the VaR and ES increases to EUR 998 million and EUR 1.431

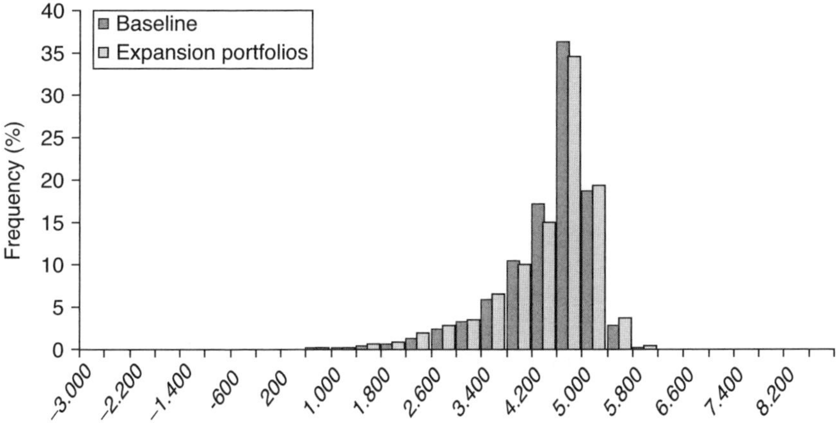

Figure 4.23 Expansion portfolios – capital and reserves probability distribution (representation of all 15,000 simulations) in EUR million

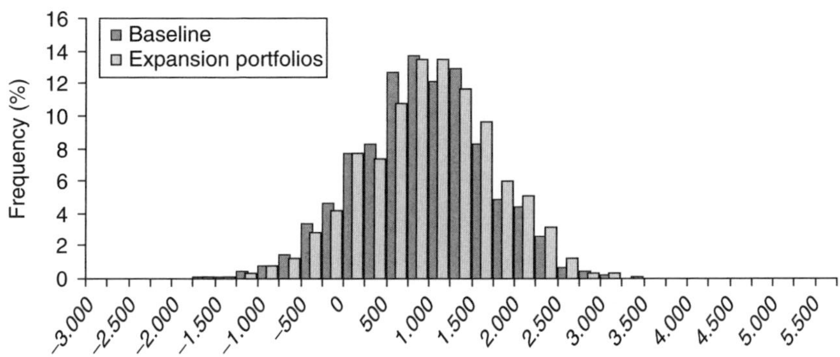

Figure 4.24 Expansion portfolios – P&L probability distribution (sample of 1000 simulations representing year 2010) in EUR million

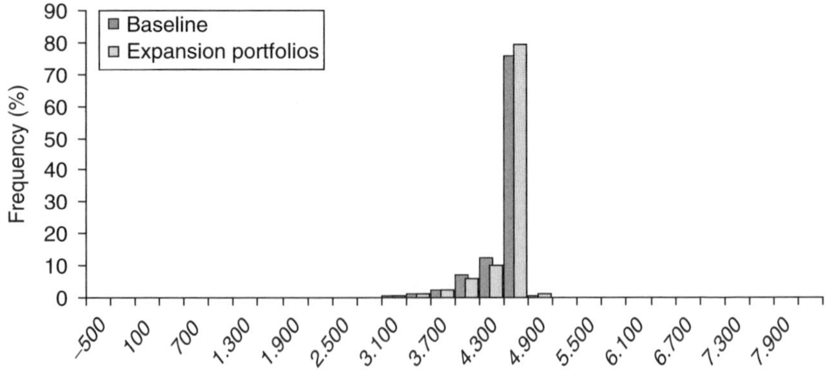

Figure 4.25 Expansion portfolios – capital and reserves probability distribution (sample of 1000 simulations representing year 2010) in EUR million

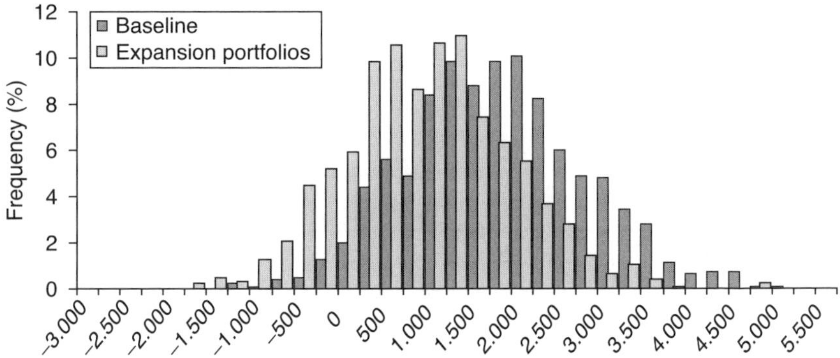

Figure 4.26 Expansion portfolios – P&L probability distribution (sample of 1000 simulations representing year 2020) in EUR million

billion, respectively. Both the increased profit and the decreased capital may be anticipated intuitively. The pattern of the profit and capital behavior can be explained by the profitability and the volatility, wherein profitability dominates in the short run and volatility dominates on the long run. The clustering of the best-cases and absence of this clustering in the worst cases is also confirmed by the skewness of the probability distributions for capital.

4.5.2 Hedging exposure to currency risk of the USD fixed-income portfolio

In this strategy the foreign exchange exposure of the USD fixed-income portfolio is hedged, with the costs of hedging being taken into account. Hedging currency risk is expected to lower volatility (spread). The graph

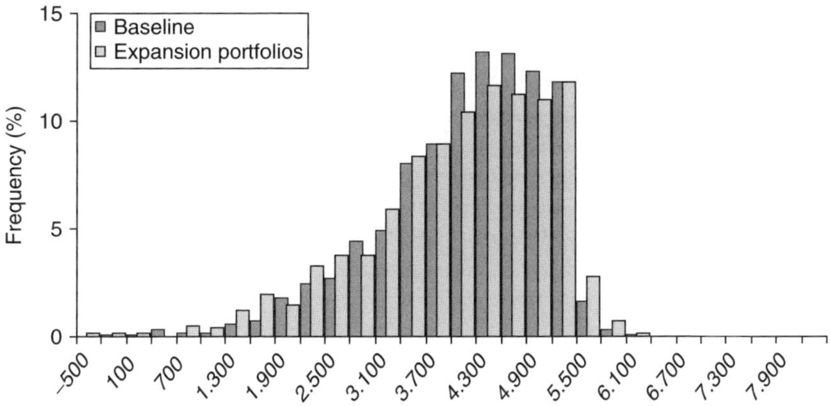

Figure 4.27 Expansion portfolios – capital and reserves probability distribution (sample of 1000 simulations representing year 2020) in EUR million

in Figure 4.28 shows an upward-sloping median, but tends to bend downwards (the median of the base scenario showed a downward-sloping trend). Furthermore, the graph is less divergent, and the spread decreases to 372 million, reducing the downside risk as a consequence. This is in line with the observation that reduced spread leads to increased profit and therefore increased capital. However, the increase in profit is not so obvious. Also the probabilities of losses and consecutive losses decrease appreciably (see Table 4.5).

Lower spread and increased profit are also confirmed by the respective probability distributions. The P&L graph (Figure 4.29) shows a slight shift to the right, mimicking increased profit as mentioned before. In addition, downside risk decreases, since the spread of the capital distribution reduces. Moreover the shift to the right of the capital distribution means less erosion of capital. In this case, the VaR decreases to 388 million and the ES decreases to 700 million. Both the increased profit and the increased capital may be anticipated intuitively, which is confirmed by the model. The clustering of the best-case scenarios and absence of this clustering in the worst-case scenarios are also confirmed by the skewness of the probability distributions for capital.

4.5.3 Implementing a Hold-to-Maturity portfolio

In this strategy a Hold-to-Maturity (HTM) portfolio with a 4-year duration is implemented. The size of the portfolio is EUR 4 billion and financed through the liquidity shortage. Note that the size of the other portfolios remains unchanged. HTM portfolios may be implemented to reduce volatility. The impact of implementing a HTM portfolio seems to result in a median remaining at a constant level (the baseline had a downward-sloping trend). Second, spread decreases to EUR 562 million; the graph

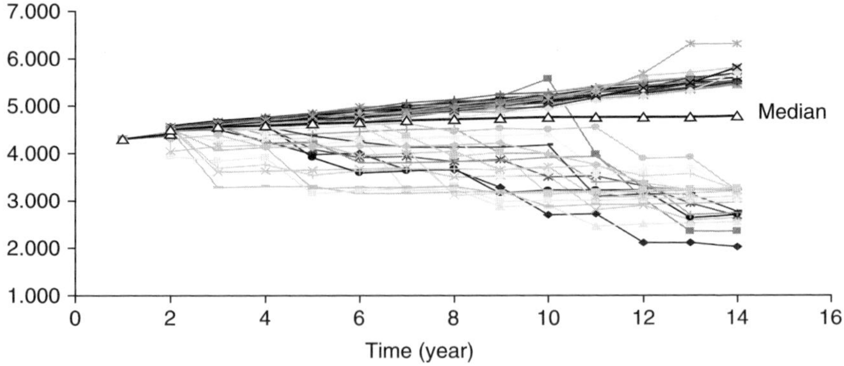

Figure 4.28 Hedging USD FI portfolio – capital development (median, 25 best-case and 25 worst-case scenarios) in EUR million

Table 4.5 Hedging USD FI portfolio – useful statistical measures

Statistics		
Measure	**Base Line**	**Hedge**
Pr{loss}	19.7%	9.9%
Pr{loss, two years in row}	3.6%	0.8%
Pr{loss > 1,000}	1.7%	0.1%
Average growth rate capital	–1.3%	2.2%
Standard deviation capital	745	372
Expected profit	691	862
Standard deviation profit	868	764

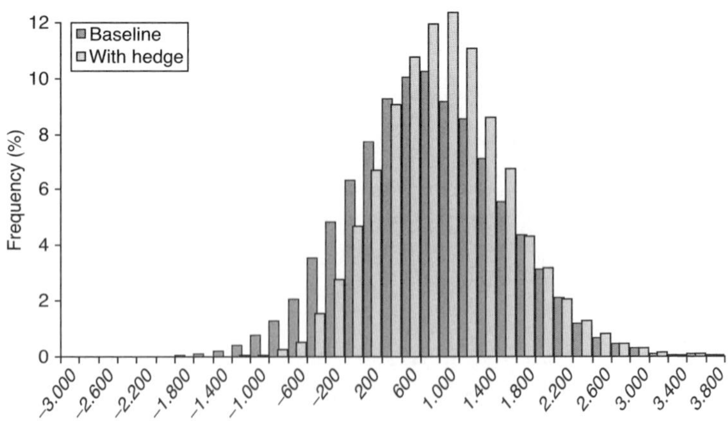

Figure 4.29 Hedging USD FI portfolio – P&L probability distribution (representation of all the 15,000 simulations) in EUR million

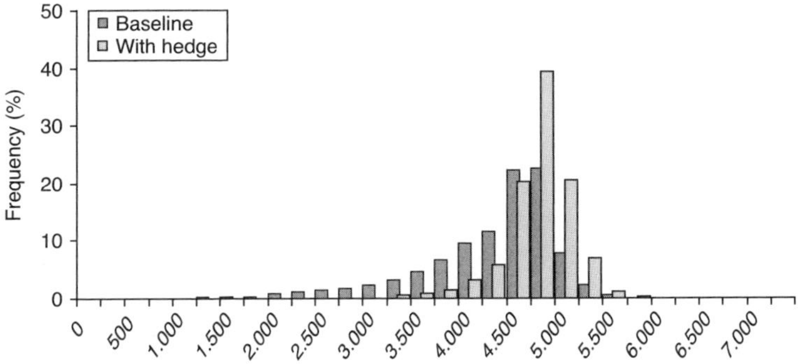

Figure 4.30 Hedging USD FI portfolio – capital and reserves probability distribution (representation of all the 15,000 simulations) in EUR million

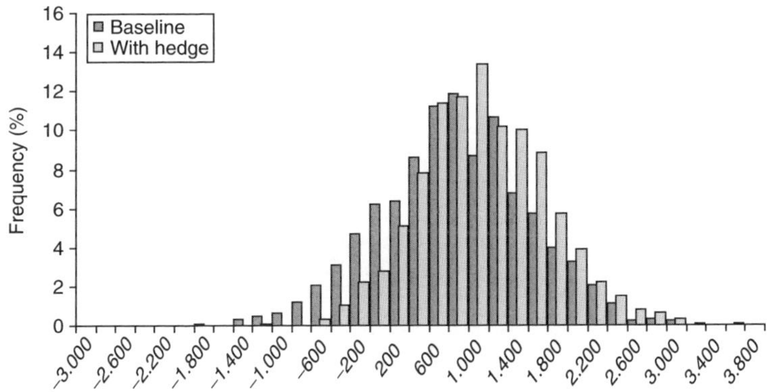

Figure 4.31 Hedging USD FI portfolio – P&L probability distribution (sample of 1000 simulations representing year 2010) in EUR million

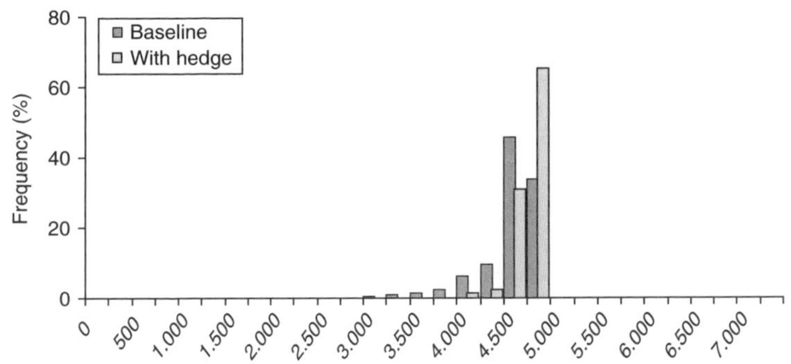

Figure 4.32 Hedging USD FI portfolio – capital and reserves probability distribution (sample of 1000 simulations representing year 2010) in EUR million

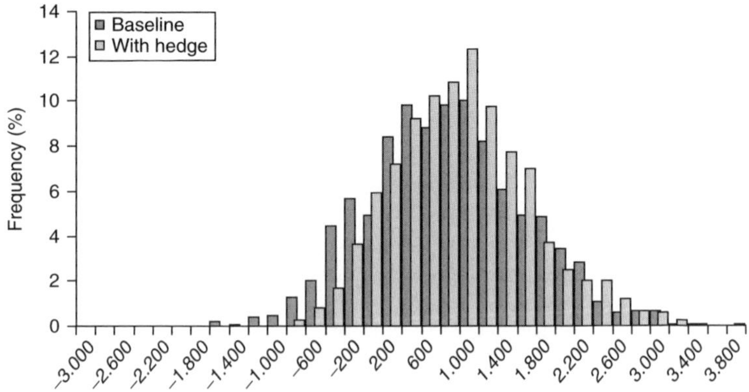

Figure 4.33 Hedging USD FI portfolio – P&L probability distribution (sample of 1000 simulations representing year 2020) in EUR million

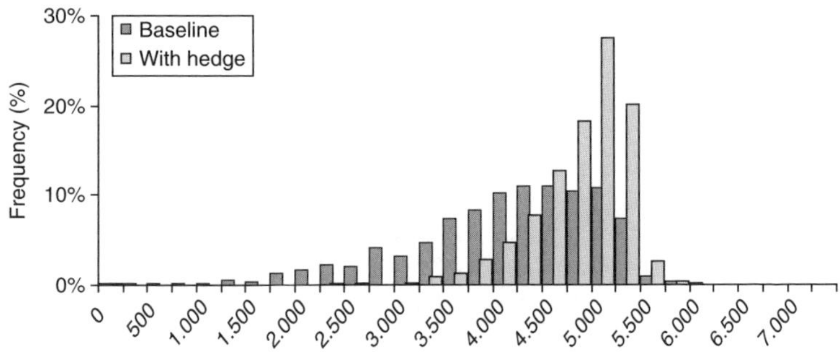

Figure 4.34 Hedging USD FI portfolio – capital and reserves probability distribution (sample of 1000 simulations representing year 2020) in EUR million

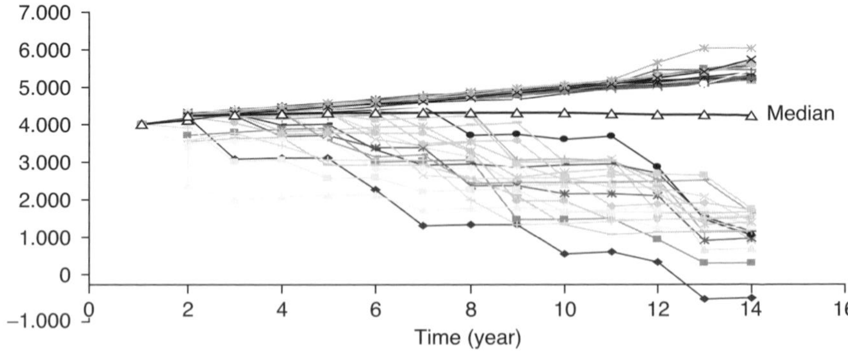

Figure 4.35 HTM portfolio – capital development (median, 25 best-case and 25 worst-case scenarios) in EUR million

Table 4.6 HTM portfolio – useful statistical measures

Statistics		
Measure	**Base Line**	**HTM**
Pr{loss}	19.7%	13.2%
Pr{loss, two years in row}	3.6%	1.8%
Pr{loss > 1,000}	1.7%	0.7%
Average growth rate capital	–1.3%	–0.1%
Standard deviation capital	745	562
Expected profit	691	856
Standard deviation profit	868	832

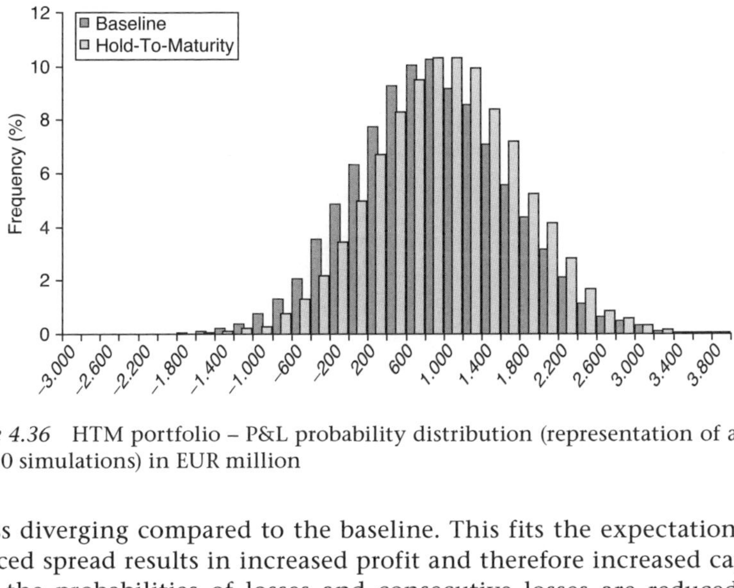

Figure 4.36 HTM portfolio – P&L probability distribution (representation of all the 15,000 simulations) in EUR million

is less diverging compared to the baseline. This fits the expectation that reduced spread results in increased profit and therefore increased capital. Also the probabilities of losses and consecutive losses are reduced (see Table 4.6).

Lower spread and increased profit are also confirmed by the respective probability distributions. The P&L graph (Figure 4.36) shows a slight shift to the right, mimicking increased profit. Moreover, the shift to the right of the capital distribution means reduced erosion of capital. In this case, the VaR decreases to EUR 624 million and the ES decreases to EUR 966 million. Both the increased profit and the increased capital may be anticipated intuitively, which is confirmed by the model. The clustering of the best-case scenarios and absence of this clustering in the worst-case scenarios are confirmed by the skewness of probability distributions for capital.

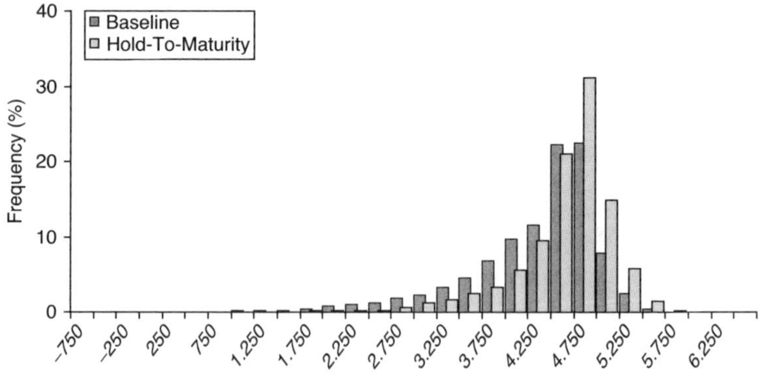

Figure 4.37 HTM portfolio – capital and reserves probability distribution (representation of all the 15,000 simulations) in EUR million

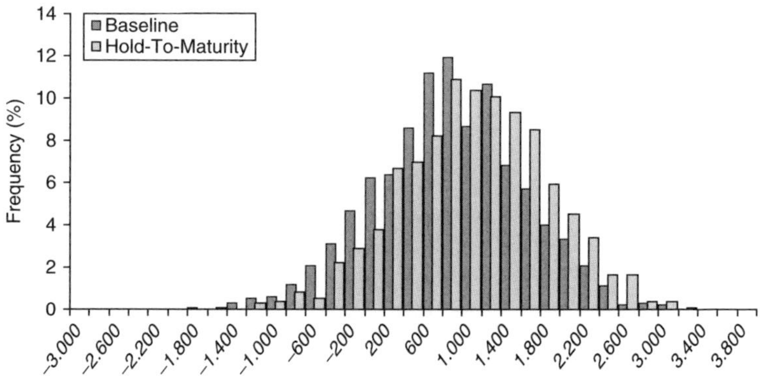

Figure 4.38 HTM portfolio – P&L probability distribution (sample of 1000 simulations representing year 2010) in EUR million

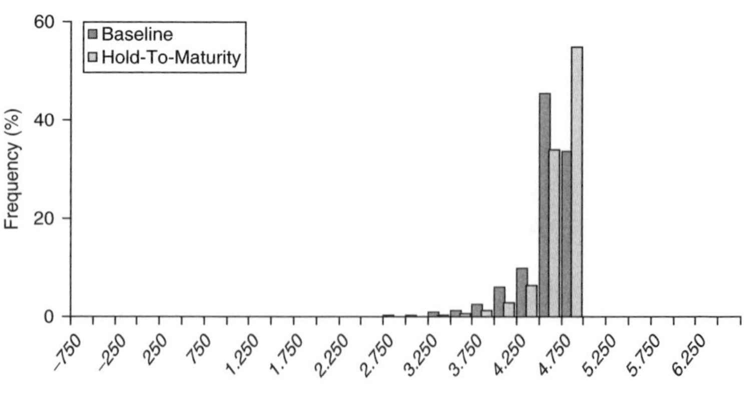

Figure 4.39 HTM portfolio – capital and reserves probability distribution (sample of 1000 simulations representing year 2010) in EUR million

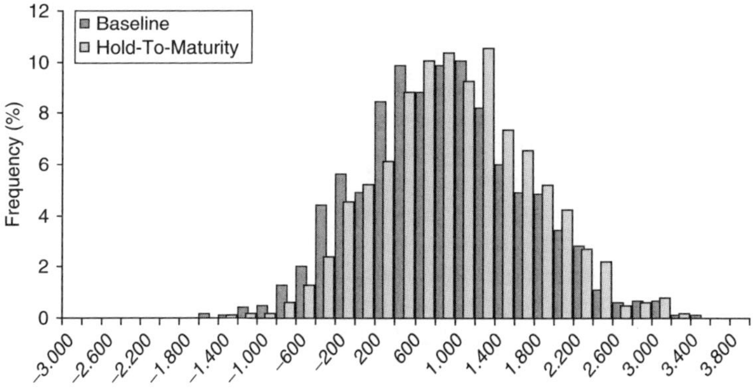

Figure 4.40 HTM portfolio – P&L probability distribution (sample of 1000 simulations representing year 2020) in EUR million

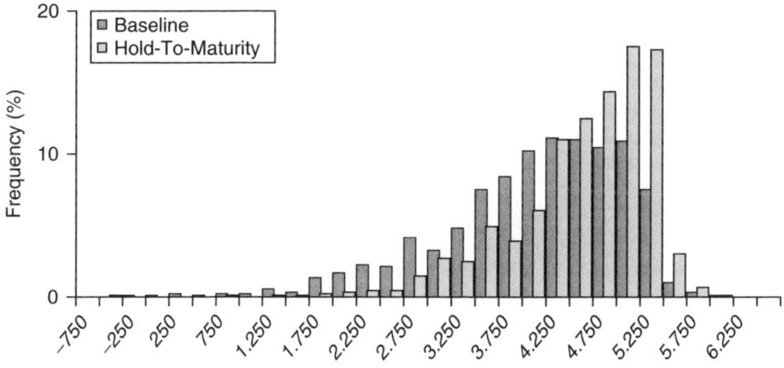

Figure 4.41 HTM portfolio – capital and reserves probability distribution (sample of 1000 simulations representing year 2020) in EUR million

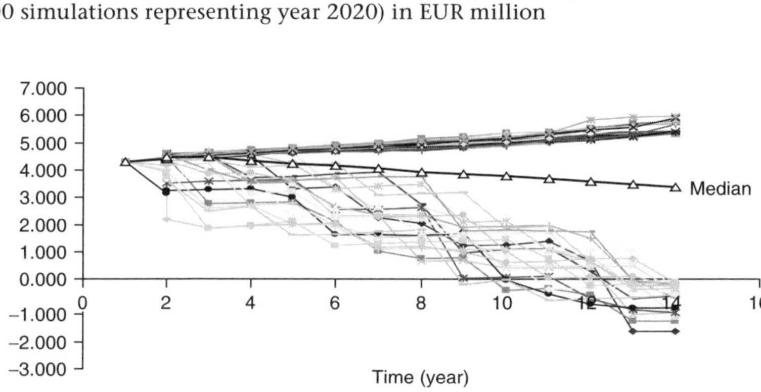

Figure 4.42 Increasing durations – capital development (median, 25 best-case and 25 worst-case scenarios) in EUR million

4.5.4 Higher duration fixed-income portfolios

In this strategy a fixed-income portfolio is implemented with higher durations for both EUR and USD portfolios. Note that the size of the other portfolios remains unchanged. Increasing the duration of fixed-income portfolios by one year can be a strategy to obtain a stronger balance position, because of better risk-return characteristics which may increase profit. Increased duration of the portfolios has the opposite effect on the trend of the median, i.e. the median is yet more downward-sloping. Even so, while increasing the spread, higher durations indeed increase profit. Profit increases slightly and spread seems to increase to 944 million. This is also visible in the graph below, which diverges more than the baseline. Moreover, the probabilities of losses and consecutive losses increase (see Table 4.7).

Increased spread and profit are also confirmed by the respective probability distributions. The P&L graph (Figure 4.43) shows a slight shift to

Table 4.7 Increasing durations – useful statistical measures

Statistics		
Measure	**Base Line**	**Duration**
Pr{loss}	19.7%	23.0%
Pr{loss, two years in row}	3.6%	3.8%
Pr{loss > 1,000}	1.7%	3.8%
Average growth rate capital	−1.3%	−2.0%
Standard deviation capital	745	944
Expected profit	691	704
Standard deviation profit	868	1007

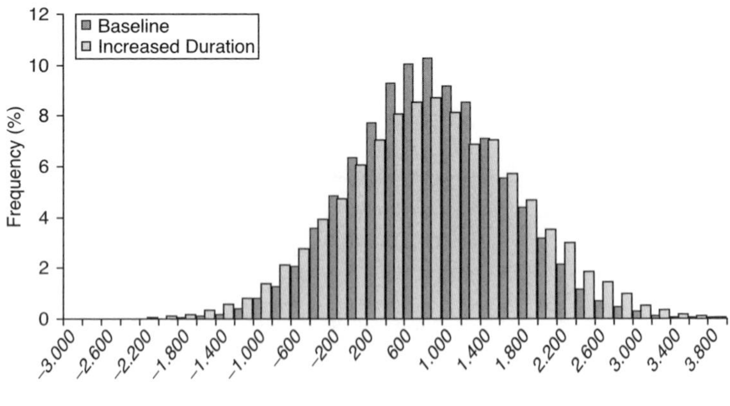

Figure 4.43 Increasing durations – P&L probability distribution (representation of all the 15,000 simulations) in EUR million

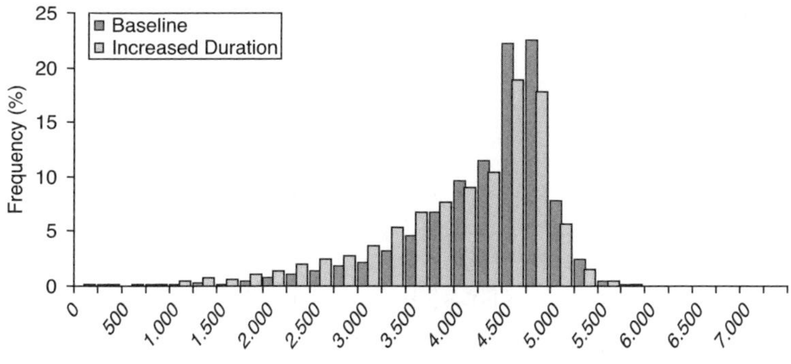

Figure 4.44 Increasing durations – capital and reserves probability distribution (representation of all the 15,000 simulations) in EUR million

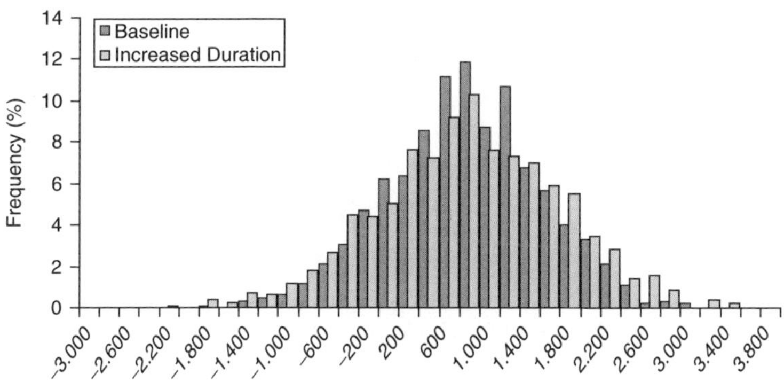

Figure 4.45 Increasing durations – P&L probability distribution (sample of 1000 simulations representing year 2010) in EUR million

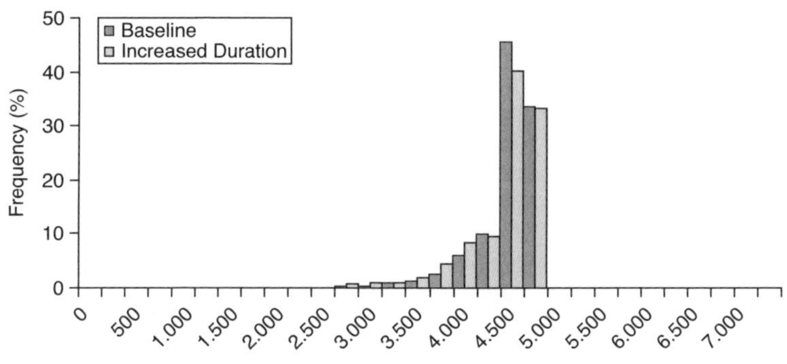

Figure 4.46 Increasing durations – capital and reserves probability distribution (sample of 1000 simulations representing year 2010) in EUR million

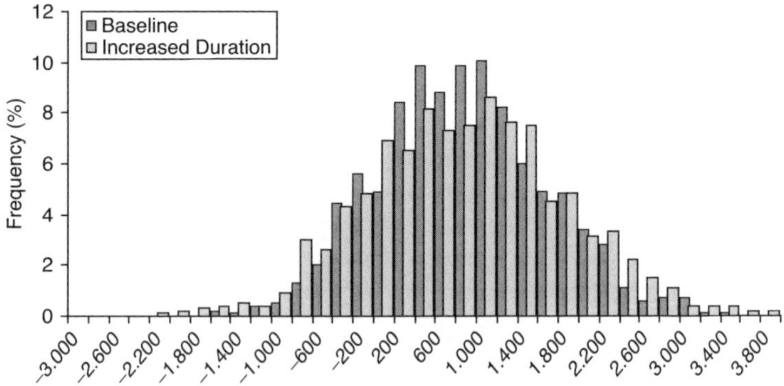

Figure 4.47 Increasing durations – P&L probability distribution (sample of 1000 simulations representing year 2020) in EUR million

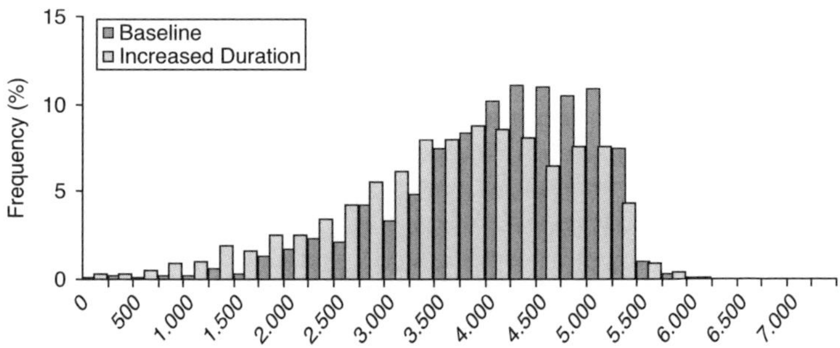

Figure 4.48 Increasing durations – capital and reserves probability distribution (sample of 1000 simulations representing year 2020) in EUR million

the right, mimicking increased profit. The increased spread shows a shift to the left of the capital distribution, since increased spread leads to erosion of capital. In this case the VaR increases to EUR 1.136 billion and the ES increases to EUR 1.466 billion. Both the increased profit and the increased spread may be anticipated intuitively, which is confirmed by the model. The clustering of the best-case scenarios and absence of this clustering in the worst-case scenarios are also confirmed by the skewness of probability distributions for capital.

4.5.5 Gold sales

In this strategy 65 tons of gold is sold over a four-year period. Selling gold is expected to increase capital, since in this study it is assumed that income from gold sales flows directly into the capital. Selling gold leads to a diverging pattern of capital development, spread increases to EUR 1.093 billion. The noticeable increase in the spread of the capital (see Figure 4.49) is due

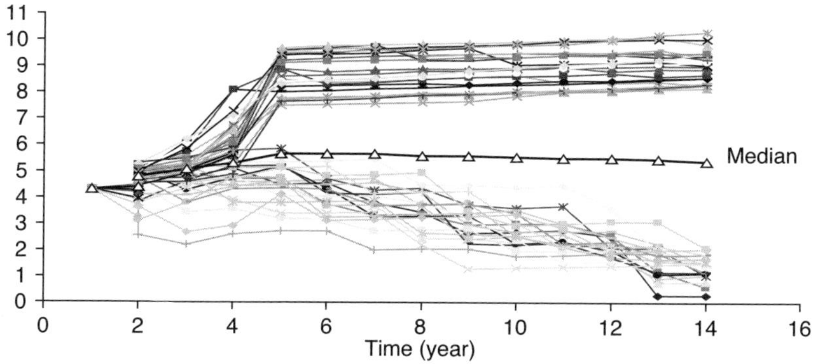

Figure 4.49 Gold sales – capital development (median, 25 best-case and 25 worst-case scenarios) in EUR million

Table 4.8 Gold sales – useful statistical measures

Statistics		
Measure	**Base Line**	**Goldsales**
Pr{loss}	19.7%	18.7%
Pr{loss, two years in row}	3.6%	3.3%
Pr{loss > 1,000}	1.7%	1.6%
Average growth rate capital	–1.3%	1.6%
Standard deviation capital	745	1093
Expected profit	691	732
Standard deviation profit	868	881

to gold sales. The spread of capital reflects the volatility in gold prices (stochastic). Some scenarios yield extremely high and others extremely low returns of these gold prices and, therefore, extremely high and extremely low market values of gold. Selling gold affects the capital, since income from the gold sales flows into the capital. Not selling gold means unrealized gains flowing into the revaluation account and thus not affecting the capital. This is the case in the baseline scenario.

The median is upward-sloping when gold is sold, but the trend bends downward when gold sales end. The effect of selling gold seems to be postponement of the capital decrease. The probabilities of losses and consecutive losses decrease (see Table 4.8).

Increased spread and profit are also confirmed by the respective probability distributions. The P&L graph (Figure 4.47) shows a slight shift to the right, mimicking increased profit. The capital distribution has a distinct shift to the right. This effect of shift in capital is obvious, since income

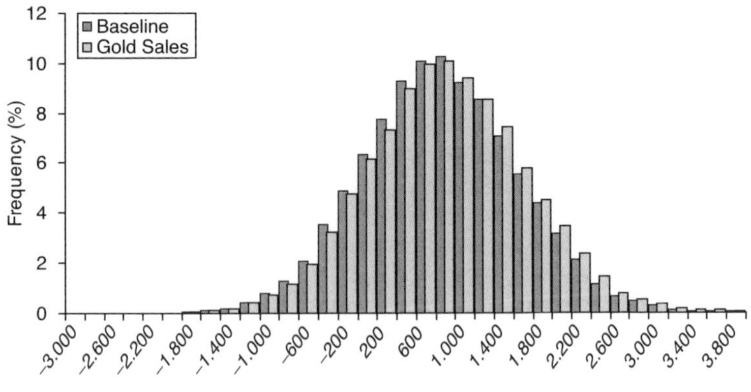

Figure 4.50 Gold sales – P&L probability distribution (representation of all the 15,000 simulations) in EUR million

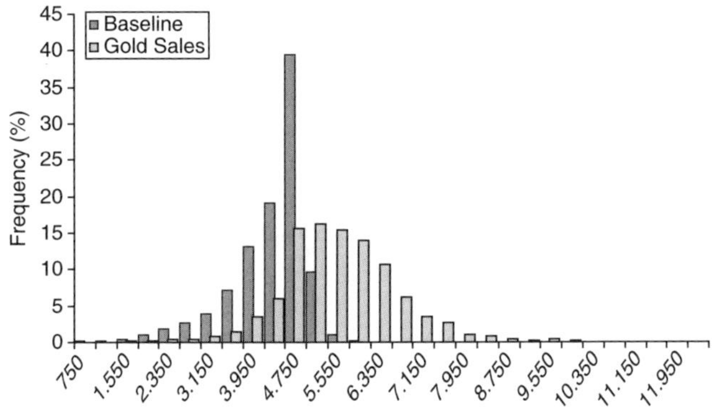

Figure 4.51 Gold sales – capital and reserves probability distribution (representation of all the 15,000 simulations) in EUR million

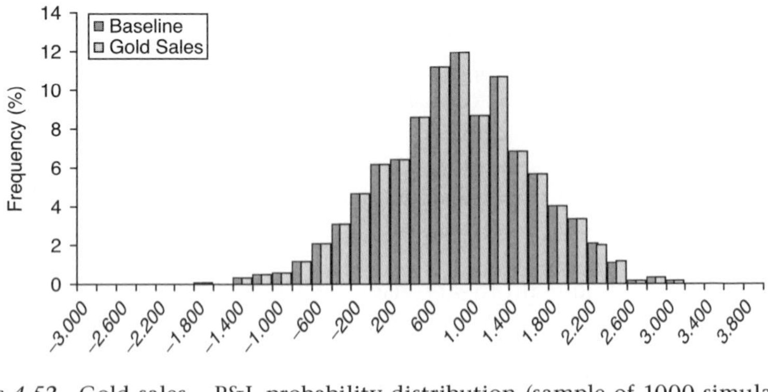

Figure 4.52 Gold sales – P&L probability distribution (sample of 1000 simulations representing year 2010) in EUR million

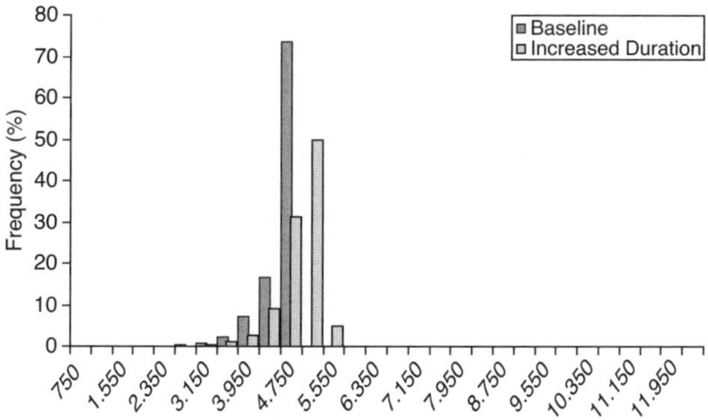

Figure 4.53 Gold sales – capital and reserves probability distribution (sample of 1000 simulations representing year 2010) in EUR million

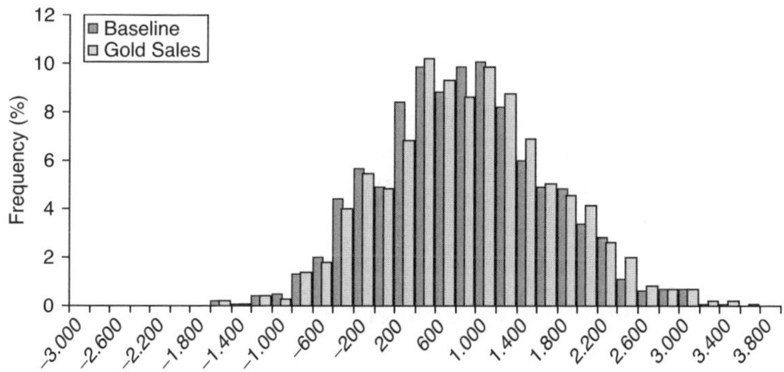

Figure 4.54 Gold sales – P&L probability distribution (sample of 1000 simulations representing year 2020) in EUR million

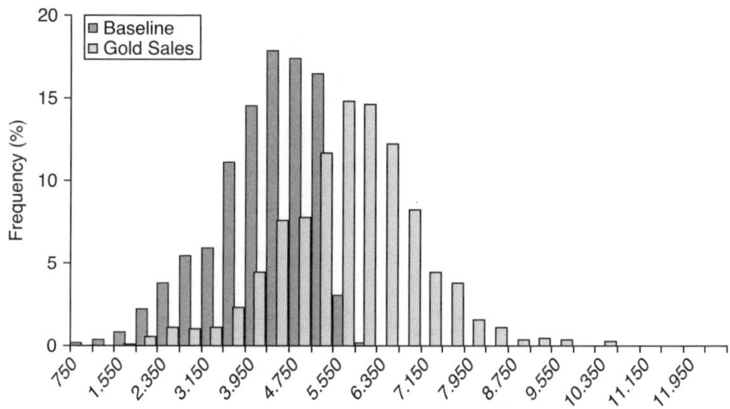

Figure 4.55 Gold sales – capital and reserves probability distribution (sample of 1000 simulations representing year 2020) in EUR million

from gold sales is assumed to flow directly into the capital. In this case, the VaR decreases slightly to EUR 812 million and the ES remains the same (EUR 1.184 billion). Both the increased profit and the increased spread may be anticipated intuitively, which is confirmed by the model. The clustering of the best-cases and absence of this clustering in the worst-cases are confirmed by the skewness of probability distributions for capital.

4.6 Conclusion

DNB's ALM model is built in such a way that it can be customized to address specific issues of the individual institution. This flexibility enables the user to implement different institutional arrangements, such as accounting rules, rebalancing rules and dividend policy. All these arrangements can easily be adjusted in the input sheet. Furthermore, it is possible to model different investment strategies, such as hedging foreign exchange risk, expanding the portfolios selling gold and converting trading portfolios to HTM portfolios. Moreover, it is possible to look at the benefit of adding asset classes in terms of profitability and volatility.

Feeding deterministic or stochastic scenarios into the model yields specific information that will be stored in the output module, which will then serve as a source for deriving meaningful statistics to support investment decisions or decisions on the institutional design. To understand in greater detail a book entry change in the balance sheet, it is important to have a transparent model. This means that the model allows one to track the effect of the strategy not only on the aggregated level, but also on the level of every single book entry. This makes it possible to unravel the complex interactions of the balance sheet and to prevent the drawbacks of a black box model. To be able to support either a policy or investment decision and also to validate the model it is important to understand the factors driving the resulting output of the ALM model (impulse response functions). A look at the median will give an idea of the trend that follows from that particular decision.

However, to quantify the effects of the decision in terms of significance it is helpful to have statistical output measures at one's disposal. For this reason, we created a statistical analysis module that calculates relevant statistical measures for capital and dividend development. For our purpose, we currently concentrate on the mean, median, standard deviation, VaR, ES, probability of loss in a given year, probability of loss in two years in row and the probability of losing more than a certain amount. Sometimes, it is the entire P&L distribution and/or the entire capital distribution which is relevant for the decision at hand. The advantages of this statistical module are its easy customizability and its ability to produce any given statistical output measure one might require.

An assets & liabilities simulation technique, if used correctly, can be a powerful tool. It is important to interpret the results with the following caveats in mind. First of all, the ALM model only focuses on the long-term exposure to market risks. Risks like credit risk or any other risks which follow from DNB's responsibility as banking supervisor are not taken into account. For example, in the case of the implementation of an HTM portfolio, the slightly upward-sloping trend of the median could easily tip over to a negative trend if credit risk is also in play, as is clearly the case in today's market.

Second, the current financial turmoil also points out the importance of keeping the economic dataset up to date. Otherwise, the results will not reflect current economic reality. Constructing good quality simulations of economic variables is specialized and time consuming work. In order to focus our attention on central bank ALM issues, we therefore acquired economic scenarios from a professional provider of simulation models.

Finally, it is important to understand that an ALM model is not a prediction tool, but only calculates the probability distributions of future outcomes. It only defines the change required for a possible outcome to happen to the whole population.

Notes

1. A previous ALM study done in 2003 is outlined in the working paper "How ALM techniques can help Central Banks" by Hoorn, H.H.J. van der and L. Zwikker, (2005).
2. We used the scenarios from the Economic Scenario Generator (ESG) of ORTEC Finance bv .
3. The Nelson and Siegel model: $r(t) = \beta_0 + (\beta_1 + \beta_2)\left[1 - e^{-t/\tau} \big/ {-t/\tau}\right] - \beta_2 e^{-t/\tau}$, where t is the maturity and $r(t)$ is the zero yield to maturity.
4. A Monte Carlo simulation is a computational algorithm that relies on repeated random sampling and aggregates the results of the individual computations into the final result. In finance Monte Carlo methods are used to quantify the various sources of uncertainty. One advantage of the Monte Carlo method over other techniques is that its solution stays tractable even for multi-dimentional problems, provided that there is sufficient computer power. Another advantage of the Monte Carlo technique is that problems can be modeled in a flexible and realistic way.
5. The Value at Risk (VaR) in this study includes all effects resulting from policy rules, investment rules and accounting rules. The Expected Shortfall (ES) represents the probability distribution of a loss exceeding VaR.

References

Boender, C.G.E., C. Dert, F. Heemskerk and H. Hoek (2007) "A Scenario Approach of ALM", in Mulvey and Ziemba (eds) *Handbook on Worldwide Asset Liabilities Management, part II.[Mulvey and Ziemba's initials? Publication info for the book?]*

Nelson, C.R. and A.F. Siegel (1987) "Parsimonious Modelling of Yield Curves", *The Journal of Business*, 60, 473–489.

Hoorn, H.H.J. van der and L. Zwikker (2005) "How ALM Techniques Can Help Central Banks", Working paper.

5
Combating Intervention Risk

Stephen John Fisher

5.1 Introduction

Central Banks (CB) hold foreign reserves to intervene in the currency market. The trigger for currency intervention depends on many factors that cannot be predicted – trade flows, domestic shocks, foreign shocks, speculative attacks and financial crises, as well as the monetary and fiscal policies of domestic and foreign governments. 'Intervention risk' – the sudden need to buy or sell foreign exchange to defend the currency – is the major risk facing a CB's reserve holdings.

This chapter examines intervention risk and the financial tools that can be employed to combat it. Specifically, the chapter focuses on the interaction between intervention risk on the one hand and the investment risks contained in a CB's reserves portfolio. The major finding of the chapter is that intervention risk can be effectively managed, and even diversified away, by careful asset choice. Intervention is just another asset (or liability) in a CB's portfolio that has its own return and risk characteristics. Asset allocation and benchmark selection are key to combating intervention risk.

The intervention and investment model presented in this chapter can be used to help answer many of the burning questions confronting a Central Banker. Common questions include the following:

1. How large should our reserves be?
2. How actively can we intervene in currency markets?
3. What is the risk of insolvency and how likely are we to call in the IMF?
4. How should our reserves be invested?
5. How often do we need to revise our benchmark?
6. Should rich Central Banks approach investments differently from poor Central Banks?

It turns out that all these questions are related. The level of reserves is the fundamental state variable determining a Central Bank's ability to intervene.

Managing this level of reserves can be achieved through several channels. The traditional channel is by directly buying or selling foreign currency in the market. The problem with this channel is that while the supply of domestic currency to buy foreign currency is unlimited, the supply of foreign reserves to buy domestic currency is finite. Another channel is through investment policy. The opportunities offered by a broad array of the foreign capital markets enables a CB to both smooth and grow the level of reserves. Adopting a more efficient and structured asset allocation is another, more subtle, way to manage reserve holdings. This diversification and growth effect can allow a CB to either hold fewer reserves for intervention or to be more active in currency markets.

This chapter examines these questions in a fully articulated, dynamic stochastic model of intervention and investment risk. The model assumes that the CB adopts an intervention policy that is triggered by random events such as trade outcomes, domestic shocks, foreign shocks, financial crises and so forth, that are out of the CB's control. The CB also faces a set of investment opportunities on offer from the international capital markets. Importantly, the model can be calibrated to reflect a number of realistic policy regimes. Monte Carlo simulations are then conducted to explore the quantitative predictions from the model for the various intervention regimes. The regimes studied are the following,

1. Latin Volatility: A small amount of reserves with a high probability of speculative attack.
2. Asian World Dominance: A large amount of reserves with a high level of continuing inflow.
3. 'Hands Off' NZ: A small amount of reserves with a small probability of intervention to defend the currency in extreme events.

The main findings of the chapter are the following:

1. Intervention risk is significantly diversified by accessing investment markets.
2. Intervention risk will be diversified with a more aggressive investment policy for all Central Banks, regardless of their current initial reserve levels.
3. Adopting a more aggressive investment policy reduces the probability of insolvency. For example, in the Latin Volatility case, the probability of insolvency drops from 5% to 0.3% in the simulations.
4. A more aggressive investment policy will reduce the expected cost of intervention.
5. Optimal asset allocation is quite stable over time, despite the risk of intervention.

It is often argued that CBs with lower levels of reserves should adopt a more conservative investment policy than those with high levels of reserves. The findings in this chapter suggest otherwise. In fact, the diversification effect is strongest for the poorer CBs with more aggressive investment policies offering them a greater chance of successfully defending their currency.

The chapter is organised as follows. Section 5.2 sketches a fully articulated dynamic stochastic model of intervention and investment risk. The full model is detailed in the Appendix. Section 5.3 calibrates the model and reports the results of the experiments designed to mimic real world intervention policies. Section 5.4 concludes the chapter.

5.2 A dynamic stochastic model of intervention and investment risk

This section describes the basic model of intervention and investment risk. The model is later calibrated and numerically simulated to provide some quantitative insights into the interaction between intervention risk and investment policy. The description in this section is intended to motivate model intuition. Technical details are confined to the Appendix.

Intervention risk is at the centre of the model. In any period, the CB is out of the market, buying reserves or selling reserves. If the CB is out of the market then the reserve portfolio earns the (stochastic) market rate of return given by its asset allocation. If the CB is buying reserves then it simply adds new reserves to its foreign investment portfolio, which continues to earn the market rate of return. If the CB is selling reserves, alternatively, it must raise foreign cash to provide liquidity. Selling reserves triggers a 'liquidity constraint' in the model that must be met to give effect to intervention. In this event, the CB either uses existing foreign cash resources or sells foreign securities to raise cash to finance its intervention. When selling reserves, the foreign reserve portfolio declines by the amount of intervention, while the remainder of the portfolio continues to earn the market rate of return. At the end of each period, the portfolio is rebalanced back to the benchmark asset allocation.

Technically, intervention risk is modelled as a 3-state discrete stochastic process that is descriptive of CB policy. A probability transition matrix describes the dynamics for the 'intervention state' linking one period to the next. The dynamics of the system depend on the transition probabilities used to calibrate the matrix. Empirical evidence suggests that intervention policy is positively serially correlated – that is, if a CB is buying currency this period it is more likely to be buying next period than if it was not buying currency. The transition matrix calibration is a reflection of policy stance. The model therefore allows me to characterise intervention risk under many different policy approaches to exchange rate management. For simplicity, investment risk is modelled with time invariant expected returns and variances. I choose this basic structure since the main focus of the chapter is to show how a simple investment portfolio can diversify intervention risk.[1]

The structure of the investment problem facing the CB is to choose an asset allocation each period consistent with the CB's risk aversion, and so that sufficient liquidity is available to finance intervention in the market. The formal problem is a multi-period optimisation described in the Appendix. The interesting features of the model are the following,

$$
\begin{aligned}
&F(t+1) = A(t)\left(1+\mathbf{w}'(s,t)\mathbf{R}\right)\\
&F(t) = A(t) + L(t)\\
&L(t) \geq \Gamma(s,t)\\
&\Pr\left(s(t+1) \mid s(t)\right) = \Pi
\end{aligned}
$$

where $F(t)$ is the level for foreign reserves, $A(t)$ the level of investible assets, $L(t)$ the level of liquidity and $\Gamma(s,t)$ is the required liquidity needed for intervention in state s. $(1 + w(s,t)R)$ is the realised market rate of return on the portfolio in state s at time t, and Π is the probability state transition matrix. The first constraint is a difference equation which specifies that foreign reserves increment or decrement by the rate of return on the level of investible assets plus the level of intervention in that period. The second equality condition stipulates that foreign reserves are comprised of risky assets and liquidity holdings. Importantly, the third constraint shows that the level of liquidity has to be at least sufficient to finance intervention at each point in time, so that asset sales may be required in some cases. The final equation describes the probability transition matrix representing intervention risk in the model.

Intervention risk is central to the model. It is partly a function of policy, as it reacts to stochastic events in the model. It is useful to examine the state transition probability matrix more closely for better understanding. For a 3-state discrete process, the transition matrix would look like the following,

$$
\Pi = \begin{bmatrix} \pi_{11} & \pi_{12} & \pi_{13} \\ \pi_{21} & \pi_{22} & \pi_{23} \\ \pi_{31} & \pi_{32} & \pi_{33} \end{bmatrix}
$$

where the first probability in the matrix, π_{11}, is the probability of being in state 1 in period t+1 given that the system is in state 1 in period t. The second probability, π_{12}, is the probability of being in state 2 in period t+1 given that the system is in state 1 in period t and so forth. The probabilities must sum to one along each row. The transition matrix contains conditional probabilities describing the dynamics of the system. The stationary or unconditional probabilities represent the average proportion of time spent in each state over the long run. The stationary probabilities are easily calculated as,

$$\Pi_{stat} = \lim_{t \to \infty} \Pi^t$$

Another important feature of the model is the liquidity constraint $L(t) \geq \Gamma(s,t)$. This stipulates the level of liquidity that needs to be held for intervention. This is a function of the intervention state 's' that is stochastic in the model. The constraint requires the CB to raise sufficient liquidity to finance their operations on realisation of an intervention state.

Calibrating the transition matrix and state vector enables me to examine many different policy stances. LeBaron (1999) has estimated the transition matrix for the US Federal Reserve during the 1980s and 1990s using historical data. More recently, Delomier and Fisher (2005) estimate the transition matrix for a selection of Asian and Latin American countries. The approach in this chapter is to specify probabilities and levels of intervention that are consistent with perceived foreign reserve policies, and then simulate distributions for different levels of foreign reserves and asset allocations.

5.3 Foreign reserves intervention policy experiments

This section calibrates the model and studies the interaction of intervention and investment risk under three policy stances. Section 5.3.1 presents the calibration of the investment parameters in the model. Section 5.3.2 presents the results of the experiments.

5.3.1 Calibrating the investment parameters

The optimisation portion of the model requires me to specify a set of returns and risk characterising the capital markets, together with the CB's attitude to risk.

For simplicity, and without loss of generality, I assume that the CB can invest in only three asset markets, namely (i) international cash, (ii) international bonds and (iii) international equities. The expected returns, risks and correlations for these assets are assumed to be as shown in Table 5.1

These risk and return assumptions are roughly in line with long run historical averages. The expected return to equities of 10% represents a risk premium over cash of 6%. This is in line with the long run realised equity premium for a diversified stock portfolio. The expected return for bonds of 6% represents a 2% risk premium over cash. The risk expectations of 22% for equities, 8% for bonds and 0.5% for cash reflect longer run annualised

Table 5.1 Expected risk and return assumptions

	E(return) (in %)	Risk(in %)	Correlation		
Equities	10	22	1		
Bonds	6	8	0.4	1	
Cash	4	0.5	0.1	0.4	1

Note: This table shows the expected risks and returns employed in the model calibration. These are chosen to broadly match the long-run equity premium over cash, bond premium over cash, standard deviations and correlations.

standard deviations for these asset classes. The correlations across asset classes show that equities and bonds are positively correlated with reasonable coherence while equities and cash have lower correlation. The short and long end of the bond market is also positively correlated. The fact that the cross-correlations range between 0.1 and 0.4 means that there is significant opportunity for portfolio diversification.[2]

The risk aversion parameter in the CB's utility function determines how aggressive their investment portfolio will be in terms of exposures to cash, bonds and equities. The parameter λ in the optimisation is the coefficient of risk aversion. A low value for λ implies that the CB is willing to take investment risk, substituting low volatility assets such as cash and bonds for equities. A high value for λ implies that the CB is more risk averse, preferring to invest in a low duration portfolio of cash and bonds. In the simulations, we allow λ to take on two values, namely,

$$\lambda = \begin{cases} 2 \\ 10 \end{cases}$$

representing relatively low and high risk aversion parameters.

5.3.2 Foreign reserves intervention policy experiments

This section studies three policy experiments for the conduct of foreign reserves intervention. The three scenarios are the following,

1. Latin Volatility: A small amount of reserves with a high probability of speculative attack.
2. Asian World Dominance: A large amount of reserves with a high level of continuing reserves accumulation
3. 'Hands Off' NZ: A small amount of reserves with a small probability of intervention to defend the currency in extreme events.

In each case, I first calibrate the transition matrix and intervention parameters. I then perform the experiments and examine (i) the distribution of foreign reserves over a 20 year horizon, (ii) selected sample paths for the level of reserves, (iii) the optimal asset allocations over time and (iv) the minimum level of reserves required to support the policy without bankruptcy.

5.3.2.1 Latin volatility

Latin America's exchange rate history is one of moderate to low foreign reserve holdings and currency crises triggered by speculative attack. The Latin experience has seen the CB regularly spending reserves to defend the currency. Calibrating the Latin policy experience has the following features, (i) moderate initial levels of foreign reserve holdings, (ii) sales of foreign reserves more likely than purchases and (iii) a significant probability of intervention.

The calibration applies to intervention probabilities at a monthly frequency. I assume the following,

$$\text{Initial reserve holdings} = \$15\text{billion}$$

$$\text{Liquidity needed for intervetion, I(s)} = \begin{bmatrix} 0 \\ -\$500\text{million} \\ \$250\text{million} \end{bmatrix}$$

$$\text{Probablity transition matrix, } \Pi = \begin{bmatrix} 0.9 & 0.08 & 0.02 \\ 0.48 & 0.5 & 0.02 \\ 0.68 & 0.02 & 0.3 \end{bmatrix}$$

The interpretation of this policy calibration is the following. I assume that the country's CB initially holds $15billion in reserves. The vector $I(s)$ shows the 3 intervention states. No intervention means that there are 0 purchases or sales of reserves in that month. If the sell state occurs, then a monthly sale of –$500million is required to support the currency. If the buy state occurs, then monthly purchases of $250million take place.

The probability transition matrix is interesting. The first row shows that there is a 90% chance that the CB will not intervene next month if it was not intervening this month, an 8% chance that it will have to sell reserves if not intervening this month and a 2% chance that it will buy reserves if not intervening this month. The second row dictates a 48% chance of no intervention next month if the CB was selling reserves, a 50% chance that it will continue to sell reserves and only a 2% chance that it will purchase reserves. The final row dictates a 68% chance of no intervention next month following reserve purchases this month, a 2% chance of sales and a 30% chance of continued purchases. The intervention dynamics implied by the transition matrix are quite rich and there is a varying degree of positive persistence in each intervention state. The stationary distribution for this transition matrix is the following,

$$\text{Stationary distribution} \quad \Pi_{stat} = \begin{bmatrix} 0.837 & 0.135 & 0.028 \\ 0.837 & 0.135 & 0.028 \\ 0.837 & 0.135 & 0.028 \end{bmatrix}$$

which shows that, over the long run, under this policy the CB spends 83.7% of its time out of the market, 13.5% selling reserves and only 2.8% buying reserves. Defining the 'return to intervention' as,

$$\text{Return to intervention} = \frac{\Pi_{stat} I(s)}{\text{Initial Reserves}}$$

$$= -0.40\% \text{ per month}$$

then it is clear that the long run expectation is for a *decline* in foreign reserves due to intervention for this policy calibration. In this case it is an expected decline of –0.40% per month.

These statistics draw out the first important point – that intervention policy carries both a long run risk and rate of return of its own. The CB has some influence over the return to intervention when framing its policy stance, but may also access the capital markets to help manage and diversify the risk of intervention. Put more simply, if a CB dips into reserves it has got to put them back to remain solvent – either through purchases, investment returns or, more optimally, both. These policy questions are quantified in the simulations.

The simulations examine the path for reserves over a 20-year horizon. 1000 sample paths are generated for each model calibration, and the distribution for final reserve holdings is calculated. The model is path dependent since future investment and intervention capabilities depend on the past evolution of the system. I also examine some individual sample paths to compare the level of reserves under different investment policies.

Figure 5.1 shows a pair of histograms with the distribution of final reserve positions after 20 years for a CB with risk aversion of 2 and 10 respectively. It should be stressed that each CB faces the same set of intervention and investment risks so that they differ only in respect of their attitude to investment risk.

This result is striking. The left hand panel shows that a risk averse CB facing the type of intervention risk in the calibration has a 5% chance of

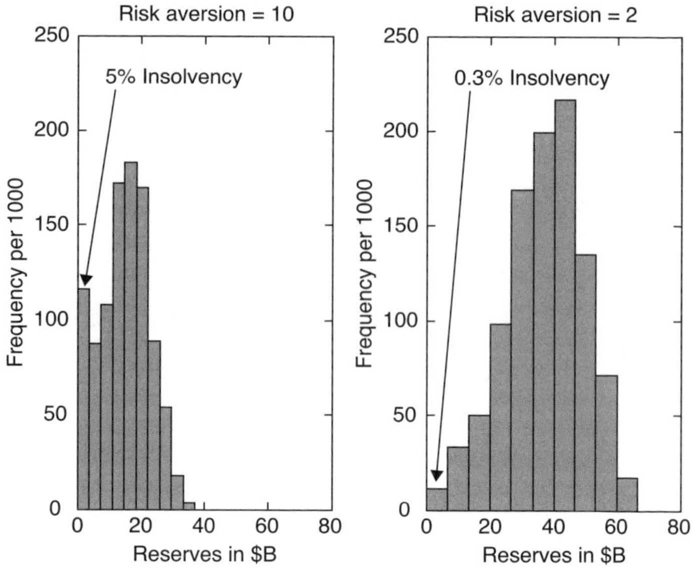

Figure 5.1 Case 1: Latin Volatility: The distribution of foreign reserves over a 20-year horizon: 1000 simulations

Note: This figure presents histograms for final period reserve holdings based on Monte Carlo simulations for the Latin Volatility case using 1000 sample paths and a 20 year horizon. The high risk aversion calibration (risk aversion = 10) shows a 5% chance of insolvency at some point during the 20 year time horizon. The more aggressive investment strategy associated with the low risk aversion calibration (risk aversion = 2) shows a substantial decline in insolvency to just 0.3% at some point during the 20 year time horizon. This is the main result of the chapter.

becoming insolvent within the 20 year horizon for the simulations. The panel also shows that the distribution of reserves at the end of 20 years is skewed toward the left and to some extent bimodal. The right hand panel shows a completely different story. A CB that is less risk averse is more likely to grow reserves over time and stave off insolvency. Only 0.3% of outcomes resulted in insolvency for a CB with a risk aversion of 2. Moreover, the average level of reserves at the end of the 20-year period is over 2.5 times that as under the conservative investment policy.[3]The reason this occurs is because adopting a more aggressive investment policy has the joint effect of raising the rate of return and diversifying intervention risk. The expected decline in reserves from intervention is offset by higher returns and risks are smoother. To illustrate this point, Figure 5.2 shows the time series for reserves and average asset allocation for one sample path in the simulations. The left-hand side of this figure shows a single sample path from the simulations for a CB with risk aversion of 10. The top panel shows the path for reserves over the 20-year period. In this case, the CB was repeatedly forced to intervene in the markets to sell reserves and therefore

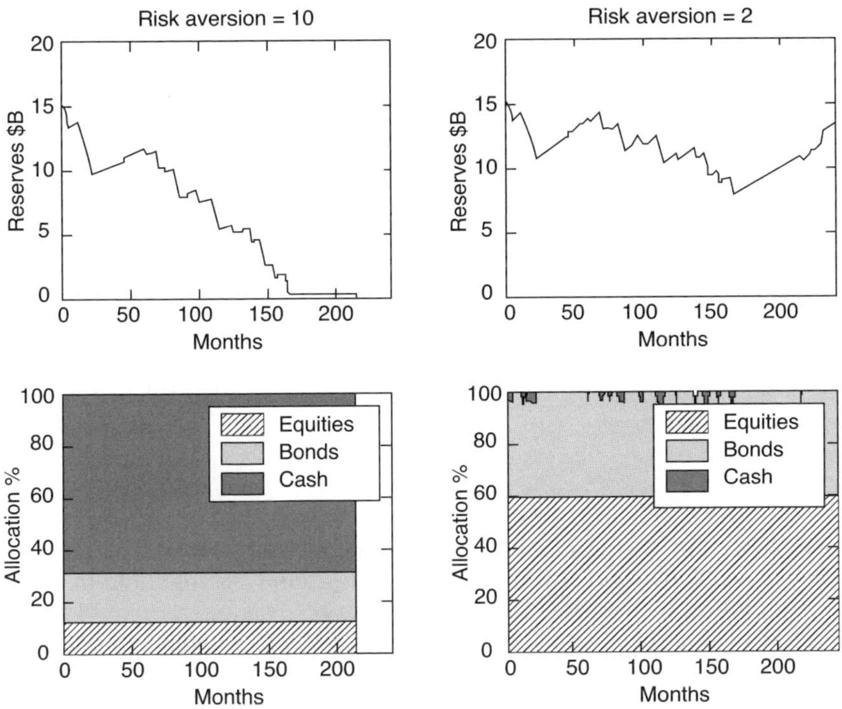

Figure 5.2 Case 1: Latin Volatility: Time series for reserves and asset allocations: single sample path

Note: This figure presents the time-path for reserves and associated asset allocations for a single Monte Carlo sample path from the Latin volatility case. The sample path is chosen to illustrate the comparative diversification and portfolio effects associated with high risk aversion (risk aversion = 10) versus the more aggressive low risk aversion calibration (risk aversion = 2). The chosen sample path demonstrates insolvency after 17 years and 8 months with an asset allocation skewed toward cash and bonds under the risk aversion = 10 calibration. Conversely, the chosen sample path demonstrates that there are always sufficient reserves to fund intervention under the more aggressive equity skewed asset allocation with risk aversion = 2.

experienced a significant drain on its resources. In fact, the risk averse CB became insolvent after 17 years and 8 months. The lower panel shows that throughout this period the CB invested most of its reserves in cash and bonds. In fact, the optimal asset allocation for the risk averse CB barely changed since, by and large, it was able to finance its intervention activities out of existing cash resources. Despite its 'conservative' investment policy, however, it still went broke.

The right hand side shows the path for reserves for a CB with risk aversion of 2. Note that this CB confronts exactly the same intervention and investment risks as the first CB. By adopting an investment policy heavily skewed toward risky assets, the path for reserves is relatively stable and the

CB remains solvent for the entire period, *despite having to intervene in exactly the same way as for the risk averse CB*! In addition, the lower panel shows that CB selling risky assets to raise cash to finance intervention – the liquidity constraint in the model became binding when required for intervention.

The conclusions from the Latin Volatility case are the following:

1. Adopting a more aggressive investment policy reduces the chance of insolvency significantly.
2. Adopting a more aggressive investment policy helps offset the expected cost of intervention.
3. Adopting a more aggressive investment policy makes foreign reserves more stable due to risk diversification.
4. Optimal asset allocation is stable in the dynamic framework, irrespective of risk aversion.

5.3.2.2 Asian world dominance

Over 70% of the world's foreign reserves are owned by Asian CB's amounting to over $1.7trillion. There are now seven Asian CB's that hold in excess of $100billion in reserves. This is the result of an explicit policy to grow reserves through international trade dominance and currency management. Asian currencies are very dirty floats in most cases, with several currencies effectively fixed to the USD (the HKD, RMB and MRG). This policy can be reflected in the framework with the following features, (i) high initial levels of foreign reserve holdings, (ii) purchases of foreign reserves significantly higher in magnitude and more likely than sales and (iii) a significant probability of intervention.

The calibration applies to intervention probabilities at a monthly frequency. I assume the following,

$$\text{Initial reserve holdings} = \$100\text{billion}$$

$$\text{Liquidity needed for intervention, I(s)} = \begin{bmatrix} 0 \\ -\$2\text{billion} \\ \$5\text{billion} \end{bmatrix}$$

$$\text{Probability transition matrix, } \Pi = \begin{bmatrix} 0.3 & 0.2 & 0.5 \\ 0.6 & 0.2 & 0.2 \\ 0.2 & 0.1 & 0.7 \end{bmatrix}$$

This policy calibration is interpreted in the same way as the previous example. The notable features are that the CB commences with $100billion in reserves and that the sales and purchases associated with intervention activity are higher in absolute terms due to the more managed exchange rate policy. In addition, the probability transition matrix is now more skewed toward foreign reserve accumulation. This is reflected in the stationary distribution for the intervention states and the expected return to intervention,

$$\text{Stationary distribution } \Pi_{stat} = \begin{bmatrix} 0.286 & 0.143 & 0.571 \\ 0.286 & 0.143 & 0.571 \\ 0.286 & 0.143 & 0.571 \end{bmatrix}$$

$$\text{Return to intervention} = 2.6\% \text{ per month}$$

which shows that under this policy the CB spends 28.6% of its time out of the market, 14.3% selling reserves and the majority 57.1% of its time

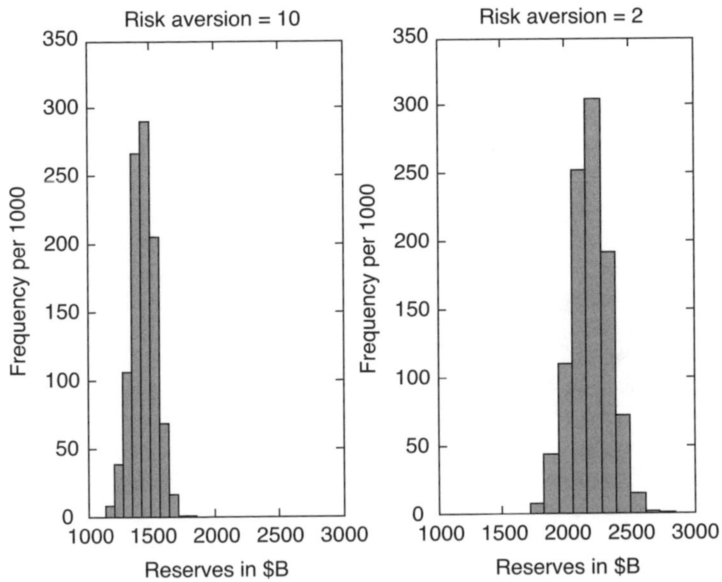

Figure 5.3 Case 2: Asian World Dominance. The distribution of foreign reserves over a 20-year horizon: 1000 simulations

Note: This figure presents histograms for final period reserve holdings based on Monte Carlo simulations for the Asian World Dominance case using 1000 sample paths and a 20 year horizon. The high risk aversion calibration (risk aversion = 10) shows a relatively tight distribution of reserves centred around $1500billion at the end of the 20 year time horizon. The more aggressive investment strategy associated with the low risk aversion calibration (risk aversion = 2) shows a substantial increase in the level and spread of reserves at the end of the 20 year time horizon.

buying reserves. The return to intervention now implies long run reserve accumulation of a staggering 2.6% per month.

With such a rapid reserve growth policy, it is not difficult to predict what the simulations will show at the end of the 20 year time horizon. Figure 5.3 compares histograms for the distribution of reserves under the conservative and aggressive investment policies.

The first observation is that the probability of insolvency is zero for both the conservative and aggressive investment policy. In fact, the only difference between the two histograms is the scale of final reserve holdings. For a risk aversion of 10, the average reserve level is \$1.4trillion whereas the average reserve level is \$2.2trillion for a risk aversion of 2.

Intervention risk does not matter much when adopting a reserves accumulation policy of the scale depicted in the Asian World Dominance

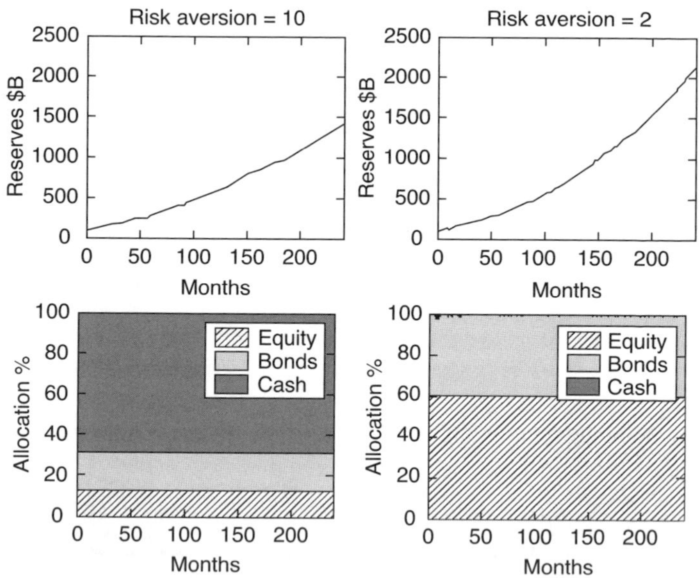

Figure 5.4 Case 2: Asian World Dominance. Time series for reserves and asset allocations: single sample path

Note: This figure presents the time-path for reserves and associated asset allocations for a single Monte Carlo sample path from the Asian World Dominance case. The sample path is chosen to illustrate the comparative diversification and portfolio effects associated with high risk aversion (risk aversion = 10) versus the more aggressive low risk aversion calibration (risk aversion = 2). The chosen sample path demonstrates a steady increase in reserves with an asset allocation skewed toward cash and bonds under the risk aversion = 10 calibration. The more aggressive equity skewed asset allocation with risk aversion = 2 produces a much faster appreciation.

scenario. Investment policy serves to determine how much faster reserves will accumulate and eventually this will dominate day-to-day FX market activities.[4] This is shown in figure 5.4. The figure examines one sample path for reserves accumulation and asset allocation for CBs differing only by their risk aversion. The top panel on the left side of the figure shows that reserves tend to grow quite smoothly over time with the bumps referring to periods of intervention. The bumpiness is smoothed out toward the end of the period as investment returns tend to dominate market activity. The lower panel shows that the optimal asset allocation is exactly the same as for the first case studied earlier. This is because the richer Asian CBs are facing exactly the same set of investment risks as any other CB.

The right side of the figure shows a much faster and arguably smoother rate of reserves accumulation for a CB with risk aversion of 2. The lower panel shows that this CB dips into non-cash reserves in months where it is buying domestic currency by liquidating its bond holdings. Notably, equity allocations are stable throughout the period.

The conclusion from the Asian World Dominance case is that these CBs will own the majority of assets in the world if their policy continues. The role risk aversion and investment play in this case is determining how rapidly these CBs achieve world dominance.

5.3.2.3 'Hands off' NZ

The Reserve Bank of New Zealand is famous for having been absent from the FX[Author Query: will readers know this term? If not, spell out on first use.] markets since 1985. This 'hands off' policy is correctly based on the belief that a small economy is unable to defend a currency against attack from speculators with significantly more resources than the CB can afford. Nevertheless, there is a small chance that the CB will have to intervene to avert a systemic breakdown and this should be factored into policy. Framing this policy is quite difficult since it is unclear at what point a declining exchange rate threatens the financial system and triggers intervention. The following model calibration is an attempt to capture these policy risks.

The calibration assumes the following,

$$\text{Initial reserve holdings} = \$5\text{billion}$$

$$\text{Liquidity needed for intervention, I(s)} = \begin{bmatrix} 0 \\ -\$2\text{billion} \\ \$1\text{billion} \end{bmatrix}$$

$$\text{Probability transition matrix, } \Pi = \begin{bmatrix} 0.999 & 0.0005 & 0.0005 \\ 0.5 & 0.5 & 0.0 \\ 0.5 & 0.0 & 0.5 \end{bmatrix}$$

This policy calibration is interpreted in the same way as the previous example. The notable features are that the CB commences with only \$5billion in reserves. If called upon to intervene, sales of reserves are relatively high at \$2billion reflecting the systemic nature of the risk. Purchases of foreign reserves are sporadic and smaller at \$1billion. The probability transition matrix now factors in only a tiny chance of having to intervene, only 1 month in 1000. However, in the event of intervention, there is a 50% probability that it will have to continue in the following month. This is reflected in the stationary distribution for the intervention states and the expected return to intervention,

$$\text{Stationary distribution } \quad \Pi_{stat} = \begin{bmatrix} 0.998 & 0.001 & 0.001 \\ 0.998 & 0.001 & 0.001 \\ 0.998 & 0.001 & 0.001 \end{bmatrix}$$

$$\text{Return to intervention} = -0.02\% \text{ per month}$$

which shows that under this policy the CB spends 99.8% of its time out of the market, 0.1% selling reserves and 0.1% buying reserves. The return to intervention now implies long run expected reserve depletion of only −0.2% per month, but this masks the 'systemic risk' in the dynamics. This is because the CB stays out of the market for the great majority of the simulated time paths (there are 240 months with 1 chance in 1000 of intervening in any month), however when they do intervene it is a significant proportion of total assets.

Figure 5.5 compares the distribution of final reserve holdings after 20 years for the CB with risk aversion of 10 and 2 respectively.The interesting feature of this figure is that investment policy now has little impact on the CB's ability to avoid insolvency when it is forced to intervene. Insolvency probability is 1.1% for a risk aversion of 10 and 0.7% for a risk aversion of 2. The main difference is that the level of reserves is significantly higher when a more aggressive investment policy is adopted.

It is disappointing that the capital markets have little ability to diversify intervention risk in a situation such as the 'Hands Off' NZ scenario. However it is interesting that the simulations suggest that the CB might as well be more aggressive with its investment policy if, for no other reason, it can make some money for the government!

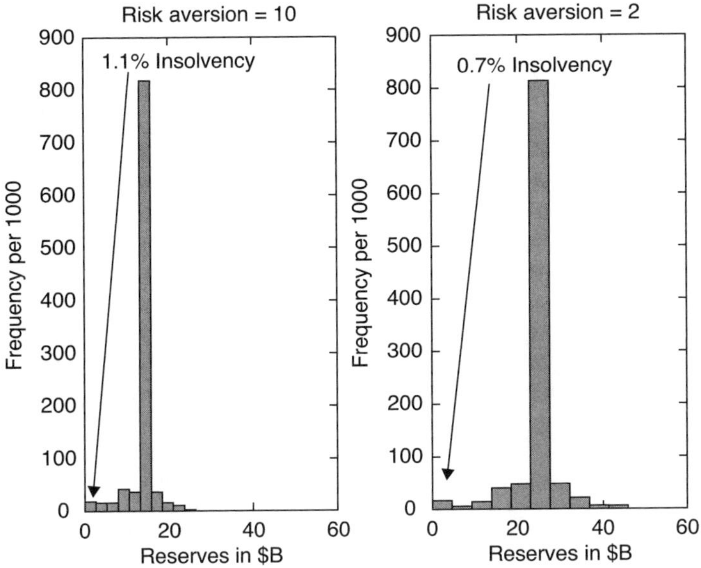

Figure 5.5 Case 3: 'Hands Off' NZ. The distribution of foreign reserves over a 20 year horizon: 1000 simulations

Note: This figure presents histograms for final period reserve holdings based on Monte Carlo simulations for the 'Hands Off' NZ case using 1000 sample paths and a 20 year horizon. The high risk aversion calibration (risk aversion = 10) shows a 1.1% chance of insolvency at some point during the 20 year time horizon. The more aggressive investment strategy associated with the low risk aversion calibration (risk aversion = 2) shows a small decline in insolvency to 0.7% at some point during the 20 year time horizon.

Figure 5.6 shows that the time series for reserves accumulation and optimal asset allocation are more volatile under the 'Hands Off' NZ scenario. Figure 5.6 chooses one of the few sample paths where the conservative investment policy leads to insolvency while an aggressive policy allows the CB to survive. The top panel on the left hand side shows that the risk to intervention clearly dominates the nation's reserves. A succession of financial crises leads to rapid reserve depletion. In contrast, the top right panel shows that a more aggressive investment policy allows for a build up in reserves in the first few years of the simulation providing a reserve cushion in later years to withstand both crises that hit the FX market.

The lower panels show the time series for asset allocations. In this case, the more aggressive CB dips into their equity investments on two occasions to generate cash for liquidity purposes. Following successful intervention, however, the asset allocation reverts back to the original benchmark despite the depletion in reserves.

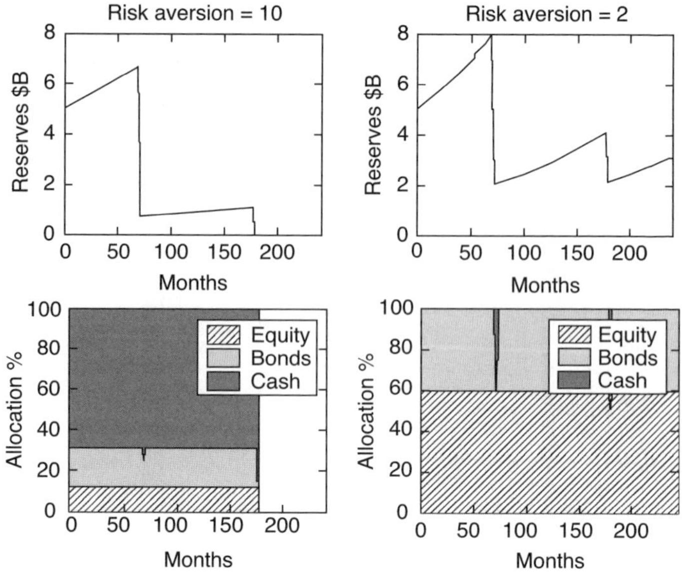

Figure 5.6 Case 3: 'Hands Off' NZ. Time series for reserves and asset allocations: single sample path

Note: This figure presents the time-path for reserves and associated asset allocations for a single Monte Carlo sample path from the 'Hands Off' NZ case. The sample path is chosen to illustrate the comparative diversification and portfolio effects associated with high risk aversion (risk aversion = 10) versus the more aggressive low risk aversion calibration (risk aversion = 2). The chosen sample path demonstrates insolvency with an asset allocation skewed toward cash and bonds under the risk aversion = 10 calibration. Conversely, the chosen sample path demonstrates that there are always sufficient reserves to fund intervention under the more aggressive equity skewed asset allocation with risk aversion = 2. In both cases, intervention risk clearly dominates investment risk in its impact on reserves.

Table 5.2 Case 3 'Hands Off' NZ: Minimum level of reserves to avoid insolvency: 1000 simulations

Risk aversion parameter	10	2
Minimum level of reserves	$16.5billion	$15.5billion

Note: This table calculates the minimum level of reserves required to avoid insolvency for the 'Hands Off' NZ case. The minimum level for the risk aversion = 10 calibration is $16.5billion but falls to $15.5billion when a more aggressive equity skewed asset allocation is chosen under a risk aversion = 2 calibration.

Of interest for the 'Hands Off' NZ case is the minimum level of reserves that needs to be held for each level of risk aversion in order to avoid insolvency. Additional simulations were conducted with the following results shown in table 5.2. The table shows that a significant increase in the level of reserves is required to be in a position to withstand the systemic crisis depicted in the 'Hands Off' NZ scenario. Reserves holdings would have to more than triple to \$15.5billion with risk aversion of 2 and rise further still to \$16.5billion under the more conservative investment policy with risk aversion of 10. While these are significant increases, the results show that adopting the more aggressive investment policy would allow the CB to hold \$1billion fewer in reserves.

In summary, the 'Hands Off' NZ case shows little opportunity to diversify intervention risk associated with extreme events. The results do suggest however, that a more aggressive investment policy can reduce the amount of reserves needed for intervention.

5.4 Conclusion

This chapter examines the relation between intervention risk and investment risk. The chapter demonstrates that intervention risk can be effectively diversified using investment policy. The chapter studies three hypothetical CBs that differ in terms of the level of reserves and their intervention policies. The Latin Volatility case examines a CB with relatively small reserves and that is relatively active in the FX markets on a monthly basis. The Asian World Dominance case examines a CB with significant reserves and with a reserves accumulation policy. The 'Hands Off' NZ case examines a small CB that is reluctant to intervene except in extreme financial stress.

In general, the results strongly encourage CBs to adopt more aggressive asset allocations for their reserves. This means that a CB should decrease its allocation to short term bonds and increase its allocations to longer maturity assets, higher yielding assets and even equities. This finding applies to each of the cases studied, regardless of the level of reserves. Accessing the capital markets has the effect of increasing the rate of return on the portfolio and smoothing the impact of purchases and sales of FX in the market. Higher returns and greater diversification reduces the probability of a CB becoming insolvent.

In reality, it is impractical to suggest that all CBs suddenly buy equities. CB practice has a long tradition with conservatism and capital preservation a cornerstone of reserves management. Nevertheless, the chapter provides significant justification for the CB community to adopt incremental steps toward adding return to portfolio and increased risk-taking. The striking finding is that this will be beneficial to all CBs, irrespective of the level of reserve holdings. Practical steps, such as moving out of short dated government bonds and into longer maturities, Asset-Backed Securities, Mortgage-Backed Securities and corporate bonds, are advisable. The richer CBs in Asia are already gravitating toward these asset classes. This chapter suggests that CBs in all parts of the world should follow suit, regardless of their reserve position.

Another conclusion from the findings is that it is optimal to formulate intervention policy and investment policy simultaneously. Exploiting the diversification opportunities of the capital markets will allow a CB to be more active in FX markets if they wish, or to hold fewer reserves. This finding potentially makes a case for combining the foreign exchange department with the reserves management function within a CB, since close coordination is optimal. It also makes a case for reintegrating the Central Banking function and Investment Corporation function in countries that have split these in two.

Appendix

This appendix describes an asset allocation framework consistent with a CB's joint objective for (i) maximising returns on their reserve holdings for a given level of risk and (ii) being prepared to intervene in FX markets.

There are 3 states of nature: (i) no intervention, (ii) buy foreign reserves and (iii) sell foreign reserves. In the event of intervention, the CB must either add to or liquidate a portion of its portfolio to facilitate its foreign exchange activities. In the no-intervention state, the CB is free to invest its assets without a liquidity constraint. A probability transition matrix is used to model the state transitions. This means that there is a distinction between the expected returns for the portfolio conditional on the intervention and no-intervention states. The unconditional expected return on the portfolio can also be evaluated. The conditional and unconditional probabilities implied by the transition matrix are key to the analysis.

This appendix first constructs a general model where expected returns, risk parameters and liquidity requirements are time varying and dependent on the intervention state. A simpler version follows which specialises the model structure to hold expected return and the risk parameters constant through time.

A general model

Let there be $i=1,\dots,I$ risky assets, a single liquidity asset denoted by L, three states denoted by $s=\{\text{No intervention, Buy reserves, Sell reserves}\}$ and an infinite investment horizon for dates $t=1,\dots,\infty$. The objective of the CB is to choose portfolio weights $\mathbf{w}(s,t)$ to maximise future expected returns subject to the liquidity requirement, a risk constraint and any other relevant constraints.

Formally, the optimisation problem is the following.

$$\underset{\{w(s,t)\}}{Max}\, E\sum_{t=1}^{\infty}\left[\mathbf{w}'(s,t)\mathrm{R}(s,t)-\lambda(s,t)\mathbf{w}'(s,t)\mathbf{V}\mathbf{w}(s,t)\right]$$

$$s.t.$$

$$F(t+1)=A(t)\left(1+\mathbf{w}'(s,t)\mathbf{R}(s,t)\right)$$

$$F(t)=A(t)+L(t)$$

$$L(t)\geq\Gamma(s,t)$$

$$\mathbf{w}'(s,t)\mathbf{1}=1$$

$$\mathbf{w}(s,t)\geq 0$$

$$F(0)=F$$

$$\Pr\left(s(t+1)\mid s(t)\right)=\Pi$$

The notation in the equation system is the following. $\mathbf{R}(s,t)$ is a vector of I+1 asset returns in each state s, $\mathbf{w}(s,t)$ a vector of portfolio weights, $\lambda(s,t)$ a risk aversion coefficient, $\mathbf{V}$ a covariance matrix, $F(t)$ is the level for foreign reserves, $A(t)$ the level of risky assets, $L(t)$ the level of liquidity and $I(s,t)$ is the required liquidity needed for intervention in state s. Π is the probability transition matrix. Note that in this general formulation, expected returns, the level of risk aversion and portfolio weights are all time varying and state dependent, i.e. they depend on whether the CB is intervening or not intervening in the market.

The interpretation of the optimisation problem is the following. The objective function is to maximise the expected return to the portfolio subject to a level of risk as measured by the quadratic penalty function. The interesting feature of the problem is the liquidity requirement in the third constraint. $\Gamma(s,t)$ determines how much of the portfolio has to be held in liquid securities for intervention purposes and is dependent on the state s. $\Gamma(s,t)$ is governed by a probability transition matrix Π and constitutes the forcing variable in the system that may lead to significant portfolio re-allocations. The transition matrix must be calibrated to reflect CB intervention policy.

A simplified model

In order to make the model more transparent, the simplifying assumption is made that expected returns and the risk aversion coefficient are independent of whether the CB is intervening and independent of time. This means that,

$$\mathbf{R}(s,t)=\mathbf{R}$$

$$\lambda(s,t)=\lambda$$

Making these substitutions, the simplified problem then becomes,

$$\underset{\{\mathbf{w}(s,t)\}}{Max}\, E\sum_{t=1}^{\infty}\left[\mathbf{w}'(s,t)\mathbf{R} - \lambda\mathbf{w}'(s,t)\mathbf{V}\mathbf{w}(s,t)\right]$$

$$\begin{aligned}
&s.t.\\
&F(t+1) = A(t)\mathbf{w}'(s,t)\mathbf{R}\\
&F(t) = A(t) + L(t)\\
&L(t) \geq \Gamma(s,t)\\
&\mathbf{w}'(s,t)\mathbf{1} = 1\\
&\mathbf{w}(s,t) \geq 0\\
&F(0) = F\\
&\Pr\left(s(t+1)\,|\,s(t)\right) = \Pi
\end{aligned}$$

In this formulation, the only feature driving portfolio reallocations is the forcing variable $\Gamma(s,t)$ which indicates the liquidity required when the CB is either intervening or not intervening. The intuition for this result is that when returns, risks and risk aversions are constant through time, the multi-period asset allocation problem collapses to a sequence of single period problems. Thus the only reason a CB would need to change its asset allocation would be when an external disturbance forced it to liquidate or purchase additional assets.

Path dependent portfolios

Solving the model algebraically is difficult since the level of reserves depends on the evolution of the intervention state variable. In addition, the amount of assets needed to intervene is a fixed $-value whereas the level of reserves may rise or fall over time depending on intervention and asset returns. For this reason, solutions to the problem need to be calculated using numerical methods such as Monte Carlo simulation.

The model is solved using the optimisation package in Matlab with realisations for the intervention state variable generated using Monte Carlo simulation.

Notes

1. In the experiments, intervention risk is independent of investment risk. This simple assumption does not change the character of the conclusions. In fact, the model framework enables a richer interaction between intervention policy and market behaviour to be explored.
2. While there may be considerable debate over the appropriate calibration for expected returns and risks, I can report that the main findings in the paper are robust to a wide range of these parameters.

3. Average reserves for risk aversion 10 are \$14.6 billion versus \$37.1 billion for risk aversion = 2.
4. Investment return will eventually dominate intervention risk in the model since the latter is a fixed \$ quantity that becomes relatively small as reserves rise.

References

Delomier, E. and S. Fisher (2005) "Central Bank Intervention Risk: An Empirical Study", JPMorgan Asset Management White Paper.

LeBaron, B. (1999) "Technical Trading Rule Profitability and Foreign Exchange Intervention", *Journal of International Economics*, 49, 125–143.

6
Reserves Adequacy and Composition

Coche Joachim and Vahe Sahakyan

6.1 Introduction

Establishing the reserves management strategy comprises decisions on the level of reserves (reserves adequacy) and on the composition of reserves (reserves allocation). Both in literature and practice, the reserves management strategy is often the result of a fragmented, hierarchical decision making process. The objective of this chapter is to analyze the optimal reserves management strategy for a central bank that simultaneously decides about adequacy and composition.

We present a model to analyze the optimal reserves management strategy for a small country that is subject to external liquidity shocks. Long-term capital investments in this country are funded by short-term borrowing in foreign currency. In this setting the central bank aims at mitigating adjustment costs to the economy implied by the external liquidity shocks by providing foreign currency loans to the private sector. In deciding the reserves management strategy, the bank balances adjustment costs, costs of funding foreign reserves as well as investment risks and returns. While investment returns and liquidity shocks are exogenous, funding costs are endogenous and are a function of the country's external vulnerability. In our model, decisions on reserves adequacy and diversification take policy and investment considerations simultaneously into account. This is in contrast to existing literature and reserves management practice where policy considerations dominate in the reserves adequacy discussion, while reserves composition is typically discussed against both policy and investment considerations.

6.1.1 Reserves adequacy

In the discussion of reserves adequacy, academic literature focuses on a trade-off between marginal benefits and costs of holding reserves. Starting with Heller (1966) the level of reserves is derived from optimizing behavior of decision makers. Utility arises from the potential use of reserves holdings to smooth consumption and production in times of balance of payment deficits while opportunity costs arise in times the reserves are held idle. Assuming that reserves are invested in foreign assets of highest liquidity, opportunity costs correspond to the differential between the return from an investment in a country's productive resources and the return from highly liquid investments.

Despite this broad concept of reserves functions in early literature, in practice, prior to globalization, countries held reserves mainly to manage foreign exchange demand and supply arising from current account transactions. Therefore, indicators used to measure reserves adequacy related primarily to the level and variability of imports. Three to five months of imports was often cited as a rule of thumb to indicate an adequate level of reserves (e.g., De Beaufort Wijnholds and Kapteyn (2001)).

Reserves adequacy was reassessed in the aftermath of the Asian crisis of 1997. On top of the management of current account transactions, additional motives for holding reserves were introduced. In particular, self-insurance motives for holding reserves gained popularity. For example, in the context of sudden stops of capital inflows, Feldstein (1999) proposes reserves accumulation to insure the risks of currency attacks. Reserves adequacy in the context of exchange rate volatility is discussed for example by Calvo and Reinhart (2000) and Flood and Marion (2002). Aizenman and Marion (2004) focus on the stabilization of fiscal expenditures in countries with limited taxing capacity and sovereign risk. Output stabilization in general is discussed by Ben-Bassat and Gottlieb (1992), Aizenman et al., (2004) and García and Soto (2004). Jeanne and Ranciere (2006) develop a model for the optimal level of international reserves for a small open economy that is vulnerable to sudden stops.

In practical reserves management, this discussion is mirrored by the Guidotti/Greenspan rule according to which reserves should correspond to at least the level of short-term foreign debts (with maturities of up to one year). Pointing to the possibility of capital flight by residents, De Beaufort Wijnholds and Kapteyn (2001) augment the Guidotti/Greenspan rule by suggesting that the optimal level of reserves should be established taking also into account broad money, the country's exchange rate regime and a country-specific risk factor.

In the context of massively increasing reserves holdings over the last years, the level of reserves is also discussed against additional, non-standard reserves functions such as fostering export growth and serving as a store of national wealth. Dooley, Folkerts-Landau, and Garber (2003) suggest that an important rational for reserves accumulation may be the preservation of export competitiveness. In this context Aizenman and Lee (2008) use the term monetary mercantilism.

6.1.2 Reserves composition

The composition decision comprises the allocation of reserves holdings to currencies, asset classes within a currency and individual financial instruments. In practice, the allocation decision is decomposed into strategic and tactical elements. The strategic elements are established by the central banks' top decision makers and are expected to be unchanged over a prolonged period (e.g. one to five years) while tactical decisions are delegated to staff and are reviewed more frequently.

The strategic decision is often divided into three separate parts. That is, first the reserves' currency composition, second the decision about exposure to interest rate, liquidity, credit and other market risk and finally the decision about the leeway by which tactical decision making is allowed to deviate from the strategic parameters. Usually tactical deviations are allowed to take advantage of market opportunities over the short to medium term.

In this process, the currency composition receives the most attention in academic literature. It is mostly related to policy considerations, however occasionally investment considerations are discussed. Dooley, Lizondo and Mathieson (1989) and Eichengreen and Mathieson (2000) relate the currency composition to the exchange rate regimes, the composition of trade, and the currency of foreign debt. Chinn and Frankel (2005) consider the size of the financial markets, inflation rates and exchange rate volatility as additional determinants. Dooley, Folkerts-Landau and Garber (2003, 2004) discuss the currency composition in the context of a trade-off between macroeconomic factors (trade-flows, exchange rate regimes) and investment considerations. Eichengreen (2005) points toward a trade-off between market, liquidity and investment risks in the decision of the currency composition. While liquidity considerations point toward concentrated holdings in the one currency, the management of investment risks would point toward broader diversification. Furthermore, from an investment perspective Papaioannou et al. (2006) use a portfolio optimization framework to devise currency compositions for alternative scenarios.

The currency composition is also occasionally discussed in the context of structural market changes. To this end, the currency composition was discussed over the past years with regard to the effects of the introduction of the euro as well as massive reserves accumulation in some countries, the rising current account and fiscal deficits of the United States, or the decrease in the issuance of US Treasury instruments as expected in the late 1990s and early 2000s.

Beyond the currency component, there are few contributions addressing the reserves instrument composition. Fung and McCauley (2000) analyze trends in the instrument composition of the US dollar reserves over the past 40 years. These authors also analyze the significance of tactical decision making. McCauley (2005) focuses on the allocation of US dollar reserves to investments in the United States and offshore. Coche et al. (2006) analyze the reserves composition assuming a policy objective to keep the exchange rate above a given target rate. Fisher and Lie (2004) use mean variance analysis to identify the optimal reserves composition. An example of a practical process to establish reserves' instrument composition is outlined in Cardon and Coche (2004). In practice, the optimal instrument composition is mostly established separately from the decision about the optimal level of reserves and currency composition. That is, the instrument composition is determined after decisions on the level of reserves and currency allocation are made. Furthermore, the instrument composition is decided for each currency sub-portfolio separately.

Thus, with a few exceptions, the reserves management strategy is seen as the result of a fragmented, hierarchical decision making process. Both in practice as well as in academic literature, reserves adequacy and reserves composition are treated independently of each other. Also different facets of reserves composition such as currency composition, interest rate risk exposure and leeway for active management are dealt with in isolation. Furthermore, parts of the reserves management strategy are closely linked to policy objectives while others take mainly investment considerations into account.

6.1.3 Integrated reserves management strategy

Against this background, the purpose of this chapter is to understand better potential interrelations between reserves adequacy and reserves diversification. The central question we aim to address is how a central bank that decides simultaneously about reserves adequacy and diversification establishes its reserves management strategy as a function of external liquidity shocks and adjustment costs, the characteristics of available investment instruments, and the institutions' risk aversion. To shed light on this question we construct a small, two-sector, two-period model comprising a firm which is funded by an international investor and a central bank managing foreign exchange reserves. Furthermore the central bank is assumed to maximize utility over aggregated private sector and central bank profits. The private sector profits are a function of the value of the firm's production as well as funding and adjustment costs. The central bank's profits constitute investment returns over funding costs. The level of reserves and diversification affects the aggregated profit distribution in various ways. First, a higher level of reserves improves the central bank's ability to buffer external shocks and thereby potentially improves the expected value and reduces the variability of private sector profits. Second, depending on reserves allocation, a higher level of reserves increases investment risks to be borne by the central bank and might increase or decrease the bank's expected profits. In addition to these direct effects, the level and composition of reserves have indirect effects which operate through the funding costs. That is, international investors demand a compensation for the probability of default which in turn depends on and affects the country's profit distribution.

The remainder of this chapter is organized as follows. The model is introduced in Section 6.2. Section 6.3 presents the results. Section 6.4 tentatively concludes the chapter by discussing some implications of the presented framework.

6.2 Model

Inspired by the work of Aizenman and Lee (2005), we construct a two-period economy comprising a firm and a central bank. The firm funds long-term capital investment by borrowing from a foreign investor in foreign currency. The international borrowing is subject to shocks, according to which the foreign investor recalls part of the loan prior to its maturity. The central bank may buffer these liquidity shocks by proving foreign currency loans to the firm. The central bank funds these loans from its foreign reserves holdings. Prior to the materialization of the liquidity shock, the central bank has to decide about the level of foreign reserves as well as its composition. The model considers only foreign currency positions.

6.2.1 Firm

At the beginning of period 0 the firm obtains from an international investor a foreign currency loan, which is normalized to be 1 and is invested during this period in production capital. Period 0 is the gestation period of the capital investment thus there is no production yet. At the end of period 0 a liquidity shock Z materializes with probability p and the international investor recalls amount τ, whereby $0 < \tau < 1$ and

$$Z = \begin{cases} \tau & \text{with probability } p \\ 0 & \text{with probability } 1-p \end{cases}$$

The firm redeems the amount Z either by disinvesting and/or by borrowing from the central bank the amount L. Central bank foreign currency lending is bounded by a maximum amount of reserves R, that the central bank holds. Disinvesting implies a cost θ which is assumed to be greater than the costs of the central bank loan i. Thus the firm borrows from the central bank $L = \min(Z, R)$. In other words, the firm prefers to borrow the whole amount from the central bank to cover the claim of the foreign investor if the reserves of the central bank are sufficient to do so. If they are not sufficient the firm will liquidate some of its capital to cover the rest of the claim. Therefore, after disinvesting $\max(0, Z - R)$ the capital K available to the firm in period 1 is

$$[1] \quad K = 1-(1+\theta)\max(0, Z-R)$$

We assume that there is no depreciation and at the end of period 1 the capital investment can be reversed at no costs. Furthermore, we assume that the one-factor production function has the form $Y(K) = \beta \ln(1 + K)$. The profit of the firm at the end of period 1 is given by

$$\Pi^F = Y(K) - \underbrace{i(1 - Z)}_{\text{Cost of foreign borrowing}} - \underbrace{i \min(Z, R)}_{\text{Cost of central bank borrowing}} - \underbrace{\theta \max(0, Z - R)}_{\text{Cost of disinvestment}}$$

6.2.2 Central bank

In order to mitigate the exposure of the country to external vulnerabilities the central bank holds foreign reserves and grants loans in foreign currency in case demanded by the firm.

During period 0 the central bank decides about the level of the foreign reserves holdings R. This decision is made before the random liquidity shock Z materializes. The foreign reserves are funded by foreign borrowing at an interest rate i. After possibly granting a loan to the firm, the central bank will invest any remaining foreign currency in international financial markets. To this end, two alternative assets are available – a risk free and a risky asset. Fraction α is invested in the risk free asset with return r_f and $(1 - \alpha)$ is invested in the risky asset, with return r. We assume that the return of the risky asset has a logistic distribution with location (μ) and scale (σ) parameters. The total return ρ on the international holdings is therefore

$$\rho(\alpha) = \alpha r_f + (1 - \alpha) r$$

Furthermore, the counterpart of the central bank's equity E is invested alongside the reserves internationally. At the end of period 1 the central banks profit is

$$\Pi^{CB} = \underbrace{i \min(Z, R)}_{\text{Interest on loan to firm}} + \underbrace{(\alpha r_f + (1 - \alpha) r)(R + E - \min(Z, R))}_{\text{Investment return}} - \underbrace{iR}_{\text{Cost of holding reserves}}$$

In determining the level of reserves R and investment strategy α, we assume the case of welfare maximizing, whereby the central bank focuses on the aggregated profits of the private and public sectors. We furthermore assume that the central bank is risk averse and maximizes mean–variance utility function

$$[2] \quad U(\Pi) = \mathrm{E}[\Pi] - \gamma Var[\Pi]$$

where γ is the risk aversion coefficient.

6.2.3 International investor

The investor finances both the central bank and the firm at interest rate i. The investor demands compensation for the possibility that the borrowers fail to redeem the foreign currency loans at the end of period 1. Therefore we decompose interest rate i into a risk free component r_f and a credit spread s.

Under the assumption that the central bank guarantees the firm's external liabilities, the probability of default can be analyzed by aggregating the balance sheets of the firm and the central bank. Default occurs at the end of period 1 if the aggregated asset value of the firm and the central bank

$$A = K + Y(K) + (1+\rho)(R + E - \min(Z, R))$$

undercuts the face value of aggregated liabilities

$$D = (1+i)(1 - Z + R)$$

The spread the investor requires for compensating this risk corresponds to the loss given default weighted by the probability of default, i.e.

$$[3] \quad s = P(\max(0,A) \le D) E\left[\left(1 - \frac{\max(0,A)}{D}\right) \mid \max(0,A) \le D\right]$$

The limited liability assumption, so that the assets can not become negative, is incorporated in the function $\max(0, A)$.

6.3 Results

Knowing model structure and parameters, the central bank can infer the spread the international investor demands.

Proposition 1 The spread s the international investor demands satisfies the following equation:

$$s = p\Delta_\tau(s) + (1-p)\Delta_0(s)$$

where

$$\Delta_k(s) = \frac{\sigma C_k}{D_K(S)} \ln\left[\frac{\exp\left(\frac{B_k}{\sigma C_k} + \frac{\mu}{\sigma}\right) + \exp\left(\frac{D_k(s)}{\sigma C_k}\right)}{1 + \exp\left(\frac{B_k}{\sigma C_k} + \frac{\mu}{\sigma}\right)}\right], \quad k = 0, \tau$$

and

i. for $0 \le R < \tau$

[4] $B_\tau = (1-(1+\theta)(\tau-R)) + \beta\ln(1+(1-(1+\theta)(\tau-R))) + (1+\alpha r_f)E$

[5] $C_\tau = (1-\alpha)E$

[6] $D_\tau(s) = (1+r_f+s)(1-\tau+R)$

[7] $B_0 = 1+\beta\ln(2)+(1+\alpha r_f)(E+R)$

[8] $C_0 = (1-\alpha)(E+R)$

[9] $D_0(s) = (1+r_f+s)(1+R)$

ii for $\tau \le R$

[10] $B_\tau = 1+\beta\ln(2)+(1+\alpha r_f)(E+R-\tau)$

[11] $C_\tau = (1-\alpha)(E+R-\tau)$

[12] $D_\tau(s) = (1+r_f+s)(1-\tau+R)$

[13] $B_0 = 1+\beta\ln(2)+(1+\alpha r_f)(E+R)$

[14] $C_0 = (1-\alpha)(E+R)$

[15] $D_0(s) = (1+r_f+s)(1+R)$

Proof of Proposition 1 Simplifying the right hand side of 3, we obtain

[16] $P(\max(0,A) \le D)E\left[\left(1-\frac{\max(0,A)}{D}\right)\middle|\max(0,A) \le D\right] =$

[17] $\mathrm{E}\left[\left(1-\frac{\max(0,A)}{D}\right)\mathrm{I}_{\{\max(0,A)\le D\}}\right] =$

[18] $\mathrm{E}_Z\left[\mathrm{E}\left[\left(1-\frac{\max(0,A)}{D}\right)I_{\{\max(0,A)\le D\}}\middle|Z\right]\right] =$

[19] $\mathrm{E}_Z\left[\mathrm{E}\left[\left(1-\frac{\max(0,A)}{D}\right)\mathrm{I}_{\left\{1-\frac{\max(0,A)}{D}\ge 0\right\}}\middle|\mathrm{Z}\right]\right]$

Conditional on Z, the asset A is affine with respect to r and, hence, has logistic distribution with location parameter $\tilde{\mu}$ and scale parameter $\tilde{\sigma}>0$, where

[20] $\tilde{\mu} = B_Z + \mu C_Z$

[21] $\tilde{\sigma} = \sigma C_Z$

and

[22] $B_Z = K + Y(K) + (1 + \alpha r_f)(R + E - \min(Z, R))$

[23] $C_Z = (1-\alpha)(R + E - \min(Z, R))$

Using Lemma 1 from the Annex we can compute the inner expectation, which is $\Delta_Z(s)$. Next, note that Z takes two values τ and 0, with probabilities p and $(1-p)$, respectively, and computing the outer expectation yields the required results.

Remark: $\Delta_k(s)$ as a function of s is bounded by $1 \geq \Delta_k(s) \geq \frac{1}{\left(1+\exp\left(\frac{B_k}{C_k}\right)\right)} \geq 0$. To see this, note that

$$\lim_{x\to 0} x \ln\left[\frac{K+\exp\frac{1}{x}}{1+K}\right] = 1$$

and

$$\lim_{x\to 0} x \ln\left[\frac{K+\exp\frac{1}{x}}{1+K}\right] = \frac{1}{1+K} \geq 0$$

for some $K \geq 0$, which does not depend on s. Given the expressions for $D_\tau(s)$ and $D_0(s)$ the expression $\Delta_k(s)$ converges to 1 if $s \to \infty$ and converges to the lower bound if $s \to -(1 + r_f)$. The above discussion suggests that the optimal solution s^* will be bounded by

$$\frac{p}{1+\exp\left(\frac{B_\tau}{C_\tau}\right)} + \frac{1-p}{1+\exp\left(\frac{B_0}{C_0}\right)} < s^* < 1.$$

Proposition 2 The strategy of the central bank (α, R) satisfies the following system of equations:

i. for $0 < R \leq \tau$

$$[24] \quad \begin{cases} [0 \quad 1 \quad 2\alpha] \bullet \mathrm{M}_1 \bullet [1 \quad R \quad R^2]^T = 0 \\ [1 \quad \alpha \quad \alpha^2] \bullet \mathrm{M}_1 \bullet [0 \quad 1 \quad 2R]^T = 0 \end{cases}$$

ii. for $\tau < R$

$$[25] \quad \begin{cases} [0 \quad 1 \quad 2\alpha] \bullet \mathrm{M}_2 \bullet [1 \quad R \quad R^2]^T = 0 \\ [1 \quad \alpha \quad \alpha^2] \bullet \mathrm{M}_2 \bullet [0 \quad 1 \quad 2R]^T = 0 \end{cases}$$

where $\mathbf{M}_1$ and $\mathbf{M}_2$ are two conformable matrices and are functions of the parameters.

Proof of Proposition 2 Using the Law of Iterated Expectations and the Law of Iterated Variances we have

$$U(\Pi) = \mathrm{E}(\Pi) - \gamma Var[\Pi] = E_Z[\mathrm{E}[\Pi \mid Z]] \\ -\gamma(\mathrm{E}_Z[Var[\Pi \mid Z]] + Var_Z[\mathrm{E}[\Pi$$

Next, we have

$$E[\Pi \mid Z] = Y(K) - i(1 - Z + R) - \theta \max(0, Z - R) + \alpha r_f(E + \max(0, R - Z))$$

$$Var[\Pi \mid Z] = (1 - \alpha)^2 (E + \max(0, R - Z))^2 \frac{\pi^2}{3}$$

Denote,

$$[26] \quad a_\tau^k = \mathrm{E}[\Pi \mid Z]\,|_{Z=\tau}, \; a_0^k = \mathrm{E}[\Pi \mid Z]\,|_{Z=0}$$

$$[27] \quad b_\tau^k = Var[\Pi \mid Z]\,|_{Z=\tau}, \; b_0^k = Var[\Pi \mid Z]\,|_{Z=0}$$

where $k = 1$, for $0 < R \leq \tau$ and $k = 2$, for $\tau < R$. Then

$$U(\Pi)^k = pa_\tau^k + (1-p)a_0^k - \gamma\,(pb_\tau^k + (1-p)b_0^k + p(1-p)(a_\tau^k - a_0^k)^2)$$

Some computations and simplifications yield

$$U(\Pi)^k = \begin{bmatrix}1 & \alpha & \alpha^2\end{bmatrix} \bullet M_k \bullet \begin{bmatrix}1 & R & R^2\end{bmatrix}^T$$

Computing the first derivatives of $U(\Pi)^k$ with respect to α and R yields the required results.

The solution to the system of equations [9]–[22] and [28]–[29] gives the equilibrium spread (s), level of reserves (R) and portfolio weight (α). The system of equations is highly nonlinear, thus no exact analytic solutions exists.

To proceed we focus on an approximate analytic solution to the system of equations. To this end we first find an approximate analytical solution for α and R, as functions of s, using the equations [28]–[29]. Plugging the solutions $\alpha(s)$ and $R(s)$ into equations [9]–[22], we find an approximate analytic solution for s as a function of the parameters. The next proposition summarizes the above discussion.

Proposition 3 Assume that $\alpha^j s^k R^l \approx 0$, when $k \geq 2$ or $j + k + l \geq 3$. Then the solution to the equations (9)–(22) and (28)–(29) for α, R and s is given by

i. for $0 < R \leq \tau$

[28] $\alpha(s) = \bar{\Lambda} - s\tilde{\Lambda} \qquad R(s) = \check{\Lambda} - s\hat{\Lambda}$

[29] $$s = \frac{\Omega\,(\bar{\Lambda}, \check{\Lambda}, 0)}{1 - \Omega^{(3)}\,(\bar{\Lambda}, \check{\Lambda}, 0) + \check{\Lambda}\Omega^{(2)}(\bar{\Lambda}, \check{\Lambda}, 0) + \check{\Lambda}\Omega^{(1)}(\bar{\Lambda}, \check{\Lambda}, 0)}$$

where

[30] $$\bar{\Lambda} = \frac{2\Lambda_{31}\Lambda_{41} + \Lambda_{21}\Lambda_{51}}{4\Lambda_{31}\Lambda_{61} - \Lambda_{51}^2} \qquad \tilde{\Lambda} = \frac{\Lambda_{22}\Lambda_{51}}{4\Lambda_{31}\Lambda_{61} - \Lambda_{51}^2}$$

[31] $$\check{\Lambda} = \frac{2\Lambda_{21}\Lambda_{61} + \Lambda_{41}\Lambda_{51}}{4\Lambda_{31}\Lambda_{61} - \Lambda_{51}^2} \qquad \hat{\Lambda} = \frac{2\Lambda_{22}\Lambda_{61}}{4\Lambda_{31}\Lambda_{61} - \Lambda_{51}^2}$$

Λ_{jk} are functions of parameters and $\Lambda_{21} \gtreqless 0$, $\Lambda_{22} > 0$, $\Lambda_{31} > 0$, $\Lambda_{41} > \Lambda_{61} > 0$ and $\Lambda_{51} \gtreqless 0$. The sufficient condition for maximum requires that .

ii. for $\tau < R$

[32] $\alpha = \bar{\Gamma} - s\tilde{\Gamma} \quad R = \check{\Gamma} - s\hat{\Gamma}$

[33] $$s = \frac{\Omega\,(\bar{\Gamma},\check{\Gamma},0)}{1-\Omega^{(3)}\,(\bar{\Gamma},\check{\Gamma},0)+\tilde{\Gamma}\Omega^{(2)}(\bar{\Gamma},\check{\Gamma},0)+\hat{\Gamma}\Omega^{(1)}(\bar{\Gamma},\check{\Gamma},0)}$$

where

[34] $$\bar{\Gamma} = \frac{2\Gamma_{31}\Gamma_{41}+\Gamma_{21}\Gamma_{51}}{4\Gamma_{31}\Gamma_{61}-\Gamma_{51}^2} \qquad \tilde{\Gamma} = \frac{\Gamma_{51}-2\Gamma_{31}\Gamma_{42}}{4\Gamma_{31}\Gamma_{61}-\Gamma_{51}^2}$$

[35] $$\check{\Gamma} = \frac{2\Gamma_{21}\Gamma_{61}+\Gamma_{41}\Gamma_{51}}{4\Gamma_{31}\Gamma_{61}-\Gamma_{51}^2} \qquad \hat{\Gamma} = \frac{2\Gamma_{61}-\Gamma_{42}\Gamma_{51}}{4\Gamma_{31}\Gamma_{61}-\Gamma_{51}^2}$$

Γ_{jk} are functions of parameters and $\Gamma_{21} \gtreqless 0$, $\Gamma_{31} > 0$, $\Gamma_{42} > 0$, $\Gamma_{41} \gtreqless 0$, $\Gamma_{61} > 0$ and $\Gamma_{21} \gtreqless 0$. The sufficient condition for maximum requires that $4\Gamma_{31}\Gamma_{61} - \Gamma_{51}^2 > 0$.

In addition,

[36] $$\Omega(\alpha(s), R(s), s) = p\Delta_\tau(\alpha(s), R(s), s) + (1-p)\Delta_0(\alpha(s), R(s), s)$$

and $\Omega^{(h)}(\cdot,\cdot,\cdot)$ is the first derivative with respect to argument h, $h = 1, 2, 3$.

Proof of Proposition 3 Below we provide the proof for $0 < R \le \tau$ and skip the case $0 < \tau < R$, as it is similar to the one provided below. Under the assumption $\alpha^j s^k R^l \approx 0$, for $k \ge 2$ or $j + k + l \ge 3$ the matrix M_1 becomes

$$M_1 = \begin{pmatrix} \Lambda_{11} + s\Lambda_{12} & \Lambda_{21} - s\Lambda_{22} & -\Lambda_{31} \\ \Lambda_{41} & \Lambda_{51} & 0 \\ -\Lambda_{61} & 0 & 0 \end{pmatrix}$$

where Λ_{jk} are some functions of model parameters. Then the necessary and sufficient conditions for the maximum are given by

$$\begin{cases} \dfrac{\partial U(\Pi)}{\partial \alpha} = \Lambda_{41} + R\Lambda_{51} - 2\alpha\Lambda_{61} = 0 \\ \dfrac{\partial U(\Pi)}{\partial R} = \Lambda_{21} - s\Lambda_{22} - 2R\Lambda_{31} + \alpha\Lambda_{51} = 0 \end{cases}$$

and

$$4\Lambda_{31}\Lambda_{61} - \Lambda_{51}^2 > 0$$

The solution to the equation (50) yields the required result for $\alpha(s)$ and $R(s)$. As the next step we plug expressions for $\alpha(s)$ and $R(s)$ into

$$\Omega(\alpha, R, s) = p\Delta_\tau(\alpha, R, s) + (1-p)\Delta_0\,(\alpha, R, s)$$

and obtain Taylor series expansion of $\Omega(\alpha(s), R(s), s)$ around $s_0 = 0$. Applying our assumption to the series, equalizing to s and solving with respect to s yields also the required result for s.

6.4 Implications

To tentatively summarize the chapter's rather technical discussion, we conclude by focusing on a number of possible policy implications. The analysis shows that the size (τ) and the probability (p) of potential liquidity shocks impact the optimal level of reserves and reserves allocation. There is also a strong link between the institution's risk tolerance and the reserves management strategy.

1. In the presence of liquidity shocks, the demand for reserves and the risky assets depends on the size (τ) and the probability (p) of liquidity shocks as well as on the institution's risk aversion. Also, a highly risk averse central bank would hold reserves and would invest part of these reserves in the risky asset.
2. In the absence of economically meaningful liquidity shocks, the demand for reserves and consequently for the risky asset is lower. Banks with lower risk aversion hold reserves and invest these in the risky asset based on risk–return considerations. The demand for reserves and consequently for the risky asset approach zero when banks are highly risk averse.

These results show that reserves adequacy and diversification are interlinked decisions. Liquidity shocks have implications not only for the size of reserves but also for the reserves composition. Likewise, the bank's risk tolerance impacts not only the reserves composition but also its level. These results are in contrast to how decisions are made in practice. Here reserves adequacy is primarily discussed against the backdrop of external vulnerabilities and primary input for the reserves allocation decision is the institution's risk tolerance.

The results also indicate that a differentiation between core reserves and excess reserves might be difficult to make. As discussed in the introduction, traditionally the split is made by taking indicators of the country's external vulnerability into account. Conventionally, it is assumed that core reserves are invested conservatively in assets with low market and credit risk exposure while excess reserves are invested more aggressively. However, under some parameter constellations we have observed that a highly risk averse central bank holds reserves lower than the highest foreign currency loan possibly demanded by the firm while the reserves are invested in the risky asset.

Appendix

Lemma 1 Let f_y be the density function of y random variable. Assume that

$$f_y = \frac{\exp\left(-\frac{y-\mu}{\sigma}\right)}{\sigma\left(1+\exp\left(-\frac{y-\mu}{\sigma}\right)\right)^2} I_{\{-\infty<y<\infty\}}$$

Then for any $a > 0$ and $a \in \mathrm{R}$ we have

$$\mathrm{E}\left[\left(1-\frac{\max(0,y)}{a}\right)\mathrm{I}_{\{\max(0,y)\le a\}}\right] = \frac{\sigma}{a}\ln\left[\frac{\exp\left(\frac{\mu}{\sigma}\right)+\exp\left(\frac{a}{\sigma}\right)}{1+\exp\left(\frac{\mu}{\sigma}\right)}\right]$$

Proof of Lemma 1

$$E\left[\left(1-\frac{\max(0,y)}{a}\right)\mathrm{I}_{\{\max(0,y)\le a\}}\right] =$$

$$= \left[\left(\frac{a-\max(0,y)}{a}\right)\mathrm{I}_{\left\{\frac{a-\max(0,y)}{a}\ge 0\right\}}\right] =$$

$$= \int_{-\infty}^{\infty}\left(\frac{a-\max(0,y)}{a}\right)\mathrm{I}_{\left\{\frac{a-\max(0,y)}{a}\ge 0\right\}} f_y dy =$$

$$= \int_{-\infty}^{0} f_y dy + \int_{0}^{\infty}\left(\frac{a-y}{a}\right)\mathrm{I}_{\left\{\frac{a-y}{a}\ge 0\right\}} f_y dy =$$

$$= \frac{1}{1+\exp\left(\frac{\mu}{\sigma}\right)} + \left(\frac{\sigma}{a}\ln\left[\frac{\exp\left(\frac{\mu}{\sigma}\right)+\exp\left(\frac{a}{\sigma}\right)}{1+\exp\left(\frac{\mu}{\sigma}\right)}\right] - \frac{1}{1+\exp\left(\frac{\mu}{\sigma}\right)}\right) =$$

$$= \frac{\sigma}{a}\ln\left[\frac{\exp\left(\frac{\mu}{\sigma}\right)+\exp\left(\frac{a}{\sigma}\right)}{1+\exp\left(\frac{\mu}{\sigma}\right)}\right]$$

References

Aizenman, Joshua and Jaewoo Lee (2005) "International reserves: Precautionary versus mercantilist views, theory and evidence", NBER Working Papers 11366, National Bureau of Economic Research, Inc.

Aizenman, Joshua and Jaewoo Lee (2008) "Financial versus monetary mercantilism: Long-run view of large international reserves hoarding", *The World Economy,* 31(5): 593–611.

Aizenman, Joshua and Nancy Marion (2004) "International reserve holdings with sovereign risk and costly tax collection", *Economic Journal,* 114(497): 569–591.

Aizenman, Joshua, Brian Pinto and Artur Radziwill (2004) "Sources for financing domestic capital – is foreign saving a viable option for developing countries?", NBER Working Papers 10624, National Bureau of Economic Research, Inc.

Ben-Bassat, Avraham and Daniel Gottlieb (1992) "Optimal international reserves and sovereign risk", *Journal of International Economics,* 33(3–4): 345–362.

Calvo, Guillermo A. and Carmen M. Reinhart (2000) "Fear of floating", *SSRN eLibrary.*

Cardon, Pierre and Joachim Coche (2004) "Strategic asset allocation for foreign exchange reserves", in Bernadell, Carlos, Pierre Cardon, Joachim Coche, Francis X. Diebold and Simone Manganelli (eds) *Risk Management for Central Bank Foreign Reserves.*[Author query: citation information for this book?]

Chinn, Menzie and Jeffrey Frankel (2005) "Will the euro eventually surpass the dollar as leading international reserve currency?", Working Paper 11510, National Bureau of Economic Research.

Coche, Joachim, Matti Koivu, Ken Nyholm and Vesa Poikonen (2006) "Foreign reserves management subject to a policy objective". *SSRN eLibrary.*

de Beaufort Wijnholds, J. O. and A. Kapteyn (2001) "Reserve adequacy in emerging market economies". *SSRN eLibrary.*

Dooley, Michael P., David Folkerts-Landau and Peter Garber (2003) "An essay on the revived Bretton Woods system". Working Paper 9971, National Bureau of Economic Research.

Dooley, Michael P., David Folkerts-Landau and Peter Garber (2004) "The revived Bretton Woods system: The effects of periphery intervention and reserve management on interest rates and exchange rates in center countries", Working Paper 10332, National Bureau of Economic Research.

Dooley, Michael P., Saul Lizondo and Donald Mathieson (1989) "The currency composition of foreign exchange reserves", *IMF Staff Papers,* 36.

Eichengreen, Barry J. (2005) "Sterling's past, dollar's future: Historical perspectives on reserve currency competition", Working Paper 11336, National Bureau of Economic Research.

Eichengreen, Barry J. and Donald J. Mathieson (2000) "The Currency Composition of Foreign Exchange Reserves: Retrospect and Prospect", *SSRN eLibrary.*

Feldstein, M. S. (1999) A Self-Help Guide for Emerging Markets. *Foreign Affairs* 78(2): 93–109.

Fisher, Stephan and Min Lie (2004) "Asset allocation for central banks: optimally combining liquidity, duration, currency and non-government risk", in Bernadell, Carlos, Pierre Cardon, Joachim Coche, Francis X. Diebold and Simone Manganelli (eds) *Risk Management for Central Bank Foreign Reserves.*

Flood, Robert P. and Nancy P. Marion (2002) "Holding international reserves in an era of high capital mobility", *SSRN eLibrary.*

Fung, B. and R. N. McCauley (2000) "Composition fo US dollar foreign exchange reserves by instrument", *BIS Quarterly Review*, November, 59–60.

García, Pablo and Claudio Soto (2004) "Large hoardings of international reserves: Are they worth it?", Working Papers Central Bank of Chile 299, Central Bank of Chile.

Heller, Heinz Robert (1966) "Optimal international reserves", *The Economic Journal*, 76(302): 296–311.

Jeanne, Olivier and Romain Ranciere (2006) "The optimal level of international reserves for emerging market countries: Formulas and applications", *SSRN eLibrary*.

McCauley, Robert (2005) "Distinguishing global dollar reserves from official holdings in the United States", *BIS Quarterly Review*.

Papaioannou, Elias, Richard Portes and Gregorios Siourounis (2006) "Optimal currency shares in international reserves: The impact of the euro and the prospects for the dollar", Working Paper 12333, National Bureau of Economic Research.

Part II

Sovereign Wealth Management

7
Strategic Asset Allocation and Portfolio Construction for Sovereign Wealth Managers*

Bernard Lee, David Rogal and Fred Weinberger

7.1 Introduction

Increasing numbers of nations are facing a new challenge in managing significant accumulations of national wealth. The amount of external reserves accumulated by many countries exceeds that which even conservative central bank managers deem necessary to effect desired monetary and foreign exchange policies. According to an IMF survey in April 2008, sovereign wealth funds are projected to grow from $2–3 trillion in assets today to over $6 trillion in 2013. There is an increasing consensus that the appropriate investment policy for such excess assets, which are commonly regarded as having the luxury of a longer-term investment focus, is one that is less conservative than the traditional strategies for central bank reserves. The emphasis has shifted from a singular focus on safety and liquidity toward the achievement of higher levels of return, albeit by accepting higher levels of short-term risk. In fact, leading sovereign fund managers and central banks have already made commitments to an expanded range of asset classes. The expansion of investment latitude includes maturity extensions along the sovereign yield curves that form the core of traditional central bank liquidity portfolios, as well as investments in fixed income sectors such as corporate bonds and mortgage-backed securities, and even asset classes such as public and private equities, real estate, and hedge funds. Most recently, in light of the credit turmoil impacting financial institutions, a number of sovereign wealth funds have made direct investments in troubled institutions and have purchased commercial real estate overseas.

7.1.1 Outline of discussion

This chapter discusses several of the unique investment challenges facing sovereign wealth managers and analytical frameworks to address them. The

*This chapter is derived from previous works by the authors, published in Sovereign Wealth Management, in 2007 by Central Banking Publications Ltd.

IMF and the Sovereign Wealth Institute have broadly categorized sovereign wealth funds into five groups: (i) stabilization, (ii) savings, (iii) reserve investment corporations, (iv) pension reserve, and (v) development. Many funds, however, are hybrid in nature and serve multiple purposes. In this chapter, we focus on pure stabilization and savings funds.

We begin with the strategic asset allocation problem and demonstrate that appropriate policy-setting should incorporate the inflow and outflow characteristics of a country's national accounts. We discuss how risk should be viewed differently over short versus long horizons, and most importantly, how a shift in perspective may influence asset allocation preferences. We highlight the shortcomings of the Markowitz efficient frontier paradigm over multiple periods, and propose Monte Carlo simulation, using shortfall-based risk measures, as a practical alternative for determining optimal asset allocations over longer horizons.

The simulation approach is then illustrated with an example of a stabilization fund. The purpose of a stabilization fund is to smooth a country's budgetary and fiscal policies by isolating them from often volatile government revenues derived from royalties on the export of a country's natural resources. For example, when resource prices are high and state revenues grow rapidly, some of the extra revenues are diverted from the current budget into a stabilization fund where they remain until needed to make up budgetary shortfalls from declining resource revenues.

We next discuss savings funds, where discretionary spending is a key differentiator from the stabilization case. The spending decision should, however, not be arbitrary, and we focus on the question of how a spending rule might be developed in conjunction with an asset allocation policy to meet the objective of 'intergenerational equity' while achieving the highest possible level of real spending.

The strategic decision results in selecting a portfolio benchmark from an efficient opportunity set that offers a desirable combination of long-term return and risk. In the final section, we address the practical elements of portfolio construction using a wider array of asset classes with more complex risk attributes. Modern approaches to tactical asset allocation are discussed, beginning with a discussion of reverse optimization using a Black-Litterman style framework. We subsequently discuss proprietary extensions of such a framework that account for the risk of extreme events, a topic that is particularly relevant given the financial climate in 2008. We conclude with an application to real-world portfolio construction, using a pre-determined group of active fund managers.

7.1.2 Economic framework

We propose a basic configuration for the world economy that sets the stage for subsequent analyses and characterizes the salient features of different national accounts. We assume that the global economy is primarily populated by three types of countries, as shown in Figure 7.1.

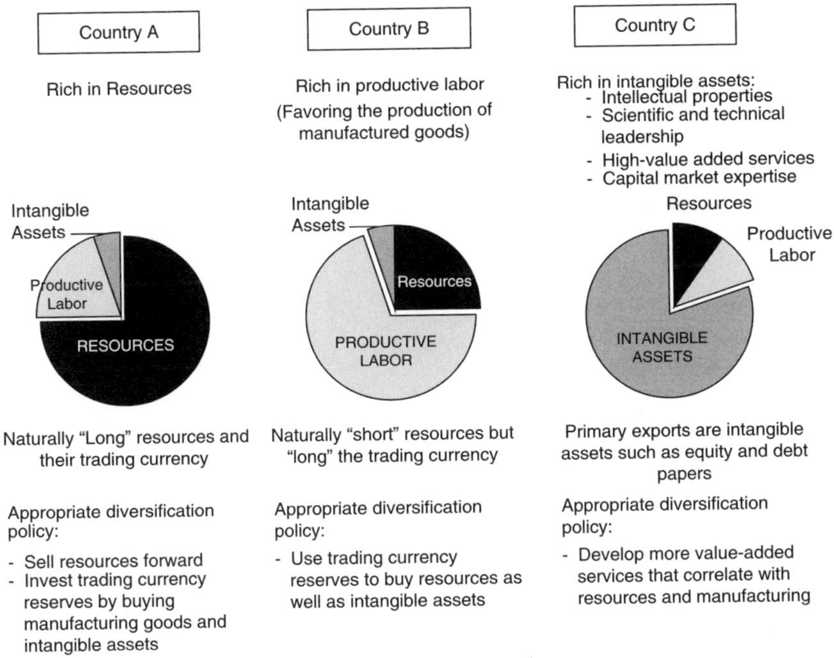

Figure 7.1 A three country model of the global economy

7.2 Strategic asset allocation

If we think about setting benchmarks and investment guidelines for any portfolio of assets, the question of what is on the other side of the balance sheet arises. That is, what are the desired payments that will be made over time from the funds available in the portfolio? It is typically easier to structure a portfolio against liabilities, which are contractually defined obligations, for which present values and bond-like risk characteristics, such as duration, can be measured. The claims on sovereign wealth portfolios, however, will typically be more equity-like, for which defining an investment approach is more difficult. While the equity beneficiary may have a well-defined objective in mind, often, the more discretionary purposes that equity interests address are conditional on the performance results of the portfolio. Thus, the specific guidelines from one fund to the next will largely reflect the manager's particular sense of the acceptable return/risk tradeoff.

An additional consideration for setting strategic benchmarks is suggested by Merton (1998), who describes how long-term wealth managers should also consider the potential substitution effects on portfolio allocations due to the characteristics of the inflows and outflows of a fund. For example, suppose that there is an ideal blueprint for the asset allocation for university endowments. Merton argues that a liberal arts university should reduce its stock allocations relative to this blueprint, under the expectation that alumni donations tend to rise in strong stock markets. The net impact creates inflow characteristics to the endowment that are strongly correlated to the stock market. The same logic can be applied to anticipated outflows. It makes financial sense for a university located in a cold climate with high energy consumption, or one located in an urban center with needs for subsidizing faculty housing, to invest directly in energy or local real estate as natural hedges to its cost base. In fact, it should do so above and beyond what would be needed under any ideal asset allocation blueprint. Consistent with Merton's proposed economic framework, sovereign wealth managers should understand the dynamics of their national accounts and the anticipated inflow and outflow characteristics of their portfolios.

7.2.1 The mean–variance efficient frontier paradigm

The asset allocation decision is typically a challenging one for most investors. Although much academic research has been devoted to the question of portfolio choice, for practitioners, the reigning paradigm for making asset allocation decisions is still the mean–variance efficient frontier. Its origins go back to the von Neumann-Morgenstern *Expected Utility Maximization Hypothesis* (1947), whose goal is not the maximization of terminal wealth, but the expected value of a function of that wealth conditioned on certain probable scenarios. This work was followed by the *Modern Portfolio Theory* (MPT), inspired by Markowitz (1952), which described how rational investors might express their preference in terms of expected return and portfolio risk as measured by variance, or standard deviation.

Figure 7.2 shows a simple efficient frontier for two asset classes, equities and bonds. Risk is measured along the horizontal axis by the standard deviation of annual returns and corresponding levels of expected annual return are along the vertical axis. Asset class return and risk assumptions are as labeled, and annual returns are assumed to be uncorrelated. In practice, econometric analysis is required to quantify the statistical attributes of different assets classes over the horizon of interest. Once statistical parameters are estimated, the efficient frontier presents the set of portfolio allocations that minimize risk at each level of expected return. The decision-maker is left to determine exactly where he/she is comfortable in the return–risk space.

Shortfall risk is an important concept for multi-period asset allocation, and even in the one-period case, it is a useful alternative to standard deviation. There are a variety of different shortfall-based risk measures, including probability of shortfall, expected shortfall, and downside variance. For

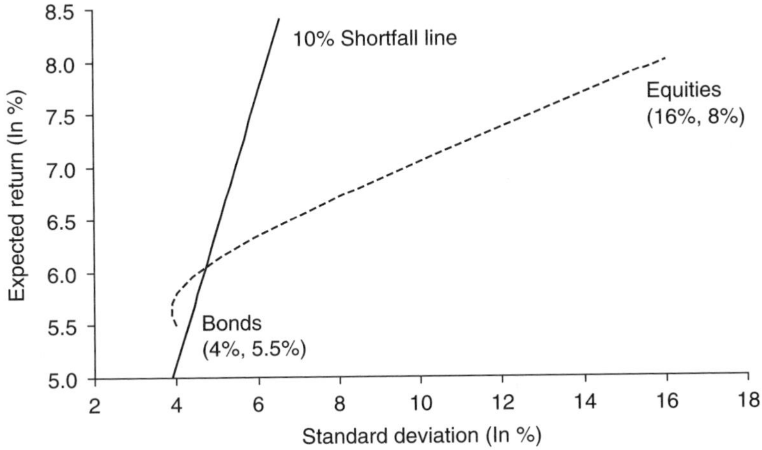

Figure 7.2 The efficient frontier: bonds and equities

illustration, we superimpose a shortfall line[12] upon the efficient frontier in Figure 7.2, which, for this example, requires 90% confidence of achieving a positive return. The highest return portfolio that satisfies this requirement occurs where the shortfall line crosses the efficient frontier.

We will return to the discussion of short-term portfolio construction in the third section of this chapter and will introduce modern tools that go beyond the standard Markowitz framework. We show how these tools mitigate some of the commonly recognized drawbacks of mean–variance analysis, namely, estimation error in the means and covariance matrix, as well as the normality assumption for asset returns. We offer practical results that portfolio managers may find helpful.

7.2.2 Shortcomings of mean–variance analysis for multi-period asset allocation

When considering portfolio choices for official institutions such as sovereign funds, and indeed in many other multi-period contexts, efficient frontier analysis does not effectively capture the return/risk tradeoffs involved. The efficient frontier is a one-period model and in its original form takes no account of liabilities. In contrast, the strategic benchmark for a sovereign fund must address risk over an extended horizon, in the presence of potentially differing liability characteristics.

The single-period metrics for return and risk – mean and standard deviation – become less relevant over multiple periods. For a one-year horizon, return and fund balance distributions are reasonably symmetric, for which mean and standard deviation effectively capture central tendency and dispersion. However, as the investment horizon increases,

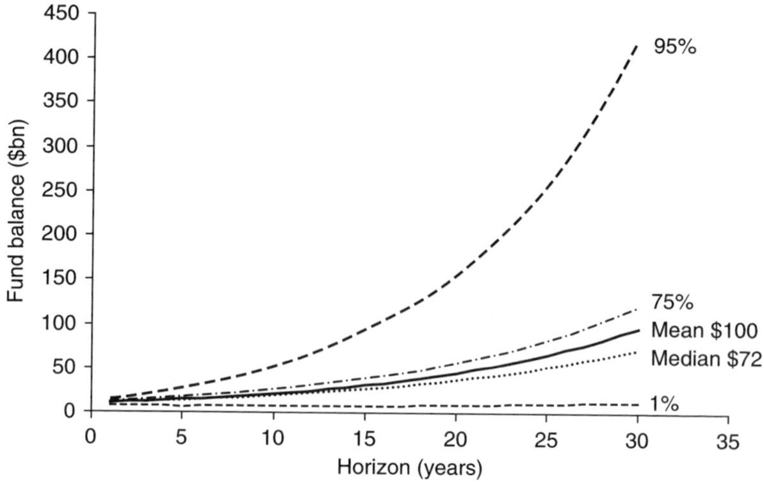

Figure 7.3 Probability distribution of the horizon equity fund balance

the distribution of total return develops increasing positive skew due to compounding. Figure 7.3 shows the horizon probability distribution of an equity fund balance assuming annual returns, as shown in Figure 7.2, are independently and identically distributed. As the horizon extends, the mean becomes biased upward by the long positive tail of very high outcomes and is no longer a good representation of the central outcome. In fact, at 30 years, there is almost a 70% probability that the portfolio's performance will fall below the mean. Similarly, standard deviation is biased by these high outcomes.

For multi-period distributions, a reasonable substitute for the mean return is the median. For risk, we will use the probability of shortfall versus the returns of a low risk baseline strategy. Specifically, we will require that alternative allocations have a tenth percentile horizon return greater than or equal to the tenth percentile return of an all bond strategy.

7.2.3 Monte Carlo simulation for multi-period analysis

Monte Carlo simulation is a common approach for computing multi-period return and risk metrics. As such, we have created simple models of stabilization and savings funds that permit us to specify different asset allocations, revenue, and spending behavior through time. We simulate asset allocations from the efficient frontier displayed in Figure 7.2, which comprises various mixes of bonds and equities of a representative Type C country. Each year the portfolio is assumed to be rebalanced to the selected asset allocation. A more comprehensive description of the simulation model is contained in the Appendix.

7.2.4 Multi-period risk measures and portfolio selection

Given our specified return and risk measures of median and shortfall probability, we now illustrate how the allocation decision will differ with the investment horizon. As the investment horizon increases, so too does the fund's ability to capture the additional risk premium offered by more volatile asset classes. The risk measure, as mentioned earlier, is defined relative to the percentiles of horizon return achievable with a baseline bond strategy. This bond baseline seems a natural choice given that excess reserves should achieve long-term returns that are greater than that of central bank fixed-income reserve portfolios. In the analysis that follows, risk is described as the 'breakeven percentile', which occurs at the crossover point of the cumulative densities of the respective horizon return distributions for the portfolio and baseline allocations.[3] Allocations with higher median returns are accepted only if their breakeven percentile is less than or equal to 10% (the 'risk budget'). A breakeven percentile greater than 10% implies that the allocation's tenth percentile horizon return is worse than that of bonds. If the breakeven percentile does not exist the allocation is either strictly superior (or inferior) to the baseline, such that the allocation achieves every possible baseline return with greater (or lesser) probability. This approach can be adapted to achieve higher levels of confidence; for example, we might demand that the breakeven percentile be less than 5%, or even 1%, depending on the decision-maker's risk tolerance.

7.2.5 Simulation results without exogenous flows

We begin with a simple analysis of portfolio performance when there are no intermediate inflows or outflows in the fund. In Figure 7.4 , we present optimal portfolio allocations at different horizons using our 10% risk budget, as well as two additional budgets of 5% and 15%, for illustration. At each horizon date we select the portfolio allocation on the efficient frontier in Figure 7.2 that maximizes median return subject to the risk budget constraint. For example, at year 1, the optimal portfolio allocation with a 10% risk budget is 20/80 (equities/bonds). In other words, the 20/80 allocation has a breakeven percentile of exactly 10% at year 1 and a higher median than the bond baseline. Allocations with more equity content have even higher median returns but would violate the risk budget via breakeven percentiles greater than 10%. Extending the horizon to 30 years, the 20/80 allocation is no longer optimal under our risk measure. In fact, the 20/80 allocation offers a 30-year breakeven percentile of almost zero, meaning, on an absolute basis, it will achieve almost every total return offered by bonds with greater probability. Clearly, with a 30-year horizon, the fund can tolerate additional risk and still meet the 10% criterion. In fact, the optimal allocation at 30 years is 55/45. Over 30 years, the median total return of the 55/45 allocation is about 36% greater than that of bonds alone.

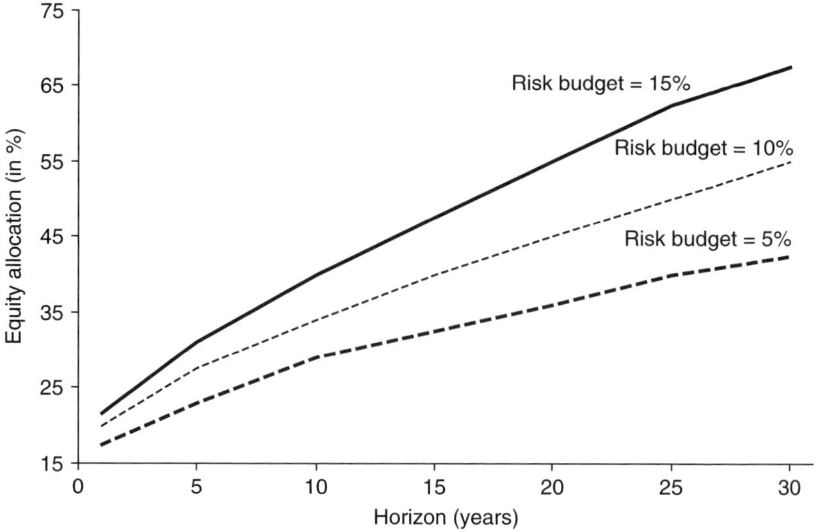

Figure 7.4 Optimal equity allocation at different horizons

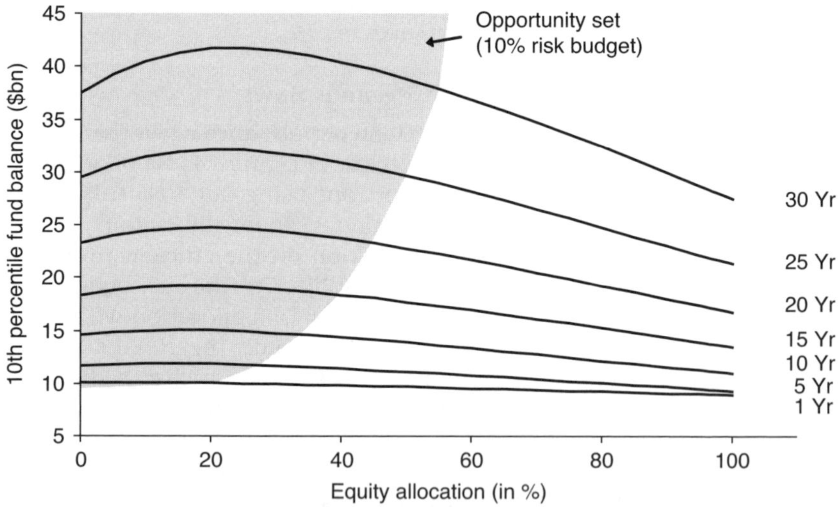

Figure 7.5 10th percentile fund balances

An alternate illustration is presented in Figure 7.5. The solid lines show tenth percentile fund balances at different horizons, as a function of the equity allocation. The shaded region represents the opportunity set of portfolios that satisfy the 10% risk-budget constraint. Portfolios on the boundary of the opportunity set are exactly the allocations plotted on the middle line of Figure 7.4. That is, the boundary allocations have breakeven percentiles exactly equal to 10% (they are at the same level as the tenth percentile fund balance on the Y-axis, that of the 100% bond allocation) and offer the highest median return achievable within the risk budget.

7.2.6 Strategic asset allocation for stabilization funds

In the following analysis, we examine a stabilization fund that experiences intermediate cash flows. Here, selecting a strategic benchmark requires careful consideration of the specific characteristics of possible future flows. Similar insight is now commonplace among pension funds and insurance companies, where investment policy is often driven by the attributes of an estimated liability stream. As we will show, liability-driven considerations may result in changes to the benchmarks that are derived in an 'asset-only' framework. Specifically, the expected direction of flows changes the effective investment horizon, variability alters standalone return/risk tradeoffs, and dependence with investment asset returns can result in substitution effects.

We focus on the stabilization fund of a Type A country with abundant natural resource wealth. The fund begins with $10 billion in financial assets and the government's future revenues, in excess of tax receipts, come principally from crude oil exports. In years with a fiscal surplus (or deficit), government funds are directed into (or out of) the stabilization fund. If the fund depletes, the government must issue debt at the prevailing sovereign interest rate to meet budget deficits. For simplicity, real fiscal spending and tax revenue are constant at $1.0 billion and $0.25 billion, so that annual oil revenues of $0.75 billion exactly balance the budget. We assume that domestic oil production is deterministic, so that changes in the annual budget are perfectly correlated with the changes in the market clearing oil price. The relationship between flows and the investment assets can then be determined through historical data analysis. Specifically, we have examined annual changes in the spot price of oil and the levels of major developed equity and bond indices over a 50 year period. We estimate that annual changes in spot oil, and consequently the annual flows in the fund, have correlations to annual equity and bond returns of –0.20 and –0.40, respectively. While different economic regimes existed during the past 50 years, our model, which has stationary statistical properties, can only capture the 'average' experience. In this general sense, the analysis is intended to provide relatively basic intuition for long-term strategic planning.[4]

The analysis considers two scenarios for natural resource revenues. In a flat scenario, the country expects annual real oil revenues of $0.75 billion, exactly enough to balance the budget. In this case, on average, the stabilization fund will not experience any net flows. In a declining scenario, the country expects gradually declining domestic production, such that, on average, the fund will experience outflows. It is assumed that the country's production alone cannot influence global supply and therefore cannot impact the market clearing oil price.

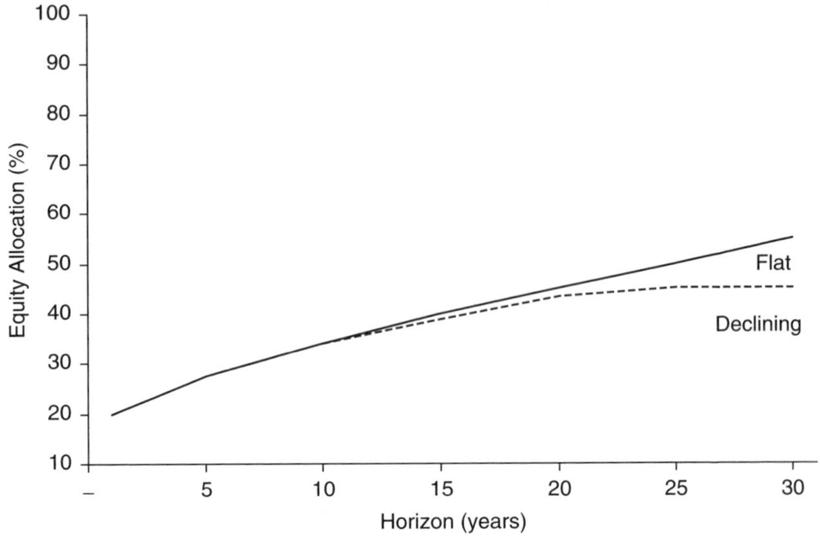

Figure 7.6 Optimal equity allocations with deterministic oil revenues

For intuition, we first examine the case of deterministic natural resource revenue, where oil prices can be projected with perfect certainty. With this simple case, we can isolate the effect of directional flows on asset allocation policy. Figure 7.6 presents results for flat and declining revenue scenarios. As before, we enforce a 10% constraint on the breakeven percentile, using the bond baseline. The flat scenario is a simple reference point – in a deterministic setting, it is exactly the case of a fund that does not experience flows, and thus matches the results shown on the middle line in Figure 7.4. In the declining scenario, sustained cash outflows shorten the effective horizon of the stabilization fund, requiring a more conservative asset allocation policy. For 30 years, the equity allocation must be reduced from 55% to 45% in order to satisfy the risk budget constraint. Larger outflows would demand ever more conservative policies.

Since real world flows in a stabilization fund are volatile and difficult to predict, we now introduce uncertainty in annual oil prices and examine the resulting impact on the asset allocation decision. As before, we assume that domestic production is known and either flat or declining. However, oil prices are now randomly sampled concurrently with asset returns. We emphasize that introducing uncertain oil prices, and therefore uncertain cash flows in the fund, increases the dispersion of the stabilization fund balance, irrespective of the asset allocation. Furthermore, and critical to our asset allocation selection criterion, uncertain cash flows increase the volatility of bond-heavy portfolios relatively more than equity-heavy portfolios.

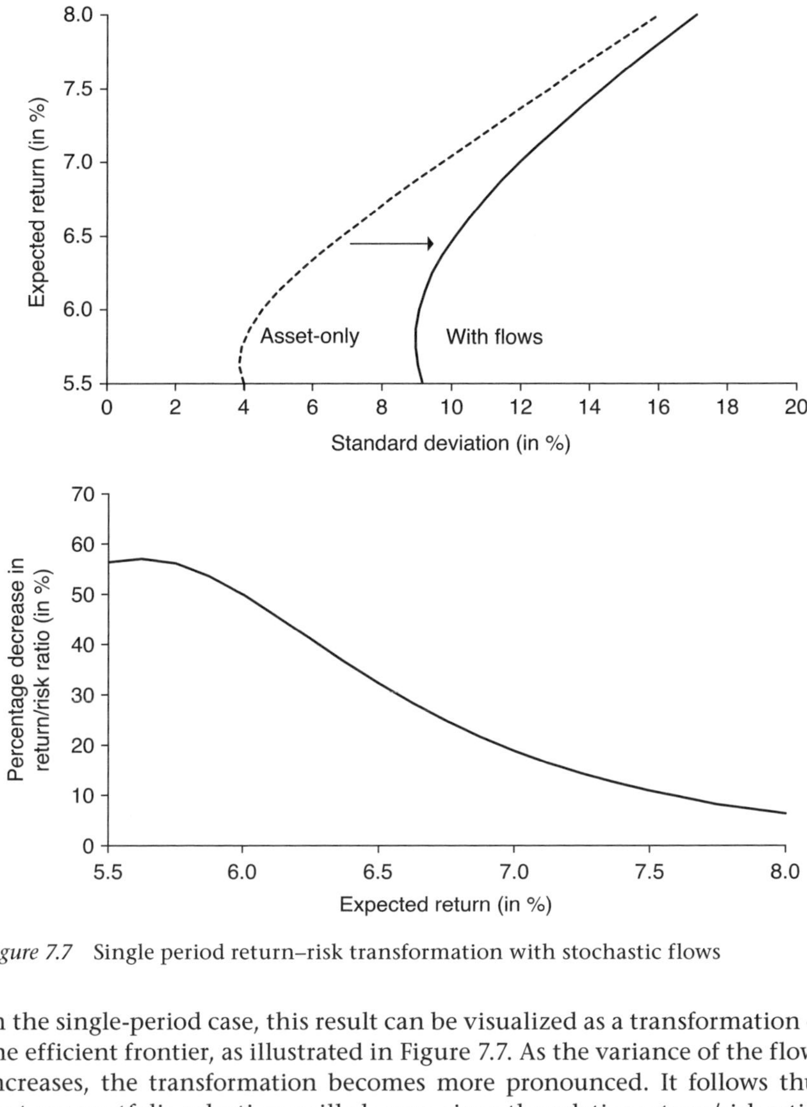

Figure 7.7 Single period return–risk transformation with stochastic flows

In the single-period case, this result can be visualized as a transformation of the efficient frontier, as illustrated in Figure 7.7. As the variance of the flows increases, the transformation becomes more pronounced. It follows thus that our portfolio selections will change, since the relative return/risk ratios along the frontier change.

For illustration, Figure 7.7 assumes that oil price changes are on average zero and have a standard deviation of 10%. As is evident, the volatility of the 100% bond portfolio increases from 4% to over 9%, and in fact the flows have a marginal contribution of 90% to this volatility. By contrast, the volatility of the 100% equity allocation increases comparatively less, from 16% to about 17%, and the flows have a smaller marginal contribution to total volatility – only 23%. Clearly, for the bond baseline, the majority of risk over a single period comes from uncertainty in the fund's cash flows. The right chart in Figure 7.6 shows the percentage decline in the return-to-risk ratio when stochastic flows are included. As shown, the decline is greater for portfolios concentrated in bonds.

The conclusions of the one-period case extend to multiple periods. However, with a growing or shrinking fund, flow variability will not be a fixed percentage of the fund over time. If the absolute mean and variance of the flows remain constant, the impact on risk may be exaggerated (diminished) if the fund is shrinking (growing) through time. Because of these complexities, we rely on simulation techniques to draw conclusions over extended horizons. Figure 7.8 presents the results for uncertain oil revenues. As is evident, the optimal equity allocations are substantially greater than those shown for the deterministic case. These results make intuitive sense; the return/risk tradeoff diminishes relatively more for the baseline allocation compared to the higher returning alternatives.

As we have shown, the interrelationship of the cash flows and asset returns impacts the return/risk tradeoffs achievable for horizon fund balances. In fact, the interrelationships between flows and assets can actually result in different one-period efficient frontiers, compared with 'asset-only' frontiers – that is, where there are no flows. Recall that we wish to select our optimal multi-period allocations from portfolios that are one-period efficient. Given that we have used a simple two asset frontier, we are assured that this is in fact the case, even in the presence of flows. More generally,

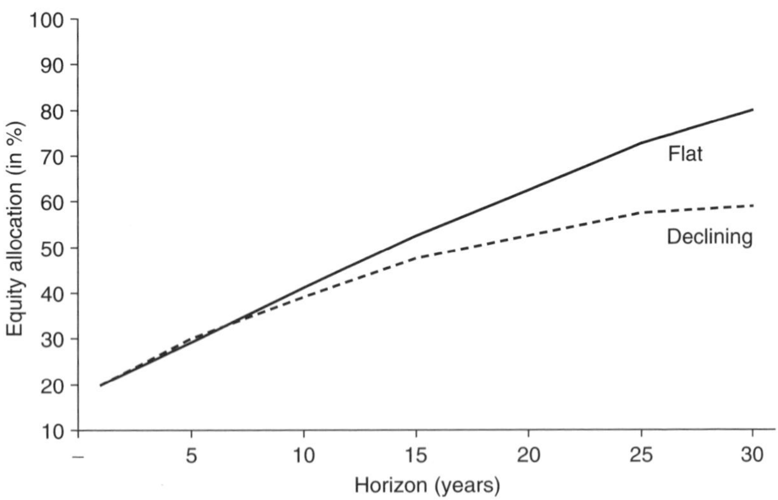

Figure 7.8 Optimal equity allocations with stochastic oil revenues

however, with more than two asset classes from which to create portfolios, we cannot be assured that the asset-only frontier remains efficient in the presence of exogenous flows.

The most significant effect of the exogenous oil revenues on the asset-only frontier could be expected in the allocations to asset classes that exhibit high positive or negative correlations with oil prices. These allocations will be most impacted by substitution effects from the flows either through reduced or increased levels in the portfolio. To understand this substitution effect, we introduce a third financial asset, an energy sector fund, which may be viewed as a substitute for the stabilization fund's intrinsic long oil exposure. In actuality, these two assets, while closely related, are not fungible. As described earlier, the country's intrinsic position arises from future oil revenues determined by future production and oil prices. The present value of these revenues can be thought of as a nontradable allocation to oil, provided forward sales are not executed via long-term supply contracts. In this case, financial allocations to the energy sector fund are less attractive than in the asset-only context.

The introduction of a third asset requires additional modeling complexity. In order to tackle this problem, we have used a scenario optimization approach with a modified risk measure that (i) expedites the optimization procedure and (ii) accounts for both the probability and magnitude of shortfalls. A detailed exposition of this model is beyond the scope of this current article. We present summary results in Figure 7.9 below. As shown, properly accounting for flows suggests substantial reductions to the energy fund allocations that are derived in an asset-only framework.

In summary, stabilization fund managers should consider at least three factors when determining the strategic asset allocation benchmark. First,

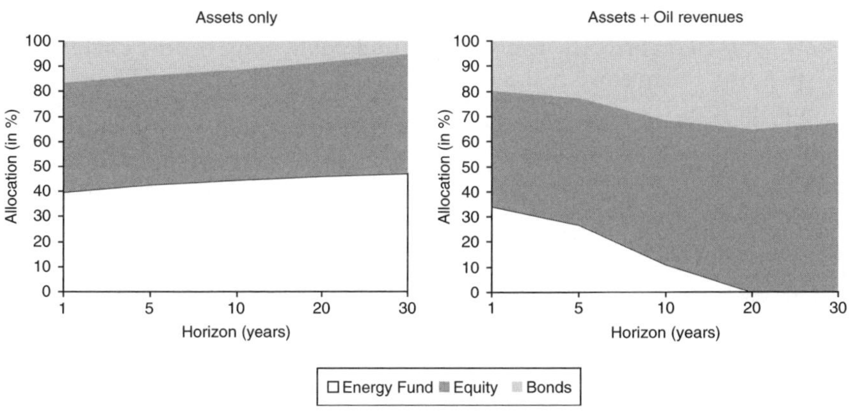

Figure 7.9 The substitution effect and optimal allocations for three financial assets

the investment horizon should be established. Longer horizons will enable the fund to capture the additional risk premium offered by higher volatility allocations. Second, the mean and volatility of potential future cash flows should be estimated. Expected outflows shorten the effective horizon of the fund and thus demand a more conservative asset allocation policy. Larger, more uncertain flows reduce the appeal of less volatile asset allocations. Third, the relationship of the cash flows to available investments should be estimated, to account for substitution effects. Assets that on average behave differently than the underlying flows will act as a natural hedge and will mitigate volatility in the fund balance.

7.2.7 Strategic asset allocation and spending rules for savings funds

Savings funds also receive contributions from the excess revenues received by the government, but their purpose is to share the country's resource wealth with future generations. These funds are referred to as intergenerational funds and are commonly viewed similarly to private sector endowments. Like endowments, these funds are often intended as permanent funds, designed to provide spending in an equitable manner over many generations. The establishment of an appropriate spending policy needs to consider the risk profile of the asset portfolio. All else being equal, the higher the volatility of asset returns, the more likely the same spending rate will result in the fund experiencing declines in real value, resulting in potentially adverse political outcomes for policy makers. Moreover, the establishment of a spending policy needs careful consideration because once established, it may be difficult to revise in an expeditious manner.

As noted, the purpose of savings funds is to share the wealth accumulated from the extraction and sale of a nation's nonrenewable resources with future generations. In the strictest sense, to provide equity across generations means that spending in real terms should be constant each year. If the portfolio's return volatility were low and the average real rate of return on assets estimated correctly, the savings fund could achieve this goal simply by spending the average real return of the portfolio each year. Under these circumstances, the real fund value would remain fairly constant. Just the same, if on average a fund could achieve higher, albeit more volatile, spending such a strategy might be preferred.

The pursuit of intergenerational equity implies a careful coordination of spending with the returns earned on the fund's assets. In a world where portfolio returns and the real value of the savings fund are volatile, the challenge is to devise both an asset allocation strategy and a spending rule that can offer a relatively high level of spending while affording as much stability to both spending and ongoing fund value as possible. An objective spending rule should be devised and articulated, rather than making annual ad hoc spending decisions that might be subject to political influences.

The selection of an appropriate spending rule is a challenging issue faced also by universities and other private sector endowments. In research literature, three common rules are often mentioned. The first is to adjust spending each year by inflation, which will result in a constant amount of real spending over time. The problem with such a rule is that it is disconnected from what is occurring to the fund's real value. If the amounts being spent do not properly reflect the portfolio's real return, the fund can substantially grow or decline over time. The second basic approach is to spend the estimated long-term real rate of return of the portfolio multiplied by the fund value. Here, spending becomes a function of actual near-term performance. The difficulty with this approach is that it can result in volatile spending patterns, as spending will be fully determined by the potentially volatile fund balance. Volatile spending patterns may present both budgetary and political challenges. A third approach that has gained considerable favor is the so-called Yale-Stanford mixed rule, which is a weighted average of the first two approaches:

$$S_t = W_i \cdot \pi_{t-1} \cdot S_{t-1} + W_a \cdot R \cdot V_t$$

S_t, Spending in the current period
S_{t-1}, Spending in the previous period
π_{t-1}, Inflation in the previous period
W_i, Weight given to "inflation" element, typically 60–70%
W_a, Weight given to "asset" element, typically 30–40%
R, Long-term spending rate
V_t, Three period moving average of the fund value

The mixed approach adjusts for inflation, which promotes stability in real spending and preserves intergenerational purchasing power. However, it also pulls spending in the direction of the fund balance, which prevents the overspending that is typical of exclusively inflation-based rules.

As compared with a stabilization fund, there are more variables that can be adjusted in attempting to achieve a satisfactory return/risk tradeoff for a savings fund. In addition to asset allocation, there is also room to adjust the spending rule. In the following analysis, we will use the Yale-Stanford rule and fix the inflation and asset weights in the above formula, W_i and W_a, at 70% and 30% respectively. In the search for a satisfactory spending rule, we will adjust the long-term spending rate, R, particularly when we depart from the baseline bond strategy.

Our stated objective for a savings fund is achieving intergenerational equity, or stable real spending through time. In practice, there are many real-world complexities that arise when judging success. For example, what measure of inflation is used to adjust annual spending? How should policy change if we allow for regime shifts in required spending? What if outsized contributions enable sustained increased welfare (through higher real spending) going forward? Consideration of these realities is beyond the scope of this chapter. Given uncertain outcomes for realized portfolio returns and for inflation, we will seek to achieve intergenerational equity in a probabilistic sense. The statistic we will focus on will be the median real spending achieved at future horizons. We will seek to stabilize median spending over time at the highest possible level that is consistent with acceptable risk. Risk will again be measured as the breakeven percentile using a bond portfolio as the baseline allocation. For the sake of intergenerational equity, we will seek to achieve a relatively stable level of risk through time. Clearly, decision -akers will have a number of simultaneous objectives that need to be traded off against one another in arriving at a total policy that integrates the asset allocation decision and the spending decision.

7.2.8 Optimizing the spending rule

We begin our analysis of spending policy by setting the long-term spending rate, R, equal to the expected real return of the asset allocation chosen. To measure real returns, we introduce a mean-reverting inflation process with a long-term average annual inflation rate of 2.0%. We continue with our earlier assumptions for asset returns, so that the average real returns are 6.0% and 3.5% respectively for equities and bonds.[5] As before, the baseline allocation is a bond portfolio and we will use the expected real bond return, 3.5%, as the baseline spending rate. If we spend the expected real portfolio return, how will different asset allocation strategies perform through time? Can we increase real spending with greater allocations to equities, or will we jeopardize future generations' welfare?

Figure 7.9 shows median real spending at different horizons for various combinations of bonds and equities. As is evident, the bond baseline provides steady, modestly increasing results. The equity strategy, which offers a higher expected real return, initially provides substantially higher spending than bonds. This is a consequence of using a higher long-term spending rate, R, in the spending formula. However, as the horizon lengthens, the increased volatility of equities dominates and median spending diminishes substantially, since spending is a function of a diminishing (median) fund balance. After 40 years, the median begins to fall below that of bonds. With the requirement of stable real spending, the equity strategy is a sure failure; we have skewed benefits to early generations, at the expense of future welfare.[6] Results for intermediate allocations are shown with the dotted lines. Clearly, some intermediate allocations can provide stable median spending higher than that of the bond baseline. To determine if such strategies are viable alternatives to bonds, we must determine if they fall within the established risk budget.

Figure 7.11 shows the corresponding intergenerational risk profiles of the asset allocations in Figure 7.10. Allocations that fall within the risk budget

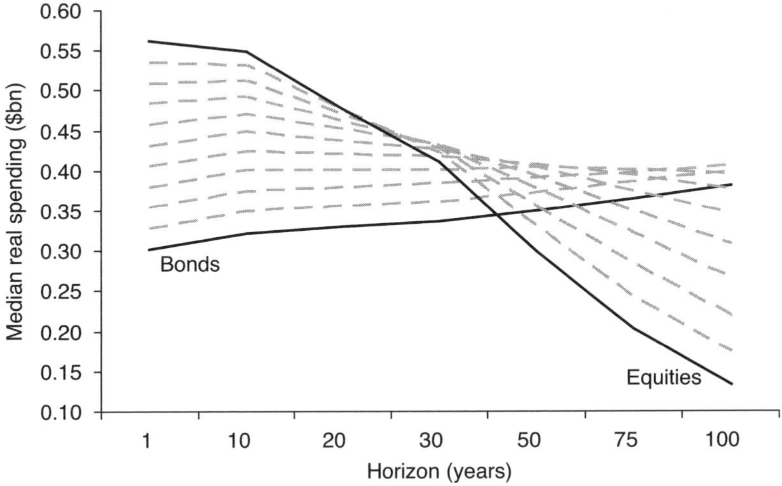

Figure 7.10 Median real spending, R = expected real return

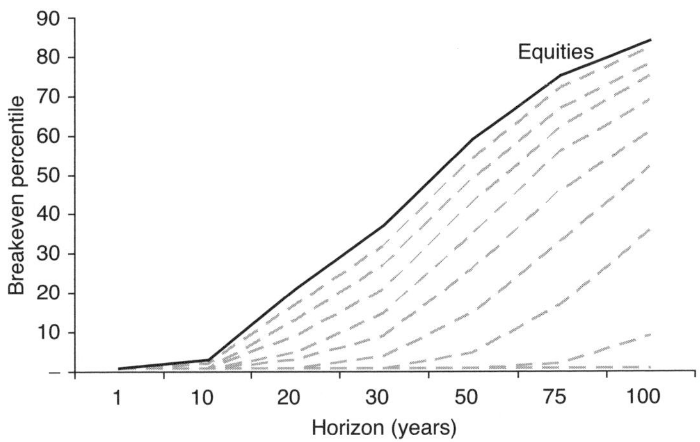

Figure 7.11 Breakeven percentile for annual real spending, R = expected real return

must have breakeven percentiles for real spending that are less than or equal to 10%. As is evident, spending the expected real return on equities presents substantial risk over long-horizons, compared to bonds. Furthermore, even allocations that provided attractive and stable median spending profiles in Figure 7.10, for example the 30/70 allocation, violate the 10% risk budget at longer horizons.

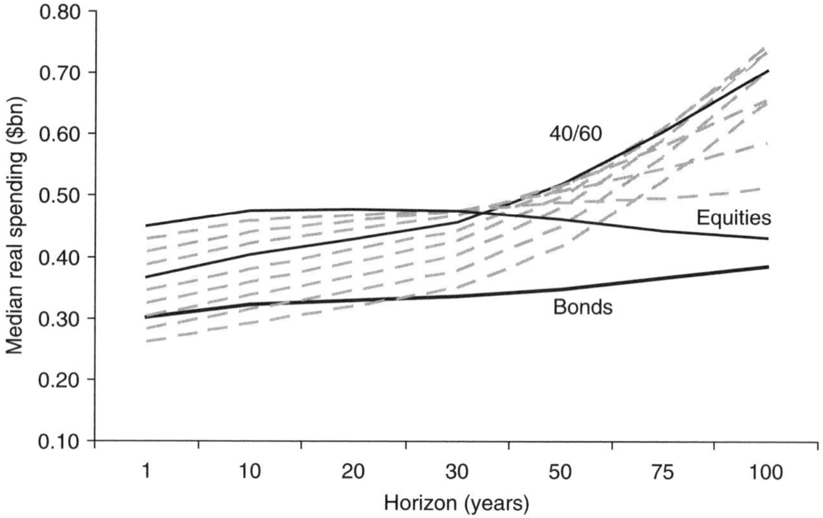

Figure 7.12 Median real spending, R = 80% of expected real return

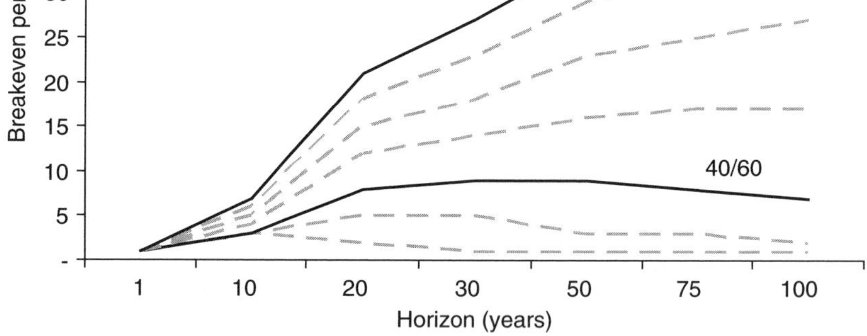

Figure 7.13 Breakeven percentile for annual real spending, R = 80% of expected real return

Notwithstanding these disappointing results, the case for higher returns is not lost. We need not, in our spending formula, spend the full expected real return. Figure 7.12 shows results when setting R, the long-term spending rate, equal to 80% of the expected real return. Here, the median real spending on equities is fairly stable and remains greater that that of bonds (for which we continue to spend the full real return) over a 100 year horizon. For intermediate allocations, the median is steady or increasing with time.

To determine which of the allocations in Figure 7.12 are satisfactory under our risk budget, we again examine the horizon breakeven percentiles. The results are shown in Figure 7.13. The equity allocation violates the risk budget at 12 years, and has a breakeven percentile as high as 45 percent at 100 years. Without a doubt, even as we target 80% of the expected real return, equities present future generations with undue risk. The 40/60 allocation, which is highlighted in Figures 7.12 and 7.13, stays within the 10% risk budget. It also achieves median real spending well above bonds at all horizons. While spending is substantially skewed in favor of future generations, this may be viewed as quite acceptable, since the intergenerational risk profile is exceptionally stable.

In conclusion, savings fund managers have two main tools at their disposal, the spending rule and the asset allocation decision. We have shown how a judicious management of these tools can create attractive real spending and risk profiles. As noted earlier in our introduction to this section, with a low volatility bond strategy we can achieve an equitable spending profile over different horizons by spending the expected real rate of return. However, by selecting allocations with higher returns and higher volatility, we can spend a portion of the real return and achieve median spending that exceeds that of bonds at all horizons, at acceptable and relatively stable intergenerational risk.

7.3 Portfolio construction

Once the appropriate strategic benchmark is determined, the next step is constructing actual portfolios and monitoring their risk through time. The financial markets exhibit volatility around their intrinsic values determined with all available information. This may be caused by information asymmetry, irrational agents, liquidity squeezes, asset bubbles, and a host of other potential causes. It thus stands to reason that there may be periods of disequilibrium and dislocation, where investors may capture additional profit relative to an established strategic benchmark. Importantly, to ensure risk limits are maintained, tactical and manager allocation decisions should be made in the context of the fund's strategic benchmark. Portfolio allocations, returns, and risk are thus defined in a relative sense, and a predetermined risk budget guides methodical deviations. In practice, the techniques required to incorporate market views and to quantify relative risk are quite sophisticated, and we spend the next part of this chapter discussing them in some detail.

7.3.1 The Black-Litterman approach to portfolio construction

The Black-Litterman approach is derived from the classical mean–variance asset allocation framework. In order to circumvent MPT's tendency to maximize those positions with the highest estimation errors, Sharpe (1974) introduced the methodology of *reverse optimization*. Instead of constructing optimal portfolios based on risk and expected returns, this concept is about understanding the set of expected returns that would make the current portfolio weights optimal. A practical twist on this concept was proposed by Black and Litterman (1992), who suggest that one way to apply the concept of reverse optimization was to understand the "implicit bets" of a portfolio – such as an implied yield curve as described in Lee (2000). This information can then be used to structure or rebalance a portfolio based on forward-looking views.

There are three clear advantages to using the Black-Litterman approach.

1. It enforces consistency between risk and return expectations.
2. It provides the investor with the ability to conduct pre-trade analysis on possible portfolio decisions, thereby making sure that returns of any potential investments are proportional to their marginal contributions to risk.
3. It enables the investor to mix implied views with statistical or his/her own fundamental portfolio management views, and thus achieve far more stable and sensible optimized results.

One important limitation of this approach is that it assumes normality of assets returns. The fact that these implied returns are computed purely from variance and correlation limit their relevance to asset classes that show prominent tail risk behavior. This is particularly true over the short to medium term (the tactical horizon) where nonnormality in markets can become an important consideration. This failure to capture tail risk behavior can expose investors to extreme downside risk, often without fair compensation, a concern that is particularly important to decision-makers in the current market environment.

7.3.2 Capturing the risk of extreme events

BlackRock has implemented an enhanced asset allocation framework which permits portfolio risk to be portrayed more realistically by incorporating the non-normal tail risk behaviors of more complex asset classes. The approach computes implied returns that reflect the true risk of the portfolio, ultimately leading to better asset allocation decisions that are based on a more realistic assessment of risk and returns.

The BlackRock model was originally developed to provide a robust quantitative approach to making hedge fund allocation decisions. Our empirical research shows that the classic Black-Litterman model consistently leads to counterintuitive allocation results for certain asset classes, such as hedge funds. It is well-known that while hedge funds tend to produce absolute returns that are less correlated with the overall market, some might also suffer substantially during low-probability, extreme events. The classic Black-Litterman framework would fail to properly evaluate such funds. For example, fixed income arbitrage funds would be evaluated as if they are certificates of deposit, and their tail risk characteristics would remain unaccounted for. Table 7.1 presents the example of an equally-weighted portfolio using common hedge fund indices, including a proxy fixed income arbitrage manager.

When tail events are correctly accounted for, as shown in Table 7.2, the implied returns of the fixed income arbitrage fund will be significantly higher.

When constructing portfolios that consist of a mix of complex asset classes, this technique allows the decision-maker to account for higher-order cross moments and thus mitigate the tail risk behavior of the overall portfolio. Essentially, these higher-order cross moments are statistical parameters expressing how one manager may perform when another suffers from an extreme market event. In many cases, this performance can be surprisingly different from what one may infer from the correlation matrix alone. For instance, during the Long-Term Capital Management debacle in October of 1998, many fixed income arbitrage funds suffered from significant draw-downs due to the depletion of liquidity in the fixed income market. Meanwhile, certain equity hedge funds actually showed positive performance. During that period, the significant spike in volatility and risk aversion benefited equity hedge funds that were long volatility, or traded as if they were replicating long equity options. In short, an intelligent combination of a fixed income arbitrage fund and an equity volatility fund would have created a portfolio

Table 7.1 Using implied returns WITHOUT tail risk adjustment

Sleeve	Weight %	Marginal Contribution to Risk (MCR %)	Ratio of (MCR % ÷ Weight %)	Implied Returns (IR %)
HFRI Convertible Arbitrage Index	12.50	5.93	0.47	6.27
HFRI Distressed Securities Index	12.50	13.34	1.07	10.66
HFRI Equity Hedge Index	12.50	23.36	1.87	16.60
HFRI Equity Market Neutral Index	12.50	5.42	0.43	5.97
HFRI Macro Index	12.50	19.33	1.55	14.21
Fixed Income Proxy Manager	12.50	15.39	1.23	11.87
CISDM CTA Index	12.50	10.21	0.82	8.80
HFRI Relative Value Arb. Index	12.50	7.02	0.56	6.91

Table 7.2 Using implied returns WITH tail risk adjustment

Sleeve	**Weight %**	**Tail Risk Contribution (TRC %)**	**Ratio of (TRC % ÷ Weight %)**	**Implied Returns (IR %)**
HFRI Convertible Arbitrage Index	12.50	6.51	0.52	7.75
HFRI Distressed Securities Index	12.50	12.04	0.96	11.95
HFRI Equity Hedge Index	12.50	1.41	0.11	3.07
HFRI Equity Market Neutral Index	12.50	4.73	0.38	6.34
HFRI Macro Index	12.50	6.74	0.54	7.65
Fixed Income Proxy Manager	12.50	66.06	5.29	38.65
CISDM CTA Index	12.50	–7.14	–0.57	–3.12
HFRI Relative Value Arb. Index	12.50	9.64	0.77	10.20

that exhibited the desirable statistical properties of the fixed income arbitrage fund, and mitigated some of its undesirable tail risk characteristics. In the context of the market environment in 2008, applying this technique would suggest using equity volatility products as a hedge against the extreme market moves experienced by mortgage and credit-linked products.

From the early days of MPT, at the heart of all portfolio performance metrics are the fundamental definitions of risk and return. Therefore, once we understand the statistical properties of more complex asset classes, the next step is to define a more advanced portfolio performance metric that can correctly make a distinction between desirable and undesirable statistical properties. For returns, we use the portfolio gain process introduced by Karatzas and Shreve (1998) to account for the impact of a second-order effect known as correlation correction. For risk, we use the *Cornish-Fisher* expansion (1936) to correctly account for skewness, kurtosis as well as the higher-order cross moments in returns (sometimes also known as co-skewness and co-kurtosis). The question then is, 'Is there a better way to combine the two besides the simplistic return to risk ratio?' Knowing that the return to risk ratio provides a functional form that is roughly correct, such a ratio is modified to produce mathematical properties that are similar to those of the Omega Function proposed by Keating and Shadwick (2005).[7] These characteristics include the following:

1. If a particular manager in the portfolio shows upside characteristics, then the portfolio performance metric will improve.

2. If a particular manager in the portfolio contributes to portfolio tail risk, then the portfolio performance metric will worsen.
3. If all managers in the portfolio are normal, then the portfolio performance metric will gradually revert to a Sharpe-Ratio-like measure.

The end result is a performance metric called the *Alternative Sharpe Ratio* (ASR), as described in Lee and Lee (2004). This metric exhibits mathematical properties similar to those of the Omega function, as well as the touch and feel of the Sharpe Ratio with which most portfolio managers are familiar. The ASR equivalent for long-only portfolios is called the *Adjusted Information Ratio* (AIR), which uses the same functional form on measures of active returns in order to address their nonnormality. We find it instructive to use active returns, because a key driver of nonnormality appears to be idiosyncratic risk. The ability to go long (assets) and short (benchmarks) cancels out a portion of systematic risk, leaving idiosyncratic risk as the primary driver of nonnormality. The long-short characteristics of hedge funds essentially produce the same effect. This advanced performance metric is at the heart of the BlackRock proprietary portfolio construction approach. In practice, optimal manager allocations could be determined by maximizing the ASR or the AIR relative to the strategic benchmark, within any practical portfolio constraints.

In Figure 7.14, the empirical distribution of weekly returns of a portfolio of real-life managers rebalanced using both the classical mean–variance and the BlackRock approaches shows how the BlackRock approach attempts

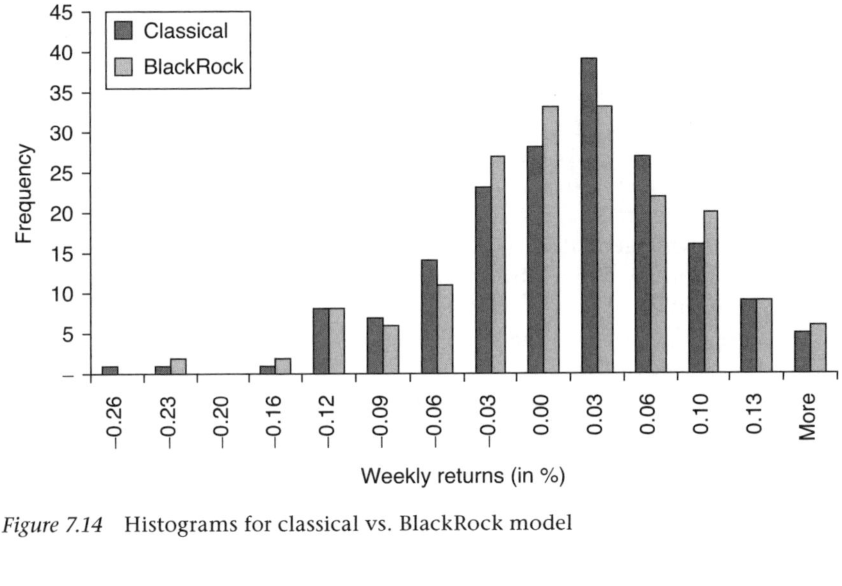

Figure 7.14 Histograms for classical vs. BlackRock model

Table 7.3 Portfolio statistics

	Classical	BlackRock
Mean Active Return (Ann.)	0.26%	0.26%
Volatility (Ann.)	0.53%	0.53%
Skewness	–0.502	–0.422
Kurtosis	1.084	0.848
97.5% Exp. Tail Loss (Ann.)	–1.15%	–1.37%

to "shift" the mass of the return distribution to the right. While in this case both the approaches assume an identical mean active return (identical "centers of gravity"), it will be desirable to choose the one with more masses to the right of the mean.

The corresponding portfolio statistics are in Table 7.3. As is evident, the BlackRock model provides more desirable skewness and kurtosis characteristics.

7.3.3 Allocating managers to fit a strategic benchmark

Once strategic benchmarks are ascertained, a sovereign fund's logical next step is to allocate assets to actual fund managers. It should be noted that while some sovereign funds do employ internal managers to manage a minor portion of the portfolio and to run active overlays, most allocate the majority or even all of their portfolios to external managers. A core part of their mandate is the selection of superior managers and the construction of a portfolio that can withstand the shocks of challenging environments.

Instead of the 40/60 strategic benchmark previously discussed for the savings fund, suppose the chief investment officer (CIO) has decided to make a tactical allocation to equities that would result in a 50/50 allocation. A deviation of 10% from the strategic benchmark is not unusual, and, in this case, is motivated by the relatively attractive valuations present in the current market environment. If the savings fund has chosen to invest in the bonds and equities of Type C countries, we could define the target allocation as in Table 7.4.

The first investment decision made by the CIO is to deviate from the 40/60 allocation to 50/50. This change would be considered a 'broad allocation' decision and is typically a significant contributor to the active risk of the portfolio, as we will see later. The second investment decision is that within the 50% equities, the CIO may want to make increased allocations to European and Asian equities that are different from the stipulated 20% total. Similar country and sector decisions might also be applied to bond allocation. In practice, these decisions rely on a certain amount of 'look through' analytics, since it is rare for active managers to adhere completely to their purported management styles. For example, a small cap manager

Table 7.4 Portfolio target allocation

Index	**Weight (in %)**
S&P 500	30
MSCI EAFE	20
Lehman Aggregate	50

Table 7.5 Equity portfolio managers

Manager focus	**Benchmark**
European	MSCI Europe
Global	60% S&P500 + 40% FTSE World ex-US
Latin American	MSCI Latin America
Pacific	MSCI Pacific
Capital appreciation	Russell 1000 Growth
US basic value	Russell 1000 Value
US small cap	Russell 2000 Total Return
US large cap	Russell 1000 Total Return

Table 7.6 Bond portfolio managers

Manager focus	**Benchmark**
Total return bond	Lehman aggregate total return
High yield bond	Lehman high yield
International bond	Citi non-US WGBI
Inflation protected bond	Lehman global real return

may not hold 100% small cap equities and may choose to use a large cap index such as the S&P 500 as an overlay. While some managers may make security-level look through available, others may choose not to do so for commercial reasons. Therefore, any practical analytical approach should be flexible enough to accommodate either case.

For the equity allocation, the manager research team of the savings fund has selected the group of managers listed in Table 7.5.

For the bond allocation, group of managers listed in Table 7.6 is selected.

A simple approach is to equal-weight these managers in their respective equity and bond sleeves, and then rebalance the portfolio every quarter, as shown in Table 7.7.

Alternatively, we may choose to optimize such a portfolio using a performance measure such as the AIR as discussed earlier. In order to do so, we must have a view on the expected performance of each manager. There are many sophisticated ways by which we can express such a view. Without getting into excessive technical details, one straightforward approach is to assume that no single manager will have a significant edge over another in the long run. This could be achieved by assuming that each manager has a Sharpe Ratio of 0.5. Such an assumption is open to

Table 7.7 Equal-weighted portfolio allocations

Manager focus	Asset type	Weight (in %)
European	Equities	6.25
Global	Equities	6.25
Latin American	Equities	6.25
Pacific	Equities	6.25
Capital appreciation	Equities	6.25
US basic value	Equities	6.25
US small cap	Equities	6.25
US large cap	Equities	6.25
Total return bond	Bonds	12.5
High yield bond	Bonds	12.5
International bond	Bonds	12.5
Inflation protected bond	Bonds	12.5

Table 7.8 Portfolio allocations optimized using the adjusted information ratio

Manager focus	Asset type	Q1'07 Weight (in %)	Q2'07 Weight (in %)	Q3'07 Weight (in %)	Q4'07 Weight (in %)	Q1'08 Weight (in %)	Q2'08 Weight (in %)	Q3'08 Weight (in %)	Q4'08 Weight (in %)
European	Equities	1	10	6	6	1	10	9	10
Global	Equities	1	1	20	1	1	1	6	4
Latin American	Equities	10	7	1	1	1	1	1	1
Pacific	Equities	10	8	1	1	1	1	5	8
Capital appreciation	Equities	14	8	8	1	2	8	7	2
US basic value	Equities	14	8	15	14	14	8	10	14
US small cap	Equities	1	14	5	1	1	6	3	6
US large cap	Equities	13	8	8	20	20	8	8	8
Total return bond	Bonds	9	9	9	28	32	30	26	21
High yield bond	Bonds	9	9	9	9	9	9	9	10
International bond	Bonds	9	9	9	9	9	9	9	10
Inflation protected bond	Bonds	9	9	9	9	9	9	7	6

debate, since certain managers are known to exhibit consistently higher Sharpe or Information Ratios than their peer universe. For the purpose of this illustration, we will live with this imperfect assumption. Accordingly, we rebalance the portfolio each quarter, starting in January 2007, using the expected return of each manager as computed using a Sharpe Ratio of 0.5. The volatility of each manager is computed from their fund's prior 2 years of returns on the rebalancing date. In short, we are performing a forward-looking backtest. The weights computed at each rebalancing date are listed in Table 7.8.

The minimum allocation for each manager is 1%, and allocations are made in discrete 1% intervals. The maximum permissible allocation for each manager is specified based on limits often deemed reasonable by sovereign policy makers. For example, the allocation to Total Return Bond must be less than or equal to 35%. The cumulative profit and loss (P&L) of the simulated portfolios (equally-weighted vs. optimized) is plotted in Figure 7.15.

Some basic statistics from the two simulations are listed in Table 7.9.

Overall, the optimization results in superior characteristics in terms of return, volatility, drawdown, skewness and kurtosis. Figure 7.16 plots the histograms for the weekly P&L based on the two simulations.

Once again, the histogram verifies that the optimization procedure shifts the mass of the return distribution to the right. The discerning reader might suggest that the extent of this improvement may not be significant enough to justify the substantial fluctuations in allocation weights, which would be costly and impractical to implement. In practice, the estimation of expected returns is usually built from asset class returns using bottom-up econometric techniques, and portfolio changes over the rebalancing interval will be less

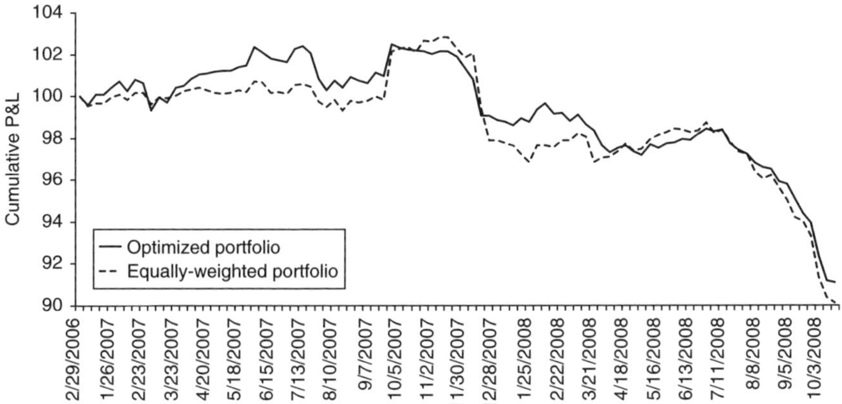

Figure 7.15 Cumulative profit and loss for simulated portfolios

Table 7.9 Portfolio statistics

	Equally-Weighted Portfolio	Optimized Portfolio
Return from 12/29/06 to 10/17/08	–9.9%	–8.9%
Volatility from 12/29/06 to 10/17/08	4.1%	3.6%
Credit Crisis Drawdown from 6/27/08 to 10/17/08	8.7%	7.5%
Skewness	–0.81	–0.51
Kurtosis	7.51	2.50

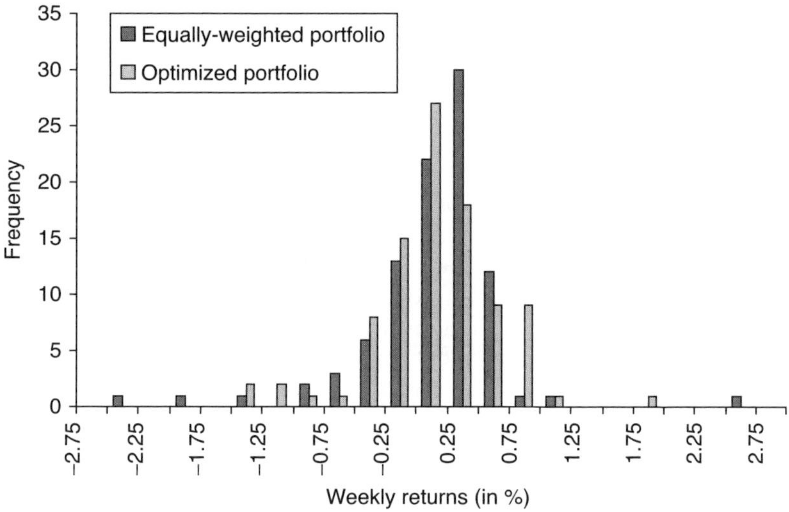

Figure 7.16 Histograms of weekly profit and loss (12/29/06–10/17/08)

dramatic. To cite a recent example, throughout 2008 the adverse outcomes in the credit markets were fairly well broadcasted and the poor performance of inflation-linked Treasuries in the early fourth quarter was forecasted by some well-known bond managers. Such insights can be incorporated to improve the expected return assumptions for individual fund managers included in the optimization, which may lead to a significant performance improvement. Finally, owing to the considerable size of typical sovereign wealth funds, even marginal improvements will make a meaningful difference.

7.3.4 Risk contribution analysis

It is important for the CIO to fully understand and appreciate the active risk of the portfolio relative to its original long-term strategic benchmark. In the

Table 7.10 Strategic asset allocation benchmark

Index	Weight (in%)
S&P 500	24
MSCI EAFE	16
Lehman Aggregate	60

Table 7.11 Breakdowns of portfolio active risk and expected tail loss

Manager Focus	Asset Type	Weight (in %)	Active Risk Contribution (in %)	Implied Alpha (in %)	Expected Tail Loss (ETL) Contribution (in %)	Implied Alpha w/ ETL (in %)
European	Equities	10	−1.37	8.23	−0.09	1.46
Global	Equities	4	−3.63	0.26	−3.43	0.91
Latin American	Equities	1	0.48	31.41	0.16	48.02
Pacific	Equities	8	−3.04	1.07	−1.09	2.52
Capital appreciation	Equities	2	−0.89	0.29	−0.90	3.53
US basic value	Equities	14	4.73	1.75	3.40	4.88
US small cap	Equities	6	−3.20	4.25	−4.02	4.85
US large cap	Equities	8	−0.50	1.16	−2.21	3.36
Equity allocation		*53*	*10.41*		*16.87*	
Total return bond	Bonds	21	2.10	3.63	2.25	3.88
High yield bond	Bonds	10	2.32	5.26	1.74	5.19
International bond	Bonds	10	2.78	6.15	0.24	−0.91
Inflation protected bond	Bonds	6	−0.03	4.37	0.27	9.67
Bond allocation		*47*	*9.00*		*0.53*	
Broad allocation			*80.81*		*86.31*	
Total		100	100.00		100.00	

previous example, the target portfolio allocation is 50/50, but the benchmark, shown in Table 7.10, is 40/60.

Using portfolio weights at the beginning of Q4 2008, the annualized active risk of the portfolio is 2.98% while its annualized 99% expected tail loss is 15.25%. The breakdowns of portfolio active risk and expected tail loss are given in Table 7.11.

'Broad allocation' refers to the portfolio's deviation from its 40/60 long-term strategic benchmark (which is +13% in equities and –13% in bonds in this case). Not surprisingly, the significant deviation accounts for over 80% of both active risk and expected tail loss. We can also compute 'bond allocation', which refers to the deviation of the composite benchmark of individual bond managers relative to the overall bond benchmark (Lehman Aggregate). The same methodology is applied to 'equity allocation'. The manager's risk contribution refers to the risk contributed by its 'alpha' component relative to its benchmark. Finally, the implied alpha of each manager, which can be thought of as the breakeven return of the manager to justify his/her active (tail) risk contribution to the portfolio, combines the proportional contributions from all of the above risk buckets. Implied alphas can be quite useful to the CIO. For instance, the high implied alphas required by the Latin American manager suggest that it is probably a poor choice for the portfolio even at its minimum 1% allocation.

It should be noted that this framework has been extended to incorporate alternative asset classes such as hedge funds, private equity, and real estate. In addition, an implementation of this framework has successfully incorporated other features, such as hedge overlays and performance attributions.

7.3.5 Other practical considerations

Practitioners may also use tactical portfolio construction techniques to dynamically adjust for unexpected changes to the long-term strategic assumptions. In the discussion of Type A stabilization funds in Section 7.2.6, intrinsic oil wealth is transformed into financial wealth through time as oil is extracted from the ground. As discussed, the 30 year strategic allocation of 50/50 assumes a certain future path of annual production. However, suppose that extraction difficulties lead to production delays, such that the intrinsic oil wealth not yet extracted at year 15 is 10% higher than expected. Clearly the revenues to the fund have not been lost, but simply delayed. The expected increase in future production revenue is equivalent to a long oil

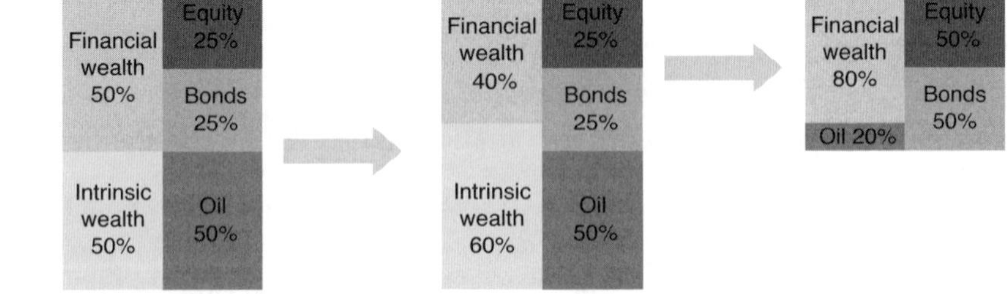

Figure 7.17 Total wealth breakdown after a production delay

position, since any delayed production, much like the rest of the intrinsic allocation, is subject to the volatility of the spot oil market. Mathematically, this problem is equivalent to optimizing a tactical allocation based on a combined portfolio of 80% financial wealth and 20% oil, relative to the original 50/50 equity-bond strategic benchmark. This approach allows tactical adjustments for temporary production surpluses or deficits with respect to the original production path assumed for long-term strategic planning, as shown in Figure 7.17.

One simple solution for this sovereign fund manager is to neutralize the 20% long oil position by selling it forward. However, if selling a large oil position forward would strain the market, the manager could alternatively avoid allocating to energy and related managers in the 80% financial portfolio, as shown in Table 7.12.

The 'BEFORE' Q4'08 weights from the simulation in Section 7.3.3 are included for comparison. The 'AFTER' weights (scaled to 100% for the financial portfolio) are the recomputed weights with crude oil included in the sovereign fund's total asset mix. As expected, the Global Resources manager is not selected in this portfolio. One other notable change is the Global Equity portfolio's reduced weight, whose investments in international energy companies are accounted for by the model. To avoid all doubt, we have significantly relaxed the constraints on each manager and rerun the simulation. The portfolio with 'RELAXED' weights also does not include the Global Equity manager. These analytical results are consistent with common sense expectations.

This adjustment technique is not limited to the case of a production delay. Suppose the opposite scenario occurs, where production in the

Table 7.12 Tactical allocations with delayed oil production

Manager focus	**Asset type**	**Q4'08 'BEFORE' Weight (in %)**	**Q4'08 'AFTER' Weight (in %)**	**Q4'08 'RELAXED' Weight (in %)**
Global resources	Commodity-related	N/A	0	0
European equities	Equities	10	6	5
Global equities	Equities	4	0	1
Latin American	Equities	1	1	1
Pacific	Equities	8	8	7
Capital appreciation	Equities	2	2	2
US basic value	Equities	14	14	8
US small cap	Equities	6	10	10
US large cap	Equities	8	8	20
Total return bond	Bonds	21	25	24
High yield bond	Bonds	10	10	1
International bond	Bonds	10	10	10
Inflation protected bond	Bonds	6	6	11

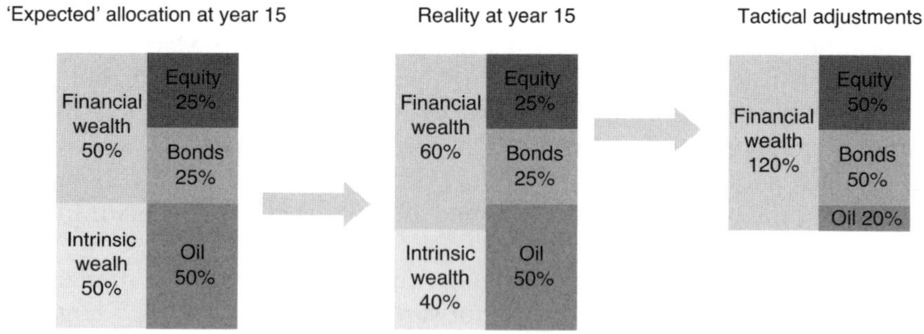

Figure 7.18 Total wealth breakdown after oil production peaks

country's main oil field unexpectedly peaks at year 15, a well-recognized geological phenomenon, and the fund therefore expects to extract less oil in the future. Mathematically, as shown in Figure 7.18 this situation is equivalent to a sovereign fund holding 120% of financial wealth but having sold 20% of its oil forward.

In reality, large deviations from the original strategic assumptions will merit rerunning the long-term simulations, so that a new strategic benchmark can be determined based on production assumptions that reflect the most current geological inputs. These simplistic examples are created to illustrate how a sovereign fund manager can combine long-term strategic planning with tactical allocation.

Appendix

Simulation Methodology

To perform our analysis of stabilization and savings funds over multiple periods, we implemented a discrete-time simulation model using one year steps. For both funds, the initial capital investment is $10 billion. For each year going forward, randomly generated inputs, listed below in Table 7.13, determine changes in the fund balance. These inputs are drawn from probability

Table 7.13 Overview of input variables

Input	Stabilization	Savings
Asset returns	X	X
Natural resource revenue	X	
Spending (Rule-based)		X
Inflation		X

distributions that are described below. Output statistics are based on 10,000 randomly generated scenarios.

Asset returns

Each period, the logs of asset price relatives are *i.i.d.* draws from a multivariate normal distribution, as follows:

$$\log(R_t) \sim N(\mu, \Sigma) \quad \text{for any } t = 1, 2, \dots, T$$

where R_t is the vector of price relatives for n assets at time t, $S_{i,t}$ is the price of asset i at time t, μ is the vector of instantaneous drifts, and Σ is the instantaneous variance–covariance matrix:

$$R_t = \begin{pmatrix} R_{i,t} \\ \vdots \\ R_{n,t} \end{pmatrix} = \begin{pmatrix} S_{1,t} / S_{1,t-1} \\ \vdots \\ S_{n,t} / S_{n,t-1} \end{pmatrix}, \mu = \begin{pmatrix} \mu_1 \\ \vdots \\ \mu_n \end{pmatrix}, \text{ and } \Sigma = \begin{pmatrix} \sigma_{11} & \cdots & \sigma_{1n} \\ \vdots & \vdots & \vdots \\ \sigma_{n1} & \cdots & \sigma_{nn} \end{pmatrix}$$

R_t is therefore multivariate log-normal with mean and variance as follows:

For any $i, j = 1, 2, \dots, n$

$$E_i = E(R_{i,t}) = e^{\mu_i + \frac{\sigma_{ii}}{2}}$$

$$V_{ij} = Cov(R_{i,t}, R_{j,t}) = e^{\mu_i + \mu_j + \frac{\sigma_{ii} + \sigma_{jj}}{2}} \left(e^{\sigma_{ij}} - 1\right)$$

The log-normal means, E, and covariance matrix, V, were specified as follows:

$$E = \begin{pmatrix} 1.08 \\ 1.055 \\ 1.02 \end{pmatrix}, \text{ for the assets, } \begin{pmatrix} Stocks \\ Bonds \\ Oil \end{pmatrix}$$

$$V = vcv, \text{ where } v = \begin{pmatrix} 0.16 & 0 & 0 \\ 0 & 0.04 & 0 \\ 0 & 0 & 0.10 \end{pmatrix} \text{ and } c = \begin{pmatrix} 1 & 0 & -0.2 \\ 0 & 1 & -0.4 \\ -0.2 & -0.4 & 1 \end{pmatrix}$$

In our analysis, we test various fixed-mix strategies where the portfolio weights, w_i, are constant over time. As such, the portfolio is assumed to be rebalanced at the end of each period. Subsequently, if applicable, cash flows are disbursed or reinvested, *pro rata*. The portfolio value, P_t, after current period cash flows, C_t, is then as follows:

$$P_t = P_{t-1} \cdot \left(w_1 R_{1,t} + w_2 R_{2,t}\right) + c_t \qquad \text{for } P_{t-1} \geq 0$$
$$P_t = P_{t-1} \cdot (1 + r_b) + c_t \qquad \text{for } P_{t-1} < 0$$

Where $w_1, w_2 \geq 0$ and $w_1 + w_2 = 1$, $R_{1,t}$, $R_{2,t}$ are the price relatives for stocks and bonds, respectively, and r_b is the risk free sovereign interest rate, which is a constant in this analysis.

Natural resource revenues

For the stabilization fund, annual oil revenue, N_t, is the product of deterministic annual oil production and the stochastic market clearing oil price, as follows:

$$N_t = Q_t S_{3,t}$$

where Q_t is the level of domestic annual production at time t, and $S_{3,t}$ is the market clearing oil price, described above.

Cash flows in the stabilization fund are determined by subtracting government spending from tax and natural resource revenue. As mentioned, government spending, G, tax revenue, T, and production, Q, are deterministic, as described below. Nominal spending and tax revenue are assumed to grow at an annual rate of 2%, which is the assumed long-term expected annual change in the oil price. This rate may be viewed as long-term expected annual inflation, so that average real oil prices and real government spending are constant. We randomize inflation for the savings case only.

$$G_t = G_0 \cdot (1.02)^t$$
$$T_t = T_0 \cdot (1.02)^t$$

For the flat production case,

$$Q_t = Q_0, \text{ for any } t = 1, 2, \ldots, T$$

For the declining production case,

$$Q_t = Q_0 . \max\left(1 - \frac{t}{25}, 0\right)$$

so production declines linearly to zero over 25 years. Initial parameters are set so that the annual budget is balanced at inception and $N_0 + T_0 - G_0 = 0$.

Inflation

For the savings fund, we require an inflation variable to measure real spending and fund balances, and to implement the Yale-Stanford spending rule, which is a function of prior realized inflation. For modeling simplicity and because it is difficult to find in the historical data a significant and consistent relationship to contemporaneous inflation, we have assumed that annual asset returns are independent of inflation shocks. However, because we model inflation as a mean-reverting process with a long-term average of 2%, we are assured that on average over the long horizons of interest in our analysis, both equities and bonds will provide real rates of return, which is consistent with historical evidence.

Inflation was generated with a mean-reverting, auto-regressive process. In the formulas below, ϕ_π is the speed of reversion, $\bar{\mu}_\pi$ is long-run average annual inflation, and σ_π is the standard deviation of annual inflation shocks. For our analysis, we assumed a 2.0% long run average, a mean reversion speed of 10.0%, and a standard deviation of 0.50% per year.

For π_t = current period inflation and π_{t-1} = prior period inflation,

$$\pi_t = \pi_{t-1} + \phi_\pi \cdot (\bar{\mu}_\pi - \pi_{t-1}) \cdot \Delta t + \sigma_\pi N\left(0, \sqrt{\Delta}\right.$$

And using $\Delta t = 1$,

$$\pi_t = \pi_{t-1} + \phi_\pi \cdot (\bar{\mu}_\pi - \pi_{t-1}) + \sigma_\pi N(0,1$$

Savings fund spending rule

For the savings fund, cash flows each period are based on the spending rule described previously in the chapter.

BlackRock Asset Allocation Model

Active Return and Active Volatility – *Active Return* is the returns of an investment after subtracting the returns of its Benchmark. *Active Volatility* is the volatility computed from active returns.

Adjusted Information Ratio and **Alternative Sharpe Ratio** – The *Adjusted Information Ratio* (AIR) is defined as:

$$\text{AIR} = \frac{\sum_i \pi_i e_i}{z_\pi^- \sigma_\pi} + \frac{1}{2} \frac{\sum_i \pi_i \left(z_i^+ \sigma_i\right)^2}{z_\pi^- \sigma_\pi} - \frac{1}{2} z_\pi^- \sigma_\pi$$

where e_i and σ_i are the active return and active volatility of the *i*-th investment respectively, $z^+ = \max\{z_{cf}(z_c^+), 0\} / z_c^+$ with z_c^+ being the critical value for probability α (e.g., 2.33 at 1%), $z^- = \min\{z_{cf}(z_c^-), 0\} / z_c^-$ with z_c^- being the critical value for probability $1 - \alpha$ (e.g., –2.33 at 99%), and the subscript π is used to denote portfolio-level metrics. The definition of the *Alternative Sharpe Ratio* (ASR) is identical, except that all parameters are computed from excess returns instead of active returns.

Expected Tail Loss – The expected critical value under *Cornish-Fisher Expansion* above a certain *Confidence Level*, such as 97.5% in this example, can be approximated by

$$z_{cf,97.5\%} \approx \frac{1}{5}\left(z_{cf,99.5\%} + z_{cf,99\%} + z_{cf,98.5\%} + z_{cf,98\%} + z_{cf,97.5\%}\right)$$

If the returns are sampled from weekly data, then the **Weekly Expected Tail Loss** is simply $z_{cfm}\sigma_m$, and the **Annualized Expected Tail Loss** can be estimated by

$$z_{cf}\sigma = z_{cfm}\sigma_m\sqrt{52} + E(R)$$

with the last term being the Annualized Expected (Active) Returns That term is assumed to be zero for daily or weekly calculations.

Implied Alpha and Implied Excess Return – Conceptually, *Implied Alpha* is the active returns required to compensate for the Active Tail Risk contributed by an investment to the portfolio. Instead of computing the *Implied Alpha* computed from the traditional Information Ratio, the AIR is used instead. Define the Implied Excess Return of the fund *i* as

$$e_i^* = \left(\mathrm{AIR} + z_\pi^-\sigma_\pi\right)\frac{\partial z_\pi^-\sigma_\pi}{\partial \pi_i} - \frac{1}{2}\left(z_i^+\sigma_i\right)^2$$

Tail Risk Contribution can be written as

$$TRC_i = \pi_i\frac{\partial z\sigma}{\partial \pi_i} \Leftrightarrow \frac{TRC_i}{\pi_i} = \frac{\partial z\sigma}{\partial \pi_i}$$

Substitute the $\partial z_\pi^-\sigma_\pi / \partial \pi_i$ in the expression of e_i^*, the *Implied Alpha* under the AIR can be written as

$$e_i^* = \left(\mathrm{AIR} + z_\pi^-\sigma_\pi\right)\frac{TRC_i}{\pi_i} - \frac{1}{2}\left(z_i^+\sigma_i\right)^2$$

Roughly speaking, *Implied Alpha* can be approximated as the difference of the Implied Excess Return for each investment and the Implied Excess Return of the benchmark, i.e.

$$IA_i \approx IR_i - IR_{BM}$$

The *Implied Excess Return* is defined similarly, except that the ASR instead of the AIR is used.

Marginal Contribution to Risk – The *Marginal Contribution to Risk* of investment i is defined as

$$RC_i = \pi_i \frac{\partial \sigma_\pi}{\partial \pi_i}$$

where π_i is referred to the weights and σ_π is the volatility of the portfolio. It can be shown that $\Sigma_i RC_i = \sigma_\pi$. The percentage *Marginal Contribution to Risk* is defined as $RC_i\% = RC_i/\sigma_\pi$.

Tail Risk Contribution – In contrast to *Marginal Contribution to Risk,* the tail risk measure $z_{cf}\sigma$ is used for *Tail Risk Contribution* instead of portfolio volatility σ. That is,

$$TRC_i\% = \frac{\pi_i \frac{\partial z_{cf}\sigma}{\partial \pi_i}}{z_{cf}\sigma} = \frac{\pi_i}{z_{cf}\sigma}\left(z_{cf}\frac{\partial \sigma}{\partial \pi_i} + \sigma \frac{\partial z_{cf}}{\partial \pi_i} \right)$$

where z_{cf} is the Cornish-Fisher coefficient. In order to compute $TRC_i\%$, the term $\partial\sigma/\partial\pi_i$ can be computed from the *Marginal Contribution to Risk* formula above. Moreover, $\partial z_{cf}/\partial\pi_i$ can be derived from the definition of *Cornish-Fisher Expansion* as the follows,

$$\frac{\partial z_{cf}}{\partial \pi_i} = \frac{1}{6}\left(z_{\bar{c}}^2 - 1\right)\frac{\partial S}{\partial \pi_i} + \frac{1}{24}\left(z_{\bar{c}}^3 - 3z_{\bar{c}}\right)\frac{\partial K}{\partial \pi_i} - \frac{2}{36}\left(2z_{\bar{c}}^3 - 5z_{\bar{c}}\right)S\frac{\partial S}{\partial \pi_i} + \ldots$$

where the partial derivatives for S (skewness) and K (kurtosis) with respect to π_i are

$$\frac{\partial S}{\partial \pi_i} = 3\sum_j \sum_k \pi_j \pi_k E\left\{\left[\frac{R_{j,t} - ER_{j,t}}{\sigma}\right]\left[\frac{R_{k,t} - ER_{k,t}}{\sigma}\right]\left[\frac{R_{i,t} - ER_{i,t}}{\sigma}\right]\right\} - 3\frac{S}{\sigma}\frac{\partial \sigma}{\partial \pi_i}$$

and

$$\frac{\partial K}{\partial \pi_i} = 4\sum_j \sum_k \sum_m \pi_j \pi_k \pi_m \; E\left\{\left[\frac{R_{j,t} - ER_{j,t}}{\sigma}\right]\left[\frac{R_{k,t} - ER_{k,t}}{\sigma}\right] \times \left[\frac{R_{m,t} - ER_{m,t}}{\sigma}\right]\left[\frac{R_{i,t} - ER_{i,t}}{\sigma}\right]\right\} - 4\frac{K+3}{\sigma}\frac{\partial \sigma}{\partial \pi_i}$$

Acknowledgments

The authors would like to thank Dr. Xi Zhang, a statistician in BlackRock's Risk and Quantitative Analysis Group, for her help in generating many of the tedious computational examples shown in this chapter, as well as Emily Fruchter and Mattias Skjorshammer for their careful proofreading. Further, the authors want to thank Dr. Bennett Golub and Lili Forouraghi of BlackRock for their insightful guidance in the drafting of this chapter. All errors and omissions remain the authors' own.

Notes

1. Assuming that portfolio returns are normally distributed, all combinations of standard deviation and expected return on this line result exactly in a 10% probability of falling below a 0% return.
2. We note that the risk measure as defined does not address the distribution of a portfolio's relative return using the stochastic bond baseline. This definition would rely on the joint probability distribution of portfolio and baseline returns and is a different conceptualization of risk. That is, a breakeven percentile of X% does not imply that there is 'X% probability of underperforming the baseline'. Rather, since we have chosen to define risk on an absolute basis, it implies that there is 'X% probability of being below a return achievable by the baseline with (1-X)% certainty'.
3. We note that future regimes, which will likely be defined by increasingly dearer oil and other nonrenewable resources, could be vastly different than the historical data indicates. Unfortunately, the scope of this chapter does not allow us to address these possibilities here.
4. We have assumed zero correlation between asset returns and inflation shocks. For further details, please refer to the Appendix.
5. Given our objective of trying to maintain a stable level of median real spending, spending the expected real equity return is a less successful strategy than spending the expected real bond return. This somewhat paradoxical result is a consequence of the higher volatility of equity returns. It should be noted, however, that if our objective were to stabilize mean real spending, the equity strategy would provide stable results at a higher level than bonds. However, with a goal of stable mean spending (instead of stable median spending), the probability of successive generations achieving at least the mean outcome would decrease significantly with time.
6. The Omega function is a technique in allocating hedge fund risk that has gained popularity among the pension industry in Europe. Its roots lie in actuarial science, which has dealt with tail risk for well over a century.

References

Black, F. and R. Litterman, "Global Portfolio Optimization," *Financial Analysts Journal*, Sep/Oct 1992.

Cornish, E.A. and R.A. Fisher, "Moments and Cumulants in the Specification of Distributions," *Revue de l'Institut International de Statistique*, Vol. 5, 307–320, 1936.

Karatzas, I. and S.E. Shreve, *Methods of Mathematical Finance*, Springer, 1998.

Keating, C. and W.F. Shadwick, *Omega: Functions and Metrics*, Gilmour Drummond, 2005.

Lee, B., "A Practitioner's Guide to Active Portfolio Management Using Implied View," *Journal of Risk Finance*, Fall 2000.

Lee, B. and Y. Lee, "The Alternative Sharpe Ratio," *Intelligent Hedge Fund Investing*, Risk Books, 2004.

Markowitz, H.M., "Portfolio Selection," *Journal of Finance*, Vol. 7, 77–91, 1952.

Merton, R.C., "Optimal Investment Strategies for University Endowment Funds," *Worldwide Asset and Liability Modeling*, Cambridge University Press, 1998.

Sharpe, W.F., "Imputing Expected Returns from Portfolio Composition," *Journal of Financial and Quantitative Analysis*, 463–472, June 1974.

von Neumann, J. and O. Morgenstern, *Theory of Games and Economic Behavior*, Princeton University Press, 1944.

8
A Note on Portfolio Choice for Sovereign Wealth Funds

Bernd Scherer

8.1 Introduction

For many oil exporting countries, crude oil or gas reserves are the single most important national assets. Any change in the value of reserves directly and materially affects these countries' wealth, and thus the wellbeing of their citizens. Figure 8.1 serves as an illustration for the violent nature of oil price changes that can have a destabilizing effect on the economy via volatile real exchange rates.

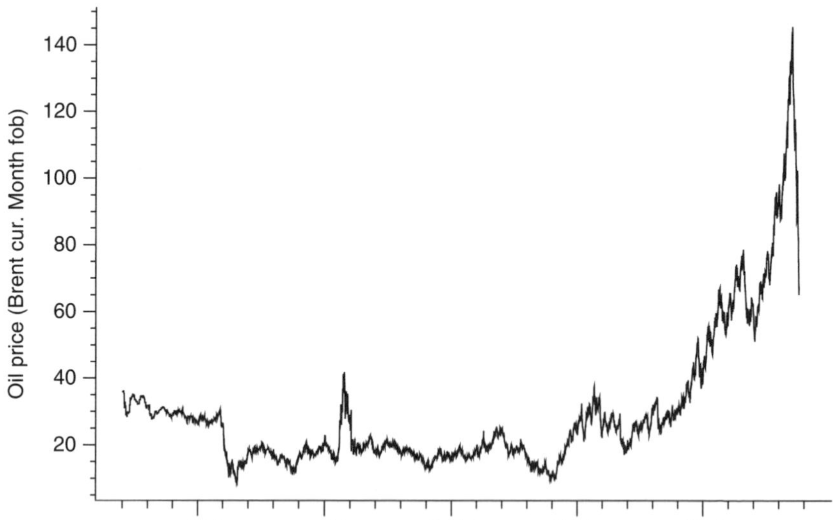

Figure 8.1 Daily oil price movements from January 1982 to September 2008

Note: The underlying total wealth position of an oil rich country can vary dramatically over time and needs management to smooth intergenerational consumption patterns.

In recognition of this problem, a number of oil exporting countries have been depositing oil revenues in funds dedicated to finance future expenditures. Gintschel and Scherer (2008) identified the optimal asset allocation problem for a sovereign wealth fund (SWF) as an asset allocation problem with nontradable wealth that bears a strong resemblance to portfolio choice in the presence of human capital. According to their one-period framework, assets with negative correlation to oil wealth are well suited to improve the efficiency of total wealth for an oil rich investor. We will extend their analysis into a multi-period setting with return predictability. This allows us to investigate the term structure of hedging demand for equities, bonds and listed real estate as an illustrative example.[1]

The outline is as follows. Section 8.2 applies the portfolio choice problem for an oil based SWF into a multi-period setting using the framework of Campbell and Viceira (2002). We establish three-fund portfolio separation. This also extends Doskeland (2007) that focused on social system liabilities and stopped at two-fund separation. Section 8.3 describes our data and data generating process. Section 8.4 presents the term structure of optimal hedging demand, while Section 8.5 concludes.

8.2 Three-fund separation – incorporating the SWF into government budgets

As in Gintschel and Scherer (2008), we view the optimal asset allocation problem of an SWF as a decision-making problem for an investor with nontradable endowed wealth (oil reserves). To transform their solution into the multi-period framework of Campbell and Viceira (2002), let x_t denote our vector of asset excess returns (including oil) over cash as well as cash and s_t the vector of economic state variables, i.e. conditioning information. The idea here is that only unexpected variations (those not explained by state variables) pose a risk. To fix notation we denote the (conditional) annualized n-period return and risk by

$$[1] \quad \mu^{(n)} = n^{-1}E\left[\sum_{i=1}^{n} x_{t+n} \mid s_t\right]$$

$$[2] \quad \Sigma^{n} = n^{-1}Var\left(\sum_{i=1}^{n} x_{t+n} \mid s_t\right)$$

where $\mu^{(n)}$ and $\Sigma^{(n)}$ represent n n-period expected returns. We can also define sub-vectors and sub-matrices. To extract the required n-period risk and return measures we use $\mu_a^{(n)}$ for the expected excess returns for assets, $\sum_{aa}^{(n)}$ for the covariance matrix of asset returns, $\sum_{ao}^{(n)}$ for the covariance vector of asset and oil returns and $\sum_{ac}^{(n)}$ for the covariance of asset excess returns and short-term cash rates. Equations [1] and [2] describe the term structure of risk and return. This information is used to specify the mean reversion properties of various asset classes in order to introduce a time dimension into portfolio choice. If, for example we would find considerable mean reversion in equity returns, long run investors could more aggressively invest into equities than short-term investors. Suppose a sovereign holds both financial assets in an SWF as well as oil assets underground and let $0 < \theta \leq 1$ denote the fraction of financial wealth to total wealth (oil plus financial assets).[2] Given CRRA (Constant Relative Risk Aversion) preferences with risk aversion parameter γ, it is easy to show that the optimal portfolio for horizon n is given by[3]

$$w_t^{(n)} = \frac{1}{\gamma}\left(\frac{1}{\gamma}\sum_{aa} + \frac{(\gamma-1)}{\gamma}\sum_{aa}^{(n)}\right)^{-1} \left[\frac{1}{\theta}\left(\mu_a^{(n)} + \frac{1}{2}\sigma_a^2\right) - (\gamma-1)\frac{(1-\theta)}{\theta}\sum_{ao}^{(n)} - \frac{1}{\theta}(\gamma-1)\sum_{ac}^{(n)}\right] \quad [3]$$

This is equivalent to three-fund separation.[4] The SWF wants to hold a leveraged ($1/\theta > 1$) speculative portfolio that purely depends on expected asset excess returns, $w_{spec.}^{(n)}$, an equally leveraged hedging portfolio, $w_{hedge,\ cash}^{(n)}$, (as changes in the risk free rate can only be managed via the asset portfolio, even though they affect total wealth), $w_{hedge,\ cash}^{(n)}$ that protects against intertemporal variations in short-term rates and another hedging portfolio that protects against oil price shocks, $w_{hedge,\ oil}^{(n)}$.[5]

$$[4] \quad w_{\text{spec}}^{(n)} = \left(\frac{1}{\theta}\right)\left(\frac{1}{\gamma}\right)\left(\frac{1}{\gamma}\sum_{aa} + \frac{\gamma-1}{\gamma}\sum_{aa}^{(n)}\right)^{-1}\left(\mu^{(n)} + \frac{1}{2}\sigma_a^2\right)$$

$$[5] \quad w_{hedge,\ cash}^{(n)} = -\left(\frac{1}{\theta}\right)\left(\frac{\gamma-1}{\gamma}\right)\left(\frac{1}{\gamma}\sum_{aa} + \frac{\gamma-1}{\gamma}\sum_{aa}^{(n)}\right)^{-1}\sum_{ac}^{(n)}$$

$$[6] \quad w_{hedge,\ oil}^{(n)} = -\left(\frac{1-\theta}{\theta}\right)\left(\frac{\gamma-1}{\gamma}\right)\left(\frac{1}{\gamma}\sum_{aa} + \frac{\gamma-1}{\gamma}\sum_{aa}^{(n)}\right)^{-1}\sum_{ao}^{(n)}$$

For $\theta = 1$ we arrive at the optimal solution for an investor with financial wealth only, while for $\gamma \to \infty$ we get $w_{hedge,\ cash}^{(n)} = -(1/\theta)[\Sigma_{aa}^{n}]^{-1}\Sigma_{ac}^{n}$ and $w_{hedge,\ oil}^{(n)} = -[(1-\theta)/\theta][\Sigma_{aa}^{n}]^{-1}\Sigma_{ao}^{n}$. Also it is interesting to note that for $\gamma = 1$, i.e. a log investor, we arrive at the familiar solution that there is no hedging demand and the optimal solution degenerates to the one-period myopic speculative demand $w_{spec}^{(n)} = 1/\theta\,\Sigma_{aa}^{-1}(\mu^{(n)} + 1/2\,\sigma_a^2)$. Note that this framework is extremely general and its application is not limited to equities or bonds, but can easily be applied to hedge funds, private equity investments etc.[6]

8.3 Return dynamics and the data generating process

8.3.1 Model and data

Our model is incomplete without a specification for [1] and [2]. We start with assuming a first order vector auto-regression as our data generating process (DGP):

$$[7] \quad z_{t+1} = a + Bz_t + \varepsilon_{t+1}, \quad \varepsilon_{t+1} \sim N(0,\Omega)$$

where $z_t = [x_t \quad s_t]^T$, and Ω represents the residual covariance matrix of our VAR with a vector of constants, a, and a coefficient matrix B. From [7] we can easily work out the multi-period expressions for risk and return in [1] and [2] as[7]

$$[8] \quad \Sigma^{(n)} = \sum_{i=1}^{n}\left[\left(\sum_{j=0}^{i-1} B^j\right)\Omega\left(\sum_{j=0}^{i-1} B^j\right)^T\right]$$

where again $\Sigma^{(n)}$ denotes the covariance matrix of n-period returns and $B^0 = I$. Correlation, variance and covariance can be easily picked from the elements in $\Sigma^{(n)}$. Plotting variances, correlations, etc. against n provides a term structure of risk.[8]

We proxy the investment universe for an SWF contained in x_t by the CRSP Value weighted stock index, real estate investments (FTSE NAREIT real estate index), government bonds (Lehman Long US Treasury Bonds Index), one-month Treasury bills rate and real bonds (TIPS).[9] For oil wealth, we use Brent current month FOB. Economic state variables, s_t, are given by dividend yield, credit spread (difference between Baa Corporate Bond Yield and the ten-Year Treasury constant maturity rate), term spread (difference between the ten-year Treasury constant maturity rate and one-month-T-Bill rate) and nominal yield (ten-year Treasury constant maturity rate). Our analysis is based on quarterly returns from 1973 I through 2007 IV. Table 8.1 summarizes

Table 8.1 Summary Statistics

	Symbol	Mean (μ)	Volatility (σ)	Sharpe $\left(\frac{\mu - rc}{\sigma}\sqrt{4}\right)$	Min	Max	Skew	Kurtosis
Assets								
Oil	ro_t	−0.37	19.23	−0.04	−0.89	0.82	−0.27	6.33
TIPS	rr_t	0.42	0.60	1.40	−0.02	0.02	−0.94	2.29
T–Bill	rc_t	1.29	0.59		0.00	0.03	0.32	0.12
Long bonds	rb_t	1.33	4.97	0.54	−0.09	0.17	0.51	0.37
Equities	re_t	1.69	8.14	0.42	−0.28	0.18	−0.79	1.46
Real estate	ri_t	1.42	7.03	0.40	−0.17	0.19	0.00	0.05
State variables								
Nominal	yn_t	7.15	2.56		0.04	0.15	0.96	0.36
Credit spread	cs_t	1.96	0.50		0.01	0.04	1.04	0.67
Time Spread	ts_t	1.75	1.25		−0.01	0.05	−0.05	−0.62
Dividend Yield	dy_t	−3.66	34.24		−4.55	−2.97	−0.21	−0.58

We report descriptive statistics for all endogenous (assets and state variables) variables in our VAR. Only the Sharpe-ratios have been annualized.

the data and our notation. It is noteworthy that oil returns are statistically not different from cash rates, i.e. excess returns are not statistically different from zero. This supports the Hotelling-Solow rule under perfectly integrated capital markets. Natural resource prices should grow at the world interest rate such that countries are indifferent between depletion (earning the interest rate) and keeping oil underground (earning price changes). Our state variables are common in the academic literature and motivated by time variation in investment opportunities[10] and the investment universe will span most of the investment opportunity set for an SWF.

8.3.2 Return dynamics

We start with calibrating our DGP in [7] to the data in Table 8.1. Coefficient estimates and R^2 s are given in Table 8.2. while Table 8.3. provides estimates for Ω with the main diagonal representing quarterly volatility. Unexplained quarterly real estate volatility amounts to 6.65%, which is only marginally smaller than unconditional volatility of 7.03%. This is hardly surprising given the R^2 for the real estate equation is extremely low. Dividend yields have significant forecasting power for equities and bonds, while bonds can also be forecasted using last quarters nominal yields. Shocks on the dividend yields show negative contemporaneous correlation (–0.27) with equity returns. At the same time rising dividend yields impact future equity returns positively (positive significant regression coefficient of 0.12). In summary: positive shocks to dividend yields (an increase) negatively impact current returns but positively impact next

Table 8.2 Results from first order VAR: parameter estimates

	z_t									
	x_t						s_t			
	rr_t	rc_t	rb_t	re_t	ro_t	ri_t	yn_t	cs_t	ts_t	dy_t
a	0.04	−0.00	−0.41	0.57	0.62	−0.02	0.01	−0.01	0.05	−1.30
	0.01	0.00	0.11	0.18	0.46	0.17	0.01	0.00	0.01	0.36
	3.23	−0.61	−3.73	3.08	1.34	−0.12	2.13	−2.02	4.76	−3.64
rr_{t-1}	0.08	−0.06	2.28	−4.29	−5.77	−1.13	0.06	−0.02	0.14	−1.61
	0.13	0.03	1.14	1.90	4.76	1.77	0.07	0.05	0.12	3.70
	0.65	−1.97	2.00	−2.26	−1.21	−0.64	0.85	−0.37	1.24	−0.44
rc_{t-1}	−0.22	1.45	−8.42	−5.27	−7.36	−12.23	0.65	−0.22	−5.65	15.38
	0.44	0.11	3.97	6.59	16.53	6.16	0.24	0.17	0.40	12.83
	−0.51	13.51	−2.12	−0.80	−0.45	−1.99	2.76	−1.36	−14.04	1.20
rb_{t-1}	−0.02	−0.01	0.10	0.42	−1.25	0.13	−0.10	0.03	−0.03	−0.32
	0.01	0.00	0.11	0.18	0.44	0.16	0.01	0.00	0.01	0.34
	−1.51	−5.14	0.95	2.43	−2.86	0.78	−16.22	7.52	−2.88	−0.94

Continued

Table 8.2 Continued

	z_t									
	x_t						s_t			
	rr_t	rc_t	rb_t	re_t	ro_t	ri_t	yn_t	cs_t	ts_t	dy_t
re_{t-1}	−0.01	0.00	0.12	0.05	−0.12	0.04	0.00	−0.01	0.00	−0.05
	0.01	0.00	0.07	0.11	0.29	0.11	0.00	0.00	0.01	0.22
	−1.71	0.10	1.75	0.45	−0.41	0.36	0.28	−3.41	0.71	−0.24
rb_{t-1}	−0.00	0.00	0.02	0.12	−0.09	0.04	0.00	−0.00	0.00	0.09
	0.00	0.00	0.03	0.05	0.12	0.05	0.00	0.00	0.00	0.09
	−0.71	0.75	0.52	2.55	−0.75	0.98	0.12	−0.19	0.54	1.01
ri_{t-1}	0.00	0.00	−0.16	−0.24	0.08	−0.01	0.01	−0.01	−0.01	0.04
	0.01	0.00	0.09	0.15	0.37	0.14	0.01	0.00	0.01	0.28
	0.50	0.67	−1.84	−1.63	0.23	−0.11	1.03	−2.16	−0.88	0.13
yn_{t-1}	−0.11	−0.11	3.33	−0.26	−0.96	2.71	0.80	0.08	1.17	−1.12
	0.11	0.03	0.95	1.58	3.96	1.48	0.06	0.04	0.10	3.07
	−1.05	−4.33	3.51	−0.17	−0.24	1.83	14.13	1.92	12.16	−0.37
cs_{t-1}	−0.02	−0.07	−1.12	−0.04	1.53	1.42	0.09	0.82	0.12	0.31
	0.11	0.03	0.99	1.65	4.13	1.54	0.06	0.04	0.10	3.21
	−0.18	−2.52	−1.13	−0.02	0.37	0.92	1.61	19.89	1.17	0.10
ts_{t-1}	0.06	0.18	−1.17	−0.80	−1.97	−1.91	0.14	−0.04	−0.60	6.74
	0.10	0.02	0.90	1.50	3.77	1.40	0.05	0.04	0.09	2.92
	0.63	7.33	−1.29	−0.53	−0.52	−1.36	2.53	−1.11	−6.59	2.31
dy_{t-1}	0.01	−0.00	−0.09	0.12	0.11	−0.00	0.00	−0.00	0.01	0.71
	0.00	0.00	0.02	0.04	0.10	0.04	0.00	0.00	0.00	0.08
	2.51	−0.98	−3.63	2.86	1.09	−0.07	2.28	−2.88	4.24	8.86
R^2	0.35	0.96	0.26	0.22	0.14	0.11	0.99	0.88	0.88	0.83
R^2	0.28	0.96	0.18	0.14	0.04	0.01	0.99	0.86	0.86	0.81

Table 8.3 Results from first order VAR: residual covariance matrix

	rr_t	rc_t	rb_t	re_t	ro_t	ri_t	yn_t	cs_t	ts_t	dy_t
rr_t	0.47	0.05	−0.45	−0.28	0.54	−0.40	0.20	−0.01	0.09	0.05
rc_t	0.05	0.12	−0.08	−0.07	0.09	−0.16	0.08	−0.19	−0.33	−0.08
rb_t	−0.45	−0.08	4.28	0.10	−0.22	0.26	−0.28	0.02	−0.24	0.04
re_t	−0.28	−0.07	0.10	7.11	−0.31	0.55	−0.15	−0.01	0.11	−0.27
ro_t	0.54	0.09	−0.22	−0.31	17.84	−0.28	−0.08	−0.01	−0.21	−0.02
ri_t	−0.40	−0.16	0.26	0.55	−0.28	6.65	−0.17	0.01	0.02	−0.31
yn_t	0.20	0.08	−0.28	−0.15	−0.08	−0.17	0.25	−0.54	0.47	0.18
cs_t	−0.01	−0.19	0.02	−0.01	−0.01	0.01	−0.54	0.18	−0.19	−0.21
ts_t	0.09	−0.33	−0.24	0.11	−0.21	0.02	0.47	−0.19	0.43	0.03
dy_t	0.05	−0.08	0.04	−0.27	−0.02	−0.31	0.18	−0.21	0.03	13.85

We report the error covariance matrix, Ω, of the VAR from [7]. The main diagonal contains (quarterly) volatility while off diagonal entries represent correlations.

period returns. This creates mean reversion and is likely to reduce long-term risks.

We report the coefficients of the VAR in equation [7] together with standard errors and *t*-values. See Table 8.1. for a description of individual variable names. The last two rows contain the "R-square" as well as "adjusted R-square" for each individual regression. Coefficients significant at the 5% level are presented in bold.

All state variables are very persistent as the high R^2 and the large highly significant autoregressive coefficients indicate. Also note that the system [7] is stable, as all Eigen-values of B have modulus less than 1 (the largest is 0.94). Hence the process is stable and therefore also stationary.

8.4 The term structure of hedging demand

In this section we will focus exclusively on the hedging demand for an SWF as $w^{(n)}_{t,spec}$ is essentially the same for an asset-only investor, an asset liability investor or an asset-only investor with nontradable wealth, and hence not specific to an SWF. We ignore effects from γ and θ as they only affect leverage. The results are summarized in Figure 8.2 and Figure 8.3. In both cases

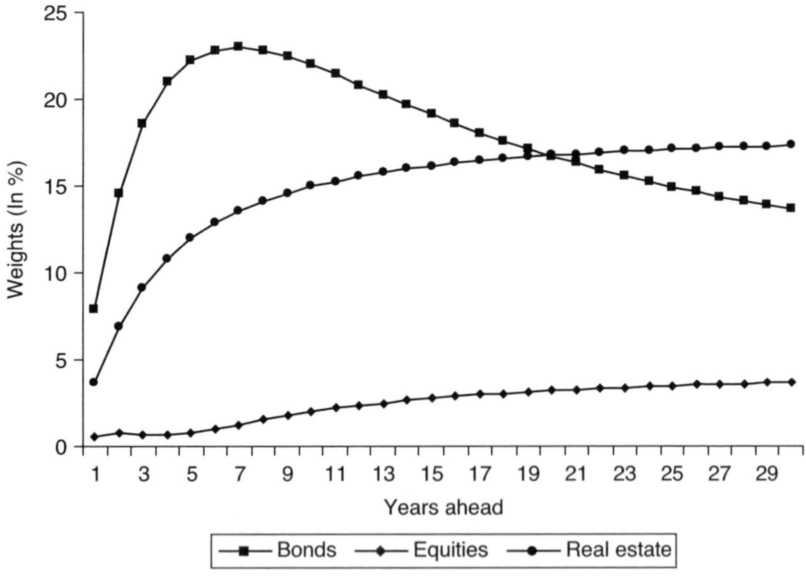

Figure 8.2 Hedging time variation in short-term interest rates

Note: We represent the hedge portfolio according to $w^{(n)}_{hedge,\,cash} = -\frac{1}{\theta}\left[\sum^{n}_{aa}\right]^{-1}\sum^{(n)}_{ac}$ for $n = 1, \ldots, 30$ and $\theta = 1/2$.

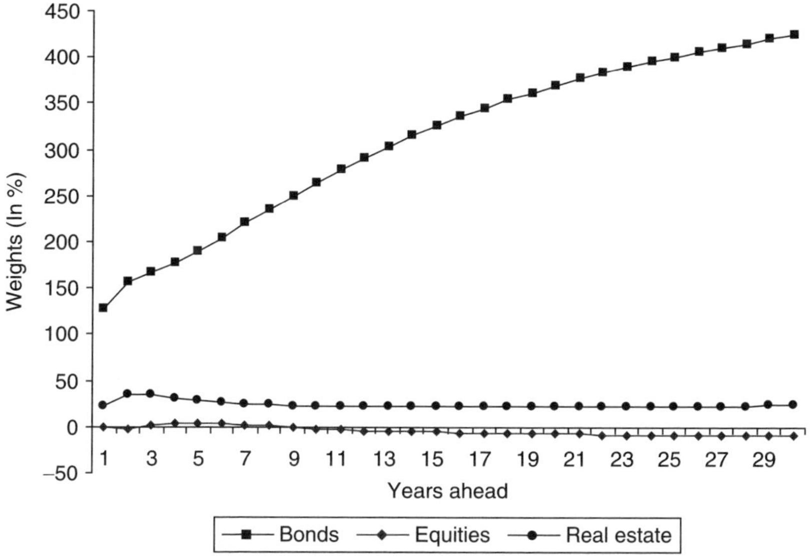

Figure 8.3 Hedging oil price shocks over time

Note: We represent the hedge portfolio according to $w^{(n)}_{hedge,oil} = -\left(\frac{1-\theta}{\theta}\right)\left[\sum^{(n)}_{aa}\right]^{-1}\sum^{(n)}_{ao}$ for $n = 1, \ldots,$ 30 and $\theta = 1/2$.

hedging demand is positive as long as the correlation between investment and risk source is negative. In other words: assets that show negative correlation with oil or time varying short rates will get positive weights. While correlation drives the sign of hedging demand, it is the relative term structure of risk (whether annualized volatility grows or decays with the time horizon) that determines hedging demand which essentially equals a "beta" estimate.

Long government bonds play the biggest role in both hedge portfolios as government bonds are both a recession hedge (they increase in value when oil prices come down in a recession) as well as a hedge against deteriorating investment opportunities, i.e. falling rates.

8.5 Conclusions

As a novelty in the academic literature we show how to derive three-fund separation in the Campbell and Viceira (2003) framework for an SWF. We provide a small empirical example for equities, bonds and listed real estate to illustrate our framework and conclude that an SWF should hold a considerable amount of assets in long US government bonds in order to hedge both the negative effects of oil price shocks as well as deteriorating short rates. Anecdotal evidence on the investment behaviour of SWFs confirms our view.

Appendix A

We can write the *n*-period return, $\mu_{t,SWF}^{(n)}$, and risk, $\sigma_{t,SWF}^{(n)2}$, as a function of our decision vector of portfolio weights, $w_t^{(n)}$, according to

$$[9]\quad \mu_{t,SWF}^{(n)} = \theta w_t^{(n)T}\left(\mu_a^{(n)} + \frac{1}{2}\sigma_a^2\right) - \frac{1}{2}\theta w_t^{(n)T}\sum\nolimits_{aa}\theta w_t^{(n)}$$

$$[10]\quad \sigma_{t,SWF}^{(n)2} = \theta^2 w_t^{(n)T}\sum\nolimits_{aa}^{(n)} w_t + 2\theta(1-\theta)\,w_t^{(n)T}\sum\nolimits_{ao}^{(n)} + 2\theta w_t^{(n)T}\sum\nolimits_{ac}^{(n)}$$

Note that we (in accordance with the literature) implicitly assume $w_t^{(n)}$ to remain constant, which equates to assuming an investor with constant time horizon *n*. Assuming CRRA we maximize $1/1-\gamma(w_{SWF,t+n})^{1-\gamma}$ and the optimization problem becomes

$$[11]\quad \max_{w_t^{(n)}}\left[\mu_{t,SWF}^{(n)} + \frac{1}{2}(1-\gamma)\sigma_{t,SWF}^{(n)2}\right]$$

Differentiating [3] we get the first order conditions

$$[12]\quad \begin{aligned}&\theta\left(\mu_a^{(n)} + \frac{1}{2}\sigma_a^2\right) - \theta^2\sum\nolimits_{aa} w_t^{(n)} + \frac{(1-\gamma)}{2}\theta^2 2\sum\nolimits_{aa}^{(n)} w_t^{(n)}\\ &+\frac{(1-\gamma)}{2}2\theta(1-\theta)\sum\nolimits_{ao}^{(n)} + \frac{(1-\gamma)}{2}2\theta\sum\nolimits_{ac}^{(n)} = 0\end{aligned}$$

We divide by θ, collect all terms involving $w_t^{(n)}$ on the left side and use the identity that $(1-\gamma) = -(\gamma-1)$ to finally arrive at

$$[13]\quad \begin{aligned}w_t^{(n)} &= \frac{1}{\gamma}\left(\frac{1}{\gamma}\sum\nolimits_{aa} + \frac{(\gamma-1)}{\gamma}\sum\nolimits_{aa}^{(n)}\right)^{-1}\\ &\left[\frac{1}{\theta}\left(\mu_a^{(n)} + \frac{1}{2}\sigma_a^2\right) - (\gamma-1)\frac{(1-\theta)}{\theta}\sum\nolimits_{ao}^{(n)} - \frac{1}{\theta}(\gamma-1)\sum\nolimits_{ac}^{(n)}\right]\end{aligned}$$

which is identical to equation [3] in the main text.

Appendix B

We want to shed more light on equation in the main text. For illustrative purposes we first present a two-period example which we will generalize afterwards. The two-period returns from a first order VAR are given by

$$[14]\quad \begin{aligned}z_{t+1} + z_{t+2} &= a + Bz_t + \varepsilon_{t+1} + a + Bz_{t+1} + \varepsilon_{t+2}\\ &= a + Bz_t + \varepsilon_{t+1} + a + B(a + Bz_t + \varepsilon_{t+1}) + \varepsilon_{t+2}\\ &= a + Bz_t + \varepsilon_{t+1} + a + BA + B^2 z_t + B\varepsilon_{t+1} + \varepsilon_{t+2}\end{aligned}$$

However uncertainty only arises from the residual terms as the model parameters are assumed to be fully known in t (no estimation error) as well as z_t. We then get

$$
\begin{aligned}
\Sigma^{(2)} &= Var\left(z_{t+1} + z_{t+2}\right) = Var\left(\varepsilon_{t+1} + B\varepsilon_{t+1} + \varepsilon_{t+2}\right) \\
&= Var\left(\varepsilon_{t+1}(I + B) + \varepsilon_{t+2}\right) \\
&= (I + B)\Omega(I + B)^T + \Omega
\end{aligned} \qquad [15]
$$

The n-period generalization follows the same logic as [15] and can be calculated via the following expression:

$$
\begin{aligned}
\Sigma^{(n)} &= \Omega \\
&\quad + (I + B)\Omega(I + B)^T \\
&\quad + \left(I + B + B^2\right)\Omega\left(I + B + B^2\right)^T \\
&\quad + \ldots \\
&\quad + \left(I + B + B^2 + \ldots + B^{n-1}\right)\Omega\left(I + B + B^2 + \ldots + B^{n-1}\right)^T \\
&= \sum_{i=1}^{n}\left[\left(\sum_{j=0}^{i-1} B^j\right)\Omega\left(\sum_{j=0}^{i-1} B^j\right)^T\right]
\end{aligned} \qquad [16]
$$

which is exactly what we find in the main text.

Notes

1. We will focus on portfolio investments. This is a narrower brief than what sovereign investors can do. Rather than investing into securities (mostly USD dominated) abroad, sovereign investors can also use their oil revenues to build exposure to future growth industries and develop the necessary infrastructure to make their country an attractive place to attract top human talent. Dubai and Qatar are prime examples of this. During the following exposition we will rely on the normality in return distributions assumption to allow us to come up with closed form solutions that provide conceptual insight into the structure of the underlying problem. While we are aware that returns on capital markets and certainly on commodities like oil are in the short run far from normal, we also believe an SWF belongs to a group of long-term investors such that the central limit theorem will come to our help to somewhat mitigate the nonnormality issue.
2. We assume θ is known and does not change over time.
3. See Appendix A for a derivation.
4. As times goes by, the investor would change her asset allocation from $w^{(n)}$ to $w^{(n-1)}$ and to $w^{(n-2)}$ etc.
5. The optimal position in risk free assets is given by $1 - I^T w^{(n)}$.
6. Including investments with less data availability can be dealt with apply standard econometric techniques to deal with time series of different length and does not

limit the practical usefulness of the above framework. It just calls for a more skilled statistician.

7. See Appendix B for a brief sketch.
8. An alternative (brute force) way to calculate the covariance of multi-period returns is to simulate $z_{t+1} + z_{t+2} \dots + z_{t+n}$ from [7] and directly calculate the required statistics.
9. TIPS are constructed using the methodology by in Kothari and Shanken (2004).
10. See Campbell and Viceira (2002).

References

Campbell, J. and L. Viceira (2002) *Strategic Asset Allocation*, Oxford University Press.

Doskeland, T. (2007) "Strategic Asset Allocation for a Country: The Norwegian Case", *Journal of Financial Markets and Portfolio Management*, 21:3, 167–201.

Gintschel, A. and B. Scherer (2008) "Optimal Asset Allocation for Sovereign Wealth Funds", *Journal of Asset Management*, 9:3, 215–238.

Kothari, S. and J. Shanken (2004) "Asset Allocation with Inflation Protected Bonds", *Financial Analysts Journal*, 60:1, 45–70.

Campbell, J. and L. Viceira (2002) *Strategic Asset Allocation*, Oxford University Press.

Doskeland, T. (2007) "Strategic Asset Allocation for a Country: The Norwegian Case", *Journal of Financial Markets and Portfolio Management*, 21:3, 167–201.

Gintschel, A. and B. Scherer (2008) "Optimal Asset Allocation for Sovereign Wealth Funds", *Journal of Asset Management*, 9:3, 215–238.

Kothari, S. and J. Shanken (2004) "Asset Allocation with Inflation Protected Bonds", *Financial Analysts Journal*, 60:1, 45–70.

9
Portfolio Choice for Oil Based Sovereign Wealth Funds

Bernd Scherer

9.1 Introduction

For the purpose of this chapter we define Sovereign Wealth Funds (SWF) as sovereign investment vehicles (returns enter the governments fiscal budget) with high foreign asset exposure, nonstandard liabilities and long (intergenerational) time horizon.[1] In this chapter we focus on SWFs sourced by oil revenue as the currently most important (biggest) fraction of this class of new investors as can be seen from Table 9.1.

Among the ten biggest SWFs we find eight funds that are sourced from oil revenues. Given an estimated market size of about 3 trillion dollars at the beginning of 2008, the three biggest oil revenue funds account for 52% of total SWF assets. Given the long term mediocre performance of spot oil (underground wealth) SWFs have been created to perform an oil to equity transformation to participate in global growth. The speed of this transformation will depend on the optimal patch of extraction which depends on the impact of increased supply on oil prices, extraction costs (technology) and oil price expectations. Given an estimated 40 trillion dollar value of underground oil compared to 50 trillion dollars in global equities, SWFs will have a major impact on global equity markets. It will also lead to a shift from traditional reserve currencies (dollar, yen) to emerging market currencies where much of the global growth is to be expected.

For many oil exporting countries, crude oil or gas reserves are the single most important national asset. Any change in the value of reserves directly and materially affects these countries' wealth, and thus the well being of their citizens. Figure 8.1 serves as an illustration. Oil price changes are of a violent nature and can have a destabilizing effect on the economy via volatile real exchange rates.

Having recognized this, a number of oil exporting countries have been depositing oil revenues in funds dedicated to future expenditure. Devising optimal investment policies for such oil revenue funds is the aim of this chapter. We analyze optimal allocations among standard partitions of the

Table 9.1 The ten biggest SWFs: size and source of funding

Sovereign	Assets	Inception	Source	Weight (in %)
UAE	880	1976	Oil	29.33
Norway	390	1996	Oil	13.00
Singapore	350	1981	Misc	11.67
Saudi Arabia	290	1981	Oil	9.67
Kuwait	245	1953	Oil	8.17
China	200	2007	Misc	6.67
Lybia	55	1974	Oil	1.83
Qatar	49	N/A	Oil	1.63
Algeria	44	2000	Oil	1.47
USA (Alaska)	39	1976	Oil	1.30

Note: All numbers are in billion dollars and based on public sources or our own estimates as of the end of 2007

investment universe, taking into account that aggregate wealth consists of financial assets and oil reserves.

An example of an oil revenue fund is Norway's State Petroleum Fund. The policy goals of the fund, as stated in the Norske Finansdepartementet's (Norwegian Ministry of Finance) Summary,[2] is "[f]irst, [...to] act as a buffer to smooth short term variations in the oil revenues [in the Fiscal Budget,...and second to] serve as a tool for coping with the financial challenges connected to an aging population and the eventual decline in oil revenues, by transferring wealth to future generations." The second objective is operationalized as "[...] invest[ing] the capital in such a way that the funds [sic] international purchasing power is maximized, taking into account an acceptable level of risk." This suggests that the benchmark of the fund is future consumption in the form of imports. The same reason also motivates the inclusion of equity, which is expected to enhance the performance of the fund. Concerning the definition of risk, it appears that the Finansdepartementet is mostly concerned with changes in the market value of the fund. We were not able to infer the Finansdepartementet's views on operationalizing the first objective, smoothing oil revenues in the short term. We believe that both objectives, smoothing revenues and maximizing long term welfare, suggest the more extensive definition of risk we propose in this chapter.[3]

More generally, our chapter is an example of how risk stemming from nonfinancial assets can be hedged, at least partially, through financial assets. In other words: we talk about asset allocation with nontradable wealth. The key is exploiting the correlation between financial and nonfinancial assets to reduce the overall risk of the portfolio, compared to an allocation that considers only the correlation structure of the financial assets. Although the general idea is straightforward, empirical or practical implementations are rare. An exception is asset/liability management, in which interest rate exposure on one side of the balance sheet is offset by interest rate exposure on the other side. This chapter applies a similar idea to a more general problem.

We will focus on portfolio investments. This is a narrower brief than what sovereign investors can do. Rather than investing into securities (mostly USD dominated) abroad sovereign investors can also use their oil revenues to build exposure to future growth industries and develop the necessary infrastructure to make their country an attractive place to attract top human talent. Dubai and Qatar are prime examples of this.

During the following exposition we will rely on the normality in return distributions assumption to allow us to come up with closed form solutions that provide conceptual insight into the structure of the underlying problem. While we are aware that returns on capital markets and certainly on commodities like oil are in the short run far from normal, we also believe an SWF belongs to the group of long term investors such that the central limit theorem will come to our help to somewhat mitigate the nonnormality issue.

The outline is as follows. Section 9.2 describes the general portfolio choice problem for an oil (commodity) based SWF together with some empirical evidence on the oil shock hedging properties for different investments. Section 9.3 extends Section 9.2 by differentiating between hedging and growth assets. In Section 9.4 we introduce background risk into the SWF asset allocation problem, by making the level of resource wealth a random variable. Section 9.5 solves the intertemporal asset allocation problem and Section 9.6 concludes.

9.2 Incorporating the sovereign wealth fund into government budgets

We view the optimal asset allocation problem of an SWF as the decision making problem of an investor with nontradable endowed wealth (oil reserves). In order to get insight into the portfolio choice problem for an SWF we assume the following analytical setup.

The SWF can invest its financial wealth into a single asset or cash. We can think of this as the choice between the global market portfolio and cash. This is certainly restrictive, but will allow us to develop our framework without the need of very complex calculations and we will relax this assumption in the following section. Returns for this performance asset are normally distributed and given by

[1] $\tilde{r}_{\alpha} \sim N\left(\mu_{\alpha}, \sigma_{\alpha}^{2}\right)$

where μ_a represents the expected risk premium (over local cash returns) of our performance asset and σ_a its volatility. At the same time the government budget moves with changes on its claim on economic net wealth. For a commodity (oil) based SWF changes in commodity (oil) prices will by far have the biggest influence on the government budget measured in economic (not accounting) terms. We assume that oil price changes are also normally distributed

$$[2] \quad \tilde{r}_o \sim N\left(\mu_o, \sigma_o^2\right)$$

and correlate positively with asset returns, i.e. $Cov\left(\tilde{r}_\alpha, \tilde{r}_o\right) = \rho_{\alpha,o} > 0$. As μ_o is empirically extremely noisy to estimate we look for an economic prior. Under perfectly integrated capital markets the Hotelling-Solow rule states that natural resource prices should grow at the world interest rate such that countries are indifferent between depletion (earning the interest rate) and keeping oil underground (earning price changes). We hence assume a risk premium on oil of zero, i.e. μ_o=0. Brent prices on 4 January 1982 were 35.9 and rose to 66.6 on 21 October 2008. This amounts to a meager 2.3% return per annum over the last 26.8 years, which makes our assumption of a zero risk premium on underground oil suddenly looking much more realistic. Even if we would instead use the maximum oil price of 145.61 this would amount to a mere 5.3% return which is even more in line with average money market returns.

How do we integrate oil wealth into a country's budget surplus (deficit)? Let θ denote the fraction of importance the SWF plays in the economy's government budget. A simple way to gauge this is the following consideration. If the SWF has a size of 1 monetary unit, while the market value of oil reserves amounts to 5 monetary units, this translates into $\theta = 1/1+5 = 1/6$ weight for the SWF asset and $1-\theta = 1-1/6 = 5/6$ weight for oil revenues.[4] In other words,

$$[3] \quad \tilde{r} = \theta w \tilde{r}_\alpha + (1-\theta)\tilde{r}_o$$

Note that 1–*w* represents the implied cash holding that carries a zero risk premium and no risk in a one-period consideration. Expressing returns as risk premium has the advantage that we do not need to model cash holdings. These simply become the residual asset that ensures portfolio weights add up to one without changing risk or (excess) return.

Suppose now the SWF manager is charged to maximize the utility of total government wealth rather than narrowly maximizing the utility for its direct assets under management. The optimal solution for this problem can be found from

$$[4] \quad \max_w \left(\theta w \mu_\alpha - \frac{\lambda}{2}\left[\theta^2 w^2 \sigma_\alpha^2 + (1-\theta)^2 \sigma_o^2 + 2w\theta(1-\theta)\rho\sigma_\alpha\sigma_o\right]\right)$$

Taking first order conditions and solving for w we arrive at the optimal asset allocation for a resource based SWF.

$$[5] \quad w^* = w_s^* + w_h^* = \frac{1}{\theta}\frac{\mu_\alpha}{\lambda\sigma_\alpha^2} - \frac{1-\theta}{\theta}\frac{\rho\sigma_o}{\sigma_\alpha}$$

Total demand for risky assets can be decomposed into speculative demand w_s^* and hedging demand, w_h^*. In the case of uncorrelated assets and oil resources the optimal solution is equivalent to a leveraged (with factor $1/\theta$) position in the asset-only maximum Sharpe-ratio portfolio or in other words w_s^*. What is the economic intuition for this leverage? For an investor with constant relative risk aversion the optimal weight of risky assets will be independent from his wealth level, which nowhere enters [4]. While a given country might have little in financial wealth in the form of SWF financial assets it might be rich in natural resources and as such it requires a large multiplier. For $\theta = 1/6$ we would require the SWF to leverage substantially (6 times). Assuming $\mu_a = 5$, $\sigma_a = 20$, and $\lambda = 0.03$ we get $(1/\theta)\left[(6/0.03)\cdot 20^2\right] = 250\%$. The second component in [5] represents hedging demand. In other words: the desirability of the risky asset does not only depend on its Sharpe-ratio but also on its ability to hedge out unanticipated shocks to oil wealth. Hedging demand is given as the product of leverage and oils asset beta, $\beta_{o,\alpha} = \rho\sigma_o / \sigma_\alpha$. The later is equivalent to the slope coefficient of a regression of (demeaned) asset returns against (demeaned) oil returns, i.e. of the form

$$[6] \quad (r_o - \bar{r}_o) = \beta_{o,\alpha}(r_\alpha - \bar{r}_\alpha) + \epsilon.$$

Hedge demand is only zero if oil price risk is purely idiosyncratic. For $\sigma_0 = 40, \rho = 0.1$, we would ***reduce*** the allocation in the risky asset according to $-[(1 - 1/6)/1/6](0.1 \cdot 40)/20 = -100\%$. Positive correlation between asset and oil price risk increases the volatility of total wealth. A 100% short position in the risky asset helps to mange total risk. However, in case the correlation was negative we would even further increase the allocation to the risky asset. The optimal position of the SWF would be 1.5 times leverage in the global market portfolio.

While the focus of this chapter is not on empirical work, we should provide some indication of the oil shock hedging properties of traditional asset classes. Without the existence of these assets that could potentially help to reduce total wealth volatility for oil rich investors equation [5] would be of little practical use. Let us look at global equities (MSCI World in USD), US government bonds (Lehman US Treasury total return index for varying maturities), and oil (Crude Oil-Brent Cur Month FOB from Thompson) for the period from January 1997 to September 2008. The selection of the above mentioned assets is motivated by some basic economic considerations. Oil tends to do well

Table 9.2 Correlation of asset returns with percentage oil price changes

	US treasury bond							
Frequency	**1 year**	**1–3 year**	**3–5 year**	**5–7 year**	**7–10 year**	**10–20 year**	**20+ year**	**Global equities**
Monthly	−8.28%	−2.38%	1.16%	2.26%	2.75%	1.18%	0.16%	9.19%
	−0.99	−0.43	0.21	0.41	0.49	0.21	0.03	1.66
Quarterly	−9.29%	−22.59%	−20.08%	−21.00%	−19.60%	−23.92%	−24.42%	−9.34%
	−0.65	−2.42	−2.14	−2.24	−2.09	−2.57	−2.63	−0.98
Annual	−38.81%	−40.70%	−50.94%	−56.52%	−59.48%	−55.04%	−51.29%	24.10%
	−1.52	−2.36	−3.13	−3.63	−3.92	−3.49	−3.16	1.31

Note: The table uses global equities (MSCI World in USD), US government bonds (Lehman US Treasury total return index for varying maturities), and oil (Crude Oil-Brent Cur Month FOB from Thompson) for the period from January 1997 to September 2008. This translates into 142 monthly, 48 quarterly and 13 annual data points. For each data frequency, the first line shows the correlation coefficient, while the second line provides its *t*-value. We calculate t-values according to $t = \rho\sqrt{\frac{n-2}{1-\rho^2}}$, where n represents the number of data points and ρ the estimated correlation coefficient. Critical values are given by the *t*-distribution with n–2 degrees of freedom. For example the critical value for 13 annual data points at the 95% level is 2.2. All significant correlation coefficients are shaded grey.

either in a political crisis (in which equities do not do well) or in anticipation of global growth (in which equities also do well). At the same time government bonds (particularly at the long end) are a natural recession hedge and will also do well if oil prices fall. There are obviously notable exceptions. Oil and bonds will move together if an oil price increase is the cause of recession fears. In this scenario shorter bonds should provide better returns than long bonds due to rising inflation fears. All asset classes move together if monetary loosening inflates a leverage driven bubble that drives equity and bond markets while bonds perform due to falling interest rates.

However we can endlessly talk about our economic priors, so we should have a look at the data instead. The results of our correlation analysis are given in Table 9.2. In the short run (monthly data) we do not find significant correlations between oil price change and the selected asset class return. However, reducing the data frequency, i.e. increasing the period to calculate returns from shows significant negative correlations between oil price changes and fixed income returns. In other words we find that long term correlations are buried under short term noise.

Both the degree of (negative) correlation and its significance (even though we reduce the sample size) rise as we move from quarterly to annual. Global equities, however, provide no hedge against oil price changes. While they could still be used as a performance asset, they are of limited use as a hedge against oil price shocks.

Proponents of equity investments might suspect that we are underselling their case as we have not been allowing for more granular equity exposures.

Table 9.3 Correlation of US Industry returns with percentage oil price changes

	Dow Jones Industries									
Frequency	**Oil & gas**	**Basic mats**	**Industrials**	**Consumer gds**	**Health care**	**Consumer Svs**	**Telecom**	**Utilities**	**Financials**	**Technology**
Monthly	45.68%	5.94%	–12.89%	–18.03%	–13.83%	–21.26%	–1.62%	–6.32%	–18.08%	–11.86%
	9.23	1.07	–2.34	–3.29	–2.51	–3.91	–0.29	–1.14	–3.30	–2.15
Quarterly	49.57%	8.11%	–6.47%	–4.17%	–28.57%	–22.69%	–4.55%	–6.20%	–24.99%	–25.03%
	5.96	0.85	–0.68	–0.44	–3.11	–2.43	–0.48	–0.65	–2.69	–2.70
Annual	51.03%	–20.03%	–11.99%	–65.36%	–37.26%	–51.40%	–44.18%	–15.84%	–13.52%	–3.47%
	3.14	–1.08	–0.64	–4.57	–2.12	–3.17	–2.61	–0.85	–0.72	–0.18

Note: The table uses Dow Jones sector returns and oil (Crude Oil-Brent Cur Month FOB from Thompson) for the period from January 1982 to September 2008. This translates into 323 monthly, 109 quarterly and 28 annual data points. For each data frequency, the first line shows the correlation coefficient, while the second line provides its *t*-value. We calculate *t*-values according to $t = \rho\sqrt{\frac{n-2}{1-\rho^2}}$, where n represents the number of data points and ρ the estimated correlation coefficient. Critical values are given by the *t*-distribution with n–2 degrees of freedom. For example the critical value for 28 annual data points at the 95% level is 2.05. All significant correlation coefficients are grey shaded.

Maybe we can identify various sectors that respond differently to oil price shock. A global equity portfolio is already a diversified portfolio that leaves no possibility to leverage these effects. The results for this can be found in Table 9.3. Our results are encouraging. We find significant negative correlation for defensive consumer and health care sectors that tend to do well when the economy does badly. Results are stable and significant for different data frequencies. At the same time the energy sector is positively related to oil and does not qualify for inclusion into SWF allocations as we would have conjectured before.

9.3 Optimal allocation between growth and hedge assets

The previous section has shown that traditional equities offer little hedge against oil price risks. At the same time fixed income investments do, but they do not offer the same long term returns and an SWF manager therefore needs to extend the investment universe into performance as well as hedge assets. We retain the setup from the previous section but extend the universe into two assets where one asset is assumed to be a hedging asset (i.e. it shows negative correlation) while the second asset provides growth orthogonal to oil wealth changes. We can summarize our setup with the following distribution,

$$[7] \quad t = \rho\sqrt{\frac{n-2}{1-\rho^2}} \quad \tilde{r}_h \sim N\left(\mu_h, \sigma_h^2\right)$$

where r_g and r_h stand for the return of growth and hedge assets with $\mu_g > \mu_h$. Our correlation assumptions are

$$[8] \quad Cov\left(r_h, r_g\right) = \rho_{h,g}\sigma_h\sigma_g > 0, \ Cov\left(r_h, r_o\right) = \rho_{h,o}\sigma_h\sigma_o < 0, \ Cov\left(r_g, r_o\right) = 0$$

Note, that our setup effectively assume that an SWF can use leverage, but will only go into long assets. The hedge asset is negatively correlated and as such will be held in nonnegative demand. This is necessary as otherwise the assumption of nontradable wealth would become meaningless. The government budget evolves according to

$$[9] \quad \tilde{r} = \theta\left[w_g\tilde{r}_g + w_h\tilde{r}_h\right] + (1-\theta)\tilde{r}_o$$

where utility (i.e. risk adjusted performance) is given by

$$[10] \quad u = E(\tilde{r}) - \frac{\lambda}{2}\left[E\left(\tilde{r}^2\right) - E(\tilde{r})^2\right]$$

We maximize [9] by setting the first order conditions to zero and solving for w_g, w_h:

$$[11] \quad w_g^* = \frac{\mu_g - \beta_{h,g} \bullet m_g}{\lambda\theta\left(1-\rho_{g,h}^2\right)\sigma_h^2} - \frac{(1-\theta)}{\theta}\frac{\beta_{o,h}}{\left(1-\rho_{g,h}^2\right)}$$

$$[12] \quad w_h^* = \frac{\mu_h - \beta_{h,g} \bullet \mu_g}{\lambda\theta\left(1-\rho_{g,h}^2\right)\sigma_h^2} - \frac{(1-\theta)}{\theta}\frac{\beta_{o,h}}{\left(1-\rho_{g,h}^2\right)}$$

where $\beta_{g,h} = \rho_{g,h}\sigma_g / \sigma_h, \beta_{o,h} = \rho_{h,o}\sigma_o / \sigma_h$. Demand for the growth asset can be split again into speculative demand and hedging demand. Speculative demand will depend on its "alpha", $\mu_g - \beta_{g,h}$, versus the hedge asset, i.e. "beta", $\beta_{g,h}$, adjusted excess return divided by the risk not explained by the hedge asset. Here $\rho_{g,h}^2$ can be interpreted as the R^2 of a regression of hedge versus growth asset returns. Hedging demand in turn will depend on the implicit hedging through the correlation to the hedge asset. The usual risk aversion and oil wealth importance scaling applies. A similar picture is given for the hedge asset. However the effect here is much more direct such that the hedge demand will always be greater than for the growth asset (by definition). A clearer picture arises when we get rid of the indirect correlation by setting $\rho_{g,h}=0$. In this case [11] and [12] become

$$[13] \quad w_g^* = \frac{\mu_g}{\lambda\theta\sigma_g^2}$$

and

$$[14] \quad w_h^* = \frac{\mu_h}{\lambda\theta\sigma_h^2} - \rho_{h,o}\frac{\sigma_o}{\sigma_h}\frac{(1-\theta)}{\theta}$$

Now both allocations can be taken independently. The growth asset is entirely driven by its Sharpe-ratio, while the hedge asset combines both speculative and hedge demand directly relating to [5]. Finally we will ask ourselves: how will the hedge demand (allocation of long term USD denominated fixed income bonds) change as θ becomes larger, i.e. as financial wealth becomes more and more dominant? In order to answer this question we calculate $\frac{dw_h^*}{d\theta}$ from [14].

All significant correlation coefficients are grey shaded.

$$[15] \quad \frac{dw_h^*}{d\theta} = \frac{-\mu_h + \lambda\rho_{h,o}\sigma_h\sigma_o}{\lambda\sigma_h^2\theta^2} < 0$$

under the assumption that μ_h, $\mu_h>0$, $\rho_{h,o}$.[5] Economies with falling levels of oil resources should therefore invest more like "traditional" investors with cash-like liabilities.

Again we ask ourselves which kind of investment strategies would show zero correlations with oil price movements such that we can separate investment decisions into building both a growth and a hedge portfolio. A natural candidate would be the hedge fund investments. Table 9.4 summarizes our results. All popular hedge fund strategies we have looked at are uncorrelated to oil price movement over medium to longer term time horizons. Hedge funds could therefore be an interesting add on to investments into long government bonds.

9.4 Background risk – the impact of resource uncertainty

There is a vast literature on background risk[6], i.e., risk that is uncorrelated to the assets you decide upon. It exists in the background of the decision maker. Pension funds for example are exposed to background risk in the form of mortality risk, that is independent from interest rate or equity risk.

How can we translate this idea into our framework for finding the optimal allocation for an SWF? To our knowledge this has not been addressed in the theoretical literature. So far we have assumed that θ (i.e. the fraction of SWF assets to total sovereign wealth) is known with certainty in [5], i.e. that the value of oil reserves is known to the decision maker. However, the size of an oil field is not known with great precision. Additionally government claims are sometimes legally disputed (among neighboring countries) and new undiscovered fields might yet be found. Hence θ might be best thought of as a random variable. We assume the fraction of financial wealth relative to total (financial and oil) wealth follows a uniform distribution around the government's estimate of $\overline{\theta}$. More precisely we assume

$$[16]\quad \tilde{\theta} \sim U\left(\overline{\theta}-\varepsilon, \overline{\theta}+\varepsilon\right)$$

It seems natural to further assume independence between background risk on the level of available oil reserves and asset risk. The joint probability density function can then be written down as

$$[17]\quad f(\theta, r_\alpha) = f(\theta) f(r_\alpha) = \frac{1}{\sigma_\alpha \sqrt{2\pi}} e^{-\frac{1}{2}\left(\frac{r_\alpha - \mu_\alpha}{\sigma_\alpha}\right)^2} \frac{1}{(\overline{\theta}+\varepsilon)-(\overline{\theta}-\varepsilon)}$$

We are looking for

$$[18]\quad Var\left(\tilde{\theta}\tilde{r}_\alpha\right) = E\left[\left(\tilde{\theta}\tilde{r}_\alpha\right)^2\right] - E\left[\tilde{\theta}\tilde{r}_\alpha\right]^2$$

Table 9.4 Correlation of hedge fund returns with percentage oil price changes

	HFR Indices									
Frequency	Distressed debt	Merger arbitrage	Equity market neutral	Quantitative directional	Short bias	Event driven	Global macro	Relative value	Fixed income arbitrage	Convertible arbitrage
Monthly	10.50%	9.41%	8.56%	19.65%	−15.19%	13.28%	23.66%	13.02%	13.39%	7.61%
	1.26	1.13	1.02	2.39	−1.83	1.60	2.90	1.56	1.61	0.91
Quarterly	−7.64%	−19.83%	−15.28%	−12.01%	12.54%	−15.15%	−17.34%	−4.22%	14.12%	−10.86%
	−0.53	−1.40	−1.07	−0.84	0.88	−1.06	−1.22	−0.29	0.99	−0.76
Annual	20.38%	6.78%	−22.43%	44.78%	−33.86%	26.77%	41.76%	28.13%	30.09%	−0.88%
	0.75	0.24	−0.83	1.81	−1.30	1.00	1.66	1.06	1.14	−0.03

Note: The table uses HFR index returns and oil (Crude Oil-Brent Cur Month FOB from Thompson) for the period from January 1997 to September 2008. This translates into 142 monthly, 48 quarterly and 13 annual data points. For each data frequency, the first line shows the correlation coefficient, while the second line provides its *t*-value. We calculate *t*-values according to $t = \rho\sqrt{\frac{n-2}{1-\rho^2}}$, where n represents the number of data points and ρ the estimated correlation coefficient. Critical values are given by the *t*-distribution with n–2 degrees of freedom. For example the critical value for 13 annual data points at the 95% level is 2.2.

in order to calculate portfolio risk. Given the joint probability density [17] this amounts to integrating over the joint probability density where

$$[19]\quad E\left[\left(\tilde{\theta}\tilde{r}_{\alpha}\right)^{2}\right]=\int_{-\infty}^{\infty}\int_{\bar{\theta}-\varepsilon}^{\bar{\theta}+\varepsilon}\left(\theta r_{\alpha}\right)^{2}f\left(\theta,r_{\alpha}\right)d\theta dr_{\alpha}=\frac{1}{3}\left(\varepsilon^{2}+3\bar{\theta}^{2}\right)\left(\mu_{\alpha}^{2}+\sigma_{\alpha}^{2}\right)$$

The expression for [18] then becomes

$$[20]\quad \begin{aligned} Var\left(\tilde{\theta}\tilde{r}_{\alpha}\right)&=\frac{1}{3}\left(\varepsilon^{2}+3\bar{\theta}^{2}\right)\left(\mu_{\alpha}^{2}+\sigma_{\alpha}^{2}\right)-\mu_{\alpha}^{2}\bar{\theta}^{2}\\ &=\bar{\theta}^{2}\sigma_{\alpha}^{2}+\varepsilon^{2}\frac{\mu_{\alpha}^{2}+\sigma_{\alpha}^{2}}{3}\end{aligned}$$

The reader will notice that for $\varepsilon\rightarrow 0$ we converge to the well known expression from undergraduate statistics $Var\left(\tilde{\theta}\tilde{r}_{\alpha}\right)=\bar{\theta}^{2}\sigma_{\alpha}^{2}$.

What does [20] imply? As long as we have background risk in the form of uncertainty around the size of oil reserves the optimal asset allocation for the SWF (we focus on the case with uncorrelated assets and oil returns for simplicity), becomes

$$[21]\quad w_{br}^{*}=\frac{1}{\lambda}\frac{\bar{\theta}\mu_{\alpha}}{\bar{\theta}^{2}\sigma_{\alpha}^{2}+\varepsilon^{2}\frac{\mu_{\alpha}^{2}+\sigma_{\alpha}^{2}}{3}}$$

We now compare this with the solution in the absence of background risk $w^{*}=\frac{1}{\bar{\theta}}\frac{\mu_{\alpha}}{\lambda\sigma_{\alpha}^{2}}$ by building the quotient

$$[22]\quad \frac{w^{*}}{w_{br}^{*}}=1+\frac{\varepsilon^{2}\left(\mu_{\alpha}^{2}+\sigma_{\alpha}^{2}\right)}{\bar{\theta}^{2}\sigma_{\alpha}^{2}}>1$$

which will always be greater than 1. An increase in background risk will lead to a decrease in risk taking for the SWF. The effect becomes stronger the more volatile our risky asset is. Empirically we should observe that SWFs with larger resource uncertainty should invest less aggressively and vice versa. Also we would expect that economies with low reserves relative to financial wealth are less affected by resource uncertainty.

9.5 Asset allocation and oil reserves over time

What will drive the optimal asset allocation for an SWF over time? How is the SWF expected to shift its assets? How fast will the financial wealth of oil rich countries accumulate? We might want the answer these questions to either solve the dynamic portfolio choice problem for an SWF or to assess the change in global financial flows for the coming years.

A brief look at the myopic one-period solution in [5] reveals that the fraction of risky assets is driven by financial wealth relative to resource wealth. For a "young" SWF where financial wealth is low relative to resource wealth a more risky asset allocation is optimal, while mature SWFs with large assets relative to natural resources should dial back their risks. To decide on the optimal asset allocation over time we therefore need to calculate the optimal extraction policy, i.e. how fast oil wealth is transformed into financial wealth. If expected oil price changes are high relative to asset returns (opportunity costs of keeping resources under ground) we would expect a slower oil extraction and therefore a lower ratio of financial wealth to resource wealth. Also if extraction technology improves (lower extraction costs) we expect a faster "oil to equity transformation".

We choose a standard dynamic programming framework (with fixed time horizon) to address this question, where optimal extraction problem is solved by recursively working backward through the well known Bellman equation where for $t=0, \ldots, n-1$,

$$[23] \quad V_t = \max_{\xi_t}\left(f_t\xi_t - \phi\xi_t^2\right) + \frac{1}{1+r}V_{t+1}\left(o_t - \xi_t\right)$$

Here f_t represents the projected oil price for period t, ξ_t stands for the level of extraction (i.e. $f_t\,\xi_t$ represents oil revenues), the state variable, o_t, denotes oil reserves, and the cost function for oil extraction is assumed to be quadratic in extraction with a calibration parameter ϕ. In order to solve [23] we also need a terminal condition, i.e. that in the last period all remaining oil wealth will be extracted (at whatever cost it takes): for $t=n$, $V_{t+n} = f_t o_t - \phi o_t^2$. In other words, each period an oil extraction decision, ξ_t, is made that leads to a reduction in oil reserves $o_t = o_{t-1} - \xi_t$ and the present value of after cost extractions is maximized. The optimal extraction policy has to counterbalance the desire to extract all the oil at once to get immediate rather than very distant cash flows against the rising extraction costs of doing so.[7]

We calibrate our calculations with the following sets of assumptions. Initial oil reserves in Norway are 9947 million barrels at an oil price of 70 USD/barrel. Current oil extraction is assumed to be around 720 million barrels a year. Assuming extraction is optimal (myopic) at current levels we can calibrate the cost function parameter from $\phi = f_0 / 2\xi_0 = 0.00000005$. This is obviously equivalent to assuming that a current (i.e. October 2008) price of 70 is equal to marginal production costs. Oil price growth is expected to be around 5% per annum, alongside a 5% risk free rate, i.e. $\beta = 1/1+r = 0.9524$. We also assume the government to be capturing 100% of revenues from oil extraction.

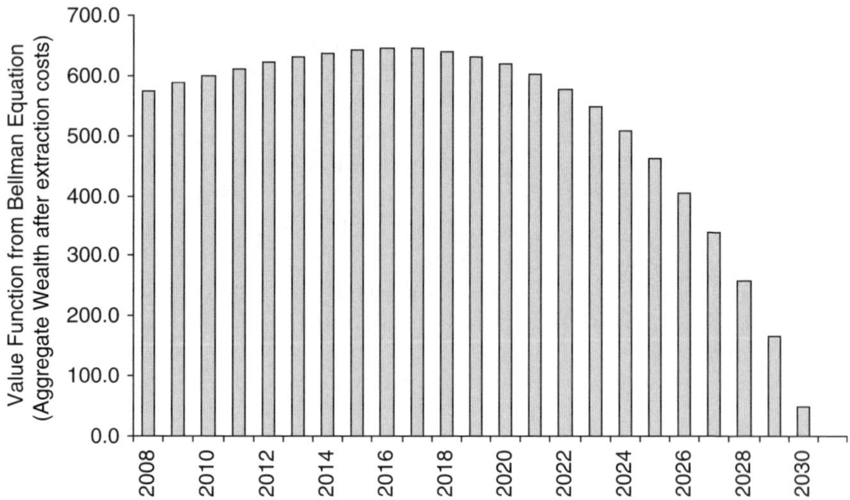

Figure 9.1 Evolution of oil wealth (adjusted for extraction costs) over time

Note: Oil wealth is directly calculated from the Bellman value function, i.e. we plot V_t^* from for $t=0,\ldots,n$ where 0 represents the year 2008. This is a better measure of wealth than simply multiplying remaining oil reserves by oil prices. After all, oil needs to be extracted first.

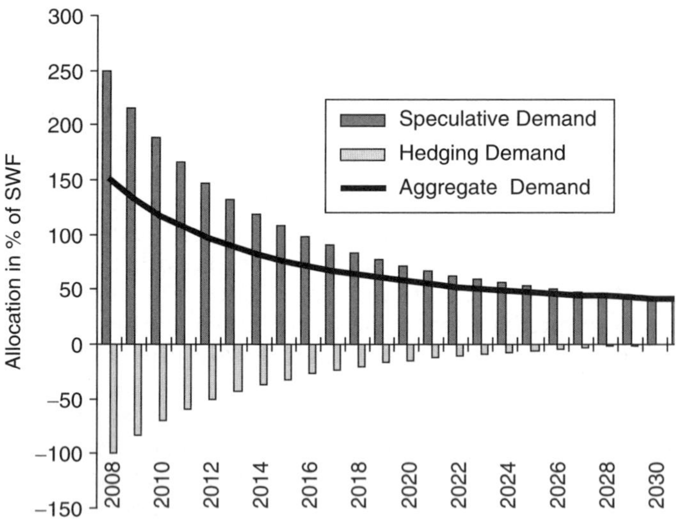

Figure 9.2 Optimal SWF allocation in risky asset over time

Note: We assume $\mu_a = 5$, $\sigma_a = 20$, $\lambda = 0.03$ as well as $\mu_o = 0$, $\rho = 5$, $\sigma = 0.1$. Aggregate demand for the risky asset arises from speculative and hedging demand. Over time hedging demand reaches zero as resources become depleted.

The result of the above calculations can be found in Figure 9.1. It is worthwhile to note that we do not equate oil wealth with the market value of oil reserves. In fact we argue that oil wealth is defined as the optimal extraction policy (whose aim it is to maximize oil wealth) and therefore can be found from V_0^* in [23]. In our example oil wealth is assumed to be 572 billion USD instead of 696 billion USD (9947 million barrels times current price of 70 USD/barrel).

As oil wealth becomes depleted the relative importance of financial assets to natural resources shifts. We simply calculate θ_t across time (assuming a starting position of $\theta=1/6$, i.e. financial wealth of 114.6 billion USD) and substitute this into [5]. This allows us to estimate the evolution of risky assets (as a fraction of financial wealth) over time. The results for speculative and hedging demand are given in Figure 9.2.

The SWF starts out as an aggressive investment vehicle with a leveraged position (150% exposure) in the risky asset. As time goes by hedging demand is reduced but so is speculative demand. Hedging demand is negative for positively correlated assets, i.e. the SWF scales back risks he would otherwise take on a stand alone basis. With no resources left the SWF would invest about 42% in the risky asset with the remaining allocation in cash.

The above framework can be easily applied to a multi-asset context. In this case it is trivial to expand [11] and [12], while the optimal extraction policy will remain the driving force for portfolio adjustments across time.

9.6 Conclusions

Sovereign wealth funds might be a new set of investors but classic portfolio choice still applies. We find that the SWF decision making problem can be modeled as optimal asset allocation with endowed, nontradable wealth. Closed form solutions are readily available and allocations can be separated with the usual two fund separation, the first fund being an optimal growth portfolio and the second an oil price risk hedging portfolio. We also investigate the impact of resource uncertainty on optimal asset allocation. An SWF of a sovereign with considerable resource uncertainty might find it optimal to invest less aggressively that an SWF with well established oil resources. Finally we show how we can model optimal asset allocation over time as a function of the optimal oil extraction policy. Maturing SWFs will invest less aggressively, while recently funded SWFs need to be run very aggressively to diversify total wealth.

Notes

1. A long time horizon does not imply low risk aversion. This is one of the most common fallacies made in asset management and usually rests with the focus on quantile based risk management.

2. Http://www.odin.dep.no/fin/engelsk/p10001617/p10002780/indexbna.html. Further information regarding the aims and policies of the Fund is in the Annual Reports; see Kjaer (2001) and Norges Bank (2002).
3. Other examples of portfolios funded by revenues from natural resources include the Alaska Permanent Reserve Fund (USD 23 billion), the State Oil Fund of Azerbaijan (USD 0.5 billion), Chad's Revenue Management Fund, the National Fund of Kazakhstan (USD 1.2 billion), Venezuela's Investment Fund for Macroeconomic Stabilization (USD 3.7 billion), the Alberta Heritage Savings Trust Fund (CAD 3.7 billion), and the Nunavut Trust (CAD 0.5 billion). Furthermore, certain central bank funds of oil exporting countries, such as Iran, Kuwait, Oman, and Saudi Arabia, are de-facto oil revenue funds. In general, stated investment objectives are similar to those of the Norwegian fund; i.e. a favorable long term tradeoff of return and risk of the financial portfolio. The risk in aggregate wealth stemming from price changes in natural reserves is typically ignored.
4. Alternatively one could incorporate all other items (tax revenues, government spending, pension liabilities, etc.) into the government budget surplus/deficit calculation as in Doskeland (2007). However, given the relatively low volatility of these positions we will ignore this problem. It will not change the nature of our findings.
5. For the more general case we get $\frac{dw_h^*}{d\theta} = \frac{-\left(\mu_h - \mu_g \frac{\rho_{h,g}\sigma_h}{\sigma_g}\right) + \lambda\rho_{h,o}\sigma_h\sigma_o}{\lambda\left(1-\rho_{g,h}^2\right)\sigma_h^2\theta^2}$. However, the intuition does not change.
6. See Gollier (2001) for a review.
7. An introduction into dynamic programming is found in Bertsekas (1976). The interested reader can get code for NUOPT™ for S-PLUS™ from the author on request.

References

Bertseas, D.P. (1976) *Dynamic Programming and Stochastic Control*, New York: Academic Press.

Doskeland, T. (2007) "Strategic asset allocation for a country: the Norwegian case", *Journal of Financial Markets and Portfolio Management*, 21:3, 167–201.

Gollier, P. (2001) *The Economics of Risk and Time*, MIT Press.

Kjaer, K. N. (2001) "A national strategy for investing resource wealth", Speech at the BSI Gamma Foundation Conference on Global Asset Management Long Term Asset Management.

Norges Bank (2002) "An appraisal of the regional weighting of the Petroleum Fund", Letter to the Ministry of Finance on 11 April 2002.

10

Strategic Investment and Risk Management for Sovereign Wealth Funds*

Stijn Claessens and Jerome Kreuser

10.1 Introduction

10.1.1 The case for analyzing Sovereign Wealth Funds' Asset Liability Management

Sovereign wealth funds (SWF)[1] have been around for a long time, at least since the 1950s. But their total size worldwide has grown dramatically over the last few years. Buoyed by rising commodity prices (at least until recently), desires to build up reserves for risk management purposes, and large capital inflows, many emerging markets as well as some developed countries have accumulated large SWFs in the last few years. The IMF now estimates that assets of SWFs will rise from \$2–3 trillion today to about \$6–10 trillion within five years (IMF 2007). Other estimates are that these SWFs can grow to \$11–14 trillion by 2012 (see McKinsey et al. (2007); note that oil and many other commodity prices have been very volatile lately, so predictions as to future size are fraught with large uncertainties). At present, China, Kuwait, Norway, Russia, Saudi Arabia, Singapore, and the United Arab Emirates are among the countries that have the largest SWFs.

This rise of sovereign wealth assets is a new phenomenon with major implications for global capital flows, cross-border investments, and international capital markets. Many international efforts are underway to analyze various aspects of SWFs. These include the desired governance and accountability arrangements for SWFs, whether there is a need (and if so in what forms) for oversight of their investments, e.g., in strategic industries, and how to mitigate concerns about a possible use of SWFs as foreign policy tools. Sets of best practices and guidelines are being developed on some of these issues (by the IMF and OECD).

---

* The views expressed in this chapter are those of the authors and do not necessarily reflect the views of the IMF or IMF policy.

These efforts do not address, however, the question as to how an SWF should manage its assets given its objectives, constraints, and (possibly) guidelines, and specifically what constitutes its best asset mix. We will analyze this question from the perspective of an SWF seeking to meet its objectives of maximizing return (or wealth) given its risk management concerns and various constraints. We will first present a very general approach, yet one that can be easily adapted since each SWF faces specific objectives and constraints, making for unique Assets Liability Management (ALM) problems. We will show how our framework avoids many of the shortcomings of other, commercial risk management systems. To demonstrate the specific benefits of our approach, we will apply our framework to the case of Norway's SWF, the Government Pension Fund – Global (NGPF or the *Fund*) of Norges Bank. Using the model, we will develop optimal benchmark asset compositions, compare our asset composition with their actual allocation (in terms of the benchmarks used), and discuss the results.[2] We end the chapter by showing how our framework is applicable to a broad class of funds, including stabilization, national pension, endowment, and development funds. Additional analysis beyond this chapter is available on the web site http://www.RisKontroller.com, which we subsequently refer to as the web version.

10.1.2 Why ALM for sovereigns and SWFs differs from the general ALM case and what our approach entails

ALM for a sovereign is not just a special case of the ALM-models developed for financial institutions, such as commercial banks or pension funds. Sovereign ALM has a number of special considerations. This importantly includes much longer horizons, as the ALM needs to address issues 10 to 30 years out, as opposed to, say, the day-by-day risk management of a commercial bank. Different objective functions will typically be involved, such as maximizing the country's overall welfare, as opposed to, say, short-term profitability. And different constraints will come into play, such as the need to observe legal constraints and report to parliament, as opposed to, say, satisfying shareholders' interests. These considerations already imply that standard ALM approaches do not suffice for the general case of ALM for sovereigns.

Yet, while a more strategic approach to risk management for sovereigns is needed, it is often not considered (Claessens 2006). This is in part the case because commercial providers tend not to provide the right type of tools. This is because it is difficult and expensive to manage and maintain customized models in a dynamic stochastic optimization (also called dynamic stochastic programming) framework (see Kreuser (2002) for various approaches to manage these models). Furthermore, there is little demand from the users' side for more sophisticated tools as the benefits of using them are often not well known and in any case are difficult to explain to the principals overseeing sovereign risk managers (which can vary from Ministers to members of parliament and the general public). As such, the tendency for sovereign risk managers is to go along with classical risk management solutions, although their needs are different from most commercial systems.

Our approach addresses many of these shortcomings. As in other ALM approaches, we incorporate assets and liabilities to create balance sheets by currency at any point in time, allow for rebalancing of the portfolio and transfers between different currencies, and include transaction costs. We deviate, however, from the standard assumptions often used in financial models, such as the reduction of the problem to a mean–variance trade-off and lognormal distributions. Different from many models, the scenario procedure we use generates trees so that at each point in time the model cannot anticipate what the future outcome will be as there will be several possibilities similar to the way uncertainty unfolds in reality. We also incorporate more capabilities than usual in the processes underlying the scenario tree generation. Specifically, we can allow the user choices of theories such as mean reversion in asset prices, Uncovered Interest Parity (UIP), expert judgment, historical estimation, or estimation of price processes from current instrument values. We can also incorporate changes in volatility and correlations depending on the level of state variables and time, the trending of currency and interest rates, the presence of fat tails in assets prices or the occurrence of extreme events. We can also account for broader changes in the international financial and economic environments and the occurrence of contingent liabilities. We then optimize the portfolio over the entire scenario tree subject to various policy and other constraints, while incorporating several risk constraints, possibly simultaneously at several points in time and at different points along the distributions of outcomes.

The very general problem we thus set up belongs to the class of dynamic stochastic optimization models which has proven to be very powerful for risk management problems. There is a literature that describes these models, either in their academic or specialized applications to central banks or ministries of finance and other institutions (Claessens and Kreuser (2007) and other papers in the same volume; Zenios and Ziemba (2007); Ziemba (2003); Ziemba and Mulvey (1998)). Ziemba and Ziemba (2007) and Mulvey et al. (2002) describe the benefits of this approach nicely, and we do not expand on that here. We do want to point out, though, that these approaches deviate from other methods of risk management.

Mean–variance approaches are often used by risk managers, but these models are very limited as they reduce the dynamics to the recurrence of a one-period problem. Multi-period models have significant advantages over single-period models, especially for long-term investors (Mulvey et al. 2002). At the same time, mean–variance approaches are sensitive to input assumptions, especially regarding expected returns. Often these models require limits on individual assets to improve diversity. The multi-period model will generally make more sensible recommendations, with more diversity. It will typically not put 100% in one asset because it hedges against all defined scenarios. Mean–variance also does not allow for periodic goals or interim constraints. In contrast, multi-period models have less need for such constraints. Single period models can not consider transaction costs in a natural way. And they do not take advantage of gains from rebalancing portfolios to target allocations (it has been shown that higher returns can be achieved by periodic rebalancing).

Sequentially applying mean–variance over time has also been proposed. But it has been shown that this approach is not optimal in the presence of transaction costs, future liquidity constraints, changing economic and financial conditions, and future binding risk or policy constraints – all factors that SWFs need to take into account.

Another version of the stochastic optimization approach is called the Fixed-Mix approach. This generates scenarios but not a tree. It does incorporate rebalancing at future dates but now the model has perfect information on what the future looks like after the initial uncertainty has been resolved. The way the approach then works is to select a fixed asset allocation over all possible rebalancing dates over all scenarios. This approach is often used because of the appeal of using scenarios which are easier to generate and conceptualize than trees. However, it does not consider changing the asset allocation over time, no matter how good or bad the scenarios have become, which is not realistic. Furthermore there is extensive evidence (e.g., Ziemba and Ziemba (2007)) that the performance of dynamic stochastic optimization dominates the Fixed-Mix approach. Another approach is called the Contingent Claims Analysis (described by Gray (2007)). This approach relies much more on asset price data to infer risk exposures and looks at the country balance sheet, but has less applicability to SWFs as it is not an optimization approach.

Overall, and especially since long-term investors like SWFs have to satisfy several objectives beyond just risk and reward, the dynamic stochastic optimization approach combined with goals, objectives, and multiple risk constraints is the best way to go.

10.1.3 Why our approach is especially applicable to SWFs

Many SWF situations represent large deviations from the world of a financial institution's ALM. And every SWF faces a special form of ALM given its particular objectives, multiple risk constraints, dynamic rebalancing, changing stochastics over time, extreme events, and often very diverse classes of assets and liabilities to be managed. This requires not one specific model but rather a framework to facilitate building models unique to each SWF, which is what our approach allows. Since it is very flexible and can be adapted to sovereigns which face a multitude of risks and objectives, many of which are not easily captured using the standard models, our approach will fit a variety of SWFs' needs.

We can show this with some examples. For one, the function to be optimized can be adjusted depending upon the objectives of the SWF. Some SWFs, for example, behave like stabilization funds, and have objectives somewhat similar to central bank reserves. Central banks generally manage their reserves with the objectives of safety, liquidity, returns, and stability; generally in that order of importance. By stability we mean the orderly transition of indicators over time. For example, it is generally preferred that no large jumps occur in the shortfall in the liquidity portfolio over time. While modest amounts of shortfall may be tolerable, large amounts are usually not. Our framework can handle these problems, even when there are multiple kinds of risks to control for and when extreme events need to be taken into account.

Other SWFs may be similar to, and in fact are, national pension funds that (also) invest in assets in foreign exchange. Pension funds may have as their primary objective having sufficient liquidity to make any interim payments on their liabilities while investing safely and maximizing long-term wealth. As for stability, they will want their funding ratio to be relatively stable over time so that there are no or very few jumps in contribution requirements. Yet investing in very safe assets will be costly, as the pension funds need to make high returns over the long term. Endowment funds on the other hand will want to maximize long-term returns but because they will also have risky asset classes, future multiple risk constraints will be essential.

The other feature that makes our model more consistent with SWFs' needs is the ability to include macroeconomic and microeconomic concerns and constraints on sovereign wealth management. Macroeconomic concerns can include issues arising from a country's currency management, debt management, and domestic financial sector stability. Microeconomic concerns can arise from legal or disclosure constraints, or may be due to institutional capacity constraints. The SWF portfolio manager will have to account for these macro- and microeconomic factors. Specifically, it means commodity price behavior, resource depletion, import and export levels, fiscal issues, GDP, population growth/decrease, benchmarks, asset universe, or other factors may need to be included. And, as a consequence, each fund will be considering differing liability profiles, different instruments, and different investment horizons. Our framework is designed to take all these factors into account.

Lastly, our framework is easy to modify both in terms of the model and in terms of the scenario tree generation. It is entirely open as the model can be easily understood by nonexperts and it is absolutely not a "black box". Information can be extracted from a solution that is suitable and can be tailored to any audience. The scenario tree generation is entirely independent of the model making it easy to generate different trees to apply to the same model. This is very important in testing sensitivity to tree generation and allows new kinds of stress tests where "stress" here means stressing the stochastics. This allows asking questions such as how to hedge against the probability of a "major" worldwide recession. We next present the framework, followed by demonstrating its application to Norway and a discussion of its general applicability.

10.2 The general analytical framework

The point of departure for this chapter is Claessens and Kreuser (2007). That paper describes our general ALM framework for central banks and ministries of finance and combined assets and liabilities management. Building on that paper, this section describes the equations used to build models for various SWFs. For ease of exposition and application to the Norway's SFW, NGPF, we will formulate the model as an asset-only model, i.e., without explicit liabilities, but with exogenous fund inflows. We will select subsets of these equations for specific kinds of SWFs and for the NGPF, which we will describe in Section 10.3.3. For the general details of scenario tree generation, we refer to Claessens and Kreuser (2007).

10.2.1 Notation, variables, and general definitions

We first present the notation and variables we will use in the models. We adopt the following notation to characterize the topology of the tree.

[1] $X^t \equiv \{e|\text{event } e \text{ occurs in time period } t\}$
[2] $AT^{t,e} \equiv \{(\tau,\varepsilon)|\text{For } \tau < t, \text{ event } \varepsilon \text{ preceeds event } e \text{ at time } \tau\}$

The set definition [1] indicates what events occur for each time period and [2] indicates the events that precede any event in any time period.[3] The sets that characterize the asset classes, the currencies, and time periods are:

$$
\begin{aligned}
& I \equiv \{\text{set of all asset classes, } i\} \\
[3] \quad & C \equiv \{\text{set of all currencies, } c\} \\
& T \equiv \{\text{set of all time periods, } t \text{ with } t = \bar{t} \text{ the last time period}\}
\end{aligned}
$$

As we will not use liabilities in the formulation of the NGPF in this chapter, we omit the notation and equations for them. Decision variables are then defined for each event with respect to the levels of assets, currencies, alternative investments (derivatives), and other cash flows. Decision variables (including shorting of assets) are all handled separately, allowing the specification of transaction costs, spreads, and limits to be individually imposed, thus increasing the stability and realism of the model.

We define the variable $A_{i,c}^{t,e,\tau,\varepsilon}$ as the holdings of asset class i in currency c purchased at time t[4] and event e and held at time τ and event ε. We use the convention of capital letters for those variables whose values are the results of the dynamic stochastic optimization model, and lowercase letters for all other variables (with the exception that capitals are also used for names of sets).

Model Variables	Definition
ALPHA	Alpha variable in definition of CVAR constraints. It will take on the appropriate VaR value in an optimal solution.
$A_{i,c}^{t,e,\tau,\varepsilon}$	Holdings at time τ and event ϵ of asset i in currency c acquired at time t and event e.
$CASH_c^{t,e}$	Cash in currency c at time t and event e.
PRF	Value of preference function.
$SG_1^{t,e}$, $SG_2^{t,e}$, $SG_3^{t,e}$	Variables for segmenting the piece-wise linear-quadratic form.
$SHF^{t,e}$	Shortfall variable representing the shortfall below some target.
$SWAPS^{t,e}$	Oil swaps in time t and event e.
$TW^{t,e}$	Total wealth in time t and event e.
$TRS^{t,e}$	Total transaction costs.
$V_{c,d}^{t,e}$	Transfer of currency from c to d at time t and event e.
W^{t}	Total expected wealth at time t in the numéraire currency.

Tree Variables	Definition
δ^t	Discount factor at time t. Used in the preference function.
$\gamma_c^{t,e}$	Exchange rate in terms of the numéraire at time t and event e.
$\eta_{i,c}^{\tau,t,e}$	The price adjustment for asset i in currency c acquired at time τ and marked-to-market at time t and event e.
$\pi^{t,e}$	The probability that event e will occur in time t.
$op^{t,e}$	Oil price at time t and event e.
$\mathrm{std}^{\mathrm{t,e}}$	Short-term debt at time t and event e.

Parameters/constants	Definition
$cliq^t$	Liquidity portfolio requirements in time t.
$ina_{i,c}$	The beginning portfolio in asset i and currency c.
liqb	Initial liquidity portfolio.
ma_c^t	Minimum activity policy constraint for currency c and time t.
$mat_{i,c}$	Maturity of asset i in currency c.
$nret^t$	Minimum return (realized or unrealized) on the portfolio for time t.

$[p^t,q^t]$	Interval for each time period t in which one wants to push the probability mass.
r_1^t, r_2^t	The beginning and ending slopes of the linear parts of the piecewise linear-quadratic at time t. The values are set to push more or less probability mass into the interval $[p^t,q^t]$ for each time t. Typically we use $[r_1, r_2]$ = p100,.01] as a starting interval for maximization.
rc	Return on cash.
$stock^t$	Oil stock in time interval t.
tc_c	Transaction cost for currency transfers in currency c.
tca_i	Transaction cost of purchase of asset i.
tcs_i	Transaction cost of sale of asset i.

10.2.2 Extending the framework to SWFs

One typical special characteristic of SWFs is the focus on long-term wealth preservation and maximization. Similar to an individual aiming to maximize wealth for his or her retirement, many SWFs aim to generate the highest wealth for the nation and its citizens. Whether it has specific liabilities, as might be the case for a fund needing to meet the formally defined pension obligations to (future and current) generations, or whether it has a more loosely defined obligation to its citizens, as might be the case for some of the more recently established funds, will vary by SWF. Whether formal or not, these differences will, of course, affect the ALM problem (in one case, the SWF will have to worry much more about downside risks; in the other case it can more easily maximize wealth with less concern for risk).

To proxy the objective of long-term wealth preservation, one might wish to maximize a log utility function (also called Kelly betting or Capital Growth Theory (Ziemba and Ziemba 2007)) as this will yield the highest long-run levels of expected wealth. However, this can also produce very high levels of volatility of wealth. In Claessens and Kreuser (2007), we developed a preference function that has some similarities with a utility function but addresses the risk of volatile final wealth. It also requires no special parameter estimation or a priori definition of a user's utility function. We describe that function below for a maximization problem (a minimization problem is similar). The function is like a utility function in that it has a positive first derivative and nonpositive second derivative. Therefore in maximizing the function (4), we will be maximizing TW^t although it operates considerably differently. The interval $[p, q]$ is the interval in which we would like to push as much of the probability mass of the density function as possible. The values r_1 and r_2 determine how strongly we wish to push the probability mass into that interval. The important aspect is that the parameters r_1, r_2, and $[p, q]$ can be defined explicitly and are not estimated.

Preference Function:

$$[4] \ \text{MAX } E\left[\sum_{t \in T} \delta^t r_1^t \left(q^t - p^t\right)\right] \Theta_{\frac{r_1^t}{r_2^t}} \left(\frac{W^t - p^t}{q^t - p^t}\right)$$

$$[5] \ \Theta_e(\lambda) = \begin{cases} \lambda & \text{for } \lambda \leq 0 \\ \lambda - \dfrac{\lambda^2(e-1)}{2e} & \text{for } 0 \leq \lambda \leq 1 \\ \dfrac{\lambda}{e} + \dfrac{e-1}{2e} & \text{for } \lambda \geq 1 \end{cases}$$

This function is a piece-wise linear-quadratic and can be solved computationally very efficiently. This allows it to be used with problems that have a very large scenario tree. It is well suited to SWFs that have wealth targets in years far off, such as might be the case for funds that behave like national pension funds. It is very computationally attractive since it is quadratic and linear.

A more general class of utility functions like $\Theta(x) = \frac{x^\gamma}{\gamma}, \gamma \leq 1$ can also be used (= $\ln(x)$ when $\gamma = 0$) but that requires obtaining the risk parameter γ and the problems become more difficult to solve, usually requiring a reduction in the size of the scenario tree. When the targeted rates of return are less well known, the SWF may wish to maximize discounted wealth over time. This is the case for endowment funds, for example, and the preference function then becomes:

$$[6] \ \text{MAX } \sum_{t \in T} \delta^t W^t$$

When there are objective functions defined in terms of shortfalls below a specified target, as might be the case for a national pension fund, the following objective might be used:

$$[7] \ \text{MAX } \sum_{t \in T} \delta^t \left(w^t - \sum_{e \in X^t} \pi^{t,e} \Gamma\left(SHF^{t,e}\right) \right)$$

The variable $SHF^{t,e}$ represents the shortfall and Γ is a convex function. This approach is often used as a proxy for controlling risk, defined as the amount of the shortfall.[5] There are several problems with this approach in general: how to define the function Γ and how to combine several shortfalls in the same objective. Furthermore, this gives a nonlinear problem unless one uses a piecewise linear approximation. We will make only use of this function for Γ linear and instead control for risk of shortfalls using conditional value-at-risk constraints.

Another characteristic of a SWF can be its specific source of assets and/or (finite) income, and its associated objectives. Many SWFs are set up by oil exporting and other natural resource rich countries. Faced with a finite amount to exploit and export, the SWFs set up by some countries (such as Kuwait and Norway) aim to accumulate wealth so as to provide sufficient income for future generations. This differs from those countries such as Brazil and China whose SWFs have accumulated foreign assets due to large capital inflows or surpluses on their current account due to nonresource exports. These countries may see their SWFs more as a tool to temporarily invest their surplus funds earning more attractive rates than as traditional foreign exchange reserves. For these SFWs, the objective of discounted expected wealth may be more relevant.

These characteristics and considerations mean adaptations to the model, which is usually complicated. Fortunately, our framework is so general that in essence we simply need to adjust the objective function, constrain the equations for the balance sheet variables, or add legal and policy constraints, along with any constraints for handling various risks.

10.2.3 Structural equations for SWFs

These are the main sets of equations that define the model and include balance sheet and cash flow equations and policy and legal constraints. Each SWF will have its own policy and legal constraints but the main balance sheet and cash flow equations are similar with the exception that, depending on the fund, some variables may not appear. The main equation defines the cash flows in each time period, for each event, and in each currency. It balances all cash flows by currency. Then given these cash flow equations, we can immediately construct the balance sheets at any time t and event e or the expected balance sheet at time t.

Cash Flows: By currency, time, and event

$$\underset{[\text{new assets}]}{\sum_{i\in I} A_{i,c}^{t,e,t,e}} \quad + \quad \underset{\begin{bmatrix}\text{transaction costs}\\ \text{on new assets}\end{bmatrix}}{\sum_{i\in I} tca_i A_{i,c}^{t,e,t,e}} \quad + \quad \underset{\begin{bmatrix}\text{transfer of}\\ \text{currency } c \text{ to } d\end{bmatrix}}{V_{c,d}^{t,e}} \quad + \quad \underset{\begin{bmatrix}\text{cash in}\\ \text{currency } c\end{bmatrix}}{CASH_c^{t,e}}$$

$$= \underset{[\text{initial portfolio}]}{\sum_{i\in I} ina_{i,c} \langle \text{if } t=0\rangle} \quad + \quad \underset{[\text{transfers of currency } d \text{ to } c]}{\sum_{d\in C, d\neq C} \frac{tc_c \gamma_c^{t,e} V_{d,c}^{t,e}}{\gamma_d^{t,e}}}$$

$$+\underset{[\text{asset sales}]}{\sum_{i\in I} \sum_{\substack{(\tau,\varepsilon)\in AT^{t,e}\\ \tau\geq t-mat_i}} \sum_{(t-1,f)\in AT^{t-1,f}} (1+tcs_i)\eta_{i,c}^{\tau,t,e}(A_{i,c}^{\tau,\varepsilon,t-1,f} - A_{i,c}^{\tau,\varepsilon,t,e})}$$

$$+ \sum_{(t-1,\varepsilon)\in AT^{t,e}} (1+rc)CASH_c^{t-1,\varepsilon} + op^{t,e} stock^t \langle \text{if } c = \text{"USD"} \rangle$$

[return on cash] [funds flows to NGPG]

$$+ \sum_{(t-1,\varepsilon)\in AT^{t,e}} \eta^{t-1,\varepsilon}_{\text{"swaps","USD"}} \; SWAPS_c^{t-1,\varepsilon} \langle \text{if } c = \text{"USD"} \rangle$$

[oil swaps flows]

[8] $\forall c \in C, t \in T, e \in X^t$

The next equation ensures that the sales of assets are properly defined in the model, i.e. are monotonic.

Monotone Asset Sales:

[9] $$\sum_{(t-1,f)\in AT^{t,e}} (A_{i,c}^{\tau,\varepsilon,t-1,f} - A_{i,c}^{\tau,\varepsilon,t,e}) \geq 0$$

[monotonicity constraint so that sales are reflected in changes in holdings]

$$\forall\, i,c,t,e,\tau,\varepsilon \ni (\tau,\varepsilon) \in AT^{t,e} \text{ and } (t-\tau) < mat_i$$

Total Wealth: In numéraire currency

$$TW^{t,e} = \sum_{i\in I, c\in C} \frac{A_{i,c}^{t,e,t,e}}{\gamma_c^{t,e}} + \sum_{i\in I, c\in C} \sum_{(\tau,\varepsilon)\in AT^{t,e}} \frac{\eta_{i,c}^{\tau,t,e} A_{i,c}^{\tau,\varepsilon,t,e}}{\gamma_c^{t,e}}$$

[*total assets*] [*new assets*] [*assets marked to market*]

[10] $$+ \sum_{c\in C} \frac{CASH_c^{t,e}}{\gamma_c^{t,e}}$$

[*cash*] $\forall\, t,e \ni e \in X^t$

The next constraint begins the definition of the preference function [4]. It allocates value to the three segmentations of the preference function according to [12] so that they are assured their proper values due to the concavity of the function under maximization defined at the horizon $t = \bar{t}$.

Segmentation: Definition 1 (the following example is for the ratio of reserves to short-term debt)

[11] $$\frac{TW^{t,e}}{std^{t,e}} - p^t = (q^t - p^t)(SG_1^{t,e} + SG_2^{t,e} + SG_3^{t,e}) \;\; \forall\, t = \bar{t}\,, e \in X^{\bar{t}}$$

The next set of constraints ensures that the segmentations take their proper values.

Segmentation: Definition 2

$$[12]\ SG_1^{t,e} \le 0, 0 \le SG_2^{t,e} \le 1, 0 \le SG_3^{t,e},\ \forall\, t = \bar{t}, e \in X^{\bar{t}}$$

Preference Function: Defined for $t = \bar{t}$ and therefore set $\delta^{\bar{t}} = 1$

$$[13]\ PRF = \sum_{t=\bar{t},\, e\in X^{\bar{t}}} \pi^{t,e}\delta^t r_1^t\,(q^t - p^t)\left(SG_1^{t,e} + SG_2^{t,e} - (SG_2^{t,e})^2\left(\frac{r_1^t}{r_2^t} - 1\right)\frac{r_2^t}{2r_1^t} + SG_3^{t,e}\frac{r_2^t}{r_1^t}\right)$$

The following defines the total expected value of the portfolio as measured in the numéraire.

Total Expected Wealth Definition:

$$[14]\ W^t = \sum_{e\in X^t} \pi^{t,e} TW^{t,e} \quad \forall\, t \in T$$

There are three separate definitions of shortfall that we use.

Shortfall Target: As might be used in targeting a funding ratio[6] for a national pension fund

$$[15]\ SHF^{t,e} \ge ratio \times target^t - TW^{t,e},\ SHF^{t,e} \ge 0,\ \ \forall t, e \ni e \in X^t$$

Shortfall in Wealth: Shortfall below expected wealth when targets are not known

$$[16]\ SHF^{t,e} \ge ratio \times W^t - TW^{t,e}, SHF^{t,e} \ge 0,\ \ \forall t, e \ni e \in X^t$$

Shortfall in Liquidity: Shortfall in meeting liquidity targets

$$[17]\ SHF^{t,e} \ge \sum_c \frac{liqreq_c - LQ_c^{t,e}}{\gamma_c^{t,e}}, SHF^{t,e} \ge 0, \quad \forall t, e \ni e \in X^t$$

The parameter *ratio* in equations [15] and [16] is used to define the percentage of the targeted value that is desired. Since shortfall appears in these three equations as an inequality, it must be part of the objective function or part of a binding constraint. We will use specific constraints to control the risk in shortfall and will incorporate it in the binding constraint there (see next section).

Asset Sales: By individual asset in time *t* and event *e*

$$[18]\quad SL_{i,c}^{t,e} = \sum_{\substack{(\tau,\varepsilon)\in AT^{t,e} \\ \tau\geq t-mat_i}} \sum_{(t-1,f)\in AT^{t-1,f}} \eta_{i,c}^{\tau,t,e}\left(A_{i,c}^{\tau,\varepsilon,t-1,f} - A_{i,c}^{\tau,\varepsilon,t,e}\right)$$

10.2.4 Policy constraints for SWFs

The policy constraints that might be imposed can be many and include limits on asset classes, portfolio rollover constraints, transaction cost limits, cash flow requirements, currency transfer constraints, market access constraints, liquidity constraints, etc. The following may be a desirable set of policy constraints:

Minimum Activity by Currency:

$$\underbrace{ma_c^t TW^{t,e}\gamma_c^{t,e}}_{\text{[minimum activity as \% of total]}} \leq \underbrace{CASH_c^{t,e}}_{\text{[cash]}}$$

$$[19]\quad + \underbrace{\sum_{i\in I} A_{i,c}^{t,e,t,e}}_{\text{[new assets]}} + \underbrace{\sum_{i\in I}\sum_{(\tau,\varepsilon)\in AT^{t,e}} \eta_{i,c}^{\tau,t,e} A_{i,c}^{\tau,\varepsilon,t,e}}_{\text{[assets marked to market]}}$$

$$\forall\, c,t,e \ni e\in X^t$$

Minimum Allowable Return:

$$[20]\quad nret^t \sum_{(t-1,\varepsilon)\in AT^{t,e}} TW^{t-1,\varepsilon} \leq TW^{t,e} - \sum_{(t-1,\varepsilon)\in AT^{t,e}} TW^{t-1,\varepsilon} \qquad \forall\, t,e \ni e\in X^t$$

Maximum Portfolio Rollover:

$$[21]\quad \sum_{(i,c)} \frac{SL_{i,c}^{t,e}}{\gamma_c^{t,e}} \leq \text{percent rollover}^t TW^{t,e}$$

Market Activity Limits:

$$[22]\quad \underbrace{A_{i,c}^{t,e,t,e}}_{\text{[new assets]}} + \underbrace{\sum_{(\tau,\varepsilon)\in AT^{t,e}} \eta_{i,c}^{\tau,t,e} A_{i,c}^{\tau,\varepsilon,t,e}}_{\text{[assets marked to market]}} \leq upperlimit_{i,c} TW^{t,e}$$

10.2.5 Risks and risk control for SWFs

An important aspect of SWF management is the control of risk or, put differently, restrictions on the desirable distribution of final wealth, rate of return, or other variables one might wish to restrict, such as shortfall. The measure we use for controlling risks or shaping distributions (or densities) is Conditional Value-at-Risk (CVaR). CVaR is defined as the expected shortfall of a target at a specified probability or confidence level of α%. It is equivalent to the concept of the average loss (gain) in the worst (best) α% cases. CVaR is related to value-at-risk (VaR) and for loss distributions, CVaR is always greater than or equal to VaR. CVaR is a more robust measure than VaR, since it provides the average loss for those α% of cases rather than the minimum loss. It therefore takes more fully into account when losses can be extreme (Rockafellar and Uryasev (2002) discuss CVaR in detail and Acerbi and Tasche (2002) discuss the relationship between CVaR, expected shortfall, worse conditional expectation, tail conditional expectation, and VaR).

CVaR has some very useful properties for modeling purposes. Specifically, CVaR constraints can be modeled as linear constraints whereas VaR constraints are nonconvex and nonsmooth and thus more complex to model and solve besides the other problems that VaR has. This makes CVaR constraints the method of choice for shaping the distributions or densities for dynamic stochastic optimization models, especially when the models are very large.

CVaR has another important property useful for SWFs: it is a coherent risk measure (McNeil, Frey, and Embrechts 2005). The property of coherence important here is its subadditivity that makes decentralization of risk management systems possible. In particular, the CVaR risk of the overall loss is less than the sum of the risks of the CVaR losses of the decentralized portfolios. This is very important for SWFs that most often have a substantial part of their portfolio managed externally with separately defined objectives and limits. There are some idealized cases where VaR is coherent as well, but most often VaR (and semi-variance) are not coherent risk measures.

CVaR Constraints can be defined for one time period, one activity, one confidence level, and one level value:

$$Z^e \geq \Lambda(X^e) - ALPHA,\ Z^e \geq 0,\ \forall e \in X^t, \text{ and for some } t$$

[23] and

$$\sum_{e \in X^t} \pi^{t,e} Z^e \leq \rho\left(clevel_\rho - ALPHA\right)$$

where Λ is a convex loss function, Z^e and $ALPHA$ are variables, $1-\rho$ is the confidence level, and $clevel_\rho$ is the value based upon that confidence level. $ALPHA$ will take the value of VaR corresponding to ρ in an optimal solution. Several CVaR constraints can also be placed on the same variable X^e at different confidence levels thereby shaping the distribution. Several CVaR constraints can be placed at different times and on different variables.[7]

CVaR allows us to translate intuitive descriptions of constraints on distributions into mathematical descriptions for use in our modeling framework. One example of a CVaR constraint can be that in the 1% worst cases, average portfolio losses should not exceed 10% of the portfolio value. Another example could be that in the 5% worst cases the average shortfall in liquidity should not exceed 20%. We may constrain a distribution of returns to certain loss levels at the 90% confidence level, the 98% confidence level, and the 99.9% confidence level, for example.

A common constraint used in SWFs is on the safety of returns, i.e., protection against extreme losses.

Wealth at Risk: shortfall is defined here as in equation [16].

$$[24]\quad \Lambda(X^e) = SHF^{t,e}_{\text{Shortfall in Wealth}},\ \rho = 1 - \text{confidence level},$$
$$clevel_\rho = \text{required expected short fall}$$

Target at Risk: Target and shortfall are defined as in equation [15] and in the case of a pension fund it is funding ratio at risk.

$$[25]\quad \Lambda(X^e) = SHF^{t,e}_{\text{Shortfall in Target}},\ \rho = 1 - \text{confidence level},$$
$$clevel_\rho = \text{required expected short fall}$$

Liquidity at Risk: Shortfall is defined as in equation.

$$[26]\quad \Lambda(X^e) = SHF^{t,e}_{\text{Liquidity}},\ \rho = 1 - \text{confidence level},$$
$$clevel_\rho = \text{required expected short fall}$$

Level of Rebalancing at Risk: This controls the distribution of sales.

$$[27]\quad \Lambda(X^e) = \sum_{(i,c)} \frac{SL^{t,e}_{i,c}}{\gamma^{t,e}_c},\ \rho = 1 - \text{confidence level},$$
$$clevel_\rho = \text{required expected short fall}$$

Unrealized Losses at Risk:

$$[28]\quad \Lambda(X^e) = \sum_{(i,c)} (1 - \eta^{t-1,t,e}_{i,c}) \frac{A^{t-1,\varepsilon,t,e}_{i,c}}{\gamma^{t,e}_c}\Bigg|_{\eta<1}$$

$\rho = 1 - \text{confidence level}$, $clevel_\rho = \text{required expected shortfall}$

10.3 Application to government pension fund – Global of Norges Bank

We next apply our model to Norway's SWF, NGPF. We will describe its purpose, the current asset mix, and the outcome of our optimization model. The model results reported here are preliminary as a more detailed study exceeds the scope and limited length of this chapter. A more detailed report appears in the online version.

10.3.1 Background

10.3.1.1 Institutional setup, management principles, and transparency

The Government Pension Fund was formally established by the Norwegian Parliament by the Act of 20 December 2005, but had been in existence in other forms for quite some time. The Government Pension Fund has two parts: the Government Pension Fund – Global (previously the Government Petroleum Fund, established in 1990) and the Government Pension Fund – Norway (previously the National Insurance Fund, established in 1967), with the second very small. The Ministry of Finance has delegated the operational management of the Government Pension Fund – Global (NGPF or the *Fund*) to the Norwegian central bank (Norges Bank), with the mandate stipulated in a regulation issued by the Ministry and a management agreement further defining the relationship. The Fund itself is managed by Norges Bank Investment Management (NBIM), a separate part of Norges Bank.[8]

The Fund's inflow consists of all state petroleum revenues, the net results of financial transactions related to petroleum activities, as well as the return on the Fund's investments.[9] The outflow from the Fund is the sum needed to cover the nonoil budget deficit, which the government aims to keep at less than 4% of the size of the Fund. The Fund's current size as of 1 January 2008 was NOK 2019 billion (some USD 375 billion at the current exchange rate of 5.4 NOK/USD) and is expected to grow to NOK 4350 billion by 2015. The Government Pension Fund is 14 billion NOK.

The Fund has no formally defined liability side and it is not specifically earmarked for pension expenditures, but it is the prime source for covering the government deficit. Its economic function can therefore best be compared to that of an endowment fund, similar to those that aim to be engaged in, say, philanthropy solely from the returns on its investments (Kjaer 2007). The Fund's strategy requires that: "it shall be securely managed based on the objective of high return subject to moderate risk in order to contribute to safeguarding the basis of future welfare, including national pensions" (from the Fund's own Articles).

10.3.1.2 Asset and liability classes

The Fund can invest solely abroad and only in financial assets. Its management strategy is laid down using a benchmark portfolio consisting of equities and fixed income instruments. In 2006 changes were proposed to the benchmark portfolio, specifically to increase the equity allocation.[10] Current asset allocations are set at 60% equity and 40% fixed income. The equity portion of the benchmark consists of equities listed on stock exchanges in Europe (50%), the Americas and Africa (35%), and Asia and Oceania (15%). The regional distribution (in terms of currency) of the fixed income benchmark is 60% Europe, 35% Americas, and 5% Asia and Oceania. Rates of return on asset classes are to be compared with those used to compute the benchmark for the Fund. These are Lehman FTSE All World indices for equities and Global indices for fixed income instruments for each of the markets/currencies USD, GBP, Euro, and Yen. The Norwegian Fund actual allocations are closely aligned with its declared benchmark allocations (NBIM 2008). As shown in Table 10.1, we make the initial asset allocation in our model to correspond to the distribution of assets by region, fixed income, and estimated duration as given in NBIM (2008).

Table 10.1 Initial asset class composition based on NBIM benchmark*

Asset classes	Percent composition	Value in NOK (billions)	Value in local currency (billions)
Equity – FTSE AW Europe (Euro) Equity	14.00	272.41	33.94
Equity – FTSE AW Americas (USD) Equity	14.00	272.41	47.96
Equity – FTSE AW Asia Pacific (Yen) Equity	6.00	116.75	2,215.77
Lehman Euro-Agg. 1–3 Year Bonds	15.75	306.46	38.18
Lehman Euro-Agg. 10+ Year Bonds	5.25	102.15	12.73
Lehman Global: US Treasury 1–3 Year Bonds	15.75	306.46	53.96
Lehman US-Agg. A+ 5+ Year Bonds	5.25	102.15	17.99
Lehman Global: Japan 1–3 Year Bonds	6.75	131.34	2,492.75
Lehman Global: Japan Long Bonds	2.25	43.78	830.92
Lehman Global: UK 1–3 Year Bonds	11.25	218.90	21.85
Lehman Global: UK Long Bonds	3.75	72.97	7.28
Lehman Global: Inflation Linked Bonds	0.00	0	0

*Total portfolio value = NOK 1,945.80 billion. This amount is used for the model as the beginning date (5 September 2008) value.

10.3.1.3 Management, follow-up, and control

Norges Bank manages assets largely internally (more than 75% of equity). NBIM hired its first external managers in January 1998, when the Government Pension Fund began investing in equity markets through index managers. The Fund reports results on a quarterly basis its rates of return in absolute terms and relative to its benchmarks. The auditing of the Fund has been assigned to the Office of the Auditor General, which bases its audit on the work performed by the Central Bank Audit. The Fund is very transparent and information up to the level of investment in specific companies is available.

10.3.2 Income, foreign exchange risks and scenario generation

The Fund receives regular transfers from the Ministry of Finance, which in 2007 totaled some NOK 314 billion or on average more than USD 300 million per trading day. As noted, most of this income is from oil related revenues and thus volatile, as the last year has again made clear. Recent events have also shown that exchange rates can affect oil prices: as the dollar depreciated (appreciated), oil (and other commodity) prices denominated in dollar terms tended to increase (decrease). Theory and empirics also strongly suggest that there is an inverse relationship between (real) interest rates and oil prices. And as oil is increasingly traded as an asset, we can expect oil prices to respond even more to the opportunity cost of capital. Given the importance of these relationships for the income stream of the Fund, we are careful about how oil prices are affected by foreign exchange and interest rates, and estimate these relationships, using Norway specific oil prices, with various econometrically robust techniques.

The foreign currency/Norwegian Kroner risk is not considered in the stated strategic ALM objectives of the Fund and, consistently, the Fund actually largely reports its performance and asset values in USD. This can be interpreted to mean that the Fund (implicitly) takes the view that its ALM should lead the Norwegian Kroner to be relatively stable or even increase in value, so as to maximize the purchasing power of the Norwegian population. Put differently, one of the main indirect objectives of the Fund will be to reduce the Norwegian Kroner exchange rate risk so as to assure a stable income and consumption pattern. We therefore have to consider the consumption basket of the Norwegian population. Foreign exchange will be available to buy imports, but these imports can be in different currencies and coming from different markets. To mimic this consumption basket we define a currency unit, called the *NKU*, using the import shares of the four major currency groups, USD, GBP, Euro, and Yen. Specifically, we classify imports from US, Latin America, and China as "USD" imports; imports from the UK as "GBP" imports; imports from all of Europe outside the UK as "Euro" imports; and all imports from other countries as "Yen" imports. Using the trade amounts for the year 2006 as weights we then create the NKU, in which we then evaluate the risk and returns on the portfolio, i.e. we rebase all securities in the NKU today and at all future dates and scenario events. We take the NKU to be 69% Euro, 12% USD, 7% Yen, and 12% GBP.

One way we generate scenarios is to use multi-factor stochastic partial differential equations:

$$[29] \quad \frac{ds_i(t)}{s_i(t)} = \mu_i(s,t)dt + \sum_j b_{ij}(s,t)\,\sigma_j(s,t)d\omega_j(t)$$

This representation underlies commonly used multi-factor models, including those with mean-reversion, such as Hull-White and Heath, Jarrow, and Morton. The parameters (μ, b, σ) of these equations can be determined from historical data.[11]

We divide the interval of time from today, $t = t_0$ to the terminal period, $t = t_T$ into intervals $[t_0, t_1]$, $[t_1, t_2]$, ... , $[t_{T-1}, t_T]$ and use an estimate of μ, b, σ for each interval separately. This allows, for example, the correlations to depend on the time and the level of the variables, allowing the generation of a very rich possibility of outcomes. The solution[12] of these equations for each interval, in which μ, b, σ are constant is:

$$s_i(t) = s_i^0 \exp\left[\left(\mu_i - \frac{1}{2}\sum_{j=1}^{n} b_{ij}^2\,\sigma_j^2\right)t + \sum_{j=1}^{n} b_{ij}\,\sigma_j\,\omega_j(t)\right]$$

$$E\{s(t)\} = (s_1^0 e^{\mu_1 t}, s_2^0 e^{\mu_2 t}, .., s_n^0 e^{\mu_n t})$$

$$\text{cov}(s_t(t), s_k(t)) = E\{s_l(t)\}E\{s_k(t)\}\left[\exp\left(t\sum_{j=1}^{n} b_{lj}b_{kj}\sigma_j^2\right) - 1\right]$$

$$\text{var}(s_l(t)) = (E\{s_l(t)\})^2\left(e^{t\sum_{j=1}^{n} b_{lj}^2\sigma_j^2} - 1\right)$$

These equations provide the first and second moments for solving the moment matching problem. The scenario trees are generated by using the above expressions and obtaining moments such that the moment matching problem is minimized and that produces the greatest possible scenario spread. Scenario trees are based on the assumptions of the distributions chosen. The distributions are not normal because they are recalibrated at each rebalancing date and because of the way scenario trees are generated. The scenarios are generated so as to avoid arbitrage possibilities (Cornuejol and Tütüncü (2007); it turns out that arbitrage is not a frequent problem).

The stochastic processes can be visually checked by looking at the scenarios generated. In Figure 10.1 we see a small number of scenarios sampled.

This diagram shows also the history of the process which was used to estimate the processes. In this case, this process is assumed to be trend reverting. The stochastic process parameters are all estimated simultaneously, including the instantaneous correlations. The smooth upward sloping line in the graph below (Figure 10.1) shows how the expected value process moves over time, from Jan 2007 to Jan 2026.

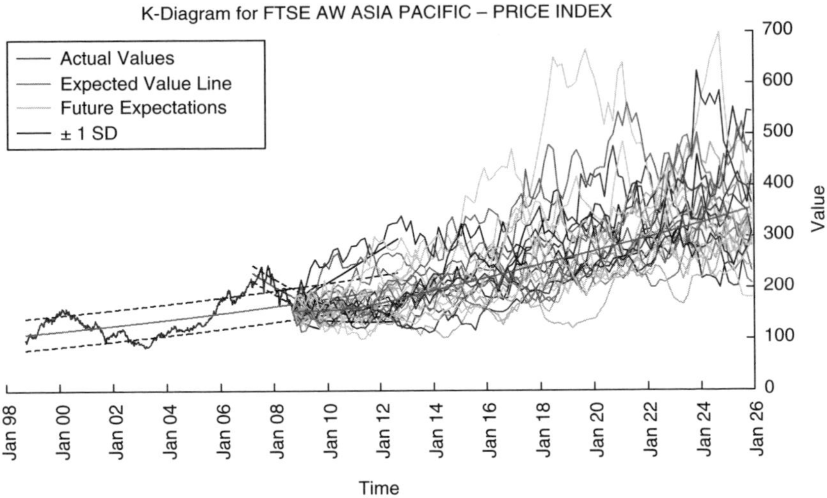

Figure 10.1 Estimated stochastic process in the short- and long-term

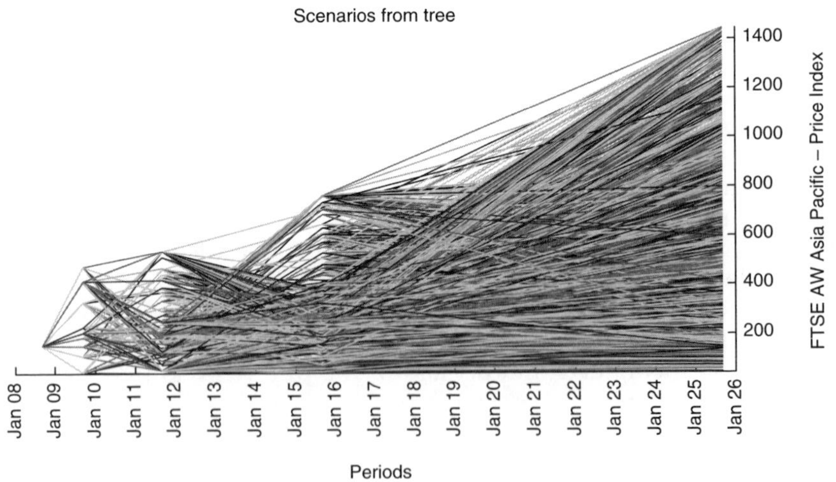

Figure 10.2 Tree created from stochastic processes

These processes are then converted into scenario trees as in Figure 10.2. The scenarios in the scenario tree are not of equal probability and this is why the scenario tree can be generated including extremes, even though there is not a large number of scenarios.

In Table 10.2 we provide some statistics for two processes.

We also estimate the oil price behavior and its correlations with the other asset classes. We use, however, a deterministic oil volume. We did not have enough information to estimate the behavior of the government deficit so we did not include that. However, both of these factors could be made stochastic. We show the graph of the distribution of the oil price over time in Figure 10.3.

10.3.3 Objective functions and policy constraints

The Fund's purpose can be stated as: maximize the expected end of period wealth in the currency basket *NKU*, given the uncertain and limited income stream of oil-related revenues, and observing risk constraints and policy constraints. This objective aims to preserve the income level of future generations when the oil revenues run out. After that the Fund is assume to have a payout ratio that will keep its overall real wealth constant over time. This ratio itself will have to vary over time as rates of return on the assets vary, but that problem is not analyzed here.[13]

Table 10.2 Stochastic process statistics

Stochastic process	05-Sep 2008	05-Sep 2009	05-Sep 2011	05-Sep 2015	05-Sep 2025
Equity – FTSE AW Asia Pacific (Yen) price index					
Mean value	155.50	155.38	166.51	212.49	342.26
Volatility %		26.97	29.73	40.27	67.05
3rd Moment		.50	.03	.64	.95
4th Moment		5.47	7.96	4.13	3.52
Annualized USD return		1.87	3.68	4.51	4.40
Annualized Basket return		–2.85	6.110	7.14	4.68
5% VaR		103.73	52.59	93.48	105.57
95% VaR		202.65	210.47	336.41	742.41
Sharpe ratio		–.003	.23	.53	.57
Lehman Global: Japan long total return index					
Mean value	124.44	125.52	132.34	149.42	195.95
Volatility %		4.70	9.69	13.16	20.36
3rd Moment		27.06	10.68	4.22	1.72
4th Moment		951.88	233.45	62.16	18.07
Annualized USD return		4.98	3.04	1.88	2.59
Annualized basket return		.80	5.04	4.35	2.88
5% VaR		122.82	125.72	122.98	146.72
95% VaR		129.53	139.37	177.10	248.30
Sharpe ratio		.18	.53	.87	1.17

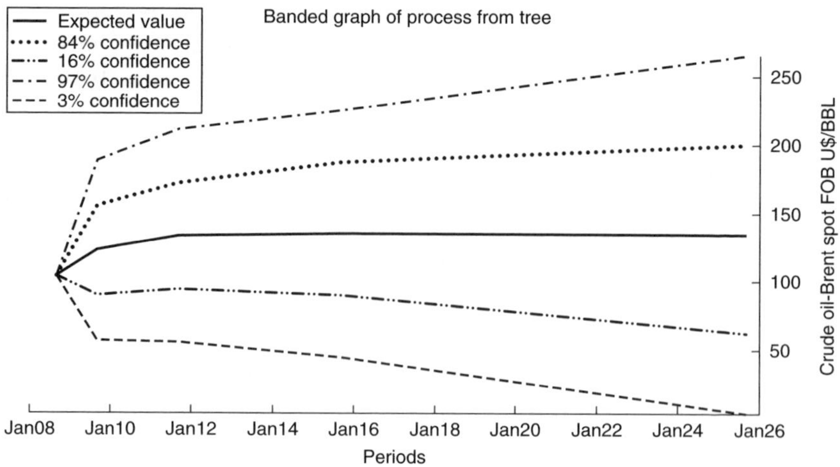

Figure 10.3 Oil price stochastics

The complete set of constraints includes:

- Maximize expected wealth (equation [6]) measured in NKU.
- Cash flows equation (equation [8]) with swaps and funds flows based upon the oil price.
- Monotone asset sales (equation [9]) to define sales properly.
- Total assets definition (equation [10]).
- Expected wealth definition (equation [14]) defines wealth in USD.
- Shortfall in wealth definition (equation [16]) to control downside risk in wealth.
- Minimum activity by currency (equation [19]) to maintain a minimum amount in each currency. These values are 30% of wealth measured in NKU for Euro, 5% for USD, 3% for Yen, and 5% for GBP for each rebalancing period and scenario.
- Maximum portfolio rollover (equation [21]) to prevent the entire portfolio from being rolled over. No more than 25% of the portfolio can be rolled over initially. After that as much as 100% of the portfolio can be rolled over at any one rebalancing date.
- Wealth at risk (equation [24]) measured in NKU; this defines the CVaR constraints such that in every period the expected tail loss at the 95% confidence level should not exceed 20% of the expected portfolio value in NKU.

10.3.4 Risks and risk control constraints

We put CVaR constraints on the downside wealth at each rebalancing point. We use separate constraints at the final date, when the oil runs out, and at the interim dates. At the final date a constraint is necessary since the Fund can not afford to have its assets fall below a certain level such that it can no longer provide a minimum "pension" to the current and future generations. The interim constraints will be necessary because the political economy may create pressures at any time to adjust the rules if the Fund were to be seen not to be able to fulfill its liabilities in the future, even when it may be expected to do so with sufficient likelihood.

We use the same asset classes the Norway fund has used as its equity and bond benchmarks, i.e. the same risk profiles. We add, however, some assets to allow for more strategic ALM. Importantly, we add a "negative oil" asset. For this we use the oil swap price to model the oil derivative price behavior. We also include some other assets. This broadening of investment classes allows a better hedging of the various risks Norway faces and is consistent with the Fund already allowing a broader class of assets (in 2007 there was an increase in equity allocation to 60% and inclusion of the small-cap sector in the benchmark portfolio, and recently investment in real estate was allowed). We estimate the correlations among the rates of return for the various asset classes and the correlations with oil prices, exchange and interest rates in a consistent fashion.

It is critical to have very good risk control when managing an endowment aggressively, such as done by the Yale and Harvard university endowment funds. This also applies to the Norway Fund, which has a large equity component and has had some years recently in which its equity net return was quite low (albeit in line with the overall benchmark rates of return). As noted, variance, semi-variance, and VaR approaches are inadequate to capture the type of extreme events that such funds are exposed to, as also shown recently by the failure of risk management approaches in many funds and banks. Using a downside penalty in the form of a convex nonlinear or piecewise linear function will work. We will use CVaR constraints at multiple points in time since they are very easy to understand and require no special estimation of parameters. It is also the technology used in the reinsurance industry to manage the tails of catastrophic loss distributions (Kreuser and Lane 2006).

10.3.5 Results[14]

We will consider and analyze four possible portfolios: the current benchmark asset allocation as given by NBIM (2008) (called "Fixed Benchmark as per NBIM"), the optimal asset allocation only considering the assets in the benchmark (called "Allowing Rebalancing"), the optimal allocation when oil funds flows are added (called "With Only Oil Funds"), and the optimal allocation when a more aggressive policy is allowed (along the lines of NBIM's planned inclusion of real estate and private equity (Kjaer 2007)) , but further adding the oil swap and funds inflows from oil exports (called "With Oil Funds, Swaps, and Assets"). The current benchmark asset allocation as given in NBIM (2008) is replicated in Table 10.1. The starting portfolio in all cases is that benchmark. We first discuss in detail the runs "Allowing Rebalancing" and "With Oil Funds, Swaps, and Assets". We then compare these two runs with two other ones in Section 10.4.1, Norway Lessons.

The first run gives the optimal allocation assuming only the benchmark asset classes, no oil swap, no alternative asset classes, and no funds flows into the fund. In the following runs, we replicate the kinds of tables that appear in NBIM (2008) in terms of their content and currency.
We note from the (scaled) third and fourth moments in Table 10.3 that the distribution is right-skewed so that the upside is much greater than the downside. This is due to the CVaR constraints, the details on which we give in the next table.

Notice that, as shown in Table 10.4, the expected loss ratio will always be less than 20% and over time more scenarios occur in which that constraint is binding.

In Table 10.5 we give the asset class composition and note that the model initially sells almost all equity classes and puts this into cash and inflation

Table 10.3 Solution statistics for wealth (billions of NOK) for the "Allow Rebalancing" case

Item	05-Sep 2008	05-Sep 2009	05-Sep 2011	05-Sep 2015	05-Sep 2025
Expected wealth	1,933.97	1,912.84	2,253.92	3,163.82	5,582.79
Volatility %		7.38	16.41	25.12	42.05
3rd Moment divided by STD cubed		31.73	34.77	25.40	11.65
4th Moment divided by 3*variance squared		987.70	740.13	536.29	176.65
Annualized Krone return		−1.09	8.55	8.84	5.84
Annualized USD return		4.19	5.66	5.37	5.19
Annualized NKU return		−0.11	7.74	7.99	5.58

Table 10.4 CVaR risk analysis (billions of USD) for "Allow Rebalancing" case for confidence level = 95% and expected tail loss = 20%

Item	05-Sep 2008	05-Sep 2009	05-Sep 2011	05-Sep 2015	05-Sep 2025
Expected value of wealth (USD billions)	344.10	358.56	400.28	493.58	818.65
CVaR value or expected tail loss limit		355.00	320.22	394.86	654.92
Corresponding VaR value		357.28	389.27	421.51	681.86
Expected loss ratio to CVaR		0.36	2.75	14.60	16.71
Worst level of wealth		352.26	201.03	375.72	483.67
Worst loss as a % of expected wealth		1.76	49.78	23.88	40.92

linked bonds. Most goes into cash in Euros giving the portfolio a 20% weight in cash. More equity would have been sold had it not been for the constraint that no more than 25% of the portfolio can be rolled over. The other point to notice is that the model increases the allocation in long bonds over the entire horizon and reduces the equity allocation.

In Table 10.6 we summarize the portfolio composition and compare it to the NBIM benchmark. Most notably the equity proportion is much smaller than in the NBIM benchmark where 60% is used. However, in the next run when we include real estate and private equity and classify them as equity we will see the ratio approaching 60% as in the NBIM benchmark. Table 10.7 shows the expected currency composition in the case where rebalancings are allowed.

Table 10.5 Expected asset class composition in solution (in %) for "Allow Rebalancing" case

Asset class	Initial prior to rebalance	05-Sep 2008	05-Sep 2009	05-Sep 2011	05-Sep 2015	05-Sep 2025
Equity – FTSE AW Europe (Euro) Equity	14.00	3.86	10.68	12.84	7.97	7.15
Equity – FTSE AW Americas (USD) Equity	14.00	0.00	1.98	1.19	2.46	2.90
Equity – FTSE AW Asia Pacific (Yen) Equity	6.00	6.05	10.52	7.80	9.12	8.66
Lehman Euro-Agg. 1–3 year bonds	15.75	15.83	1.48	0.62	0.41	0.30
Lehman Euro-Agg. 10+ year bonds	5.25	4.40	13.51	11.52	8.24	6.56
Lehman Global: US Treasury 1–3 Year Bonds	15.75	15.68	13.56	5.67	3.53	3.75
Lehman US-Agg. A+ 5+ year bonds	5.25	5.23	17.46	20.82	19.26	18.97
Lehman Global: Japan 1–3 year bonds	6.75	6.80	.00	.01	.00	.00
Lehman Global: Japan long bonds	2.25	2.27	8.09	3.22	1.21	1.07
Lehman Global: UK 1–3 year bonds	11.25	11.22	6.02	15.10	17.37	15.44
Lehman Global: UK long bonds	3.75	3.74	10.49	15.12	11.34	10.91
Lehman Global: Inflation linked bonds	0.00	5.00	.52	.51	3.04	2.80
Euro	0.00	19.94	4.41	5.06	15.18	17.54
GBP	0.00	0.00	.01	.05	.00	1.02
USD	0.00	0.00	.05	.08	.01	1.54
Yen	0.00	0.00	1.24	.40	.88	1.41

Most notably the model moves out of Euro and into USD long bonds and UK long and short bonds. The long USD bonds have the best long-term annualized return of around 6.2% and also benefit from the long-term appreciation of the USD against the Euro to its mean-reversion level around 1.12. The long-term appreciation of GBP is greater but the UK long bond has a Sharpe ratio of about half of the long USD bonds. The model has a tendency to go for a longer bond duration than the benchmark does.

We now expand the problem and add in real estate asset classes for Euro, USD, and Yen zones plus private equity measured in USD. We include oil swaps and funds flows based upon the oil price. The solution summary is given in Table 10.9. The expected value we get for terminal wealth in 2015 is NOK 6,661 billion instead of the NOK 4,350 billion expected by NBIM. But this difference can be attributed to several factors: the exact asset class set that NBIM uses, the assumptions they place on the stochastic processes, the oil funds flows they assume, and other policy constraints, especially the risk constraints, as we only use downside risk constraints and the type of model that they use. We note that oil swaps are only sold in 2009 with the flows from them accruing in 2011. The amount in swaps increases over time as the oil stock goes down and the price is more volatile.

Table 10.6 Summary of expected portfolio composition for "Allow Rebalancing" case

Item	05-Sep 2008	05-Sep 2009	05-Sep 2011	05-Sep 2015	05-Sep 2025
Portfolio composition (Billions USD)					
Overall	344.13	358.56	400.28	493.58	818.65
Equities	34.08	82.10	86.33	98.90	152.96
Fixed income	241.44	257.51	291.73	319.98	487.34
Cash	68.61	18.95	22.22	74.69	178.35
Portfolio composition (%)					
Overall	100.00	100.00	100.00	100.00	100.00
Equities	9.90	22.90	21.57	20.04	18.69
Fixed income	70.16	71.82	72.88	64.83	59.53
Cash	19.94	5.29	5.55	15.13	21.79

Table 10.7 Expected currency composition (%) for "Allow Rebalancing" case

Currency	NBIM Benchmark	05-sep 2008	05-Sep 2009	05-Sep 2011	05-Sep 2015	05-Sep 2025
Euro %	35	44.02	30.07	30.04	31.80	31.55
GBP %	15	14.96	16.53	30.27	28.71	27.37
USD %	35	25.91	33.56	28.27	28.29	29.95
Yen %	15	15.12	19.84	11.43	11.21	11.13

From Table 10.8, we note from the third and fourth moments that the resulting distribution is skewed to the right and has fatter tails than a normal distribution. The skewness to the right may be partially because of the CVaR constraints that only constrain the downside. The worst loss in 2025 is around 50% of the expected value of the portfolio but the expected loss of the portfolio is at 20% of the expected portfolio value at the 95% confidence level because of the CVaR constraint. The first period returns are negative but the funds flows help to satisfy the CVaR constraint and the returns later make up for the early low returns.

The histogram in Figure 10.4 shows how well the downside CVaR constraints have reduced the worst outcomes, i.e. the left side of the distribution.

The Table 10.10 gives the asset class composition.

Table 10.8 Solution for expectations of wealth (billions of NOK) for "With Oil Funds, Swaps, and Assets" case

Item	**05-Sep 2008**	**05-Sep 2009**	**05-Sep 2011**	**05-Sep 2015**	**05-Sep 2025**
Expected Wealth	1,934.01	2,201.22	3,404.62	6,661.86	15,382.24
Funds Flows over the Period	0.00	349.97	716.30	1,231.08	1,664.75
Swaps Flows over the Period	0.00	0.00	12.83	30.85	100.39
Volatility %		8.94	11.66	14.85	27.00
3rd Moment Divided by STD Cubed		3.28	0.53	2.34	3.17
4th Moment Divided by 3*Variance squared		32.39	19.72	10.70	8.90
Annualized Krone Return		–12.29	5.09	11.07	7.49
Annualized USD Return		–7.51	2.02	7.23	6.66
Annualized Basket Return		–11.37	4.24	10.14	7.23
5% VaR in NOK		2,026.33	2,902.40	5,335.69	11,913.09

Table 10.9 CVaR risk analysis for "With Oil Funds, Swaps, and Assets" case in NKU billions for confidence level = 95% and expected tail loss = 20%

Item	**05-Sep 2008**	**05-Sep 2009**	**05-Sep 2011**	**05-Sep 2015**	**05-Sep 2025**
Expected Wealth (NKU billions)	261.33	300.89	458.44	869.49	1,962.17
CVaR Value or Expected Tail Loss Limit		240.71	366.75	695.60	1,569.74
Corresponding VaR Value		281.80	431.06	713.17	1,619.20
Expected Loss Ratio to CVaR		6.34	5.97	17.98	17.48
Worst Level of Wealth		153.44	260.62	577.61	968.07
Worst Loss as a % of Expected Wealth		49.00	43.15	33.57	50.66

In this case, the model initially sells Euro and Yen short bonds and some US equity and invests in Yen and Euro real estate asset classes. More equity would have been sold off if it had not been for the 25% rollover constraint. We note that the Yen area real estate is positively correlated with equities

Table 10.10 Expected asset class composition in solution (in %) for "With Oil Funds, Swaps, and Assets" case

Asset class	Initial prior to rebalance	05-Sep 2008	05-Sep 2009	05-Sep 2011	05-Sep 2015	05-Sep 2025
Equity – FTSE AW Europe (Euro) Equity	14.00	14.07	9.99	1.77	1.98	1.52
Equity – FTSE AW Americas (USD) Equity	14.00	11.02	.01	2.03	.85	.88
Equity – FTSE AW Asia Pacific (Yen) Equity	6.00	6.05	7.36	3.51	5.55	4.88
Lehman Euro-Agg. 1–3 year bonds	15.75	.86	1.63	.06	.01	.01
Lehman Euro-Agg. 10+ year bonds	5.25	5.27	11.69	14.96	8.10	4.83
Lehman Global: US Treasury 1–3 year Bonds	15.75	15.68	7.99	.57	1.01	.85
Lehman US-Agg. A+ 5+ year bonds	5.25	5.23	11.68	15.32	17.91	15.06
Lehman Global: Japan 1–3 year bonds	6.75	0.00	.00	.01	0.00	.01
Lehman Global: Japan Long Bonds	2.25	1.92	1.57	.11	1.42	.94
Lehman Global: UK 1–3 year bonds	11.25	11.22	.02	.14	.66	.46
Lehman Global: UK long bonds	3.75	3.74	10.56	9.74	13.98	10.60
Lehman Global: Inflation linked bonds	0.00	.00	3.59	3.39	4.94	4.50
DJ US real estate total return	0.00	0.00	5.97	5.46	.96	.86
DJ Euro STOXX real estate total return	0.00	9.79	7.81	10.81	9.21	7.38
DJ STOXX Asia Pacific total return	0.00	15.15	8.82	10.36	4.22	3.39
Private equity total return	0.00	0.00	10.52	19.09	19.07	18.44
Euro cash	0.00	0.00	.70	2.47	10.71	17.81
GBP cash	0.00	0.00	.05	.05	.00	.83
USD cash	0.00	0.00	.00	.03	.00	6.18
Yen cash	0.00	0.00	.05	.13	.14	.60

and in the short-term is decreasing in value. But the long-term growth is very good and the appreciation with respect to the NKU is also good. The model detail shows that the Yen real estate asset class purchased in 2008 is held in many scenarios until 2025. Private equity is not purchased until 2009. Table 10.11 shows that equity approaches 60% as we add in real estate and private equity.

The expected currency composition is given in the Table 10.12. The USD percentages are high but this has more to do with the fact that the private equity is measured in USD.

Again in terms of duration, the model favors long-term bonds over short bonds.

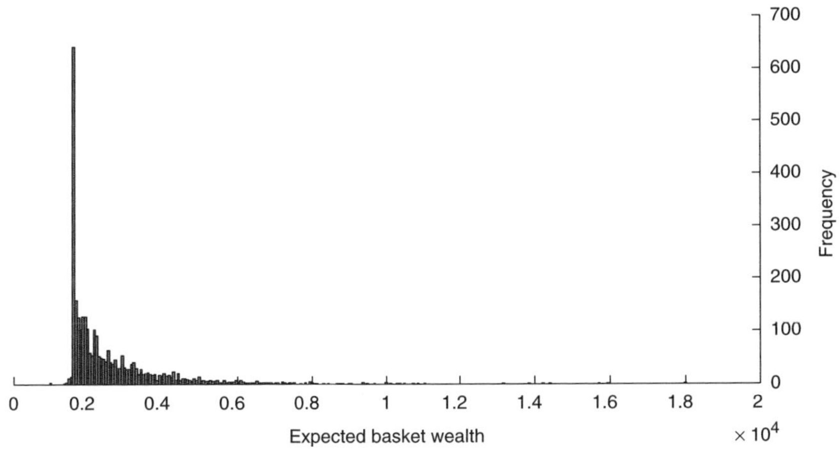

Figure 10.4 Histogram of wealth in NKU on 5-Sep-2025

Table 10.11 Optimal portfolio composition for "With Oil Funds, Swaps, and Assets" case

Item	**05-Sep 2008**	**05-Sep 2009**	**05-Sep 2011**	**05-Sep 2015**	**05-Sep 2025**
Portfolio composition (Billions USD)					
Overall	344.14	414.85	605.12	1,033.81	2,212.40
Equities	192.98	206.35	321.61	428.59	823.06
Fixed income	151.16	204.50	266.78	494.80	820.39
Cash	0.00	4.01	16.73	110.43	568.95
Portfolio composition (%)					
Overall	100.00	100.00	100.00	100.00	100.00
Equities	56.08	49.74	53.15	41.46	37.20
Fixed income	43.92	49.29	44.09	47.86	37.08
Cash	0.00	0.97	2.76	10.68	25.72

Figure 10.5 provides information on the distribution of USD flows due to swaps in each period.

In the online version we provide more details and more analysis. This includes the CVaR constraints, sensitivity of buy and sell prices, sensitivity to policy constraints, implied prices on scenarios used to price other instruments, more details on oil price funds flows and swaps, etc. We also investigate the dynamics. We also look at the relationship between returns on asset classes and break them up between returns on the assets and returns on foreign exchange. We further discuss the Sharpe Ratio and other ratios that more reasonably characterize the use of a downside risk measure, CVaR.

10.4 Discussion and general applicability

10.4.1 Norway lessons

In this section we compare different solutions and in that way emphasize the importance of dynamics, CVaR constraints, and general stochastic

Table 10.12 Expected currency composition (%) for "With Oil Funds, Swaps, and Assets" case

Currency	NBIM Benchmark	05-Sep 2008	05-Sep 2009	05-Sep 2011	05-Sep 2015	05-Sep 2025
Euro %	35.00	30.00	31.82	30.07	30.02	31.55
GBP %	15.00	14.95	10.63	9.93	14.64	11.88
USD %	35.00	31.93	39.75	45.89	44.02	46.76
Yen %	15.00	23.12	17.80	14.12	11.33	9.80

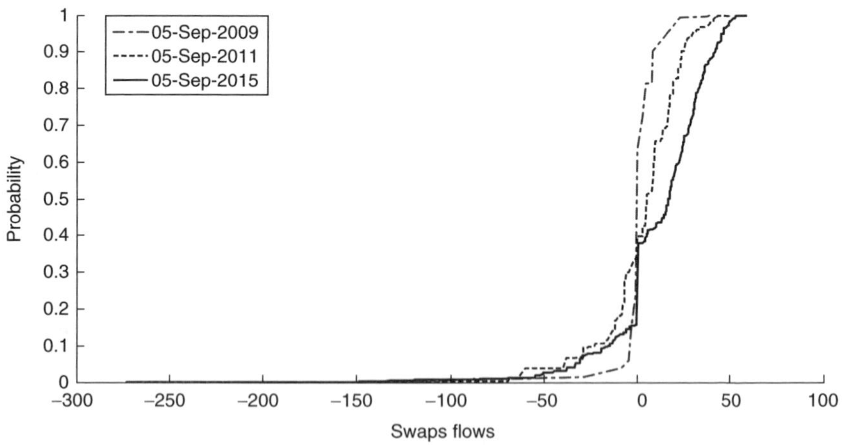

Figure 10.5 Distribution of flows due to USD swaps in each period

optimization with inequalities. We could compare our framework with the mean–variance solution, but that is a very different approach. We therefore add what we call the "Fixed Benchmark as per NBIM". In this case we assume that the proportions of asset classes remain always fixed to the benchmark proportions and compute the expected wealth over the same scenario tree as for the first case analyzed in this chapter. The next case we add is the "With Only Oil Funds" case, where the flows into the fund are based on a stochastic oil price, but the asset classes remain the same as in the "Fixed Benchmark as per NBIM" case. We can compare these cases then to the solutions presented in the previous section, the "Allowing Rebalancing" case and the "With Oil Funds, Swaps, and Assets" case.

Of course, the "Fixed Benchmark" case is suboptimal and the "Allowing Rebalancing" case dominates it in all time periods in NOK and NKU and on all indicators. We see this especially in Figure 10.6 showing how the latter distribution dominates the former. The "Allowing Rebalancing" case buys assets initially that can be held in whole or in part until 2025 and will shift them around as the economic and financial environments necessitate. It does this because the objective function is maximizing wealth at the model terminal period, 2025. Furthermore, by using the dynamics, future policy and risk constraints impact what the asset class selection is today. At the same time, interim CVaR constraints keep the downside risks from becoming too great at any rebalancing period and the distribution is shifted to the right.

Comparing the "With Only Oil Funds" case and the "With Oil Funds, Swaps, and Assets" cases, there is not much difference until 2009, but then values begin to diverge. By 2011 the "With Oil Funds, Swaps, and Assets" case dominates the "With Only Oil Funds" case in all indicators and as shown in the distributions in Figure 10.7 by 2025. The model suggests investments in the new asset classes, even though they won't pay off until later years (see annualized returns in Table 10.13). At the same time, CVaR constraint prevents the downside risks from becoming too great. The addition of the

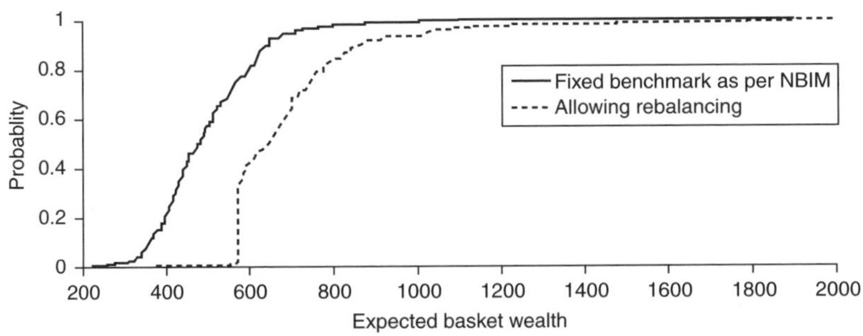

Figure 10.6 Distribution of "Fixed Benchmark as per NBIM versus "Allowing Rebalancing" in 2025

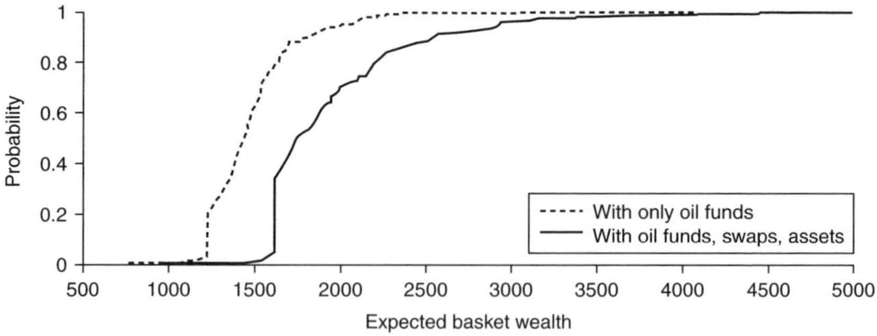

Figure 10.7 Distribution of "With Only Oil Funds" versus "With Oil Funds, Swaps, and Assets" in 2025

asset Oil Swaps allows for better risk diversification in later years. As such, the SWF helps to reduce the impact of oil price volatility on Norway's overall economy, i.e. it acts as an insurance mechanism.

10.4.2 Applying the framework to other types of SWFs

There are many types of SWFs and this framework can be applied to these cases with some adaptations. For example, national pension funds would want to invest safely and maximize long-term wealth, yet have sufficient liquidity to make interim payments on liabilities. In this case we would want to add equations [15] and [25] for target at risk, often called the funding ratio in the case of pension funds. This would be applied at each rebalancing point in time in the model as CVaR constraints. If the funds has explicit expectations of its liabilities, we could use preference functions [4] and [5] to obtain a solution with a density function as close as possible to the value of expected liabilities. This would produce a solution where the pension fund can meet its obligations safely. We could also apply a CVaR constraint to the shortfall in wealth, especially if some risky asset classes were included.

Commodity stabilization funds would want to manage their resources more like central bank reserves do for safety, liquidity, returns, and stability. To incorporate safety and returns, we could adapt equations [4] and [5] for the objective function, to obtain more narrow distributions for targeted wealth levels, while incorporating the effects of stochastic commodity prices (like we did for oil prices). For liquidity constraints, equations [17] and [26] plus associated CVaR constraints could be made a function of the stochastic commodity prices to ensure funds are available when prices fall. Stability constraints, such as [18] and [27], could be added to smooth the degree of asset sales over time.

Table 10.13 Comparison statistics for the four problems

Item	05-Sep 2008	05-Sep 2009	05-Sep 2011	05-Sep 2015	05-Sep 2025
Expected wealth (Billions of NOK)					
Fixed benchmark as per NBIM	1,935.59	1,892.51	2,099.87	2,682.83	3,943.38
Allowing rebalancing	1,933.97	1,912.84	2,253.92	3,163.82	5,582.79
With only oil funds	1,933.72	2,231.22	3,287.91	5,849.82	11,679.88
With oil funds, swaps, and assets	1,934.01	2,201.22	3,404.61	6,661.86	15,382.24
Expected wealth (Billions of NKU)					
Fixed benchmark as per NBIM	261.54	258.31	281.87	349.26	501.22
Allowing rebalancing	261.32	261.02	303.02	412.14	709.36
With only oil funds	261.29	304.82	443.22	763.07	1,488.66
With oil funds, swaps, assets	261.33	300.89	458.44	869.49	1,962.17
Annualized rate of return in % (based on NKU)					
Fixed benchmark as per NBIM		–1.23	4.46	5.50	3.68
Allowing rebalancing		–.11	7.74	7.99	5.58
With only oil funds		–1.67	6.60	7.91	5.26
With oil funds, swaps, and assets		–11.37	4.24	10.14	7.23
5% VaR (billions of NKU)					
Fixed benchmark as per NBIM		242.42	264.64	281.15	342.08
Allowing rebalancing		254.73	292.01	340.07	572.57
With only oil funds		293.81	406.78	635.72	1,238.47
With oil funds, swaps, assets		276.73	431.06	713.17	1,619.20
95% VaR (billions of NKU)					
Fixed benchmark as per NBIM		265.51	310.42	418.52	708.79
Allowing rebalancing		269.42	328.87	481.72	1,039.05
With only oil funds		318.39	485.44	905.73	2,006.05
With oil funds, swaps, assets		332.65	525.50	1,045.64	2,935.73

Development funds could be treated as endowment funds, as in this chapter, with the addition of some known or estimated liabilities, similarly to national pension funds. In addition, because of legal or other policy parameters, any of the following could be added as policy constraints: minimum level of exposure to a currency, maximum level of an asset class as a percent of wealth, maximum percentage of portfolio rollover, and unrealized losses at risk, all defined in this chapter.

10.5 Conclusions

We have presented a framework for SWF investment and risk management that combines tactical asset allocation considerations with broad macroeconomic, macroprudential risk, and sovereign investment management considerations. Our investment and risk management framework allows for very general objective definitions and does not restrict the class of eligible stochastic processes or limit the investment universe. It also allows for easy feedback between outcomes and decision variables by including various tools that can reshape densities. We show the possible applications of our approach to the Government Pension Fund – Global of Norges Bank. We compare our approach with that used by NBIM (based on their quarterly report, NBIM (2008)) and discuss differences. We illustrate with actual examples and solutions the importance of using dynamic asset allocation, CVaR constraints that only restrict the downside, and stochastic optimization.

We see our approach as an important complement to the various ALM-tools currently being used by sovereign wealth funds. Although our approach is more demanding than other approaches in terms of analytical modeling regarding objectives, constraints, and assumptions, we think this is worthwhile for several reasons. First of all, strategic allocation and the formation of benchmarks can be one of the most important determinants of portfolio returns and overall investment management objectives. It is therefore important that the strategic analysis be done incorporating all the risks and other factors in an integrated fashion. Second, a dynamic framework that allows for rebalancing is very important for benchmark creation, as we have demonstrated. It allows for incorporating longer-term effects such as mean-reversion of exchange rates, changing correlations, extreme events and contingent liabilities, and the effects of instruments such as longer duration assets and derivatives. Third, in the case of SWFs especially, it is crucial that the formulation of objectives and risk constraints captures the various considerations regarding the multiple risk at all points in time. This means the model needs to incorporate not only assets and liabilities, but all kinds of risk indicators and objectives that are important to SWFs, as we did. Lastly, the existing approaches used often do not provide the richness of sensitivity stress tests we provided, that are needed to address the various considerations facing managers.

Our approach also has important advantages because it requires a very explicit process for model development that will help clarify the strategic aspects involved in risk management. Often, these strategic aspects, including linkages between macroeconomic, microeconomic and financial risks are left out or treated only implicitly in other approaches. At the same time, the use of numerical approaches to solving using a dynamic stochastic optimization framework allows for analytical rigor while maintaining ample modeling flexibility. As implemented by using CVaR constraints and objectives that shape densities as major tools, the model retains many intuitive features attractive to policy makers. The approach not only provides the complete density functions of outcomes of a selected portfolio (instead of just summary measures), but also defines criteria for the shape of density functions in terms senior management can understand. Then, satisfying those criteria, our approach determines the strategic portfolio allocation that is optimal over time with respect to an objective – such as returns or the likelihood of meeting a target, such as a funding ratio or other liabilities. This intuitive approach can be supported at each level in an institution, while its flexibility allows adaptation to the unique requirements of each individual fund.

Notes

1. There is no unique definition of SWFs, but generally these are thought to include assets held by governments in another country's currency, i.e., held in foreign exchange. They are managed using a continuum of institutional mechanisms (Truman 2008). Toward one end of the spectrum are pure SWFs, which generally have long-term investment objectives. These may include national pension, endowment and development funds. Further along the continuum are stabilization funds accumulated from "excess" revenues from commodity exports in particular. At the other end are traditional international reserves managed by central banks and/or finance ministries, where shorter-term considerations of liquidity and low risk normally are paramount. When purely held for exchange rate management and monetary policy purposes, however, these foreign reserve positions are typically not considered SWFs, although there is no sharp dividing line.
2. Although the final version of the model was run on December 5, 2008, to obtain asset allocations we used historical data only up until September 5, 2008 and did not use any additional data or expert views since. This way we make a fairer comparison with the benchmark we assumed for NGPF as we avoid the period of extreme turmoil during the fall of 2008.
3. This mathematical notation can be directly translated into the General Algebraic Modeling system (GAMS) notation for optimization.
4. We find this notation convenient especially for asset classes most often held by sovereign institutions. The notation is different than is normally used as we measure the purchase value while others often measure the number or volume of assets. There are reasons to use either notation for specific problems.
5. See Ziemba and Mulvey (1998) for several examples. Shortfall is also called "embarrassment" to reflect the embarrassment in not meeting targets.
6. The target for a pension fund then becomes the net present value of future liabilities.
7. Since one equation is required for each event e it would seem that the model could become very large and difficult to solve. This is not usually the case since we will use linear Λ and only a small number of these constraints are in fact active making the problem much easier to handle than would otherwise be assumed.

8. NBIM also manages, besides the Government Petroleum Insurance Fund (which is small, only NOK 16 billion), the major share of Norges Bank's foreign exchange reserves.
9. According to the Government pension fund Act (No. 123 of 21 December 2005), the cash flow is the sum of (1) total tax revenues and royalty deriving from petroleum activities collected pursuant to Petroleum Taxation Act (no. 35 of 13 June 1975) and the Petroleum Activities Act (no. 72 of 29 November 1996), (2) revenues deriving from tax on CO2 emissions due to petroleum activities on the continental shelf, (3) revenues deriving from tax on NOx emissions due to petroleum activities on the continental shelf, (4) revenues deriving from the State's Direct Financial Interest in petroleum activities, defined as operating income and other income less operating expenses and other direct expenses, (5) central government revenues from net surplus agreements associated with certain production licenses, (6) dividends from Statoil ASA, (7) transfers from the Petroleum Insurance Fund, (8) central government revenues deriving from the removal or alternative use of installations on the continental shelf, and (9) any government sale of stakes representing the State's Direct Financial Interest in petroleum activities, less (1) central government direct investments in petroleum activities, (2) central government expenses in connection with the Petroleum Insurance Fund, (3) central government expenses in connection with the removal or alternative use of installations on the continental shelf, and (4) any government purchase of stakes as part of the State's Direct Financial Interest in petroleum activities. Net financial transactions associated with petroleum activities are gross revenues from government sale of shares in Statoil ASA less (1) any government purchase of shares in Statoil ASA, defined as the market price paid by the government for the shares, and (2) government capital contributions to Statoil ASA and companies attending to government interests in petroleum activities.
10. "Notice from the Governor's Staff – Investment Strategy", Norges Bank, 2006. In this change, the Fund's strategic asset allocation was compared with funds with similar objectives, two of which were the Harvard and Yale University endowment funds.
11. Because of the way we structure our model formulation, we estimate most variables in the rate-of-return space. This makes the formulation particularly consistent and applicable especially in the formulation of the stochastic estimations.
12. Solution provided by Roger J-B Wets, as in Claessens et al. (1998).
13. This is consistent with the current fiscal rule that stipulates that, over time, the central government nonoil structural deficit can not be larger than the real rate of return on the assets of the Fund, currently estimated at 4%, thus preserving the real value of the Fund.
14. Besides more detail, the online version of this chapter addresses three additional questions. The first is what else could have been done using our framework (on 5 September 2008) to improve our results and what kinds of probabilistic stress test could have been done. The second is how our hedged portfolio would have performed over the short term compared to the benchmark. Lastly, we discuss how the hedged portfolio performs with respect to the benchmark over the long term.

References

Acerbi, Carlo and Dirk Tasche (2002) "On the Coherence of Expected Shortfall", *Journal of Banking and Finance*, 26:7, July, 1487–1503. See also <http://www.risklab.ch/Papers.html>.

Claessens, Stijn (2006) "Taking Stock of Risk Management Techniques for Sovereigns", forthcoming, In Stiglitz, Joseph and Jose Antonio Ocampo (Eds) *Sovereign Debt Project*, Initiative for Policy Dialogue, Columbia University, and Department of Economic and Social Affairs, United Nations.

Claessens, Stijn and Jerome Kreuser (2007) "Strategic Foreign Reserves Risk Management: Analytical Framework", *Financial Modeling, Annals of Operations Research*, 152: 79–113.

Claessens, Stijn, Jerome Kreuser, Lester Seigel, and Roger J-B Wets (1998) "A Tool for Strategic Asset Liability Management", *World Bank Working Paper*, Research Project Ref. No. 681–23, Washington, D.C., 12 March 1998.

Cornuejols, Gerard and Reha Tütüncü (2007) *Optimization Methods in Finance*, Cambridge University Press, Cambridge University Press, New York.

Gray, Dale (2007) "A New Framework for Risk and Sovereign Wealth Management", In Jennifer Johnson-Calari and Malan Rietveld (Eds) *Sovereign Wealth Management*, Central Banking Publications Ltd, London, United Kingdom.

IMF (2008) *Global Financial Stability Report*, Washington, D.C.

Johnson-Calari, Jennifer and Malan Rietveld (2007) *Sovereign Wealth Management*, Central Banking Publications Ltd, London, United Kingdom.

Kjaer, Knut N. (2007) "Turning Oil Wealth into Financial Assets: The Case of Norway", in *Sovereign Wealth Management*, Central Banking Publications Ltd, London, United Kingdom.

Kreuser, Jerome L. (2002) "The Rapid Implementation of Asset/Liability Kodels for Sovereign Risk Management", in Soeren Nielsen, *Programming Languages and Systems in Computational Economics and Finance*, Kluwer Academic Publishers.

Kreuser, Jerome L. and Morton Lane (2006) "An Introduction to the Benefits of Optimization Models for Underwriting Portfolio Selection", *Proceedings of the 28th International Congress of Actuaries*, Paris, June, <http://riskontroller.com>.

McKinsey Global Institute, Farrell, Diana, Susan Lund, Eva Gerlemann, and Peter Seeburger (2007) "The New Power Brokers: How Oil, Asia, Hedge Funds, and Private Equity are Shaping Global Capital Markets", McKinsey & Company, <http://www.mckinsey.com/mgi>.

McNeil, Alexander J., Rüdiger Frey, and Paul Embrechts (2005) *Quantitative Risk Management*, Princeton University Press, Princeton, New Jersey.

Mulvey, John M., Bill Pauling and Ron Madey (2002) "Advantages of Multi-period Portfolio Models", *Journal of Portfolio Management*, Winter 2003, 29(2): 35–45.

Norges Bank Investment Management (2008) *NBIM Quarterly Performance Report – First Quarter 2008*, Norges Bank, 23 May, Oslo.

Norges Bank (2006) "Changes to the Benchmark Portfolio of the Government Pension Fund – Global", Governor's Staff – Investment Strategy, Oslo.

Rockafellar, R. Tyrrell and Stanislav Uryasev (2002) "Conditional Value-at-Risk for General Loss Distributions", *Journal of Banking and Finance*, 26:7, July.

Truman, Edward (2007) *Sovereign Wealth Funds: The Need for Greater Transparency and Accountability*, Peterson Institute for International Economics, Policy Brief.

Zenios and Ziemba (2007) *Handbook of Asset and Liability Management*, Vol. 1–2, Elsevier, Amsterdam.

Ziemba, Rachel E. S. and William T. Ziemba (2007) *Scenarios for Risk Management and Global Investment Strategies*, John Wiley & Sons, Ltd, West Sussex, England.

Ziemba, William T. (2003) *The Stochastic Programming Approach to Asset, Liability, and Wealth Management*, The Research Foundation of the Association for Investment Management and Research, <http://www.aimr.org>.

Ziemba, William T. and John M. Mulvey (1998) *Worldwide Asset and Liability Modeling*, Cambridge University Press, United Kingdom.

11
Optimal Scale and Asset Allocation for Sovereign Wealth Funds: China's Case

Yueyan Zhang and Xianhua Wei

11.1 Introduction

Sovereign wealth funds (SWFs) have been discussed more and more frequently and internationally nowadays. However, there is yet no clear definition of an SWF. Some well-recognized aspects of SWFs are listed as follows: sovereign wealth, in contrast with private wealth, is public wealth, generally in the form of a foreign currency and typically composed of governmental earnings from specific taxes, budget distribution, incomes from natural resources, surplus of international payments or other means. An SWF is different from a traditional government pension fund. It is also different from those government organizations that simply hold reserved assets in order to keep the value of currency stable. An SWF is a brand new investment institution with distinct professional and market characteristics.

In recent years, SWFs have developed rapidly. According to statistics from the IMF, there are more than 30 SWFs in the world, mostly established by developing countries and regions. The global amount of the SWFs' capital has also been increasing sharply. Currently the total amount is between 1,900 billion and 2,900 billion USD. It is expected that this number will be up to 10,000 billion in 2012. Among the biggest 20 SWFs in the world, the average size is over 10 billion USD. And in total, their assets amount to 2,000 billion USD. Similarly to hedge funds, the information for most SWFs is confidential. SWFs usually do not disclose their holding assets, and they do not take responsibility to publicize their investment policies, either.

There is no fixed rule on how to manage SWFs. Some countries, such as Singapore, have set up investment companies which are independent from central banks and the Ministry of Finance for their SWFs. And some countries make such institutions under their central banks to manage their SWF assets. Most SWFs have applied professional and market oriented operational methods and diversified investment strategies. They also allocate resources on a global basis in order to earn long-term investment returns.

Nonetheless, there is some disagreement regarding SWFs. Such disagreements include the following five aspects: (1) whether the purpose of the SWF is for governmental strategy or business returns; (2) whether the SWF should use passive or active investment policy; (3) how to balance transparency and business privacy; (4) whether the SWF could stabilize the financial market or would jeopardize the stability; (5) how to deal with financial protectionism. Though over time, the attitude towards SWFs is becoming accepting, doubt still exists.

The China Investment Corporation (CIC), founded in 2007, has attracted attention all over the world due to its substantial assets and the backgrounds of its shareholders. Since China's State Administration of Foreign Exchange is not professional enough to invest China's huge foreign reserve assets, it hopes that the newly established CIC could change such situation. Currently, the registered capital of CIC is 200 billion USD. In addition, there is more than 1,000 billion USD foreign exchange reserves to support. Currently, the major target investment industries of the CIC are finance and energy, which did not generate the expected return for the CIC. In addition, there are also some suspicion and concerns about the scales, investment purposes, and transparency of the CIC. Unfortunately, there is not much academic research into these issues.

This chapter stands at an academia point, and calculates the optimal scale of foreign exchange expenditures based on the trend of China's foreign exchange earnings, and then proposes the optimal size of SWF. It further discusses the optimal asset allocation for the CIC, and analyzes the investment style the CIC should assume.

At present, there has not been too much research regarding optimal scales of SWFs in academia. One representative project was published by Arrau and Claessens in 1992. They apply the precautionary saving model developed by Deaton in 1991 and use the commodity stabilization fund of Chili to calculate the optimal scale of stabilization-oriented Ffunds. As for the asset allocation, there has been much more research than for SWF scale. The investment behavior of pension plans has been studied by Boulier, Trussant and Florens (2005) and by Josa-Fombellida and Rincon-Zapatero (2004). Browne (1997) also discusses the optimal portfolios at length. There was also some research on funds with liability, for instance, Bohn (2001) researched the innovative government debt management case; Josa-Fombellda and Rincon-Zapatero (2006) also discuss this issue.

This chapter uses Deaton's model and refers to the Tauchen's (1986) model to calculate the optimal scale of foreign exchange expenditures, in order to deduce the optimal size of SWF. In contrast, we focus more on how different trends of foreign exchange earnings influence the optimal size of SWFs, and by optimization calculation we find out the most important factors that influence the optimal size of SWFs. We will also make some improvements to the models by differentiating risky assets and low-risk assets, in order to calculate the optimal strategic asset allocation of SWFs. Unlike Deaton's approach of giving an analytical solution to the precautionary model, we use dynamic optimization to solve this problem and get a more clear and intuitive result. In addition, policy suggestions are provided based on the results.

The structure of this chapter is as follows. In Section 11.2, Deaton's precautionary saving model is introduced. In Section 11.3, we explain the foreign exchange earnings statistics used in this model and simulate possible trends of future foreign exchange earnings. Section 11.4 is an important section which shows the calculation of optimal foreign exchange expenditures under different scenarios and relevant optimal sizes of SWFs. We discuss the implication of using different values for some parameters in Section 11.5. In the next section we make a differentiation between risky assets and low-risk assets, and further calculate the optimal asset allocation for SWFs under different yields and foreign exchange earnings trends. The final conclusion will be shown in Section 11.7: under the current trend that the earnings from foreign exchange are increasing in China, there is no need to expand the scale of the SWF, and the ratios of risky assets invested should be high. The fundamental way to prevent the foreign reserve from depreciating is to narrow the balance of international payments. In the future, if the foreign reserve increases slowly, the scale of the SWF and reserve for preventivepurposes should be expanded, with the premise that the SWF guarantees relevant returns. And the optimal asset allocation depends on the fluctuations of earnings and the yields of the SWF. If it is predicted that there will be a big fluctuation in China's future foreign exchange earnings, expanding the SWF's scale will be very necessary, even facing a low yield. Also, risky assets should be invested prudently.

11.2 Models

According to the research of Central Huijin Investment Ltd., SWFs could be classified into the following five categories by their incentives: (1) stabilization-oriented funds, (2) sterilization-oriented funds, (3) savings-oriented funds, (4) preventive funds and (5) strategy-oriented funds. Though the stated reason for the establishment of the CIC is to solve the problems of excess and depreciation of foreign exchange reserves, it has additional strategic meanings. The main resource of China's foreign exchange earnings is the large surplus in the current account. But, the advantages of such a surplus are slowly dying down because of the following two reasons. First, the price of China's formerly cheap resources, such as labor, are gradually rising. Second, the economies of China's main trade partners have slowed down, which will reduce the demand for exports. For example, the economy of the United States, one of China's important export objectives, incurred a heavy loss in the 2008 Wall Street financial turmoil, which decreased its imports from China. There are also some other factors that have caused a decline in China's exports, such as the appreciation of RMB, etc. The most important implications of the establishment of the CIC are to prevent utility shocks under situations in which the foreign exchange earnings of China decreases continuously due to any unexpected factors. Thus, we classify China's SWF in the Preventive Fund category.

Because of the analysis above, we use the precautionary saving model in Deaton (1991). The model is based on the notion that the individual or country faces some constraints on its borrowings which prevent it from smoothing adverse earnings fluctuations. This is very realistic especially for China because the Chinese have a long tradition of saving money against unanticipated future events.

We assume that the government has an objective function which is a function of a sequence of expenditure demands for foreign exchange – government consumption demands, provision demands for public goods, social program demands etc. – to be financed with the surplus from the foreign exchange earnings. We assume that all other expenditures, asset accumulation and policy decisions made by the central bank can be separated from the saving and expenditure decisions related to foreign exchange earnings. We further assume the central bank to be risk averse. Because of the volatile earnings stream from international trade, the borrowing constraint and the low returns from low-risk assets such as US government treasury bonds, the central bank or the government has an incentive to set up an SWF to smooth earnings fluctuations optimally. In "good" years the central bank or the government transfers some foreign exchange earnings to the SWF which invests in risky assets to make more profits for future use in "bad" years. Therefore the capital for this kind of SWFs comes from excess foreign exchange reserves, which is the surplus of foreign exchange earnings other than the optimal expenditures that maximize the utility of the country.

Formally, the government maximizes the expected value of a function of the control variable, savings, subject to budget and borrowing constraints.

$$[1] \quad \max \; E\sum_{i=1}^{n} \beta^{t-1} u(c_t)$$

$$[2] \quad s.t. \; w_{t+1} = (1+r)(w_t + y_t - c_t)$$

$$[3] \quad w_t \geq 0, t = 1, \mathrm{L} \ldots, n$$

where:

- $u(\cdot)$: Instantaneous utility function, assumed to be increasing, strictly concave, and differentiable, i.e. $u' > 0$, $u'' < 0$.
- c_t: Consumption in period t.

- y_t: Foreign exchange earnings in period *t*.
- w_t: Total value of SWF's assets in period *t*.
- β: Time preference factor, and $0 < \beta < 1$.
- *r*: Return rate of an SWF asset, assumed to be a constant, i.e. the return rate of a low-risk asset.

We assume that foreign exchange earnings follow the Autoregressive process of order 1(AR (1)) process and that the utility function is as follows:

$$[4]\ u(c_t) = \frac{c_t^{1-\alpha}}{1-\alpha}$$

where α is the relative risk aversion parameter, and the value of α grows as the degree of risk aversion increases. The typical procedures to solve this dynamic programming problem give the following Euler equation:

$$[5]\ u'(c_t) = \max\left\{(y_t + w)^{-\alpha}, r\beta E\left[u'(c_{t+1})\right]\right\}$$

That is, the optimal consumption decision makes the marginal utility of the current consumption equal to the discount value of the marginal utility of the consumption in the next period, when the budget constraint is not binding.

Our approach is different from the direction Arrau and Claessens (1992) and Deaton (1991) pursue. We simulate the possible trends of the future foreign exchange earnings, and for each trend scenario the optimal consumption (foreign exchange expenditure) series are obtained through an optimization algorithm.

Our simulation period starts from 1993. The scale of foreign exchange reserve at that time was rather small, so we set $w_1 = 0$. Because history is unchangeable, we use actual earnings and expenditures data for 1993 to 2007. We obtain the data after 2007 through simulations. Furthermore, although China has accumulated lots of reserves, considering China's reserve management policy and the strategic significance of reserves, we assume that the existing foreign exchange reserves are not disposable assets. Also, taking the convenience of the calculation into account, we assume that the wealth generated in the simulation periods would not be taken into future periods. That means all of the remaining wealth in the last simulation period would be consumed. By calculation and analysis, we find that this assumption has little influence on the earlier periods, but has some influence on the later ones (for example, the last five to ten years). So, to avoid potential error, we will mainly analyze the earlier periods.

During the model simulation, we set $\alpha = 0.5$ and $\beta = 0.9$ based on experience. We will discuss this in Section 11.5. The value of *r* mainly depends on the investment opportunities and the characteristic of the assets invested. When there are enough investment opportunities, it is generally accepted that the yield of some low-risk financial products, such as the government bonds of counties that have a good credit grade or money market funds, is less than 5 per cent, while the yield of products with slightly higher risk, such as equity funds, real estate funds, etc., is about 10 per cent, the yield of higher risk assets like stocks is about 15 per cent and products with very high risk, such as options, futures, hedge funds, PE funds, etc., usually get very high expected yields, but are associated with great volatility risk.

11.3 Data on foreign exchange earnings

Arrau and Claessens (1992) use export data for copper, since the income of copper exports is the country's major foreign exchange earnings. They applied the AR (1) process to simulate and analyze the data. This chapter uses as its basis data from the balance sheet (1993–2007) published by the Chinese bureau of state foreign exchange reserves. Based on the characteristics of the obtained data, we defined the sum of the credit portion of the current account, the credit portion of the capital account and the credit portion of direct investment as board foreign exchange earnings. The relevant debit counterpart is defined as foreign exchange expenditures. The balance is the change in foreign exchange reserve.

After the establishment of the People's Bank of China (PBoC), the central bank of China, in 1949, the Chinese government exerted strict control on foreign exchange in order to increase the amount of foreign reserves by limiting outflows and increasing inflows. Between 1950 and 1980, the amount of foreign exchange earnings increased very slowly, and sometimes decreased. At the beginning of the Reform and Opening of China, due to the lack of economic power, the foreign reserve amount continued to increase at a low speed. It was only after the 1990s that the Chinese economy started to grow rapidly and so did foreign reserves. Especially after 2000, even though China has loosened the limits on foreign exchanges, increased the amount of the state commercial bank's capital fund and appreciated RMB, China's foreign reserve amount continues to go up rapidly. Based on the discussion above, we believe that data from 1993 to 2007 can represent China's foreign exchange earnings pattern accurately.

Wang (2003) has conducted simulations and research on China's foreign exchange reserve scales. He found that the increasing amount is in accordance with AR (1) model and the statistical results were significant. Inspired by Wang's research, we also used AR (1) to simulate China's foreign reserve earnings. Results show that by using a log function on foreign exchange earnings and taking the first order differences, the result corresponds with AR (1) and the simulation results were satisfactory. Therefore, we use this model to simulate China's foreign exchange earnings process.

In the AR (1) analysis, let y_t be the foreign exchange earnings of the period *t*. We then have:

$$[6]\ \Delta\log(y_t) = a\Delta\log(y_{t-1}) + b + \varepsilon_1$$

where $\varepsilon_1 \sim N(0, \sigma_{\log(y)})$. Using the existing data, Table 11.1 shows the regression results.

Meanwhile, taking possible fluctuations of the Chinese economy and the world economy into consideration, we discuss the following three scenarios for China's future foreign exchange earnings: increase, stabilization and decrease. The simulations are as follows:

1. Stable increase of foreign exchange earnings as the graph below shows, i.e. $\Delta\ \log(y_t) = a\Delta\ \log(y_{t-1}) + b + \varepsilon_1$. In the figure, the data are historical between 1993 and 2007, and simulated from year 2008 to 2017.
2. Foreign exchange earnings stabilize as earnings growth slows down. We assume that the current upward trend can sustain for 10 years until 2017. After 2017, foreign reserves start to stabilize. Starting from 2018, the foreign exchange earnings follow:

   $$[7]\ y_t = y_{t-1} \times \exp(\varepsilon_2),\ \varepsilon_2 \sim N\left(0, \sigma_{\log(y)}\right)$$

   Simulations of this scenario is shown in the Figure 11.2.
3. Sharp drop of foreign reserves. When foreign reserves are increasing, their earnings process is an AR (1) process, which is $\Delta\log(y_t) = 0.45\Delta\log(y_{t-1}) - 0.47 + \varepsilon$. When foreign exchange earnings decrease, the process of decrease is the inverse process of increase with the assumption that the rate of decrease is the same as the rate of increase. Simulation of this scenario is shown in the Figure 11.3.

Table 11.1 AR (1) regression results on foreign exchange earnings

Variable	**Coefficient**	**Std. error**	***t*-statistic**	**Prob.**
C	0.190199	0.054993	3.458618	0.0061
AR (1)	0.408428	0.297266	1.373946	0.1995
R-squared	0.868796	Mean dependent var		0.188212
Adjusted R-squared	0.854676	S.D. dependent var		0.117038
S.E. of regression	0.112583	Akaike info criterion		−1.379236
Sum squared resid	0.126750	Schwarz criterion		−1.298419
Log likelihood	10.27542	F-statistic		1.887727
Durbin-Watson stat	1.827373	Prob (F-statistic)		0.199470

Note: The regression result shows that t-statistics are significant and the R-square is high. The AR (1) value in Table 11.1 is less than 1, meaning that the AR (1) procedure is balanced. Also, the Durbin-Watson value is close to 2. Therefore this model can be used for the simulation and prediction of foreign exchange earnings.

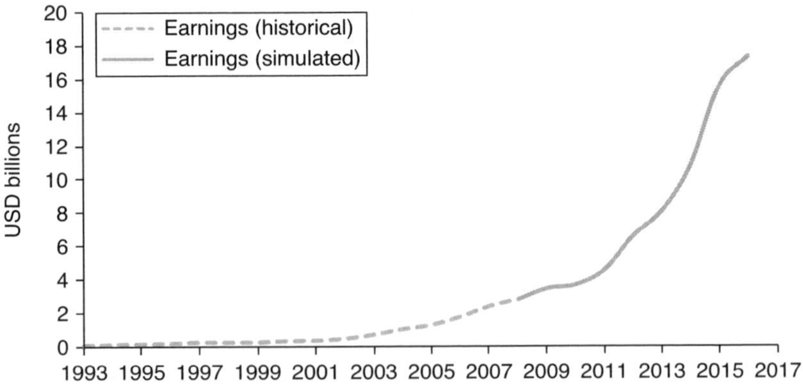

Figure 11.1 Increase of foreign revenues

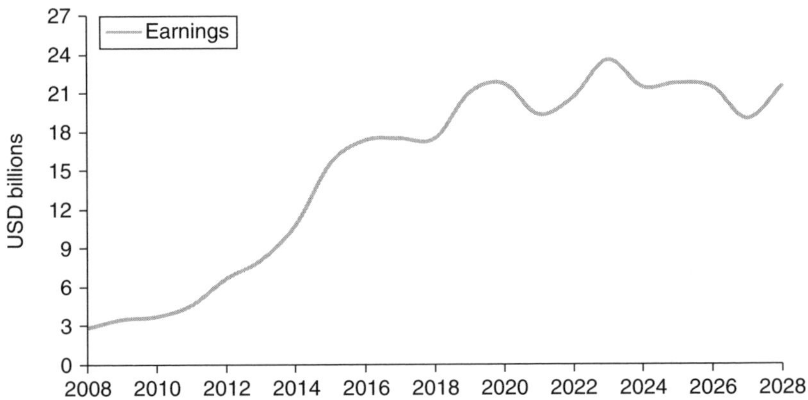

Figure 11.2 Stability of foreign exchange earnings

In the following section of the chapter, we make a comprehensive analysis based on the simulation scenarios above.

11.4 Analysis of the optimal size of funds

Case 1: Stable growth of future foreign exchange earnings

Since 1993, China's foreign exchange earnings have increased very rapidly, from 143 million US dollars in 1993 to 2,410 billion US dollars in 2007. Especially after 2002, with the gradual globalization of cross-border outsourcing and reorganization of the supply chain to accelerate development, the

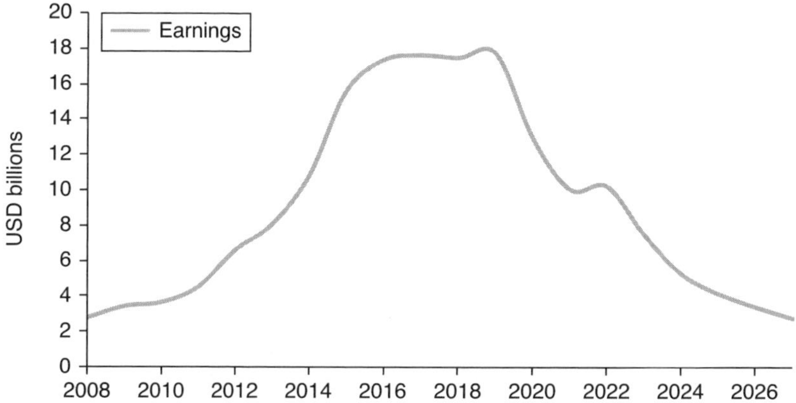

Figure 11.3 Fluctuations of earnings

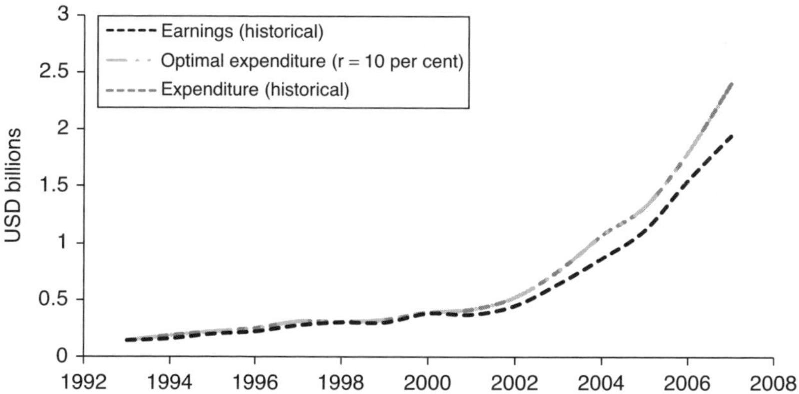

Figure 11.4 China's foreign exchange earnings, expenditure and optimal expenditure

growth rate of China's foreign exchange earnings has been above 20 per cent each year. In 2003 and 2004, it reached more than 40 per cent. At the same time, foreign exchange expenditures increased significantly. In Figure 11.4, the broken bold line stands for foreign exchange earnings, the broken line stands for foreign exchange expenditure, and the broken dotted line stands for the optimal expenditure derived from the model (as the optimal expenditure is equal to foreign exchange earnings, the broken bold line coincides with the broken dotted line). We can see from Figure 11.4 that in the past 15 years, the actual annual expenditure was less than optimal. That is to say, in the past

15 years, China's foreign exchange policy was too conservative. There was too much corresponding accumulation of a balance of international payments, which is an important reason for China's excessive current foreign exchange reserves. Therefore, in view of the present situation, China should encourage imports and overseas investment and loosen control over foreign exchange expenditures to further enhance the level of utility.

If China's foreign exchange earnings can still maintain the present upward trend in the future, we can use the previous AR (1) to simulate the growth process (from 2008 to 2017), and calculate the corresponding optimal expenditure. The result is shown in Figure 11.5 (as the amount of optimal foreign exchange expenditure is equal to the amount of earnings, these two coincide with each other). According to the results, if China's foreign exchange earnings in the next decade can maintain steady growth as in the present state and foreign exchange expenditure is still facing liquidity constraints, with the current set of parameters the rate of optimal foreign exchange expenditure is still 100 per cent. This means that China can achieve an optimal state without preventive reserves. This also means that the optimal size of the SWF is the current foreign exchange reserve minus its optimal scale, which is about 1 trillion US dollars according to Xia (2006). Also, various measures should be taken to make the expenditure of foreign exchange equivalent to the annual foreign exchange earnings, namely, relaxing foreign exchange controls to meet with various needs of the people in order to maximize social utility as a whole.

Now let us analyze investment opportunities' influence on the results of optimal foreign exchange expenditure. As the results of the optimization simulation in Figure 11.5, we set the expected yield as 10 per cent. In fact, there is only a little difference between the results when the yield

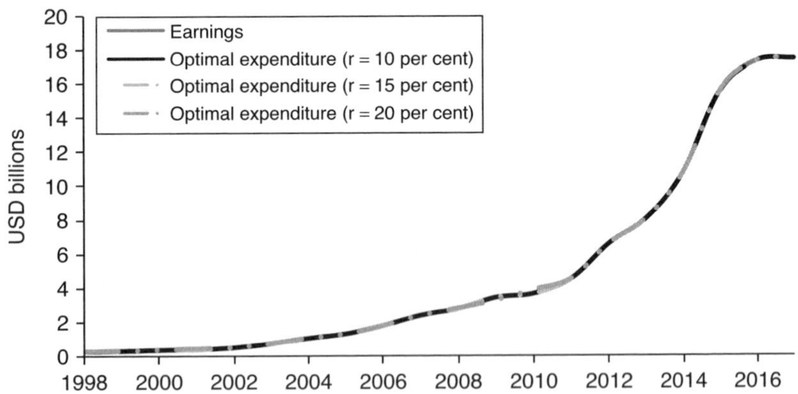

Figure 11.5 Expected future foreign exchange earnings and corresponding optimal foreign exchange expenditure.

gradually increases from 10 per cent to 20 per cent. According to the simulation results, the rate of optimal expenditure is still 100 per cent because the future foreign exchange earnings will take on an upward trend and grow sharply. That means the earnings of the next period will be much higher than the current earnings. As the marginal utility is a decreasing function, the marginal utility of the next period after a discount is always lower than the current marginal utility if the time discount factor is not low enough. Just as is shown in Euler's equation: if $u'(c_t) = \max\{(y_t + w_t)^{-\alpha},(1 + r)\beta E[u'(c_{t+1})]\}$, $u'(c_t) = (y_t + w_t)^{-\alpha}$ is a tight constraint, then the optimal expenditure rate is 100 per cent. If we do not face liquidity constraints, the optimal pre-expenditure ratio will be greater than 100 per cent.

According to Figure 11.5, if China's future foreign exchange earnings are still growing at a high rate, even if the return rate of SWF could reach 20 per cent, which is actually very hard to achieve, it is still not attractive to increase the scale of the SWF. The optimal decision should make the foreign exchange expenditure equal to the foreign exchange earnings, where utility could be maximized.

Case 2: Stability of future foreign exchange earnings

The high flow and growth of China's foreign exchange earnings mainly lies in relatively cheaper labor costs. With the rapid expand of the current cross-border outsourcing and supply chain reorganization, the demand for cheaper labor force has increased substantially. However, with the development of China's economy, workers' salaries will be gradually rising. Meanwhile the investment opportunities become less and less, coupled with the appreciation of the RMB to curb China's exports. Therefore, China's foreign exchange earnings, in the long term, may not be able to maintain such rapid growth. After a peak period of growth, foreign exchange earnings are likely to remain steady, just as the process of simulation shows in Figure 11.2. At this point, the simulation of foreign exchange earnings and the corresponding optimal expenditure are shown in Figure 11.6. We can see that even when the yield is only 10 per cent or lower, the various foreign exchange earnings require a certain scale of SWF. The preventive reserves should be higher as the yield gradually increases. Also, when the yield is higher, the expenditure line is smoother, and the expected total utility is higher.

As shown in Figure 11.6, if foreign exchange earnings tend to be stable, the size of the SWF mainly depends on its yield and the fluctuations of the foreign exchange earnings at the given level of time preference and of risk aversion. If the SWF could achieve a relatively higher yield, it should maintain a larger size for the SWF to get increased utility. On the other hand, if the SWF could not get a higher rate of return, then simply from the perspective of maximizing utility, the optimal decision is to carry out preventive savings and thus get an SWF of a smaller scale. This means that provided

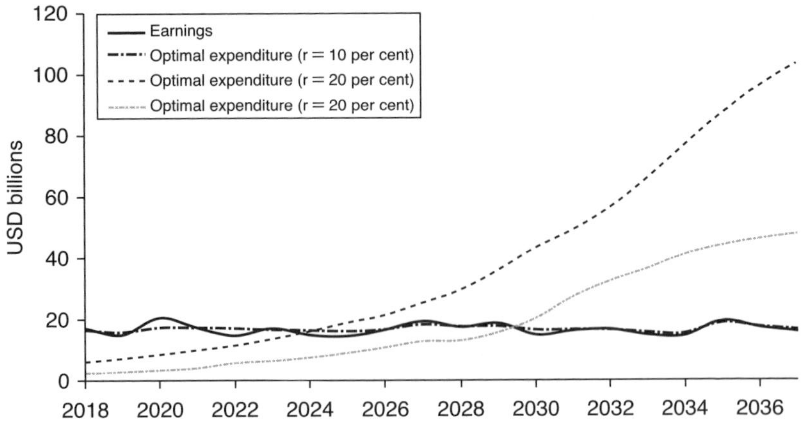

Figure 11.6 Optimal expenditure for stable future foreign exchange earnings in the future

that there is a stable tendency for future foreign exchange earnings, as long as we set up the SWF, we should be actively looking for investment opportunities with higher risk and allocating more assets in risky assets, such as stocks and stock funds. If the expected fluctuations of foreign exchange earnings are higher, then the SWF should remain relatively larger. In contrast, if the expected foreign exchange earnings fluctuations are smaller, the SWF should have a smaller scale. At the return rate of 10 per cent, for example, Figure 11.7 and Figure 11.8 below show the fluctuations of optimal expenditure and optimal size on different conditions of foreign exchange earnings for the corresponding SWFs.

As shown in Figure 11.7 and Figure 11.8, the optimal scale for SWFs obviously varies with changes in the foreign exchange earnings. To test the correlation between two elements, we first set the variable "$yratio_t$" to indicate the fluctuation of foreign exchange earnings in the period t, that is,

$$[8] \quad yratio_t = (y_t - E(y)) / E(y)$$

Then we set another variable "$wratio_t$" to indicate the ratio of preventive reserves in the period *t*, namely the percentage of foreign exchange earnings invested in the SWF, that is,

$$[9] \quad wratio_t = \triangle w_t / y_t$$

The results of the regression analysis are shown in Table 11.2.

As we can see from the Table 11.2, the result shows significant statistics for the T-test and higher R-squared. This means that on the stable

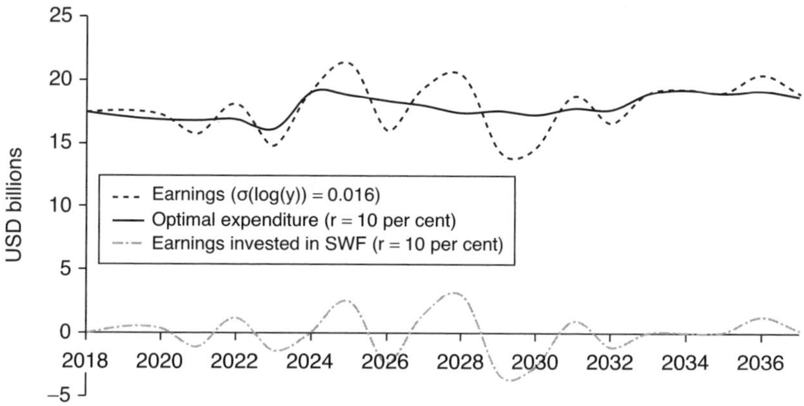

Figure 11.7 Optimal expenditure and optimal size of the SWF under low volatility of foreign exchange earnings

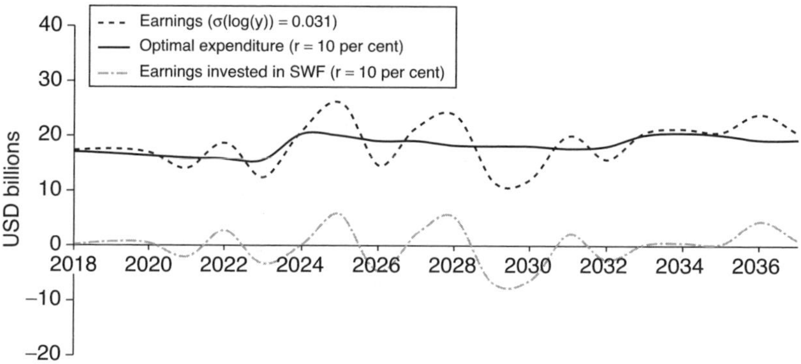

Figure 11.8 Optimal expenditure and optimal size of the SWF under high volatility of foreign exchange earnings

condition of foreign exchange earnings, the degree of volatility of earnings accounts for the percentage of annual foreign exchange earnings invested in a SWF at the given yield. For instance, when foreign exchange earnings are 10 per cent higher than the expected revenue, 8.17 per cent of foreign exchange earnings should be used for precautionary savings and investing in the SWF. By contrast, when foreign exchange earnings are 10 per cent lower than the expected revenue, 9.44 per cent of foreign exchange earnings should be withdrawn from the SWF to supply the foreign exchange expenditures.

Table 11.2 Regression results for a preventive savings rate and foreign exchange earnings volatility rate

Variable	Coefficient	Std. error	*t*-statistic	Prob.
C	−0.063936	0.017714	−3.609314	0.0011
YRATIO	0.883302	0.074786	11.81113	0.0000
R-squared	0.818185	Mean dependent var		−0.069538
Adjusted R-squared	0.812320	S.D. dependent var		0.234806
S.E. of regression	0.101723	Akaike info criterion		−1.674435
Sum squared resid	0.320775	Schwarz criterion		−1.583737
Log likelihood	29.62817	F-statistic		139.5028
Durbin-Watson stat	1.242764	Prob (F-statistic)		0.000000

Case 3: Sharp Drop in Foreign Exchange Earnings

Given China's current economic trend, it is not likely to have a sharp drop in foreign exchange earnings in the short term. However, the world economic market is unpredictable and the economies of some economically developed countries (such as the US) has shown a trend of recession. Impacted by the world economic integration and some factors of uncertainty (such as the financial crisis, the real estate bubble, etc.), it is possible for China's foreign exchange earnings to incur sharp drops. Figure 11.9 shows the simulation of this situation (assuming the foreign exchange earnings tends to be balanced after the fluctuations), and it contains the calculated corresponding optimal expenditure. The increase in foreign exchange earnings process still applies AR (1) to the simulation, and so does the inverse process of the decline.

It can be seen from Figure 11.9 that if foreign exchange earnings show great uncertainty, the high-yield investment opportunities would be slim, and the SWF would have a low yield. Thus the preventive savings would be useful and necessary. Certainly, the effectiveness and the size of the SWF depends on its yield. As shown in Figure 11.9, when the yield of the SWF reaches 20 per cent, the SWF should be kept at a high level.

Comparing Case 2 with Case 3, we can see that both optimal expenditure and optimal preventive savings actually can not be achieved if unpredictable shocks affect the foreign exchange earnings. For example, when foreign exchange earnings fall by 10 per cent, if it is expected to be normal fluctuations, and assets should be taken from the SWF to smooth expenditures. However, if it is expected to be a signal of continuous decrease, we should continue to expand the scale of the SWF. Also, incorrect expectations would inevitably cause a great loss of utility. To have rational expectations, we should take various economic indicators into account, which have an impact on foreign exchange earnings such as the RMB exchange rate, labor wages, and GDP growth rates. However, from the conservative point of view, we should make the appropriate precautionary savings

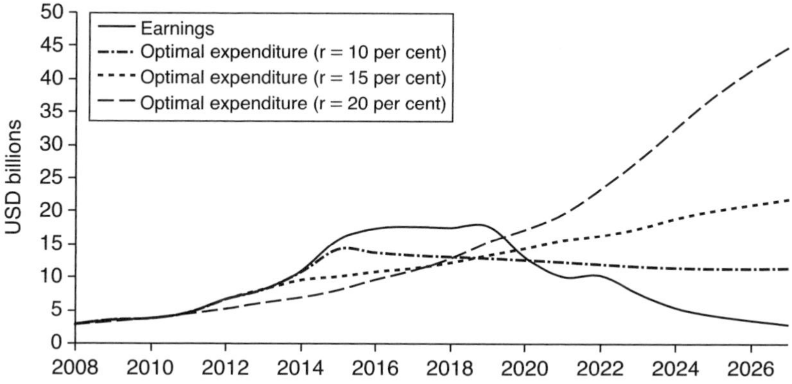

Figure 11.9 Sharp drops in foreign exchange earnings and corresponding optimal expenditure

when foreign exchange earnings are still rising, so we can cope with risks and smooth earnings even if sudden shocks affect foreign exchange earnings.

11.5 Discussion

The time preference rate also has important impacts on the optimal expenditures. In the above analysis, we take $\beta = 0.9$ and $\alpha = 0.5$. When β decreases constantly, the preference for the current period would strengthen continuously, and it would require more expenditure in the current period, and correspondingly, the size of the SWF would decrease rapidly. As shown below (when the yield reaches 20 per cent, the optimal expenditure line coincides with the foreign exchange earnings line), when β is reduced to 0.7, even in the scenario in which shocks affect the foreign exchange earnings, the preventive savings would not be attractive unless the yield reached 25 per cent or higher. This means that if current consumption was excessively preferred, it would be meaningless to increase the size of the SWF unless it had a very high yield (which is difficult to achieve). In other words, if the current preference was excessive, the SWF would have to seek investment opportunities with high-yield appeal, such as options, futures, private equities, hedge funds, etc.; otherwise, it should be downsized.

α stands for the risk aversion level. The higher the value is, the higher the degree of risk aversion is. Figure 11.11 shows the impact on the optimal expenditure when α takes on the values of 0.1, 0.5 and 0.9. It can be seen that the change of α will not have a particularly significant impact on the optimal expenditure in a large foreign exchange earnings fluctuation.

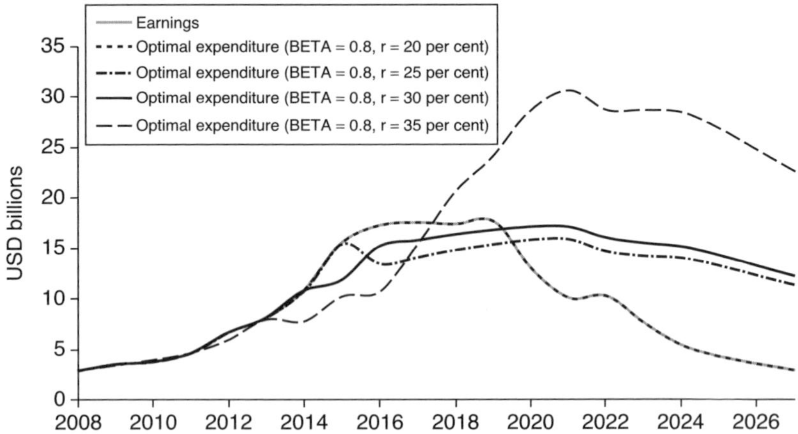

Figure 11.10 Optimal expenditure under international shocks when β = 0.7

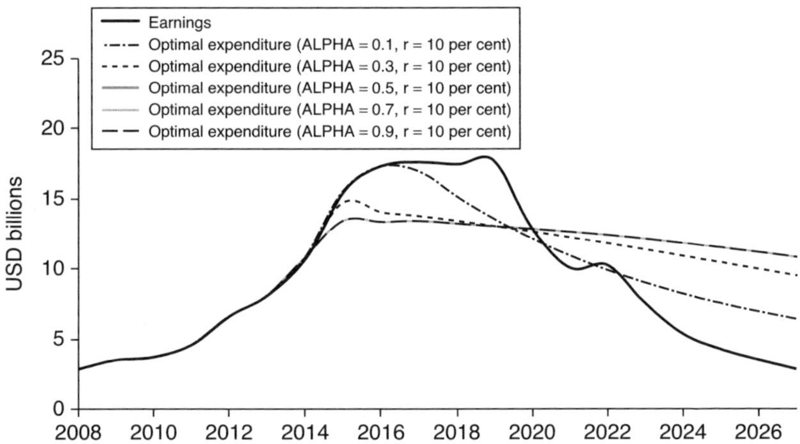

Figure 11.11 Impacts on optimal expenditure when α takes on different values

We also calculate the impact on optimal expenditure under every scenario in which alpha or beta changes. Those results are shown in Appendix A.

11.6 Strategic asset allocation

We assume that there are two investment chances for the foreign exchange assets to choose, low-risk assets and risky assets. In such a situation, how should we allocate the assets of SWF, in order to maximize the total utility of the country? To solve this problem, we have developed the following model:

$$[10]\ \max E\sum_{t=1}^{n}\beta^{t-1}u(c_t)$$

$$[11]\ s.t.\ w_{t+1}=((1-\omega)r_1+\omega r_{2t}+1)(\omega_t+y_t-c_t)$$

$$[12]\ w_t\geq 0, t=1,\text{L},n$$

where:

- $u(\cdot)$: Instantaneous utility function, assumed to be increasing, strictly concave, and differentiable, i.e. $u'>0$, $u''<0$;
- c_t: Consumption in period t;
- y_t: Foreign exchange earnings in period t;
- w_t: Total assets in period t;
- β: Time preference rate parameter, and $0<\beta<1$;
- r_1: Return rate of the low-risk assets, assumed to be consistent in all simulation periods;
- r_{2t}: Return rate of the risky assets in period t.
- $1-\omega$, ω: Ratios of the assets invested on the low-risk assets and risky assets, assumed to be consistent in the simulation periods.

We assume there are two different investment opportunities and calculate the respective optimal asset allocation for each scenario. Considering China's SWF purchases the diversification of the investment assets. To achieve this objective, it can invest in different countries or invest in different financial products.

(1) When it invests in many countries to offset single market risk, we use the MSCI World Stock Index to describe the return rate. The World Stock Index is one of the Morgan Stanley Capital International Indices, which now has 22 component markets: Australia, Austria, Belgium, Canada, Denmark, Finland, France, Germany, Greece, Hongkong, Ireland, Italy, Japan, Netherlands, New Zealand, Norway, Portugal, Singapore, Spain, Sweden, Switzerland, UK, and the USA. It is used by many individual investors, institutional investors, scholars, mediums, etc. What we use here are the yearly return rates from 1969 to 2007; the statistical characteristics of it are listed in Table 11.3.

In the process of calculation, in each given scenario of the trends of foreign exchange earnings, we did optimization calculations for $w = 0, 0.05, 0.1, \ldots, 1$. For each given w, we simulated r_{2t} 1000 times using bootstrap methods, and then obtained the relevant expected utility. The w maximizing the expected utility is supposed to be the optimal ratio of risky assets.

Table 11.3 Summary of statistical characteristics of MSCI World Stock Index

Mean	0.088388	Skewness	−0.47527
Standard error	0.026609	Range	0.669352
Median	0.127577	Minimum	−0.2783
Standard deviation	0.16403	Maximum	0.391057
Variance	0.026906	Sum	3.358762
Kurtosis	−0.32472	Count	38

According to our simulations, the optimal ratios of risky assets under different scenarios are shown in Table 11.4.

When the trend of foreign exchange earnings is upward, according to the optimization results, all earnings should be consumed, and therefore the size of the SWF should not be enlarged. And the optimal ratio for risky assets is 100 per cent. When the foreign exchange earnings tend to be stable, the optimal ratio for risky assets is 95 per cent. When the earnings decline, the optimal ratio for risky assets is 90 per cent. That means China's SWF should invest more in risky assets and pursue high return chances. In this point of this view, the CIC's investment in BlackStone could be understood as an attempt on the way to purchasing high profits. Unfortunately, it failed. But this does not mean the CIC chose the wrong investment style.

Besides, the optimization result of such high risk asset ratios is partly due to the fluctuation of earnings and characteristics of the MSCI World Stock Index. Because the fluctuation of earnings is not very large, and MSCI World Stock Index's historical data shows a relative steady return, the optimal ratio of risky assets is very high. According to our simulations, when the fluctuation of foreign exchange earnings is larger, the risky asset ratios tend to be smaller. And as for different fluctuations of return rate, we analyze this in the following section.

(2) When the SWF invests in different financial products for diversification, such as stocks, PE funds, hedge funds and so on, we use the respective financial products' return ratios to describe r_{2t}. For simplification, we assume the invested assets with higher risk will have a lower Sharpe ratio; taking related financial products' yield and fluctuation into account, we simulate r_{2t} with the following paths:

$$[13] \quad r_{2t}^1 = 10\% + 0.1 \times \varepsilon,\ r_{2t}^2 = 15\% + 0.2 \times \varepsilon,$$
$$r_{2t}^3 = 20\% + 0.3 \times \varepsilon,\ r_{2t}^4 = 30\% + 0.5\varepsilon$$

where $\varepsilon \sim N(0,1)$. We also calculated the respective optimal asset allocation which is shown in Table 11.5.

As we determined above, when the trend of foreign exchange earnings is steadily growing, the SWF should invest everything in risky assets. And

Table 11.4 Optimal weights invested in risky assets under different trends of foreign exchange earnings

Trend of foreign exchange earnings	Upward	Stable	Downward
Optimal risky asset weights	100%	95%	90%

Table 11.5 Optimal weights invested in risky assets under different trends of foreign exchange earnings and yields (in %)

Trend of foreign exchange earnings	r_2 = 10 per cent+ 0.1ε $\varepsilon \sim N(0,1)$	r_2 = 15 per cent+ 0.2ε, $\varepsilon \sim N(0,1)$	r_2 = 20 per cent+ 0.3ε, $\varepsilon \sim N(0,1)$	r_2 = 30 per cent+ 0.5ε, $\varepsilon \sim N(0,1)$
Upward	100	100	100	100
Stable	95	90	75	75
Downward	75	70	70	65

when foreign exchange earnings maintain a steady trend, the risk features of invested financial products have a large impact on the optimal ratios of risky assets invested. Generally, when the risk is low, the optimal ratio of risky assets would be relevantly high in which the foreign exchange earnings decline terribly, the optimal weight of risky assets peaks with an expected yield of 20 per cent.

According to the media the current ratio of risky assets of CIC now is about 40 per cent, which is far away from the optimal ratio. Truman (2007) reaches the same opinion. The CIC should be actively seeking high-yield investment opportunities, and increasing the ratio of risky assets.

11.7 Conclusions

We can conclude from the analysis that the optimal scale of an SWF mainly depends on the expected trend and fluctuations of the future foreign exchange earnings and yield that the SWF can get. Generally, the optimal scale of an SWF is mainly determined by the expected trend of foreign exchange earnings, and there is a positive correlation between the optimal scale of the SWF and its yield, as well as a positive correlation between the optimal scale of the SWF and the fluctuations of the foreign exchange earnings. The optimal asset allocation of the SWF is mainly determined by the expected trend of foreign exchange earnings and the yield of the fund.

The direct reason for the establishment of the CIC is that China has foreign exchange reserves much surpassing the optimal scale, the reserve assets depreciate continuously, and the opportunity cost of holding so much reserves is very high because of the depreciation of US dollars, the State Administration of Foreign Exchange being the curbstone in investment. But the essential reason lies in the growing balance of international payments and the low time preference rate, more strategically, to prevent the possibility of the foreign exchange earnings decreasing sharply. Actually, the most important and fundamental method to solve the excessive reserves problem is to minimize the payment surplus. As for the foreign exchange policy, China should increase imports, and relax and reform the existing foreign exchange management system. The current foreign exchange management system concentrates foreign exchange earnings obtained from the twin surpluses in the central bank, and also make the reserves grow sharply. But enterprises and residents cannot divert it. China should loosen control on the foreign exchange needs from the public, and further expand the civil holders of foreign exchange.

As for the CIC, it has some further strategy functions, not only to solve the problem of the excess and depreciation of foreign exchange reserves, but also to smooth the expenditures in case that shocks affect the earnings. Under the current trend in which the foreign exchange earnings grow rapidly, the optimal scale for the CIC is the gap between China's reserve scale and its optimal scale. According to Xia (2006), this gap is about 1 trillion, which means that the optimal scale of the CIC is 1 trillion. But now the scale of the CIC is 200 billion, which is far from its optimal scale. Besides, based on our analysis in this chapter, under the upward trend of foreign exchange earnings, the CIC should get a relatively high yield; otherwise it would result in losses for the country's utility. However, from the limited disclosures about the performance of SWFs around the world, the world's leading SWFs' yield is not very good. The 34-year average yields of Singapore's SWFs, Temasek and Singapore Government Investment Corporation, were 18 per cent and 9.5 per cent respectively. The 10-year average yield of the famous Norwegian Government Pension Fund is only 4.3 per cent. That means the CIC should follow Singapore's SWF investment model, learn from its investment experience, and actively seek high-yield investment opportunities. But in view of the investments that the CIC has made in recent years, seizing investment opportunities and obtaining a high yield is still a major challenge for the CIC.

According to the present performance, the CIC has not achieved its set objective. However, the future is unknown. If China's foreign exchange earnings fluctuate or shock, even with a low yield, the SWF can still play a positive role to smooth expenditures and resist the risk of fluctuations. What the CIC should do is seek high-yield investment opportunities, increase the ratio of risky assets, improve investment skills, accumulate investment experience and win in the future world.

Appendix

The impact on the optimal expenditure when α or β changes

When the foreign exchange earnings tend to be increasing stable, the optimal expenditure is to consume all earnings. In such situation, a change in beta or alpha between 0 and 1 makes no difference on the optimal expenditure, just like the Figure 11.A.1 and Figure 11.A.2.

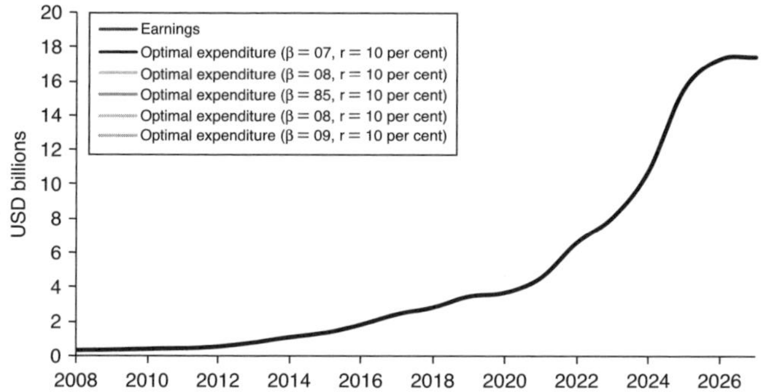

Figure 11.A.1 Optimal expenditure when β changes under the stable increasing of earnings

Note: The lines of earnings and optimal expenditure under different values of β coincide with each other.

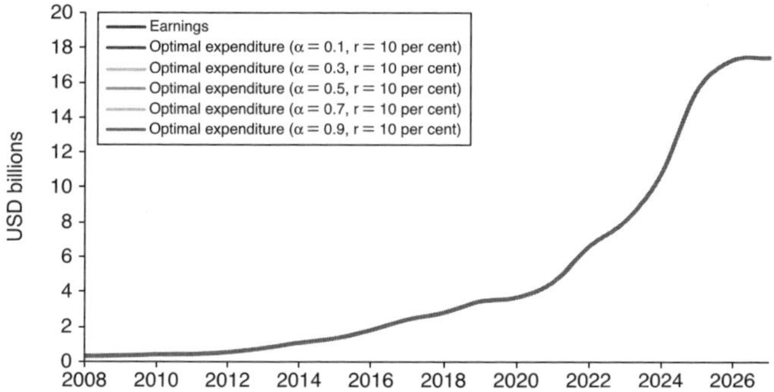

Figure 11.A.2 Optimal expenditure when β changes under the stable increasing of earnings

Note: The lines of earnings and optimal expenditure under different values of β coincide with each other.

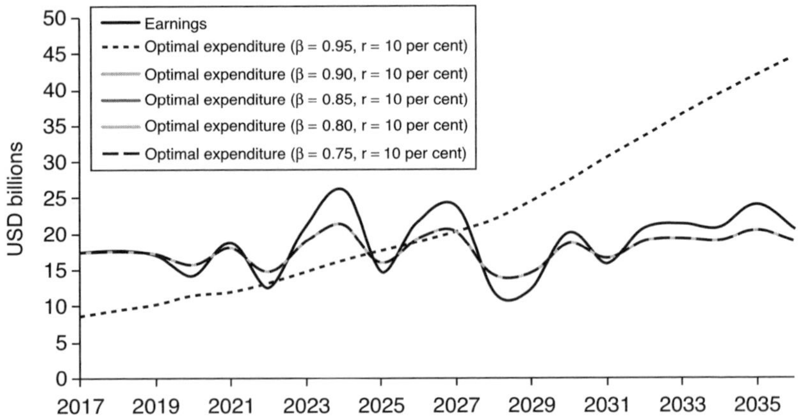

Figure 11.A.3 Optimal expenditure when β changes under low volatility of earnings

Note: The lines of optimal expenditure when β = 0.75 and 0.8 coincide with each other.

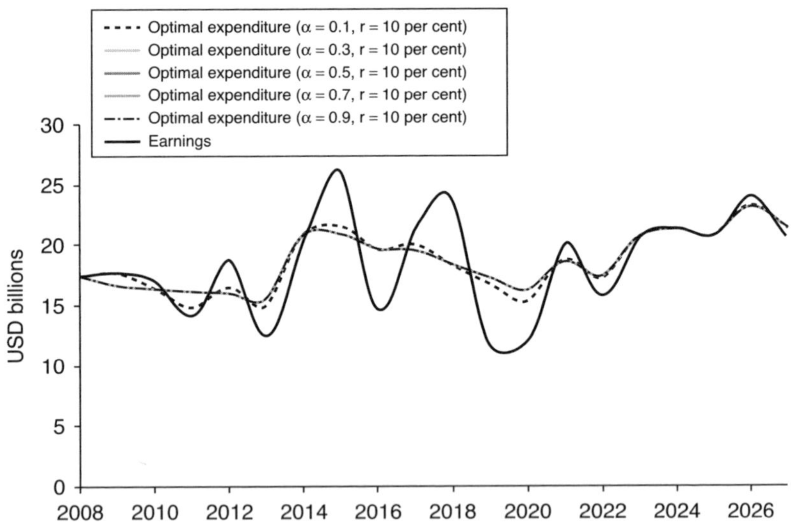

Figure 11.A.4 Optimal expenditure when α changes under low volatility of earnings

Note: The lines of optimal expenditure when α = 0.3, 0.5, 0.7 and 0.9 coincide with each other.

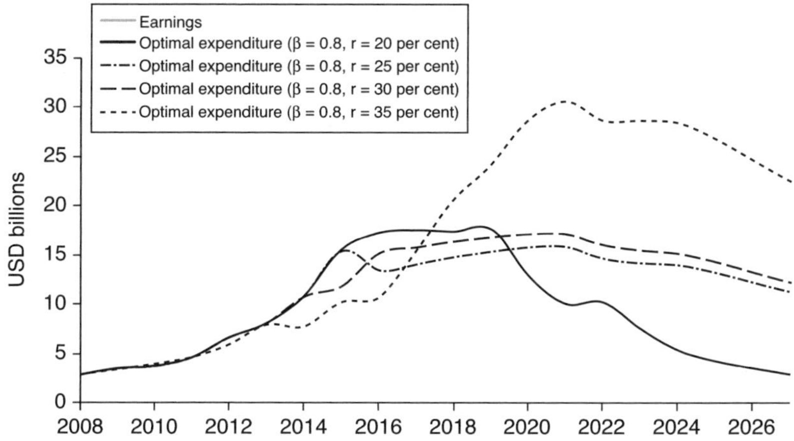

Figure 11.A.5 Optimal expenditure when β changes under shocks of earnings

Note: The lines of earnings and optimal expenditure when β = 0.8 coincide with each other.

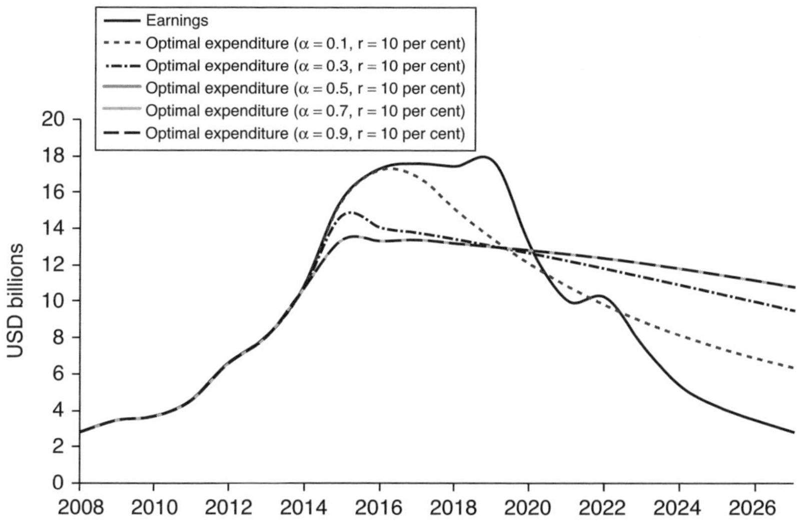

Figure 11.A.6 Optimal expenditure when α changes under shocks of earnings

Note: The lines of optimal expenditure when α = 0.5, 0.7 and 0.9 coincide with each other.

References

Arrau, P. and Claessens, S. (1992) "Commodity stabilization funds", Policy Research Working Paper Series, No. 835, the World Bank.

Boulier, J.F., Trussant, E. and Florens, D. (1995) "A dynamic model for pension fund management", In *Proceedings of the 5th AFIR International Colloquium 1*, 361–384.

Browne, S. (1997) "Survival and growth with a fixed liability: Optimal portfolios in continuous time", *Mathematics of Operations Research*, Vol. 22, 468–493.

Bohn, H. (2001) "Retirement savings in an ageing society: A case for innovative government debt management", Working Paper.

Deaton, A. (1990) "Saving in developing countries: Theory and review", Supplement, *The World Bank Economic Review*, Vol. 4, 61–96.

Deaton, A. (1991)"Saving and liquidity constraints", *Econometrica*, Vol. 59, No. 5, September, 1221–1248.

Feng, Y.F. (2006) "Scale and use of the Chinese foreign exchange reserve", *Economic Perspectives*, October.

Josa-Fombellida R. and Rincon-Zapatero, J.P. (2006) "Optimal investment decisions with a liability: The case of defined benefits pension plans", *Insurance: Mathematics and Economics*, Vol. 36, 81–98.

Josa-Fombellida R. and Rincon-Zapatero, J.P. (2004) "Optimal risk management in defined benefit stochastic pension funds", *Insurance: Mathematics and Economics*, Vol. 34, 489–503.

Tauchen, G. (1986) "Finite state Markov chain approximation to univariate and vector autoregressions", *Economic Letters*, Vol. 22, 237–55.

Truman, E.M. (2007) "The management of China's international reserves: China and a SWF scoreboard", Paper prepared for the Conference on China's Exchange Rate Policy, Peterson Institute for International Economics, 19 October 2007.

Wang, G.L. (2003), "Research of the scale of Chinese foreign exchange reserves", *Modern Finance*, Vol. 2.

Xia, B. (2006) "The optimal scale of foreign exchange reserves is 700 billion US dollars", *First Finance Daily*, 11 April 2006.

12

Foreign Exchange Reserves and Sovereign Wealth Funds: Will They Change the Global Financial Landscape?

Roland Beck and Michael Fidora

12.1 Introduction

Over the past decade, governments in emerging economies have accumulated large holdings of foreign financial assets, mostly in the form of foreign exchange reserves held and managed by central banks. More recently, sovereign wealth funds, which are special government agencies that manage sovereign wealth separate from traditional foreign exchange reserves, have grown rapidly and received considerable attention in the public debate. The policy issues arising from the emergence of sovereign wealth funds as large global financial players range from concerns over a lack of transparency and a reversal in privatisations, to risks to global financial stability. A further concern relates to the question of whether such funds might distort asset prices through non-commercially motivated purchases or sales of securities.

Against this background, this chapter first reviews the motives behind the accumulation of foreign assets by government authorities in emerging market economies, taking into account the different sources for funding such investments as well as the vehicles and instruments that governments use to channel their savings into global financial markets. It follows a factual review of trends in the accumulation of traditional foreign exchange reserves over the past decade, and takes stock of the debate on the two main related policy issues, namely the question of whether foreign exchange reserves have grown too large and to what extent shifts in the currency composition of foreign exchange reserves have taken place or are to be expected. Finally, this chapter reviews the available evidence on the accumulation of assets by sovereign wealth funds, and provides a tentative assessment of the potential impact of sovereign wealth funds on the global financial system.

While no consensus on reserve adequacy has been reached among central banks and academics, it appears that the notable rise in foreign exchange reserves among the emerging economies can be rationalised to some extent in the case of oil exporting countries in view of intergenerational equity considerations. In the case of reserve growth which is mainly a reflection of inflexible exchange rate regimes among countries in Asia, the economic rationale for large holdings of foreign assets appears less clear-cut.

The currency composition of global foreign exchange reserves has remained relatively stable over the past decade, reflecting mostly liquidity considerations by central banks. If sovereign wealth funds, however, continue to grow rapidly, official portfolios might reduce their bias towards the major reserve currencies, the US dollar and the euro. As a result, more capital flows "downhill" from rich to less wealthy economies. The potential implications of a rebalancing of international capital flows for stock prices, interest rates and exchange rates remain, however, uncertain. Moreover, the broader implications of the rise in foreign exchange reserves and assets held by sovereign wealth funds for the global financial landscape are difficult to predict. More transparency in this area would help in the study of possible global repercussions in this context and would also contribute to global financial stability.

12.2 Sources and motives for the accumulation of sovereign foreign assets

Global foreign exchange reserves and other government-owned financial assets have over the last decade grown at a remarkable pace, and are likely to exceed USD 10,000 billion today. Traditionally, the motives for holding foreign exchange reserves have been mainly rationalised with the transaction needs of the central bank. Such transaction needs encompass temporary import financing, foreign exchange interventions or the balancing of capital outflows. A related argument suggests that an insurance motive has led to the accumulation of international reserves, reflecting the desire of governments for self-insurance against future sudden stops of capital inflows, in case of which reserves can be used to help domestic firms and thus avoid a financial crisis. The financial crises in Asia and Latin America in the 1990s have indeed reaffirmed the importance of such transaction and precautionary motives for holding foreign exchange reserves. In fact, emerging economies in Asia only started to accumulate sizeable foreign exchange reserves following the sudden stop in 1997 that caused massive capital outflows.

More recently, the academic literature has explained the massive reserve build-up with mercantilist motives. According to this view, the accumulation of foreign exchange reserves is the result of managed exchange rate regimes of countries that target the international competitiveness of the exchange rate in order to promote export-led growth. The empirical literature tends, however, to find that traditional transaction and insurance motives have historically outweighed the mercantilist motive. This is perhaps not surprising given that financial crises have been a recurring event in recent years. Rothenberg and Warnock (2006) find that between 1995 and 2003 emerging economies experienced financial crises, either in the form of sudden stops of capital inflows or massive capital flight of domestic investors, in at least 36 instances. Even more recently, some emerging markets have been subject to capital outflows and reserve losses during the ongoing global financial crisis.

The accumulation of large foreign asset holdings by emerging economies mainly originates in two sources, namely net receipts of foreign exchange through trade and capital inflows. From a balance-of-payment perspective, current account surpluses – to the extent that they are not absorbed by private capital outflows – translate into fiscal surpluses that are invested abroad. In fact, many emerging economies have sharply improved their government balances during the recent years of unprecedented growth in foreign exchange reserves, suggesting that a substantial part of the fiscal gains from large trade surpluses in many emerging economies have been channelled into global financial markets through official capital outflows in the form of foreign exchange reserves or sovereign wealth funds.

One group of countries that have built up large sovereign foreign asset holdings are resource-rich economies which in recent years have benefited from high oil and other commodity prices and have thus accumulated foreign assets at a remarkable pace, well above that of non-commodity exporting emerging economies (see Table 12.1). In these countries, foreign assets partly also serve the purpose of stabilising government and export revenues which would otherwise mirror the volatility of oil and commodity prices. A second motive for accumulating foreign assets in resource-rich countries is the desire to save for future generations as natural resources are non-renewable and will be exhausted at some point.

A second group of countries, most notably in Asia, have been accumulating foreign assets through receipts from trade surpluses that are not directly

Table 12.1 Foreign exchange reserves of commodity exporters and exchange rate peggers

	in USD billion	in per cent of GDP
All emerging economies	5860	29
Commodity exporters	1719	38
Non-commodity exporters	4141	27
Fixed exchage rate regimne	2990	42
Floating exchange rate regime	2870	28

Note: Percentages of GDP are calculated as unweighted averages of individual countries.

Source: International Monetary Fund

linked to the recent hike in commodity prices, but rather to their choice of exchange rate regime. Many of these countries had experienced a strong depreciation of their currencies during the financial crises in the late 1990s, and subsequently re-pegged their currencies – de jure or de facto – to the US dollar. At the beginning of their economic recovery in the aftermath of the crises this facilitated the pursuit of policies aimed at promoting export-led growth. Savings rates in this group of countries appear large by international and historical standards.

Traditionally, governments have accumulated foreign assets mostly as official foreign exchange reserves due to transaction motives of central banks which require reserve portfolios of highly liquid foreign securities. Some governments, however, have started using sovereign wealth funds to manage their foreign investments more and more intensively over the years. Most notably, many commodity-exporters – also in mature economies – have established sovereign wealth funds or similar investment vehicles over the past 50 years. Keeping in mind the considerable uncertainty about the size of sovereign wealth fund assets, governments of commodity exporting economies appear to hold at least half of their foreign assets in sovereign wealth funds. This may to some extent reflect the fact that the transaction motive for holding foreign assets is dominated by the investment motive, as the need to save for future generations appears to have gained importance relative to macroeconomic stabilisation objectives. Countries with inflexible exchange rate regimes have until recently managed their foreign assets within the central banks' foreign exchange reserves due to the importance of transaction motives in the context of balance-of-payment stabilisation and a history of financial crises. Several of these countries, however, have also established sovereign wealth funds to manage part of their foreign assets indicating that authorities in these countries feel they have accumulated foreign assets in excess of the liquidity needed for transaction purposes or as insurance against sudden stops in capital flows.

12.3 The rise in foreign exchange reserves

12.3.1 Recent trends in foreign exchange reserve growth

Global foreign exchange reserves have risen significantly over the past decade, from around USD 1,600 billion in 1999 to more than USD 7,000 billion as of end-June 2008. During the same period, crude oil prices have risen ten-fold from around USD 12 per barrel to more than USD 120 per barrel in end-June 2008, though oil prices have declined again recently. However, while for a number of countries higher revenues from oil and other commodities are the main reason for the sharp increase in reserve accumulation, this is not the case for other emerging markets.

Disaggregating the rise in foreign exchange reserves by country groups shows that the increase in reserves has taken place almost entirely in emerging economies rather than advanced economies, with the exception of Japan, as reserves have risen from below USD 1,000 billion in 1999 to around USD 5,500 billion in June 2008. At the same time, the increase of foreign exchange reserves of emerging economies has not been limited to commodity exporting countries. To the contrary, oil exporting countries account, in absolute US dollar terms, only for a relatively small share in total reserves held by emerging economies.

In view of the large current account surpluses in oil exporting countries, this observation appears surprising at first since one would expect that authorities in these countries have accumulated foreign exchange reserves. To some extent, however, relatively moderate growth of foreign exchange reserves among oil exporting economies can be attributed to the accumulation of foreign assets in sovereign wealth funds, which are not included under the category of foreign reserves, and which will be reviewed later in this chapter.

At the level of individual countries, growth in foreign exchange reserves over the past decade has been mainly accounted for by a few countries, namely China, Japan and Russia which together account for more than 70 percent of the rise in foreign exchange reserves since 1999 (see Table 12.2). This implies that the degree of concentration of holdings of foreign exchange reserves has increased substantially over the past couple of years. In particular, the share of China's foreign exchange reserve holdings in global foreign exchange reserves has risen from around 9 percent in 1999 to around 31 percent in June 2008.

12.3.2 The debate on optimal reserve levels

The notable rise in foreign exchange reserves has also raised the question of whether foreign exchange reserves among emerging market economies have grown too large from a normative perspective. Most traditional rules

Table 12.2 The largest foreign exchange reserve accumulators

	Mar 1999 (USD billion)	**Jun 2008 (USD billion)**	**Change (USD billion)**	**Change (in %)**
1. China , P.R. Mainland	147	1757	1610	1098
2. Japan	211	974	762	361
3. Russia	7	554	547	8200
4. India	30	302	273	924
5. Taiwan	93	290	197	212
6. Brazil	31	200	169	540
7. Algeria	5	133	128	2490
8. Thailand	29	103	74	257
9. Mexico	31	93	62	202
10. Turkey	21	76	54	256

Note: June 2008 against March 1999.

Source: International Monetary Fund

of thumb for reserve adequacy suggest that foreign exchange reserve holdings have grown beyond what may be required for transactions needs. For example, foreign exchange reserves of emerging and developing economies have risen substantially beyond the amount needed to cover three months of imports or 100 percent of short-term debt or even the sum of the two (see Table 12.3), which are rules often used to assess reserve adequacy. Another benchmark that has been suggested to judge the adequacy of reserves is the stock of broad money supply since in the extreme, the demand for foreign currency during a "sudden flight" could amount to the whole domestic money supply. Applying this benchmark, foreign exchange reserves in emerging economies do not seem overly large, as indicated in Table 12.3.

Such computations should, however, be treated with caution. A more systematic assessment of reserve adequacy requires indeed a careful analysis of the costs and benefits associated with the holding of foreign exchange reserves. Large holdings of foreign exchange reserves can create sizable costs for the respective economies. From a public sector perspective, the difference between the interest rate paid on domestic government bonds and the return on foreign exchange reserves is often considered as a yardstick for the fiscal costs of holding reserves. Such costs typically arise in the balance sheet of the respective central bank that is accumulating foreign assets through sterilised interventions, i.e. through purchases of foreign assets and concomitant sales of domestic government bonds. From a macroeconomic perspective, however, the cost of holding reserves originates in the spread between the interest on private short-term external borrowing and the return on foreign assets. Some observers have also suggested measuring the social costs of holding reserves in terms of opportunity cost of not investing in the domestic economy. These costs need to be weighed against the benefits of holding foreign exchange reserves. One way of accounting for these benefits is to consider only reserves in excess of what may be needed for transaction purposes. Approximating reserves needed for balance-of-payment purposes with traditional rules of thumb such as the three-months-of-imports rule

Table 12.3 Reserve holdings and indicators of reserve adequacy in developing countries

	Actual reserve level	**Benchmark levels**		
	As of end-2007	**3 months of imports**	**100% short-term debt**	**100% broad money**
All emerging markets	4602	1274	608	12250
China	1531	257	191	4902
Russia	445	70	54	576

Source: International Monetary Fund

and considering alternative assumptions about the relevant interest rate spread suggests that the costs of holding reserves have grown to up to 1.5% of GDP in the developing countries (Rodrik 2006).

12.3.3 Foreign exchange reserve accumulation on global capital flows

A final issue is what the implications from the rapid reserve accumulation of emerging markets are for advanced economies, and in particular for the United States and the euro area, where a large part of the reserves are invested. In fact, some have argued that under the current system of fixed exchange rate of several emerging economies, emerging market central banks have increasingly contributed to the financing of the US current account deficit and exceptionally low real interest rates by investing the bulk of their foreign exchange reserves in low-yielding US government bonds. According to this line of reasoning, countries with managed exchange rates against the US dollar find it difficult to diversify their reserve portfolios as such changes would be inconsistent with their overall exchange rate policy framework. Others have stressed that the rise in reserves may offer scope for "reserve diversification". The available empirical evidence suggests though that the currency composition of global foreign exchange reserves has, following a gradual rise in the share of the euro during the first years following European Monetary Union, remained relatively stable over the past couple of years.

The currency composition of foreign exchange reserves has remained relatively stable during the rise in reserves in developing countries, according to the IMF data on the Currency Composition of Global Foreign Exchange Reserves (COFER) which covers, however, only around two thirds of global foreign exchange reserves (see Table 12.4). To some extent, the gradual decline in the share of the US dollar and the rise in the share of the euro are reflecting valuation effects, as shown when measuring the currency shares at constant exchange rates (see Table 12.4). However, the fact that the respective central banks appear to not perfectly rebalance their reserve portfolios as global exchange rate configurations change could also be interpreted as evidence of passive reserve diversification. In addition, the gradual increase in the use of the euro – in particular over the first few years of European Economic and Monetary Union – may reflect the establishment of a credible, stability-oriented monetary policy and improvements in the liquidity of euro area capital markets.

Moreover, the above patterns in the currency composition of foreign exchange reserves may also reflect the declining importance of transaction motives in central bank reserve management, as many emerging market economies may have accumulated reserve levels in excess of precautionary levels. Given that such transaction motives typically appear to favour the use of the US dollar as a reserve currency, their declining relevance in reserve management can be interpreted as one possible reason for the increase in

Table 12.4 Currency shares in global foreign exchange reserves (in %)

		2001	2003	2005	2007
At current exchange rates	USD	72	66	67	64
	EUR	19	25	24	26
	JPY	5	4	4	3
	GBP	3	3	4	5
	Other	2	2	2	2
At constant exchange rates	USD	61	62	61	63
	EUR	29	29	29	28
	JPY	5	4	4	3
	GBP	3	3	4	5
	Other	1	2	2	2

Source: International Monetary Fund

the share of the euro in the early 2000s. The relative stability of the share of the euro in recent years could reflect a convergence towards minimum variance portfolios that attribute a large weight to the anchor currency.

12.4 The rise of sovereign wealth funds

12.4.1 Sovereign wealth funds in global financial markets

Sovereign wealth funds, broadly defined as public investment agencies which manage part of the foreign assets of governments, have grown rapidly in recent years and have attracted considerable public attention. Although there exists no commonly accepted definition of sovereign wealth funds, three elements can be identified that are common to such funds. First, sovereign wealth funds are state-owned. Second, sovereign wealth funds have no or only very limited explicit liabilities and, third, sovereign wealth funds are managed separately from official foreign exchange reserves. In addition, most sovereign wealth funds share certain characteristics that originate in the specific nature of sovereign wealth funds. For example, the lack of explicit liabilities (or the stretched-out maturity of liabilities) favours the pursuit of long-term investment strategies, as implemented by most sovereign wealth funds.[1] In this respect, sovereign wealth funds differ from sovereign pension funds that operate subject to explicit liabilities and a continuous stream of fixed payments, making sovereign wealth funds more similar to private mutual funds.[2] Second, the absence of explicit liabilities also has a bearing on the willingness to take risk, as standard portfolio theory predicts a higher share of fixed income securities for funds that are subject to recurring payments. Finally, most sovereign wealth funds appear to have substantial exposure to foreign investments or are even entirely invested in foreign assets.

The largest sovereign wealth funds have more assets under management than the world's biggest hedge funds, though they continue to command significantly less market exposure than the largest global asset managers. As regards the relative size of sovereign wealth funds, total assets are relatively small compared with the more than USD 50,000 billion managed by the private asset management industry. However, the largest sovereign wealth funds already now manage portfolios that are in the order of magnitude of the biggest private investment companies and could in the future – to the extent that external surpluses are increasingly accumulated in sovereign wealth funds or that existing reserves are shifted into such funds – even exceed the largest private investment managers' portfolios.

Oil exporters, mostly from the Middle East, but also Norway's Government Pension Fund, are estimated to account for the largest part of total assets managed by sovereign wealth funds, probably between USD 1,200 and 2,200 billion, although this estimate is subject to large uncertainty (see Table 12.5). A smaller fraction, around USD 600 billion, is accounted for by Asian emerging economies, most notably Singapore, which has been running sovereign

Table 12.5 The World's largest sovereign wealth funds (in USD billion)

Country	Fund	Assets in USD billion	Foreign	Equity
Oil exporters		**1240–2220**		
UAE	Abu Dhabi Investment Council	400–800	high	high
Norway	Government Pension Fund – Global	373	high	medium
Saudi Arabia	SAMA	300	high	low
Kuwait	Kuwait Investment Authority	213	high	high
UAE	Investment Corporation of Dubai	20–80	high	high
Qatar	Qatar Investment Authority	20–60	high	high
Libya	Libyan Investment Authority	20–60	high	high
Brunei	Brunei Investment Agency	10–50	high	high
Norway	Government Pension Fund – Norway	~20	low	medium
Russia	National Welfare Fund	~24	high	high
Kazakhstan	National Oil Fund	22	high	low
Malaysia	Khazanah Nasional Berhad	~18	low	high
East Asia		**~585**		
China	China Investment Corporation	~200	high	high
Singapore	Government Investment Corporation	~130	high	high

Continued

Table 12.5 Continued

Country	Fund	Assets in USD billion	Foreign	Equity
Hong Kong	Exchange Fund Investment Portfolio	~112	high	low
Singapore	Temasek Holdings	~108	medium	high
Korea	Korea Investment Corporation	~20	high	high
Taiwan	National Stabilisation Fund	~15	low	high
Others		**~138**		
Australia	Government Future Fund	~49	medium	medium
United States	Alaska Permanent Fund	~38	medium	medium
United States	Permanent University Fund	~20	medium	medium
United States	New Mexico State Investment	~16	medium	medium
Canada	Alberta Heritage Savings Trust Fund	~15	medium	medium
TOTAL		1963-2943		

Source: Beck and Fidora (2008)

Table 12.6 Major sovereign wealth fund investments 2007–2008 (in USD billion)

Sovereign wealth fund	Acquired company	Transaction value (in USD bn)	Transaction value (in % of firm value)
GIC of Singapore	UDS	9.8	8.6
Abu Dhabi Investment Council	Citigroup	7.6	4.9
GIC of Singapore	Citigroup	6.9	4.4
Investment Corporation of Dubai	MGM Mirage	5.1	9.5
China Investment Company	Morgan Stanley	5.0	9.9
Temasek(Singapore)	Merrill Lynch	5.0	11.3
Qatar Investment Authority	Barclays	4.0	8.0
Qatar Investment Authority	Sainsbury	3.7	25.0
KIA (Kuwait)	Merrill Lynch	3.4	7.0
China Development Bank	Barclays	3.0	3.1
Others		42.1	

Source: Beck and Fidora (2008)

wealth funds since the 1970s. But mature economies other than Norway have set up sovereign wealth funds, mostly to save receipts from the exploitation of natural resources. In sum, a plausible estimate of total assets managed by sovereign wealth funds ranges from USD 2,000 to 3,000 billion.

Despite the scarce information available, two main traits of the portfolio composition of sovereign wealth funds can be identified. First, the largest part of sovereign wealth funds' holdings is accounted for by foreign investment, although some sovereign wealth funds restrict their portfolio to domestic assets. Second, the share of risky assets in sovereign wealth funds' portfolios appears to be substantial. In fact, sovereign wealth funds have over recent years acquired significant shares in many large stock corporations in advanced economies, in particular in the financial sector (Table 12.6). Overall, the share of sovereign wealth funds' equity investments exceeds in most likelihood one half of the total assets. In addition, available data on some of the more transparent funds, such as Singapore's Temasek and US endowment funds, as well as anecdotal evidence on Middle East oil exporters' investment projects, indicate that private equity, real estate and emerging market investments account for a significant part of at least some sovereign wealth fund portfolios. Hence, the information available on the world's largest sovereign wealth funds suggests that, with respect to investment style, these differ substantially from traditional foreign exchange reserves and are instead comparable to private asset managers, in particular mutual funds.

12.4.2 Sovereign wealth funds and global capital flows

An important issue arising from these considerations is whether a gradual shift of official portfolios away from traditional foreign exchange reserves to more return-oriented and diversified sovereign wealth funds might have an impact on global capital flows. While the magnitude of future capital flows is difficult to quantify, the rise of sovereign wealth funds could potentially generate large net capital flows between major regions of the global economy. In order to gauge the impact of sovereign wealth funds on global financial markets, it is useful to consider how an increasing accumulation of assets in sovereign wealth funds, rather than in traditional foreign exchange reserve portfolios, could change the pattern of global capital flows.

Assuming, by way of illustration, that authorities in emerging economies were to shift foreign exchange reserves in excess of the two oft-cited benchmark levels reviewed above (roughly USD 3,000 billion) to sovereign wealth funds, net capital flows would indeed be substantial. A diversification of such magnitude according to the capitalisation of regional capital markets would generate sizeable outflows out of US and euro area bond markets which would in most likelihood only partly be offset by inflows into advanced economies' equity markets (see Table 12.7). In such a scenario, the main counterparts of these net outflows from the euro area and the United States would be net inflows to other dollar-block economies but notably also emerging economies, reflecting the relatively larger weight of these countries in global capital markets compared with their negligible role as reserve currencies.

Major shifts in the composition of sovereign portfolios are, however, likely to only take place gradually over a longer horizon. Rapid diversification across currencies may for example be incompatible with some countries' macroeconomic and exchange rate policies, as large shifts out of US dollars could trigger an appreciation of domestic currencies against the US dollar, requiring increased intervention. In addition, liquidity considerations may still be of relevance for some sovereign wealth funds. In particular funds that have been established for macroeconomic stabilisation objectives could continue to invest in highly liquid instruments and hence remain overweight in US dollar and euro bonds.

12.4.3 The impact on exchange rates and asset prices

A direct impact on asset prices or exchange rates through price pressures triggered by sovereign wealth fund demand (e.g. equities) or supply (e.g. government bonds) is only conceivable if the demand curve in the respective markets is downward-sloping. While there is some empirical evidence for price pressures in certain markets, it remains controversial how persistent such effects are. In the earlier literature on price pressures, researchers have documented individual stock price reactions to large block trades.[3] However, these price reactions may also reflect new information about the respective stocks. Therefore, subsequent "event studies" have examined the price impact of stock inclusions into major stock market indices and found significant price pressure effects in an environment where information effects probably play almost no role.[4] Several other earlier studies, however, find little support for the price-pressure hypothesis and a downward-sloping demand curve.[5] More recently, more convincing support for downward-sloping demand curves for stocks in a case which appears unambiguously free of information has been provided by Kaul, Mehrotra and Morck (2000).

Table 12.7 Simulation of net capital flows for reallocation of reserves towards sovereign wealth funds (in USD billions)

	US	Euro area	Japan	UK	Others	Total
Stock market	538	183	115	93	281	1209
Bond market	–1073	–413	210	–100	167	–1209
Total	–534	–230	325	–7	447	

Source: Beck and Fidora (2008)

Outside the framework of event studies Levin and Wright (2006) examine downward-sloping demand curves for stocks econometrically. In addition, Froot, O'Connell and Seasholes (2001) find that portfolio inflows have positive forecasting power for future equity returns, in particular in the emerging markets.

Changes in government bond yields and the yield curve have traditionally been linked to the announcement of macroeconomic news.[6] Warnock and Warnock (2006) provide econometric evidence for foreign official purchases of US government bonds having a large and significant impact on US bond yields. Krishnamurthy and Vissing-Jorgensen (2007) study a case in which the aggregate demand curve for the convenience provided by Treasury debt (e.g. through high liquidity) is downward-sloping. Changes in the supply of Treasury debt are used to trace out the demand for convenience. Interestingly, disaggregated estimates of convenience demand suggest that the demand for Treasury debt from foreign official holders (i.e. central banks) is very inelastic, consistent with the view that a stable demand for US assets has helped finance the US current account deficit. A structural decrease of demand for US government bonds due to the rise of sovereign wealth funds would hence prompt US investors to buy these securities, but at a lower price, implying a rise in US government bond yields. Most empirical estimates on the yield impact of US Treasury buying by foreign central banks range from around 20 to 200 basis points (see Table 12.8).

In foreign exchange markets, the early portfolio balance literature has motivated downward-sloping demand curves by postulating imperfect substitutability between domestic and foreign bonds. However, the traditional portfolio balance approach enjoyed little empirical support. The resilience of foreign exchange markets is also at the core of the literature on central bank interventions. While the conceptual case for the effectiveness of sterilised interventions has remained controversial, recent empirical studies do provide evidence for an exchange rate effect of such interventions. Besides the traditional portfolio effect, central bank intervention may also have an impact on exchange rates as it reveals information about future monetary policy through a "signalling effect". Therefore, studies on central bank interventions have remained ambiguous about the nature of the exchange rate effect. The surge in gross cross-border capital flows since the 1990s has triggered renewed interest in the portfolio channel for exchange rates.[7] At the same time, the market microstructure literature has highlighted that currency order flows are strongly correlated with exchange rate returns. Finally, recent event studies on foreign exchange markets also find indications for price effects. Hau, Massa and Peress (2005) show that a redefinition of the MSCI international equity index – which has implied large changes in the representation of different countries – led to strong exogenous equity flows by index funds and an appreciation of the respective exchange rates.

Table 12.8 The effect of foreign central bank buying on US Treasury yields (in basis points)

Source	Estimated reduction
Babque de France (2005)	125
Bernanke et al. (2004)	50–100
BIS (2006)	~0
Goldman Sachs (2004)	40
IXIS (2005)	75
JP Morgan (2005)	30–50
Krishnamurthy and Vissing-Jorgensen (2007)	20–55
Merrill Lynch (2005)	30
Morgan Stanley (2005)	100–150
PIMCO (2005)	100
Roubini and Setser (2005)	200
Truman (2005)	75
Vanguard Group (2005)	~0
Warnock and Warnock (2006)	90

Source: European Central Bank (2006)

12.4.4 A case study on price pressure: Norway's Government Pension Fund

Norway's Ministry of Finance has established Ethical Guidelines that allow for the exclusion of a stock from the fund's portfolio based on non-economic considerations. Upon an Advisory Council's recommendation, the Ministry of Finance can exclude a particular company's stocks from the Fund's investment universe and instruct the central bank to divest from the respective company within a deadline of, on average, around two months. Once the stocks have been excluded from the Fund's portfolio the exclusion is announced to the public.

The exclusion of securities from the Fund's investment universe constitutes a natural experiment that is particularly well-suited for analysing the potential impact of the investment behaviour of sovereign wealth funds for two reasons: first, the exclusion is based on purely non-economic criteria. Hence, the exclusion is unlikely to reflect the Fund's expectations or private information on future performance. Second, the timing and modalities of the exclusion allow for distinguishing two potential channels through which the exclusion might have an impact on the stocks returns: (i) during the period within which the central bank divests from a particular stock abnormal returns on the company's stocks would reflect the pure impact of the decrease in demand; (ii) on the day of the public announcement of the exclusion abnormal returns can be interpreted as a signalling impact due to the reaction of other market participants to the announcement.

Abnormal returns are obtained from an augmented capital asset pricing model that relates the return of a given equity (r) to two explanatory factors: (i) the return of a domestic equity index *RM*, capturing financial market developments in the economy, and (ii) the return of a sector-specific index *RS*, capturing sector-specific developments.[8]

$$r_t = \alpha + \beta^M R_t^M + \beta^s R_t^s + \epsilon_t$$

From this equation parameter estimates are obtained for a sample of daily observations ranging from 2000 up to the date of exclusion, and expected returns *E*(*r*) are calculated for the period during which a particular equity was being removed from the Fund's portfolio as well as for the day on which the exclusion was revealed to the public. In a second step, it can be tested (i) whether the realised cumulated return over the period during which the equity was being excluded is significantly different from the expected cumulated return based on the econometric model; and (ii) whether the realised return on the day on which the exclusion was made public is significantly different from the expected return based on the econometric model.[9]

Table 12.9 reports abnormal returns during the divestment period for the 20 stocks that have been excluded during 2005–06. Overall the results indicate no significant effect of the Fund's divestment on the performance of the analysed stocks. Out of the 20 stocks, only 10 underperformed their respective benchmarks during the divestment period and only 9 stocks recorded a negative excess return on the day the exclusion was made public. None of the negative excess returns is statistically significant. Hence, there is no evidence for a financial market impact of non-economically motivated large-scale transactions by Norway's sovereign wealth fund.

12.5 Concluding remarks

Global foreign exchange reserves and foreign assets managed by sovereign wealth funds have risen substantially over the past decade as authorities in emerging markets have accumulated external assets for various reasons. Most prominently, authorities in the emerging markets have increased their holdings of foreign exchange reserves as insurance against sudden stops in capital flows. During the current turmoil in the financial markets, these high levels of reserves have reduced the vulnerability of these countries to shifts in global risk aversion.

In most oil exporting countries, foreign assets have been accumulated mainly in sovereign wealth funds as intergenerational equity considerations in the context of non-renewable resources have gained importance relative to macroeconomic stabilisation objectives. The large holders of foreign exchange reserves in Asia – where the reserve build-up is to a large extent a reflection of inflexible exchange rate regimes – have also recently started to set up sovereign wealth funds in order to improve the returns on their

Table 12.9 Stock performance during divestment period and upon announcement of exclusion

	Divestment period				Anouncement day			
	Equity return	Bench-mark return	Excess return	p-value	Equity return	Bench-mark return	Excess return	p-value
Alliant Techsystems Inc.	9.9	4.4	5.5	0.65	0.2	−0.2	0.3	0.86
BAE Systems Plc	10.3	12.9	−2.6	0.76	2.6	2.4	0.1	0.93
Boeing Co.	3.4	5.6	−2.2	0.83	0.1	0.2	−0.1	0.99
DRD Gold Ltd.	-16.0	10.5	-26.4	0.37	2.3	1.6	0.7	0.91
EADS Co.	6.3	9.7	−3.4	0.81	0.2	2.3	−2.1	0.32
Finmeccanica Sp. A.	−1.2	3.9	−5.1	0.67	0.3	−0.1	0.5	0.77
Freeport McMoRan Copper & Gold Inc.	−0.4	1.4	−1.8	0.92	−0.6	0.9	−1.5	0.58
General Dynamics Corp.	4.1	2.8	1.3	0.89	0.2	−0.3	0.5	0.73
Honeywell International Corp.	3.8	4.4	−0.6	0.96	0.0	−0.1	0.1	0.98
Kerr McGee Corp.	−4.7	2.7	−7.4	0.36	−1.2	0.5	−1.7	0.49
L3 Communications Holdings Inc.	6.5	5.1	1.3	0.93	−0.3	0.0	−0.3	0.90
Lockheed Martin Corp.	−3.0	3.4	−6.4	0.56	−0.7	−0.3	−0.4	0.83
Northrop Grumann Corp.	11.7	4.3	7.4	0.54	−0.8	0.0	−0.8	0.72
Poongsan Corp.	8.0	3.8	4.2	0.80	−1.5	0.0	−1.5	0.53
Raytheon Co.	0.0	1.4	−1.4	0.92	0.3	−0.3	0.7	0.77
Safran S.A.	5.2	2.0	3.3	0.88	1.4	−0.2	1.5	0.58
Thales S.A.	10.0	7.5	2.4	0.86	0.9	1.7	−0.7	0.72
United Technologies Corp.	11.2	6.8	4.3	0.69	1.1	0.9	0.2	0.90
Wal-Mart de Mexico S.A.	1.0	−2.6	3.6	0.75	−0.1	1.1	−1.2	0.47
Wal-Mart Stores Inc.	−1.3	−13.2	11.8	0.17	2.1	3.3	−1.2	0.50

Notes: P-values below 10%, 5% and 1% indicate statistically significant excess returns at the 10%, 5% and 1% levels, respectively.

Source: Beck and Fidora (2008)

reserve portfolios. These transfers of traditional foreign exchange reserves into national investment vehicles can be interpreted as an indication of possibly too large reserve holdings in these countries.

Given their systemic relevance, sovereign wealth funds have received considerable attention also at several international organisations and policy fora, including the International Monetary Fund and the G7, which led to the establishment of an International Working Group on Sovereign

Wealth Funds comprised of 23 investor countries as well as permanent observers including the Organisation for Economic Co-operation and Development (OECD) and the World Bank. In late 2008 the International Working Group, in consultation with representatives from mature economies and the IMF, agreed on a set of 24 Generally Accepted Practices and Principles for Sovereign Wealth Funds that are intended to guide the appropriate governance and accountability arrangements, as well as the conduct of appropriate investment practices by sovereign wealth funds. Likewise the OECD is working on issues relating to the treatment of sovereign wealth funds in capital recipient countries. These multilateral efforts aim at ensuring efficient asset management of sovereign wealth funds based on purely financial considerations, sound corporate governance standards and transparent and open capital markets, in order to promote the potentially beneficial role of sovereign wealth funds in global financial markets. Thus, sovereign wealth funds could contribute to a widening of the long-term investor base for non-government securities, including corporate bonds, private equity, emerging market assets, real estate and commodities, and more efficient sharing and diversification of risk at the global level.

As central banks and sovereign wealth funds have become large market participants in the global financial system, it is of particular importance that transparency is raised in this area. While the size of global foreign exchange reserves is public information, details about their composition is available only for around two thirds of global reserves. In the case of sovereign wealth funds, their size and composition is subject to considerable uncertainty. Improvements in this area would make an important contribution to the transparency of global financial markets.

Notes

1. The lack of explicit liabilities is not a necessary condition for financial institutions to have a long-term investment horizon. For example, traditional banks often transform short-term liabilities into long-term assets. Nevertheless, from a balance sheet perspective, a low degree of short-term liabilities favours the pursuit of long-term strategies.
2. Pension funds often match their fixed liabilities that imply a stream of future payments with investments into fixed coupon-bearing bonds.
3. See Scholes (1972), Holthausen, Leftwich and Mayers (1984) and Mikkelson and Partch (1985).
4. See Harris and Gurel (1986) as well as Shleifer (1986).
5. See Hess and Frost (1982), Jain (1987) and Kalay and Shirnrat (1987).
6. See Fleming and Remolona (1997, 1999) and Piazzesi (2003).
7. See Froot and Ramadorai (2004).
8. Sectoral and country indices are taken from Standard and Poor's.

9. Assuming identically and independently normally distributed residuals in equation [1], i.e. $\varepsilon_t \sim N(0,\sigma^2)$, excess returns over the divestment period and on the day of publication of the exclusion follow a normal distribution.

References

Beck, Roland and Michael Fidora (2008) "The Impact of Sovereign Wealth Funds on Global Financial Markets", *Review of European Economic Policy*, 43(6), 349–358.

European Central Bank (2006) "The Accumulation of Foreign Reserves", ECB Occasional Paper No. 43.

Fleming, Michael J. and Eli M. Remolona (1997) "What Moves the Bond Market?", *Federal Reserve Bank of New York Economic Policy Review*, 31–51.

Fleming, Michael J. and Eli M. Remolona (1999) "Price Formation and Liquidity in the U.S. Treasuries Market: The Response to Public Information", *Journal of Finance*, 54, 1901–1915.

Fleming and Remolona (1999) "The term structure of announcement effects," BIS Working Paper No. 71 (June).

Froot, Kenneth A., Paul G.J. O'Connell and Mark S. Seasholes (2001) "The Portfolio Flows of International Investors", *Journal of Financial Economics*, 59, 151–193.

Harris, Lawrence and Eitan Gurel (1986) "Price and Volume Effects Associated with Changes in the S&P 500 List: New Evidence for the Existence of Price Pressures", *Journal of Finance*, 41(4), 815–829.

Hau, Harald, Massimo Massa and Joël Peress (2005) "Do Demand Curves for Currencies Slope Down? Evidence from the MSCI Global Index Change", CEPR Discussion Paper No. 4862.

Hess, Alan C. and Peter A. Frost (1982) "Tests for Price Effects of New Issues of Seasoned Securities", *Journal of Finance*, 37(1), 11–25.

Holthausen, Robert, Richard Leftwich and David Mayers (1987) "The Effect of Large Block Trades: a Cross-Sectional Analysis", *Journal of Financial Economics*, 19(2), 237–267.

Jain, Prem C. (1987) "The Effect on Stock Price of Inclusion in or Exclusion from the S&P 500", *Financial Analysts Journal*, 43, 58–65.

Kalay, Avner and Adam Shimrat (1987) "Firm Value and Seasoned Equity Issues: Price Pressure, Wealth Redistribution or Negative Information", *Journal of Financial Economics*, 19, 109–126.

Kaul, Aditya, Vikas Mehrotra and Randall Morck (2000) "Demand Curves for Stocks Do Slope Down: New Evidence from an Index Weights Adjustment", *Journal of Finance*, 55(2), 893–912.

Krishnamurthy, Arvind and Annette Vissing-Jorgensen (2007) "The Demand for Treasury Debt", *NBER Working Paper* No. 12881.

Levin, Eric J. and Robert E. Wright (2006) "Downwards Sloping Demand Curves for Stock?", *Studies in Economics and Finance*, 23(1), 51–74.

Mikkelson, Wayne H. and M. Megan Partch (1985) "Stock Price Effects on Secondary Distributions", *Journal of Financial Economics* 14, 165–194.

Piazzesi, Moika (2003) "Bond Yields and the Federal Reserve", *Journal of Political Economy*, 113(2), 311–344.

Rodrik, Dani (2006) "The Social Cost of Foreign Exchange Reserves", *International Economic Journal*, 20(3), 253–266.

Rothenberg, Alexander D. and Francis E. Warnock (2006) "Sudden Flight and True Sudden Stops", NBER Working Paper No. 12726.

Scholes, Myron S. (1972) "The Market for Securities: Substitution versus Price Pressure and the Effects of Information on Share Prices", *Journal of Business*, 45(2), 179–211.

Shleifer, Andrei (1986) "Do Demand Curves for Stocks Slope Down?", *Journal of Finance*, 41, 579–590.

Warnock, Francis E. and Veronica Cacdac Warnock (2006) "International Capital Flows and US Interest Rates", NBER Working Paper No. 12560.

13
Public Investment Funds and Value-Based Generational Accounting

*Roy P.M.M. Hoevenaars, Roderick D.J. Molenaar and Eduard H.M. Ponds**

13.1 Introduction

Governments in various countries are holding large pools of resources managed for public goals. These pools are known under different names, like sovereign wealth funds, public investment funds, pension funds, saving funds, intergenerational funds and so on, reflecting their different historical roots and orientation. Mitchell et al. (2008) make a distinction between three types of publicly held funds, or of public investment funds as they call these funds: (i) reserve funds held for currency stabilization and macroeconomic stabilization purposes; (ii) sovereign wealth funds (SWF) accumulated from natural resource taxes or from fiscal surpluses aimed at sharing the revenues of the exploitation of natural resources with future generations (Norway, Kuwait, Abu Dhabi); and (iii) public pension funds built up either through an explicitly funded arrangement or the result of prefunding the foreseeable increase in social security benefits because of ageing (Japan, Canada).

SWFs and the public pension funds have in common an intergenerational dimension in their objectives (Mitchell et al. (2008) and Paulson (2009)). Questions faced by SWFs can be handled with insights derived in other fields. Universities and other private endowment funds provide guidance to public funds regarding the optimal spending rules. Lee et al. (2009) for example explore for a typical SWF how generational equity can be realized by coordination of savings, asset allocation strategies and spending rules. The challenge for a typical SWF is to define a strategy that can offer a relatively high level of spending while affording as much stability to both spending and ongoing fund value as possible. Furthermore Scherer (2009) provides a linkage between oil-funded SWFs and life cycle investing by interpreting

* The views expressed here are those of the authors only and not necessarily of the institutions with which they are affiliated.

the asset allocation problem of a SWF as the decision making problem of an investor with a nontradable endowed asset (oil reserves).

If generational equity is an important goal for SWFs and public pension funds, then one necessarily has to raise the question of how to assess a certain strategy as fair or not. Which path of wealth accumulation, asset allocation and spending over time is desirable from the perspective of various generations? This is a difficult topic belonging to the field of normative economics. Moreover there are large uncertainties in revenues, financial market rates of return, domestic economic growth and so on. These factors all have an impact on the welfare position of the various generations. Which discount factor has to be used to compare the benefit position of the various generations?

In previous papers we have discussed for real–existing pension funds the usefulness of what we have called the tool of value-based ALM. This tool is a complement to traditional ALM and it appears to be very useful to compare the positions of the various generations from the perspectives economic value (Ponds (2003) and Hoevenaars and Ponds (2008)). The main advantage of value-based ALM is its objective nature as the method is rooted in market prices and that risk can easily be handled by the use of stochastic discount factors.

We claim that the value-based ALM tool is a useful tool for SWFs and public pension funds aiming at realizing generational fairness when setting the path of wealth accumulation and spending over time. What we do in this chapter is to explain the tool of value-based ALM. Subsequently we apply the tool to a stylized pension fund considering policy changes. This pension fund is a stand-alone pension fund in which all risks now and in the future have to be borne by current and future generations. We reconstruct this fund into an aggregate of embedded generational options by making use of value-based generational accounting. Finally we discuss the helpfulness of the value-based tool for SWFs intending to establish generational equity.

13.2 Asset liability management

13.2.1 Classical ALM

In the pension industry, Asset Liability Management (ALM) is being used to come to optimal pension deals. A typical pension deal defines what is being promised, how these promises are funded (asset mix and contribution policy) and who of the stakeholders of the deal are bearing the risks in the funding process (risk allocation rules). Members of the Board of Trustees of the pension funds have to decide what the optimal combination is of funding strategy, indexation policy and investment strategy, as well as how risks best can be shared over the various stakeholders, i.e. the plan members and the employer. ALM often makes use of Monte Carlo scenario simulations to project distributions regarding contributions, indexation and funding ratios to form an opinion on the attractiveness of the different strategy options being considered.

Sensitivity analysis is usually carried out to explore specific policy variants in terms of asset mix, contribution policy and indexation rules. Policy variants are evaluated in terms of expected values and relevant risk measures for key variables – for example, the funding ratio, the contribution rate, the indexation rate and so on. Moreover one can easily take care of specific constraints, like the funding requirements of the supervisor (e.g. a minimum probability of underfunding) and a maximum level of contribution rate.

13.2.2 Value-based ALM

Despite its widespread popularity, one may feel uncomfortable with the classical ALM tool kit. Chapman et al. (2002) characterize ALM studies as producing merely 'funnels of doubt', which serve only to demonstrate that taking more risk will imply more uncertainty about key outputs. It is difficult to rank policy variants using solely the classical ALM output. Is a risky strategy with, on average, a high but volatile funding ratio to be preferred above a less risky strategy that will end up with, on average, a low funding ratio with little risk? Younger members in a plan with intergenerational risk sharing may prefer a risky strategy that could yield a high pay-out per unit contribution, whereas older members will prefer a liability-hedged investment strategy to safeguard pension fund assets in order to reduce benefit risk. Practitioners solve the ranking problem by discovering the policy setting that is most acceptable given the interests of all participants, taking into account all constraints. However in seeking this 'most acceptable' policy variant, the ALM professionals and/or the board of trustees do not usually consider whether the policy variant is fair in economic value terms for all members. In financial markets, the no arbitrage principle guarantees that the market-based compensation for a taken risk is fair, so that risk taking is accompanied by an appropriate reward compensation. Within pension funds, the no arbitrage principle of financial markets is replaced by the rules of the pension contract defining the risk and reward allocation amongst the members.

Value-based ALM can deal with the fact that indexation cuts and contribution increases typically occur in bad times. Therefore these financial adjustments are very valuable. In good times funding ratios and return of financial assets will be high giving room for contribution cuts and additional (catch-up) indexation. However these adjustments probably are not that valuable in good times.

Contingent claim analysis is fruitful to test for possible value transfers. Restating the highly stylized framework of Sharpe (1976) into a realistic setting results in what is now called value-based ALM (Kortleve and Ponds (2006) and Hoevenaars and Ponds (2008)). Value-based ALM essentially uses the same output from scenario analysis as classical ALM, but the future outcomes are discounted back to the present with an appropriate risk adjusted discount rate. This is achieved by making use of a pricing kernel specification (see Section 13.3.3 for technical details): low discount rates are assigned to bad scenarios, whereas high discount rates are assigned to good scenarios. This reflects the prevailing risk aversion in the market which implies that payoffs during bad times are more valuable than payoffs during good times. What we show in this chapter is that value-based generational accounting enables us to rewrite any institutional generational arrangement; for example a pension fund or a sovereign wealth fund can be rewritten as an aggregate of embedded generational options. This allows us to detect possible transfers of value resulting from policy changes by examining changes in the value of the various embedded generational options.

13.3 The pension fund as an aggregate of embedded generational options

13.3.1 Pension fund characteristics

Before deriving generational accounts in a pension fund setting, it is be useful to describe the specific institutional characteristics of the pension fund. All funding risks must be borne by current and future members of the pension plan. The content of the pension contract helps determine how surpluses and deficits in the funding process are allocated amongst participants. Essentially there are four ways to allocate the funding risks amongst the participants: (i) doing nothing by shifting forward in time a position of underfunding or overfunding, i.e. passing the gains/losses to future participants; (ii) adjusting the contribution rate; (iii) adjusting the indexation rate; or (iv) a reallocation of the asset mix.

The fund under study has the following features. The pension plan is an average-wage plan with indexed liabilities. Workers acquire for each year of service 2% of their pensionable wage as newly accrued liabilities. The yearly indexation of benefits and accrued liabilities aims to follow the wage growth of the sector; however the actual indexation may be contingent on the financial position of the pension fund. Workers pay yearly contributions out of their wage income in order to fund new accrued liabilities in that year. Total contributions must be equal to the present value of new liabilities, where new liabilities are calculated with the expected rate of return on assets net of wage growth as the discount rate. All workers pay the same uniform contribution rate as a percentage of pensionable wages.[1] We assume a constant mix rebalancing policy in which the investment manager rebalances to fixed asset weights at the end of each year. The investment universe consists of stocks and bonds only. The duration of the nominal liabilities is 15 years (at a nominal rate of 4.6%) and the investment horizon is 40 years. The nominal funding ratio equals 150% at the start of the analysis.

13.3.2 Generational accounts as embedded options

The value of pension fund assets A_t is equal to the value of total pension fund nominal liabilities L_t plus the pension fund residue R_t

$$[1]\quad A_t = L_t + R_t$$

The balance sheet next period ($t + 1$) expressed in present value terms at t is

$$[2]\quad A_t + V_t[C_{t+1}] - V_t[PP_{t+1}] = V_t[L_{t+1}] + V_t[R_{t+1}]$$

Inherent to the stochastic discount factors approach (see e.g. Cochrane (2001)) is that the economic value of initial assets plus investments proceeds is equal to initial assets: $V[A_t(1 + r_{t+1})] = A_t$ with r_{t+1} as rate of return in $t + 1$. The term $V_t[C_{t+1}]$ is the economic value at t of contributions C_{t+1} paid in $t + 1$ and $V_t[PP_{t+1}]$ is the economic value at t of pension payments PP_{t+1} in $t + 1$. The term $V_t[L_{t+1}]$ stands for the economic value of accrued liabilities at the end of period $t + 1$, being the sum of the accrued liabilities at the end of period t, including indexation *minus* the liabilities written off in $t + 1$, as they have been reserved for pension payments in $t + 1$ *plus* the new accrued liabilities in $t + 1$ attributable to one year of additional service of working members. The term $V_t[R_{t+1}]$ is the economic value at t of the pension fund residue at the end of period $t + 1$, R_{t+1}.

Using [1], we can rearrange [2] as

$$[3]\quad V_t[L_{t+1}] - L_t + V_t[PP_{t+1}] - V_t[C_{t+1}] + \left(V_t[R_{t+1}] - R_t\right) = 0$$

This expression says that the one year change in the value of liabilities is backed by contributions and by either an increase or a decrease in the pension fund residue. This reflects the zero-sum nature of a pension fund. However, the zero-sum feature does not hold necessarily for the different age cohorts. We can split up expression (3) by age cohort. This results in

$$[4]\quad \Delta GA_{t+1}^x = V_t\left[L_{t+1}^x\right] - L_t^x + V_t\left[PP_{t+1}^x\right] - V_t\left[C_{t+1}^x\right] + \left(V_t\left[R_{t+1}^x\right] - R_t^x\right) \neq 0$$

where x refers to cohort x. We call the term ΔGA_{t+1}^x the generational account option of cohort x, that is defined as the economic value at t of the change in the generational account of cohort x during $t + 1$.

We assume that the pension fund residue can be allocated amongst the cohorts at all times proportionately to each cohorts's stake of nominal liabilities:

$$[5]\quad R_t^x = l_t^x R_t$$

where

$$[6]\quad l_t^x = \frac{L_t^x}{L_t}$$

The sum of all generational account options must be necessarily equal to 0, reflecting that the pension fund is a zero-sum game in value terms:

$$[7]\quad \sum_{x \varepsilon X} \Delta GA_{t+1}^x = 0$$

We can split up ΔGA^x into two parts: the so-called net benefit option NB^x and the residue option ΔR^x:

$$[8]\quad \Delta GA_{t+1}^x = \underbrace{V_t\left[L_{t+1}^x\right] - L_t^x + V_t\left[PP_{t+1}^x\right] - V_t\left[C_{t+1}^x\right]}_{NB^x} + \underbrace{\left(V_t\left[R_{t+1}^x\right] - R_t^x\right)}_{\Delta R^x}$$

The net benefit option consists of the change in the value of liabilities $V_t\left[L_{t+1}^x\right] - L_t^x$ due to new nominal accruals and the writing off of planned nominal pension payments, plus the value of actual pension payments $V_t\left[PP_{t+1}^x\right]$ including indexation, and the value of paid contributions $V_t\left[C_{t+1}^x\right]$ The net residue option says that a cohort gives away the certain claim on the current residue R_t^x by participating in the fund and it receives an uncertain claim on the residue at the end of the evaluation period R_{t+1}^x, with economic value equal to $V_t\left[R_{t+1}^x\right]$.

Below, we compare some alternative policy variants to study the impact on the generational accounts of cohorts. This comparison is based on the expression:

$$[9]\quad \Delta GA_{alternative}^x - \Delta GA_{basic}^x = \left(NB_{alternative}^x - NB_{basic}^x\right) + \left(\Delta R_{alternative}^x - \Delta R_{basic}^x\right)$$

Stepping over from the current pension contract to an alternative one may lead to a change of the generational account option of cohort *x*, and this can be split up into changes in the net benefit option and the residue option held by cohort *x*.

13.3.3 Pricing embedded options

The ALM framework is based on a simulation study which projects the development of the pension fund in many future scenarios. The investment universe consists of MSCI world stocks and (German) nominal ten years zero coupon bonds. Furthermore we assume that wage inflation equals price inflation, so that real wage growth is zero.[2]

In accordance with Campbell and Viceira (2002), we describe the return dynamics by a first-order vector autoregressive (VAR) model. The relevant economic factors $\mathbf{X}_t$ in the model include the one-month interest rate ($y_t^{(1)}$), the ten-year zero coupon rate ($y_t^{(120)}$), price inflation (π_t), stock returns in excess of the one-month interest rate (xs_t), and the corresponding dividend yield (dy_t).

$$[10] \quad X_t = \left[y_t^{(1)}, y_t^{(120)}, \pi_t, xs_t, dy_t\right]^{\mathrm{T}}$$

Returns on a rolling ten-year constant maturity zero coupon bond portfolio are constructed from the nominal term structure. The VAR is written as

$$[11] \quad X_{t+1} = \Phi_0 + \Phi_1 X_t + \sum \zeta_{t+1}$$

where $\zeta_{t+1} \sim N(0, I)$. In order to value the embedded options, we specify the pricing kernel as

$$[12] \quad -\log M_{t+1} = y_t^{(1)} + \frac{1}{2}\lambda_t^{\mathrm{T}}\lambda_t + \lambda_t^{\mathrm{T}}\zeta_{t+1}$$

where M_{t+1} is the stochastic discount factor (SDF) for valuation of embedded options in the pension deal and λ_t are the time-varying prices of risk. λ_t is a linear function of the state variables X_t:

$$[13] \quad \lambda_t = \lambda_0 + \Lambda_1 X_t$$

The pricing kernel defined in [11] to [13] is thus consistent with the VAR return dynamics and results in arbitrage free term structures (see the Appendix). This approach ensures that for each stochastic scenario besides the results for the X_t series a series for the SDF is also generated. For further technical details, we refer to Nijman and Koijen (2006) and Brennan and Xia (2002).

Summary statistics of the data and scenarios are provided in Table 13.1. Monthly data (1972:09–2008:08) are used to estimate the parameters in the VAR system. MSCI world stock returns[3] and dividend yield are from Factset, German interest rates are from the Deutsche Bundesbank and the German inflation is from Datastream. Stochastic scenarios are constructed by forward iterating the VAR. The views in Table 13.1 are used for the median of the scenarios.

The ALM model provides both classical and value-based outcomes. The classical results include probability distributions for the relevant ALM output variables as e.g. the distribution of the nominal funding ratios, indexation characteristics and probabilities of underfunding. We value embedded options in the pension contract using the pricing kernel specification in [11] to [13]. Low discount rates are assigned to bad scenarios, whereas high discount rates are assigned to good scenarios. This reflects the prevailing risk aversion in the market which implies that payoffs during bad times are more valuable than payoffs during good times. Multiplication of the future payoffs k periods ahead (P_{t+k}) by the corresponding SDF $\left(M^*_{t+k} = M_{t+1}M_{t+2} \cdots M_{t+k}\right)$ and averaging over all scenarios gives the current economic value Vt[Pt+k] (i.e., the option value) embedded in the pension contract:

$$[14] \quad V_t\left[P_{t+k}\right] = E_t\left[M^*_{t+k}P_{t+k}\right]$$

13.4 Empirical results

Table 13.1 reports the summary statistics for the data. The Dickey-Fuller OLS F-statistic fails to reject the unit root at the 10% level for both interest rates and the dividend yield. We do not correct for the unit roots due to economic reasoning: it is consistent with the literature (e.g. Campbell and

Table 13.1 Summary statistics

	Mean	Stdev	SR	Min	Max	Skewness	XKurtosis	DF-test	Views
$sy_t^{(1)}$	5.31	2.53		2.00	13.10	0.93	0.05	2.17	3.75
π_t	2.88	0.91		−0.47	1.40	0.94	1.77	104.27	2.00
$y_t^{(120)}$	6.54	1.74		3.16	10.71	0.01	−0.82	0.92	4.50
xs_t	3.54	14.41	0.25	−23.15	11.84	−0.81	2.61	165.82	2.75
DY_t	2.99	1.16		1.27	5.70	0.65	−0.85	0.75	2.25

The table reports the summary statistics for the full period (1972:09–2008:08). The mean, stdev and Sharpe Ratio (SR) are annualized. The other statistics are on a monthly basis. XKurtosis is the excess kurtosis. The DF-test is the Dickey-Fuller statistic. We have adjusted the mean log returns by one half of their variances so that they reflect mean gross returns. The statistics are based on the log returns and log yields. NOTE: the statistics for dy_t are based on the original series ($DY_t = exp(dy_t)$). The last column shows the views for the (simple) yields and returns. The views are imposed by adjusting the constants Φ_0 in the VAR model and λ_0 in the pricing kernel

Viceira (2005) and Brennan et al. (1997)). Also, the Dickey Fuller test statistic has too low power.

Table 13.2 reports the parameters Φ_1 of the VAR model in [10] and the correlations and volatilities of the shocks ζ_t. The maximal eigenvalue of the coefficient matrix is 0.987. The system is stable, i.e. shocks to the system will dampen through time. The dividend yield has a significant predictive power for the stocks returns. The negative correlation between the shocks to the dividend yield and the stocks return indicates that a positive shock to the dividend yield implies a negative shock to the contemporaneous stocks return. The positive exposure of stocks to the lagged dividend yield implies that the future stocks returns will be affected positively. These effects imply mean reversion in stock returns. The high and significant coefficients of the one-month rate, the ten-year

Table 13.2 VAR estimation results

	$y_t^{(1)}$	π_t	$y_t^{(120)}$	xs_t	dy_t	R^2/p
$y_t^{(1)}$	0.95	0.03	0.04	−0.00	−0.01	0.96
	61.10	3.89	1.48	−0.56	−1.04	0.00
π_t	0.39	0.17	0.05	0.00	0.08	0.26
	4.68	3.66	0.35	0.62	2.07	0.00
$y_t^{(120)}$	0.01	0.00	0.98	0.00	−0.00	0.98
	1.69	1.02	79.20	1.02	−0.16	0.00
xs_t	−1.11	−2.18	−4.08	0.10	2.48	0.06
	−0.74	−2.57	−1.57	2.10	3.38	0.00
dy_t	0.00	0.02	0.03	−0.00	0.98	0.99
	0.19	2.52	0.97	−1.39	129.46	0.00

	$y_t^{(1)}$	π_t	$y_t^{(120)}$	xs_t	dy_t
$y_t^{(1)}$	0.04				
π_t	0.03	0.22			
$y_t^{(120)}$	0.19	0.16	0.02		
xs_t	−0.04	−0.07	−0.10	4.03	
dy_t	0.06	0.05	0.12	−0.91	0.04

The first panel reports the parameter estimates of Φ_1 in the VAR(1) model $X_{t+1} = \Phi_0 + \Phi_1 X_t + \Sigma\zeta_{t+1}$. The coefficient estimates and R^2 are in the first row, the t-values and p-value of the F-statistic of joint significance in the second. The second panel reports the cross-correlations of the shocks ζ_{t+1}. The volatility (%/month) is given on the diagonal.

rate and the dividend yield on their lagged values reflect the high persistence of these series (this is also reflected in the low values of the DF-test in Table 13.1).

Figure 13.1 shows the annualized conditional volatility of the cumulative holding period returns.[4] The results confirm the findings of Hoevenaars et al. (2008): stocks and bonds show mean reversion, while a strategy of monthly investing in the one-month rate is more risky in the long run. Stocks are less risky in the long run due to the negative correlation between the shocks to dividend yield and stocks and the positive exposure of stocks to the lagged dividend yield: a positive shock to the dividend yield implies a negative shock to the contemporaneous stocks return but a positive effect on future stocks returns. Shocks in the ten-year yield are negatively correlated to contemporaneous bond returns, but positively to future bond returns, whereas the shocks to the one-month rate are negatively correlated to both the current and the future returns. The mean reverting effect of the long yield dominates, as the ten-year yield is more persistent than the one-month rate. The increasing risk of the one-month rate reflects the reinvestment risk due to the persistent variation of both the inflation and short-term real interest rate.

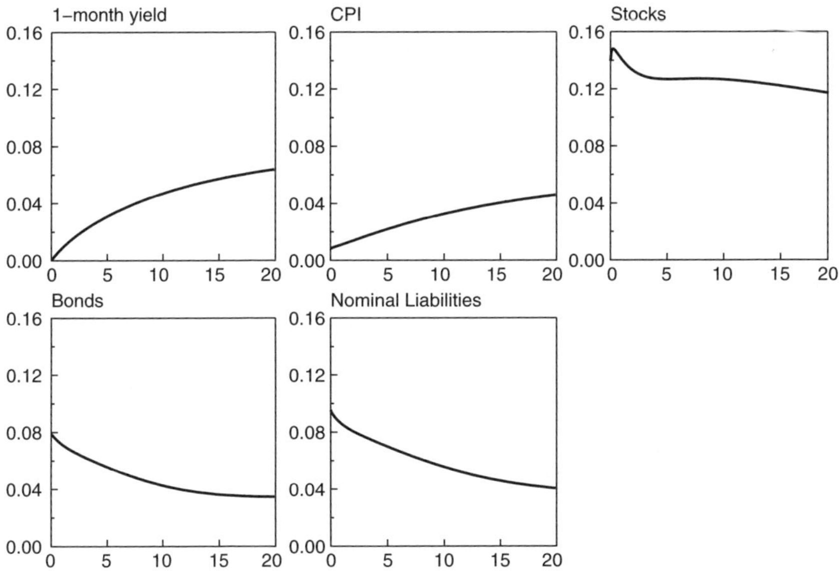

Figure 13.1 Term structure of risk: annualized volatility of cumulative holding period returns

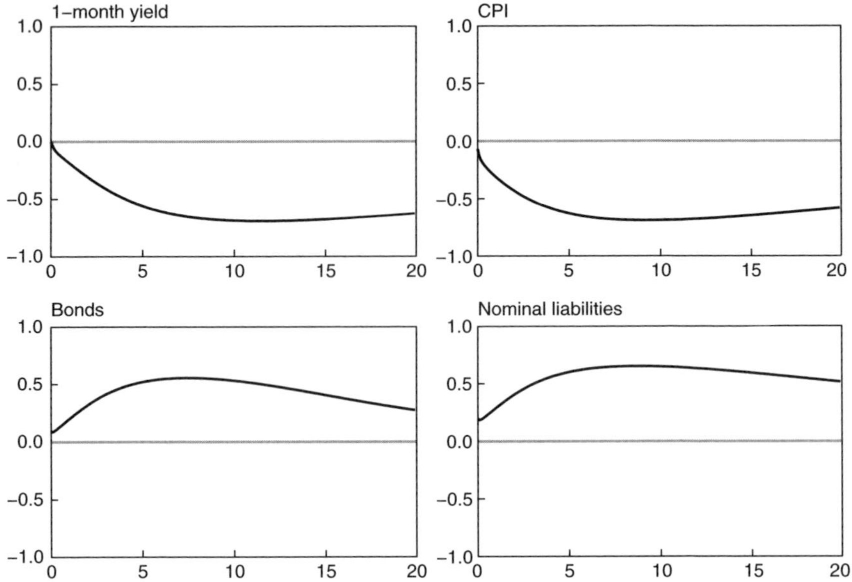

Figure 13.2 Term structure of risk (continued): correlation of cumulative holding period returns with stocks

Figure 13.2 shows the horizon dependent correlations with stocks. The diversification between stocks and bonds changes over time: in the short and long run, the correlation is low; however, in the medium term it increases to 0.55. If the ten-year yield increases unexpectedly, the bond return will decline immediately, whereas the contemporaneous effect on the stock return is small (the correlation is -0.10). The subsequent effects on the bond return are positive as the bond profits from the higher yield, whereas the majority of the decrease of the stock return will occur in the next periods (the exposure is -4.08).

Figure 13.3 shows the inflation hedging qualities of the assets: the one-month rate is the best instrument to hedge unexpected inflation shocks. Bonds will suffer for several years from unexpected inflation increases; however, they will profit ultimately from the higher yields. Increasing inflation will lead to lower real economic activity and this leads to lower stock returns. In particular, unexpected inflation is related to negative output shocks, which generally lead to falling stock prices through higher discount rates. The long run inflation hedge potential can be explained by a present-value calculation of real stock prices. The higher inflation will increase future dividends, which will boost stock prices in the long run (see e.g. Campbell and Shiller (1988)). The net effect in the long run is negative.

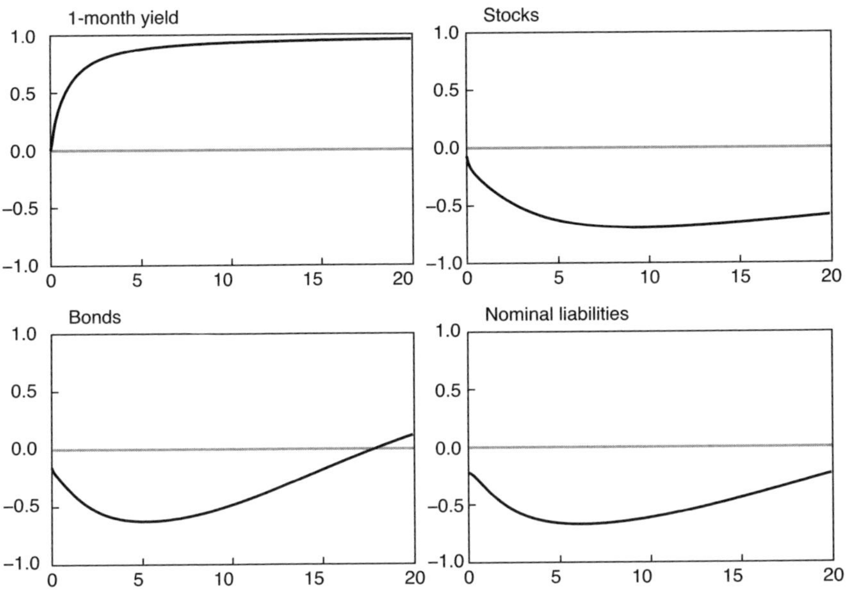

Figure 13.3 Term structure of risk (continued): correlation of cumulative holding period returns with CPI

Note: The *y*-axis shows the correlation; the *x*-axis shows the horizon in years.

13.5 Value transfers in an intergenerational fund

We demonstrate how the methodology of value-based generational accounting reveals the position of various generations for any institutional arrangement sharing revenues and losses with current and future generations. The illustration in this section is based on a stand-alone pension fund with intergenerational risk sharing, but can also be applied to sovereign wealth funds and public finance. Changes in the stylized pension contract may easily lead to sizeable intergenerational value transfers as the allocation of risk amongst stakeholders changes substantially. We evaluate three types of policy reforms that are closely related to pension reforms in the past and current debate about pension reform: improvement of solvency risk management (Section 13.5.1), the effect of a more conservative investment mix due to an ageing society (Section 13.5.2) and challenges of the life cycle theory (Section 13.5.3).

As our main purpose is about the intergenerational transfers we focus on the embedded options. The classical ALM output is in line with expectations: if we e.g. change the 50% stocks and 50% bonds portfolio to a 100% bonds portfolio (see Section 13.5.2), the median nominal funding ratios will be lower and the volatility of the assets vs. the nominal liabilities will also be lower.

13.5.1 Improvement of solvency risk management after the 2001–2003 pension crisis

Falling stock returns and declining interest rates during 2001–2003 led to a revision of financial assessment frameworks for banks, insurance companies and pension funds around the world. Fair value accounting and solvency risk management became key aspects of the financial policy of pension funds. Pension funds in the Netherlands also responded by switching from a traditional defined benefit system to a hybrid system where the inflation compensation was no longer guaranteed. In general, the indexation policy became conditional on the funding ratio as shown in Figure 13.4.

We explore how changes in pension plan design influence the embedded options held by the various age cohorts. Along the lines of the previous section, we decompose changes in the generational account options into changes in the underlying net benefit options and residue options as

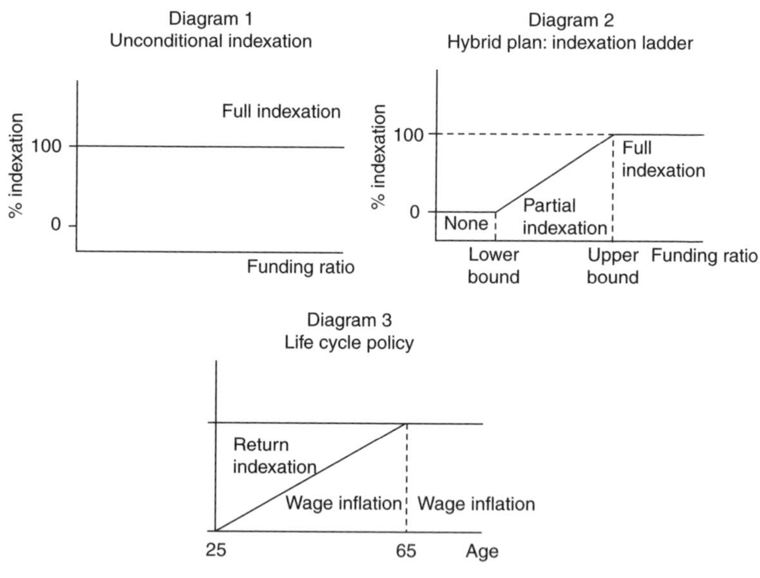

Figure 13.4 Different collective pension deals

Note: Pension deal 1 represents unconditional wage indexation; pension deal 2 is a hybrid plan with a dynamic wage indexation policy (with boundaries); pension deal 3 is a hybrid plan with dynamic indexation which depends on an age dependent combination of return indexation and unconditional wage indexation.

demonstrated in [8]. The contribution rate remains fixed in all variants at 19%.

The replacement of the full indexation rule by the hybrid plan leads to value transfer from older generations to younger ones. Figure 13.5 displays the accompanying changes in embedded options for each cohort. The introduction of the hybrid plan implies that an unconditional indexation policy is replaced by a conditional indexation policy. All members lose value from this change in indexation policy. Typically, indexation cuts will occur in bad times and these cuts will then be very valuable. Catch-up indexation is provided in good times when the funding ratio is high; however, this additional indexation in good times is not as valuable in value terms. The flexible indexation has substantial effects on both the residue and net benefit option. The residue option improves, because the downside risks reduce, but at the cost of the net benefit option which deteriorates for all cohorts. The overall impact on the generational accounting option differs considerably between young and old plan members. This option improves strongly for the younger workers, whereas the older workers must accept a severe deterioration. The net changes turn negative from the current age of 32 onwards. Hence for workers older than 32, the loss in value due to a conversion to a conditional indexation policy more than outweighs the gain in value attributable to the lower downside risks due the conditional indexation. Workers

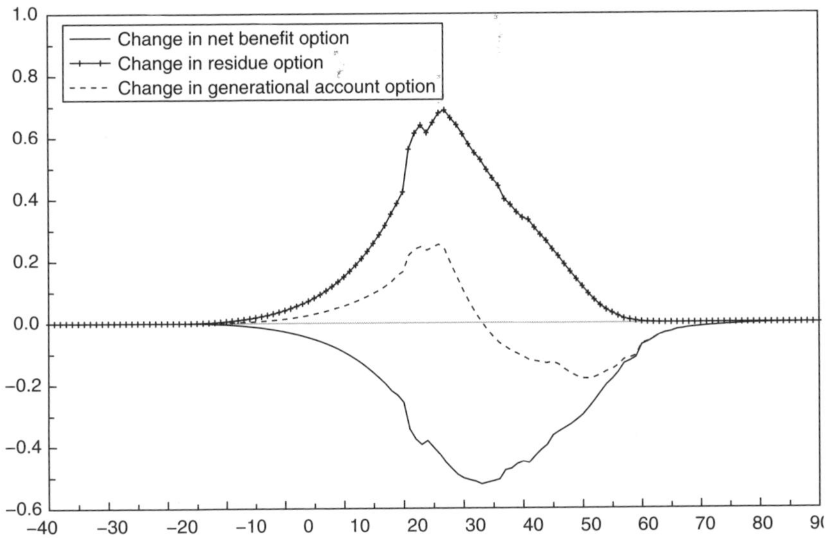

Figure 13.5 Generational effects when stepping over from the full indexation plan to the hybrid plan

younger than 32 have a longer planning horizon and thus a longer time for the indexation policy to catch up. The improved downside risks conditions are more valuable for them than the potential indexation cuts.[5]

13.5.2 Ageing society and a conservative investment mix

Most collective pension funds face problems over the coming years due to an ageing population and demographics. Mature funds may shift the focus of the investment policy to the interest of the elderly. Life cycle theory suggests a more conservative mix to safeguard payout benefits of the retirees. However, such a conservative mix might conflict with common financial planning advice for the younger plan members. An important question, arises as to who is bearing the additional risk. When a different asset mix will leads to a different financial position and indexation policy, then value transfers will inevitably occur from workers to retirees.

The analysis above has been evaluated using an asset mix of 50% bonds and 50% stocks. Figure 13.6 demonstrates the impact on the hybrid plan of moving the asset mix toward 100% bonds. As the contribution rate does not change in this setting, the return on the assets falls below the return on the liabilities in many scenarios. The significant deterioration of the residue option reveals the higher underfunding risks for all cohorts. On the other hand, the elderly benefit the most in terms of the net benefit option. Not

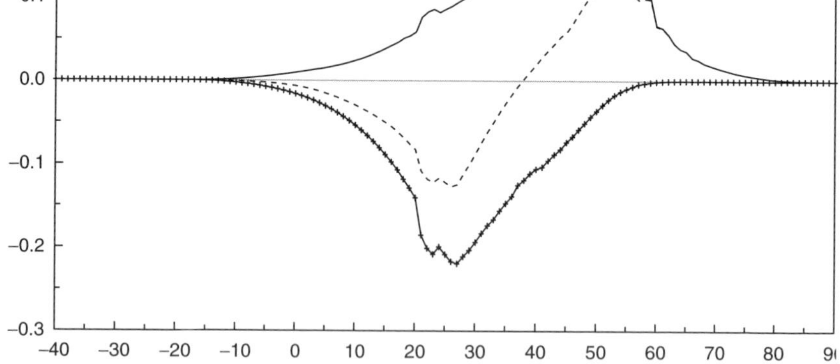

Figure 13.6 Generational effects when stepping over from the hybrid plan with 50% stocks and 50% bonds to the hybrid plan with the conservative mix (i.e. 100% bonds)

only the lower volatility of the assets mix, but also the comfortable initial funding ratio contribute to this. Younger members still benefit from the lower volatility, however, they have less upside potential because the financial position deteriorates over the years. On balance the switch to a more conservative asset mix leads to a value distribution from the young (younger than currently 35) to the elderly.

13.5.3 Challenges of life cycle theory

The theory of life cycle investing suggests that a uniform risk profile over the life cycle is not optimal from a theoretical perspective. When the human capital has a bond-like nature, the depletion of human capital over the life cycle introduces horizon effects in the optimal equity allocation. Below we propose an age-dependent indexation rule in combination with benefits of collectivity and risk-sharing (see Figure 13.4).

The proposed life cycle policy leads to substantial value transfers from the young (younger than currently 40) to the elderly (see Figure 13.7). Just as in the first setting, retirees benefit from the full wage inflation compensation. All members benefit from the higher upward potential of the indexation policy, but depending on their age are exposed to possibly severe downside risks. Low and even negative return indexation coincides with bad economic scenarios which have a high stochastic discount rate for the

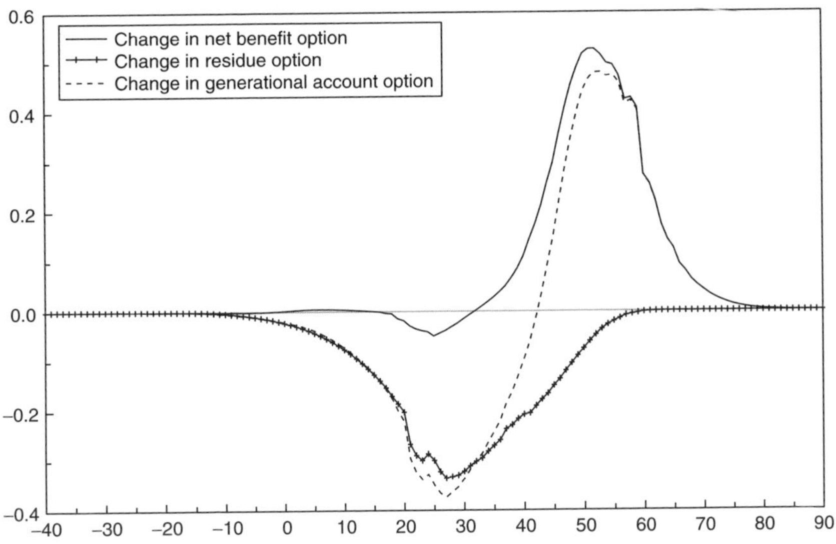

Figure 13.7 Generational effects when stepping over from the hybrid plan to the life cycle policy plan

payoffs of the indexation and especially the residue option. In particular, for the younger participants the residue option and the net benefit option interact over the planning horizon. The residue option becomes worse as the fund matures, because retirees are guaranteed full indexation at the cost of the other members which leads to a deterioration of the financial position of the fund. The results suggest that the downside risks outweigh the upward potential the most for participants who are currently in their twenties.

The proposed life cycle policy partly restores the value transfers from elderly to the young by the replacement of the full indexation system with the hybrid system after the previous pension crises. Interestingly, the value transfers from switching to a life cycle variant are in same direction as a switch to a more conservative asset mix in an ageing society. As the value transfers measured by the changes in the generational account options are much higher in magnitude in the life cycle variant than in the other two illustrations, the parameters of the life cycle elements in institutional arrangements should be twisted to find an acceptable set of value transfers between the current and future generations. For instance the change in the net benefit option will be positive for all generations and will resemble the change in Figure 13.6 if the life cycle policy is combined with a reduction of the contribution rate of 2% in order to profit from the increase of the expected indexation over the horizon. Other policy settings like the addition of a collar construction to the life cycle variant seem worth investigation to reduce downside risks. Value-based generational accounting can be used to accomplished this.

13.6 Conclusion

Sovereign wealth funds and other public funds often have the aim of sharing revenues and losses with future generations. The background of these funds varies considerably, giving a broad spectrum of government-backed funds ranging from prefunding the ageing-driven increase in social security costs to a fair distribution of oil wealth over generations.

A challenge for the funds is to arrive at a generational fair policy. The decision-making by public fund management necessarily has to take place within a long horizon context with large uncertainties regarding economic growth and capital market returns. Therefore the welfare position of the various generations is difficult to evaluate. Setting a generational fair strategy regarding the funding path, the asset allocation and the spending path over time is also hard. The traditional ALM tool is of limited value as the ALM output of probability distributions provides no guidance in ranking the various strategies. We have proposed the method of value-based generational accounting to get an objective view on the consequences of different strategies for the position of the various generations. The method is rooted in market-based valuation wherein all cash flows from and to current and future generations can be compared by making use of stochastic discount factors. The positions of the various generations can be expressed in terms of the embedded generational options. These options can be derived, as an institutional arrangement covering current and future generations has to be seen as a zero-sum game in economic value terms. A change in strategy can be evaluated on its generational effects by looking at the changes in the embedded options held by the various generations.

Appendix

The development of the state variables $\mathbf{X}_{t+1}$ is given by the VAR(1) model

$$[A.1] \quad X_{t+1} = \Phi_0 + \Phi_1 X_t + \sum \zeta_{t+1}$$

where $\zeta t_{+1} \sim N(0, I)$. The pricing kernel is log normal,

$$[A.2] \quad -\log M_{t+1} = y_t^{(1)} + \frac{1}{2}\lambda_t^\top \lambda_t + \lambda_t^\top \zeta_{t+1}$$

where M_{t+1} is the stochastic discount factor and λ_t are the time-varying prices of risk. λ_t is a linear function of the state variables $\mathbf{X}_t$:

$$[A.3] \quad \lambda_t = \lambda_0 + \Lambda_1 X_t$$

The pricing equation for an *n*-period zero-coupon treasury bond is given by

$$P_t^{(n)} = E_t\left[M_{t+1} P_{t+1}^{(n-1)}\right]$$

or in log terms:

$$[A.4] \quad p_t^{(n)} = E_t\left[m_{t+1} + p_{t+1}^{(n-1)}\right] + \frac{1}{2} Var_t\left[m_{t+1} + p_{t+1}^{(n-1)}\right]$$

where $p_t^{(n)} \equiv ln\left[P_t^{(n)}\right]$ and $m_t \equiv ln\ [M_t]$. We have

$$-p_t^{(n)} = A_n + B_n^T X_t$$

as $p_t^{(0)} = 0$ $A_0 = 0$ and $\mathbf{B}_0 = 0$. For a *1*-period bond (A-4) can be rewritten as

$$-y_t^{(1)} = p_t^{(1)} = E_t(m_{t+1}) + \frac{1}{2} Var_t[m_{t+1}]$$

Let $y_t^{(1)} = \delta_1^T X_t$. The recursive relations for A_n and $\mathbf{B}_n$ are given by

$$\text{[A.5]} \quad \begin{aligned} A_n &= A_{n-1} + B_{n-1}^T(\Phi_0 - \Sigma\lambda_0) - \frac{1}{2} B_{n-1}^T \Sigma\Sigma^T B_{n-1} \\ B_n &= \delta_1 + (\Phi_1 - \Sigma\Lambda_1)^T B_{n-1} \end{aligned}$$

The n-period log zero coupon yields $y_t^{(n)}$ are an affine function of the state variables $\mathbf{X}_t$:

$$\text{[A.6]} \quad y_t^{(n)} = -\frac{p_t^{(n)}}{n} = \frac{A_n}{n} + \frac{B_n}{n}^T X_t = a_n + b_n^T X_t$$

The real term structure can be derived along the lines in Ang et al. (2008).

The parameters of the system [A.1] to [A.3] (i.e. Φ_0, Φ_1, Σ, λ_0 and Λ_1) will be estimated using a two-step procedure (see e.g. Ang et al. (2005)). In the first step we estimate the VAR parameters (Φ_0, Φ_1 and Σ). In the second step we estimate, conditional on the VAR estimates, the parameters of the prices of risk (λ_0 and Λ_1). We assume that the yields are observed with a measurement error, i.e. $y_t^{(n)} = \hat{y}_t^{(n)} + \varepsilon_t^{(n)}$, where

$$\hat{y}_t^{(n)} = a_n + b_n^T X_t$$

and $\varepsilon_t \sim N(0, \Omega)$. We minimize the sum of squared errors:

$$\min_{\lambda_0, \Lambda_1} \sum_{n=1}^{N} \sum_{t=1}^{T} (\hat{y}_t^{(n)} - y_t^{(n)})^2$$

As the ten-year yield is included in the set of state variables, the constraint is imposed that this yield is fitted exactly. The optimization is based on yields with maturities from 1 to 15 years.[6] Tables 13.3 and 13.4 report the results of the second step.

Table 13.3 Prices of risk

	λ_0	$y_t^{(1)}$	π_t	$y_t^{(120)}$	xs_t	dy_t
$y_t^{(1)}$	0.14	−140.00	303.61	−135.54	−5.48	−11.91
π_t	−0.00	4.79	−10.39	4.64	0.19	0.41
$y_t^{(120)}$	−0.14	143.55	−37.60	−126.17	2.31	−5.79
xs_t	3.09	−21.45	−46.13	−117.31	2.47	60.99
dy_t	6.83	−65.57	−133.00	−208.24	5.60	137.78

The table reports the parameter estimates of $\lambda_t = \lambda_0 + \Lambda_1 X_t$.

Table 13.4 Volatilities of measurement errors of yields

$y_t^{(12)}$	0.67	$y_t^{(24)}$	0.71	$y_t^{(36)}$	0.68	$y_t^{(48)}$	0.60
$y_t^{(60)}$	0.50	$y_t^{(72)}$	0.39	$y_t^{(84)}$	0.28	$y_t^{(96)}$	0.18
$y_t^{(108)}$	0.09	$y_t^{(120)}$	0.00	$y_t^{(132)}$	0.07	$y_t^{(144)}$	0.14
$y_t^{(156)}$	0.19	$y_t^{(168)}$	0.24	$y_t^{(180)}$	0.28		

The table reports the volatilities of the measurement errors $\varepsilon_t^{(n)}$ in $y_t^{(n)} = a_n + b_n^{\top} X_t + \varepsilon_t^{(n)}$. The volatility of the ten-year yield ($y_t^{(120)}$) is by construction 0.00.

Notes

1. This implies that young workers pay more contributions than the present value of their new accrued liabilities, whereas older workers contribute less than their new accrued liabilities. Younger workers grow older so that at the end of their careers there will be a balance between the value of paid contributions and the value of accrued liabilities.
2. The assumption of a real wage growth of zero avoids the problem of valuation in an incomplete market. As there are no wage-indexed assets, risk relating to real wage growth is not priced into the market. De Jong (2008) discusses several methods to value wage-indexed cash flows in an incomplete market.
3. The returns are in Deutsch Mark / Euros, the USD exposure is fully hedged.
4. We refer to Campbell and Viceira (2005) for the technical details on the derivation of the term structures of risk.
5. The contribution rate has no effect here because it remains fixed. Hoevenaars and Ponds (2008) show that all workers benefit from the replacement of the flexible contribution rate in a traditional DB plan by the fixed contribution rate in the hybrid plan. Workers no longer lose value due to contribution increases in bad times.
6. The observations of the yields with maturities ranging from 11 to 15 years start in 1986:06.

References

Ang, A., Bekaert, G. and Wei, M. (2008) 'The term structure of real rates and expected inflation', *Journal of Finance*, Vol. 63(2), 797–849.
Ang, A., Piazzesi, M. and Wei, M. (2005) 'What does the yield curve tell us about GDP growth?', *Journal of Econometrics*, Vol. 131(1–2), 359–403.
Brennan, M.J., Schwartz, E.S. and Lagnado, R. (1997) 'Strategic Asset Allocation', *Journal of Economic Dynamics and Control*, Vol. 21(9), 1377–1403.
Brennan, M.J. and Xia, Y. (2002) 'Dynamic asset allocation under inflation', *Journal of Finance*, 57(3), 1201–1238.
Campbell, J.Y. and Shiller, R.J. (1988) 'Stock Prices, Earning, and Expected Dividends', *Journal of Finance*, Vol. 43(3), 661–676.
Campbell, J.Y. and L.M. Viceira (2002) *Strategic Asset Allocation, portfolio choice for long-term investors*, Oxford University Press.
Campbell, J.Y. and L.M. Viceira (2005) 'The Term Structure of the Risk-Return Trade-off', *Financial Analysts Journal*, Vol. 61(1), 34–44.
Chapman R.J., Gordon T.J. and Speed C.A. (2001) 'Pensions, funding and risk', *British Actuarial Journal*, Vol. 74, 605–663.[Author query: listed as 2002 in the text.]
Cochrane (2001) *Asset Pricing*, Princeton University Press.
De Jong, F. (2008) 'Valuation of pension liabilities in incomplete markets', *Journal of Pension Economics and Finance*, Vol. 7(3), 277–294.
Hoevenaars R.P.M.M., Molenaar R.D.J., Schotman P.C. and Steenkamp T.B.M. (2008) 'Strategic Asset Allocation with Liabilities: Beyond Stocks and Bonds', *Journal of Economic Dynamics and Control*, Vol. 32(9), 2939–2970.
Hoevenaars R.P.M.M., and Ponds, E.H.M. (2008) 'Valuation of intergenerational transfers in funded collective pension schemes', *Insurance, Mathematics and Economics*, Vol. 42, 578–593.
Kortleve N. and Ponds E.H.M. (2006) 'Pension deals and value-based ALM', in Kortleve N., Nijman Th. and Ponds E.H.M. (eds) *Fair value and pension fund management*, Elsevier Science.
Lee, B., Rogal, D. and Weinberger, F. (2009) 'Asset allocation and portfolio construction for sovereign wealth managers', in *Strategic Asset Allocation for Central Banks & Sovereign Wealth Funds*, Palgrave Macmillan.[Author query: editors?]
Mitchell, O.S., Piggott, J. and Kumru, C. (2008) 'Managing public investment funds: best practices and new questions', *Journal of Pension Economics and Finance*, Vol. 7(3), 321–356.
Nijman, Th. E. and Koijen, R.S.J. (2006) 'Valuation and risk management of inflation-sensitive pension rights', in Kortleve N., Nijman Th. and Ponds E.H.M. (eds) *Fair value and pension fund management*, Elsevier Science.
Paulson, A.L. (2009) 'Raising capital: The role of sovereign wealth funds' *Chicago Fed Letter*, January, 321–356.
Ponds E.H.M. (2003) 'Pension funds and value-based generational accounting', *Journal of Pension Economics and Finance*, Vol. 2(3), 295–325.
Scherer, B. (forthcoming) 'Portfolio choice for oil based sovereign wealth funds', in A. Berkelaar, J. Coche, and K. Nyholm (Eds) *Strategic Asset Allocation for Central Banks & Sovereign Wealth Funds*, Palgrave Macmillan.
Sharpe, W.F. (1976) 'Corporate pension funding policy', *Journal of Financial Economics*, Vol. 3, 183–193.

Conference Agenda

BANK FOR INTERNATIONAL SETTLEMENTS

TREASURY
THE WORLD BANK

EUROPEAN CENTRAL BANK

Joint BIS/ECB/World Bank

Public Investors Conference 2008

Strategic Asset Allocation for Central Banks & Sovereign Wealth Funds

24–25 November 2008
at the European Central Bank in Frankfurt

Monday 24 November

7:30 *Registration and coffee*

Welcoming remarks by the organizers
8:30 Ken Nyholm , Joachim Coche, Arjan B. Berkelaar
European Central Bank, Bank for International Settlements, World Bank

Reserves Management

Global Reserves Management
8:45 Krzysztof Rybinski and Urszula Krynska
Ernst & Young and Millenium Bank

Asset Liability Management for Central Banks
9:30 Urmila Kisoen and Ingmar van Herpt
De Nederlandsche Bank

10:15 *Coffee break*

Mortgage Backed Securities in a Strategic Asset Allocation Framework
10:30 Adam Kobor and Myles Brennan
World Bank Treasury

Comparing the Global Aggregate Index to a Blend of Global Treasuries and MBS
11:00 Lev Dynkin, Jay Hyman, Bruce Phelps
Barclays Capital Research

Combining Canadian Interest Rate Forecasts
11:30 David Bolder and Yuliya Romanyuk
Bank of Canada and Bank for International Settlements

Lunch with keynote address by Richard Bookstaber, Bridgewater Associates
12:00 *and author of* A Demon of Our Own Design

Break-Out Sessions

	Reserves Management I Chair: Pierre Cardon	**Optimization** Chair: David Bolder
14:00	*Optimal Reserves Composition in the Presence of Sudden Stops* Roland Beck and Ebrahim Rahbari European Central Bank	*Scenario Dependent Portfolio Optimization* Roberts Grava JP Morgan

14:30	*Combating Intervention Risks* Stephen John Fisher JP Morgan Asset Management	*Hidden Risks in Mean–Variance Optimization* Jose Fernandes and Jose Ornelas Banco Central do Brasil
15:00	*Reserves Adequacy and Diversification* Vahe Sahakyan and Joachim Coche Bank for International Settlements	*Efficient Portfolio Optimization in the Wealth Creation and Maximum Drawdown Space* Alejandro Reveiz and Carlos Leon World Bank Treasury and Banco de la República Colombia
15:30	*Coffee break*	

Break-Out Sessions

	Reserves Management II Chair: Jennifer Calari	**Fixed Income** Chair: Ulrich Bindseil
15:45	*Conceptual Issues in Central Bank Strategic Asset Allocation* Alex Joia and Joachim Coche Bank for International Settlements	*Dynamic Management of Interest Rate Risk Exposure* Gabriel Petre and Arjan B. Berkelaar World Bank Treasury
16:15	*Strategic Asset Allocation: Balancing Short-Term Liquidity Needs and Real Capital Preservation* Javier Bonza, Norma Gómez, Reinaldo Pabón Fondo Latinamericano de Reservas	*Updating the Yield Curve to Analysts' Views* Leonardo Nogueira Banco Central do Brasil and ICMA
16:45	*Strategic Asset Allocation with a Variable Investment Horizon* Paulo de Cacella, Antonio da Silva, Isabella Maia Banco Central do Brasil	*A Spread Risk Model for Strategic Fixed Income Investors* Fernando Monar and Ken Nyholm European Central Bank
17:15	*Strategic Asset Allocation Process at Danmarks Nationalbank* Ib Hansen Danmarks Nationalbank	

19:00 *Dinner with keynote address by Robert Litterman, Goldman Sachs*

Tuesday 25 November

8:00 *Coffee*

Sovereign Wealth Management

Chair: Arjan B. Berkelaar

The Impact of Sovereign Wealth Funds on Global Financial Markets
8:45 Michael Fidora and Roland Beck
European Central Bank

Optimal Asset Allocation for Sovereign Wealth Funds
9.30 Bernd Scherer and Andreas Gintschel
Morgan Stanley and JPMorgan

10:15 *Coffee break*

Asset Allocation and Portfolio Construction for Sovereign Wealth Managers
10.30 Fred Weinberger, Bernard Lee, and David Rogal
BlackRock

Strategic Investment and Risk Management for Sovereign Wealth Funds
11.00 Stijn Claessens and Jerome Kreuser
International Monetary Fund

Alternatives and Asset Allocation: Implications for Investment Policy of Sovereign Wealth Funds
11.30 Kurt Winkelmann
Goldman Sachs

12:00 *Lunch*

Break-Out Sessions

	Emerging Perspectives on Asset allocation	**Asset Modeling**
	Chair: Evangelos Tabakis	Chair: Sudhir Rajkumar
16:45	*Can Life-Cycle Policies Help Collective Pension Schemes?* Roderick Molenaar, Roy Hoevenaars and Eduard Ponds APG Investments	*Optimal Construction of a Fund of Funds* Petri Hilli, Matti Koivu and Teemu Pennanen Quantitative Solvency Analysis, Finnish Financial Supervision Authority, Helsinki University of Technology

15:00	*Volatility Exposure for Strategic Asset Allocation* Marie Brière, Alexander Burgues and Ombretta Signori Credit Agricole Asset Management, University Libre de Bruxelles	*Statistical Inference for Sharpe's Ratio* Rafael Schmidt Bank for International Settlements
15:00	*Copulas and Risk Measures for Strategic Asset Allocation* Cyril Caillault, Stephane Monier Fortis Investments	*Combining Financial Data with Mixed Frequencies* Torres Trovik and Couro Kane World Bank Treasury

Coffee break

Asset Modeling and Portfolio Construction

Chair: Joachim Coche

15:45 *A Frequency Domain Methodology for Time-Series Modeling*
Hens Steehouwer
Ortec Finance

16:15 *Strategic Tilting Around the SAA Benchmark*
Aaron Drew, Richard Frogley, Tore Hayward and Rishab Sethi
New Zealand Superannuation

16:45 *Using Economic Theory to Build Optimal Portfolios*
Thomas Chevrier and Robert McCulloch
State Street Global Markets

17:15 *Closing Remarks followed by a reception*

Index